Direct3D™

PROFESSIONAL REFERENCE

Michael Stein
Eric Bowman
Gregory Pierce

New Riders Publishing, Indianapolis, Indiana

Direct3D Professional Reference

By Michael Stein, Eric Bowman, and Gregory Pierce

Published by:
New Riders Publishing
201 West 103rd Street
Indianapolis, IN 46290 USA

All rights reserved. No part of this book may be reproduced or transmitted in any form or by any means, electronic or mechanical, including photocopying, recording, or by any information storage and retrieval system, without written permission from the publisher, except for the inclusion of brief quotations in a review.

Copyright © 1997 by New Riders Publishing

Printed in the United States of America 1 2 3 4 5 6 7 8 9 0

Library of Congress Cataloging-in-Publication Data

CIP data available upon request

Warning and Disclaimer

This book is designed to provide information about **Direct3D**. Every effort has been made to make this book as complete and as accurate as possible, but no warranty or fitness is implied.

The information is provided on an "as is" basis. The author(s) and New Riders Publishing shall have neither liability nor responsibility to any person or entity with respect to any loss or damages arising from the information contained in this book or from the use of the disks or programs that may accompany it.

Publisher	*Don Fowley*
Associate Publisher	*David Dwyer*
Marketing Manager	*Mary Foote*
Managing Editor	*Carla Hall*

Product Development Specialist
Sean Angus

Acquisitions Editor
Steve Weiss

Senior Editors
Sarah Kearns
Suzanne Snyder

Development Editor
Nancy Warner

Project Editor
Dayna Isley

Copy Editor
Nancy Warner
Gina Brown

Acquisitions Coordinator
Stacy Merkel

Administrative Coordinator
Karen Opal

Cover Designer
Karen Ruggles

Cover Illustration
©Ken Coffelt/SIS

Cover Production
Aren Howell

Book Designer
Sandra Schroeder

Production Manager
Kelly Dobbs

Production Team Supervisors
Laurie Casey
Joe Millay

Graphic Image Specialists
Wil Cruz
Dan Harris

Production Analyst
Erich J. Richter

Production Team
Lori Cliburn
William Huys Jr
Christopher Morris
Megan Wade

Indexer
Greg Pearson

About the Authors

Michael L. Stein was born in Baltimore, Maryland, and raised in nearby Owings Mills. He received a high school diploma from Pikesville High School. He received a Bachelor of Science degree in Mathematics and Computer Science from Carnegie Mellon University, in Pittsburgh, Pennsylvania. Michael currently resides in San Francisco.

Michael has worked in the computer industry since 1984 in a variety of jobs ranging from computer assembly and repair to game designer and programmer. He has worked on a number of published software titles including Moriarity's Revenge (Macintosh), Sesame Street: Numbers (3D0), Eco: East Africa (Windows), and Squeezils (Windows 95). Michael currently works for Electronic Arts in the EA Sports division.

Eric Bowman is a software engineer with the Maxis Core Technology Group in San Mateo, CA. In addition to 3D graphics, Eric likes designing and implementing object-oriented systems in C++. A graduate of Reed College with a degree in physics, he has since designed and implemented a number of object-oriented systems for biological simulations, multimedia, networking, and 2D and 3D graphics. He likes getting lost, reading Rilke, discovering new music, not owning a car, and watching four episodes of *The Simpsons* every day.

Gregory Pierce was born and raised in New Orleans, Louisiana. He received his high school diploma from Jesuit High School. A computer science graduate of Xavier University of Louisiana, Greg enjoys developing graphical 3D physics simulations and games. He likes Japanamation, high-speed driving, paintball, and software development. Greg is currently a Special Projects Engineer with Sytex, Inc. in Vienna, Virginia.

Trademark Acknowledgments

All terms mentioned in this book that are known to be trademarks or service marks have been appropriately capitalized. New Riders Publishing cannot attest to the accuracy of this information. Use of a term in this book should not be regarded as affecting the validity of any trademark or service mark.

Dedications

From Michael Stein

To Mom and Dad, for raising me right.

To my family, for taking good care of me. To Tracey, for her love and support.

And to the teachers of the world. Peace. —michael

From Eric Bowman

To my mother, for never losing faith; to my father, for teaching me how to push limits; and to both of them for teaching me how to find beauty in simplicity.

From Gregory Pierce

To God and my parents for raising me to believe that all things are possible.

To Deirdre and my family for their loving support.

To Nora, Brett, Ben, Art, and Lawrence for being there when I needed someone to talk to when I was totally frustrated.

To all the dreamers who want to make their game a reality.

Acknowledgments

Michael Stein's Acknowledgments

I would like to thank the following people for their help, guidance, and wisdom throughout my professional and educational career: Betsy and Jim, for giving me so many opportunities to learn about the computer industry at a very young age; Mark Stehlik, for rising above and beyond the call of duty and for supporting me 100% when no one else would; Eric Gregory, for being a great teacher as well as a great engineer; Steve Weiss, for giving me a chance to be a writer; Nancy Warner, for her support and guidance throughout the making of this book; the staff at New Riders and Macmillan, for putting this book together; and all of the teachers I've ever had.

Eric Bowman's Acknowledgments

Thanks to Jim Mackraz for everything++, and Maxis for graciously allowing me to take on the added responsibility of this book. Special thanks to the entire research community of the Esoterotica Research Institute, and to everyone who ever blew my mind.

Gregory Pierce's Acknowledgments

I would like to acknowledge: Jason Zisk for all his help in getting me started; the folks at New Riders for giving me the opportunity; the CNCMS project group for trying to give me time to do the book; the Gamedev group for providing answers; the Math, Computer Science, and Engineering Departments of Xavier University for pushing me beyond the limits that I thought I had. –A.M.D.G

New Riders Publishing would like to thank the authors for endless hours of hard work and their willingness to offer extra help. Nancy Warner for demanding high quality standards from everyone involved in the project, successfully completing this huge organizational task, and sacrificing so many hours of sleep. John De Goes for his expertise in DirectX and assistance with this and other projects. Phil Taylor from Microsoft for his guidance and support. Steve Weiss for staying actively involved in the project from its conception to the bookshelves. Sandra Schroeder for the weeks she devoted to creating an awesome interior design. And to the proofreading, layout, illustration, indexing, and editorial teams—this publishing company couldn't exist without you and your skills.

Table of Contents

Part I: Principles of Direct3D and DirectX

Introduction to 3D — 3
- Coordinate Systems 4
- 3D Geometry 5
  - Vertices 6
  - Lines 7
  - Faces 7
  - Vectors and Normals 8
  - Meshes 9
- Visual Characteristics 10
  - Materials 10
  - Lights 10
  - Textures 12
- Viewing a 3D Scene 14
  - Frames of Reference 14
  - Transformations 14
  - Viewing Volume 15
  - Viewing in 3D 16
- Rasterization 17
  - Rendering Quality 17
  - Visible-Surface Determination 18
- Animation 19

Introduction to DirectX — 21
- DirectX Structure of Today 22
- DirectX Components at a Glance 23
- DirectX and the Component Object Model 24
  - COM Fundamentals 24
  - COM and C++ 25
  - Accessing COM Objects via C 25

Introduction to Direct3D 27

History 27
Direct3D Architecture 28
    The Retained-Mode API 29
    The Immediate-Mode API 29
    The Hardware Abstraction Layer 30
    The Hardware Emulation Layer 30
    The Rendering Engine 30

Part II: Retained-Mode Function Reference

Introduction to the Direct3D Reference Section 35

Retained-Mode Function Reference 37

COM Methods 37
    AddRef 37
    QueryInterface 38
    Release 38
    CoCreateInstance 39
    CoInitialize 40
    CoUninitialize 41
Retained-Mode Functions 43
    Direct3DRMCreate 44
    D3DRMColorGetAlpha
      D3DRMColorGetBlue
      D3DRMColorGetGreen
      D3DRMColorGetRed 44
    D3DRMCreateColorRGB
      D3DRMCreateColorRGBA 45
    D3DRMMatrixFromQuaternion 46
    D3DRMQuaternionFromRotation 46
    D3DRMQuaternionMultiply 47
    D3DRMQuaternionSlerp 48
    D3DRMVectorAdd 49
    D3DRMVectorCrossProduct 49

D3DRMVectorDotProduct 50
D3DRMVectorModulus 51
D3DRMVectorNormalize 51
D3DRMVectorRandom 52
D3DRMVectorReflect 52
D3DRMVectorRotate 53
D3DRMVectorScale 54
D3DRMVectorSubtract 55

Retained-Mode Callbacks 56
D3DRMDEVICEPALETTECALLBACK 56
D3DRMFRAMEMOVECALLBACK 57
D3DRMLOADCALLBACK 58
D3DRMLOADTEXTURECALLBACK 58
D3DRMOBJECTCALLBACK 59
D3DRMUPDATECALLBACK 60
D3DRMUSERVISUALCALLBACK 61
D3DRMWRAPCALLBACK 62

ARRAY 63
GetSize 64
GetElement 64
GetPick 65

IDirect3DRM 67
AddSearchPath 68
CreateAnimation 68
CreateAnimationSet 69
CreateDevice 69
CreateDeviceFromClipper 70
CreateDeviceFromD3D 71
CreateDeviceFromSurface 73
CreateFace 74
CreateFrame 75
CreateLight 75
CreateLightRGB 76
CreateMaterial 77
CreateMesh 78
CreateMeshBuilder 78

- CreateObject 79
- CreateShadow 80
- CreateTexture 81
- CreateTextureFromSurface 81
- CreateUserVisual 82
- CreateViewport 83
- CreateWrap 84
- EnumerateObjects 85
- GetDevices 85
- GetNamedObject 86
- GetSearchPath 86
- Load 87
- LoadTexture 90
- LoadTextureFromResource 90
- SetDefaultTextureColors 91
- SetDefaultTextureShades 92
- SetSearchPath 93
- Tick 93

IDirect3DRMAnimation 95
- AddPositionKey 95
- AddRotateKey 97
- AddScaleKey 97
- DeleteKey 98
- GetOptions 99
- SetFrame 99
- SetOptions 100
- SetTime 101

IDirect3DRMAnimationSet 102
- AddAnimation 102
- DeleteAnimation 103
- Load 103
- SetTime 105

IDirect3DRMDevice 106
- AddUpdateCallback 107
- DeleteUpdateCallback 107

- GetBufferCount 108
- GetColorModel 108
- GetDirect3DDevice 109
- GetDither 110
- GetHeight 110
- GetTrianglesDrawn 110
- GetQuality 111
- GetShades 112
- GetTextureQuality 112
- GetViewports 113
- GetWidth 114
- GetWireframeOptions 114
- Init 115
- InitFromClipper 115
- InitFromD3D 116
- SetBufferCount 117
- SetDither 117
- SetQuality 118
- SetShades 119
- SetTextureQuality 119
- Update 120

IDirect3DRMFace 122
- AddVertex 123
- AddVertexAndNormalIndexed 123
- GetColor 124
- GetMaterial 124
- GetNormal 125
- GetTexture 125
- GetTextureCoordinateIndex 126
- GetTextureCoordinates 126
- GetTextureTopology 127
- GetVertex 127
- GetVertexCount 128
- GetVertexIndex 128
- GetVertices 129
- SetColor 130

- SetColorRGB 131
- SetMaterial 131
- SetTexture 132
- SetTextureCoordinates 132
- SetTextureTopology 133

IDirect3DRMFrame 135
- AddChild 136
- AddLight 137
- AddMoveCallback 137
- AddRotation 138
- AddScale 139
- AddTransform 140
- AddTranslation 140
- AddVisual 141
- DeleteChild 142
- DeleteLight 142
- DeleteMoveCallback 143
- DeleteVisual 143
- GetChildren 144
- GetColor 145
- GetLights 145
- GetMaterialMode 146
- GetOrientation 146
- GetParent 147
- GetPosition 148
- GetRotation 148
- GetScene 149
- GetSceneBackground 149
- GetSceneBackgroundDepth 150
- GetSceneFogColor 150
- GetSceneFogEnable 151
- GetSceneFogMode 151
- GetSceneFogParams 152
- GetSortMode 153
- GetTexture 153
- GetTextureTopology 154

GetTransform 155
GetVelocity 155
GetVisuals 156
GetZbufferMode 156
InverseTransform 157
Load 158
LookAt 159
Move 160
SetColor 161
SetColorRGB 161
SetMaterialMode 162
SetOrientation 163
SetPosition 164
SetRotation 164
SetSceneBackground 165
SetSceneBackgroundDepth 165
SetSceneBackgroundImage 166
SetSceneBackgroundRGB 167
SetSceneFogColor 168
SetSceneFogEnable 168
SetSceneFogMode 169
SetSceneFogParams 169
SetSortMode 170
SetTexture 170
SetTextureTopology 171
SetVelocity 172
SetZbufferMode 172
Transform 173
IDirect3DRMLight 174
GetColor 174
GetConstantAttenuation 175
GetEnableFrame 176
GetLinearAttenuation 176
GetPenumbra 177
GetQuadraticAttenuation 177

GetRange	178
GetType	179
GetUmbra	179
SetColor	180
SetColorRGB	180
SetConstantAttenuation	181
SetEnableFrame	182
SetLinearAttenuation	182
SetPenumbra	183
SetQuadraticAttenuation	183
SetRange	184
SetType	185
SetUmbra	185
IDirect3DRMMaterial	**186**
GetEmissive	186
GetPower	187
GetSpecular	187
SetEmissive	188
SetPower	189
SetSpecular	189
IDirect3DRMMesh	**190**
AddGroup	191
GetBox	192
GetGroup	192
GetGroupColor	193
GetGroupCount	194
GetGroupMapping	194
GetGroupMaterial	195
GetGroupQuality	196
GetGroupTexture	196
GetVertices	197
Scale	198
SetGroupColor	198
SetGroupColorRGB	199
SetGroupMapping	199

14 Direct3D Professional Reference

- SetGroupMaterial 200
- SetGroupQuality 201
- SetGroupTexture 201
- SetVertices 202
- Translate 203

IDirect3DRMMeshBuilder 204
- AddFace 205
- AddFaces 205
- AddFrame 207
- AddMesh 207
- AddMeshBuilder 208
- AddNormal 208
- AddVertex 209
- CreateFace 210
- CreateMesh 210
- GenerateNormals 211
- GetBox 211
- GetColorSource 212
- GetFaceCount 212
- GetFaces 213
- GetPerspective 214
- GetQuality 214
- GetTextureCoordinates 215
- GetVertexColor 216
- GetVertexCount 216
- GetVertices 217
- Load 218
- ReserveSpace 220
- Save 221
- Scale 221
- SetColor 222
- SetColorRGB 222
- SetColorSource 223
- SetMaterial 224
- SetNormal 224

```
    SetPerspective ............................................................................... 225
    SetQuality ....................................................................................... 225
    SetTexture ...................................................................................... 226
    SetTextureCoordinates ................................................................. 227
    SetTextureTopology ...................................................................... 227
    SetVertex ........................................................................................ 228
    SetVertexColor .............................................................................. 229
    SetVertexColorRGB ...................................................................... 229
    Translate ......................................................................................... 230
IDirect3DRMObject ............................................................................ 231
    AddDestroyCallback ..................................................................... 231
    Clone ............................................................................................... 232
    DeleteDestroyCallback ................................................................. 233
    GetAppData ................................................................................... 233
    GetClassName ............................................................................... 234
    GetName ......................................................................................... 235
    SetAppData .................................................................................... 235
    SetName .......................................................................................... 236
IDirect3DRMShadow .......................................................................... 237
    Init .................................................................................................... 237
IDirect3DRMTexture ........................................................................... 239
    Changed .......................................................................................... 239
    GetColors ....................................................................................... 240
    GetDecalOrigin .............................................................................. 241
    GetDecalScale ................................................................................ 241
    GetDecalSize .................................................................................. 242
    GetDecalTransparency ................................................................. 242
    GetDecalTransparentColor .......................................................... 243
    GetImage ......................................................................................... 243
    GetShades ....................................................................................... 244
    InitFromFile ................................................................................... 244
    InitFromResource .......................................................................... 245
    InitFromSurface ............................................................................ 245
    SetColors ......................................................................................... 246
    SetDecalOrigin ............................................................................... 247
```

SetDecalScale 247
SetDecalSize 248
SetDecalTransparency 248
SetDecalTransparentColor 249
SetShades 249
IDirect3DRMUserVisual 250
Init 250
IDirect3DRMViewport 251
Clear 252
Configure 252
ForceUpdate 253
GetBack 253
GetCamera 254
GetDevice 254
GetDirect3DViewport 255
GetField 255
GetFront 256
GetHeight 256
GetPlane 257
GetProjection 258
GetUniformScaling 258
GetWidth 259
GetX 259
GetY 260
Init 260
InverseTransform 261
Pick 262
Render 262
SetBack 263
SetCamera 263
SetField 264
SetFront 264
SetPlane 265
SetProjection 266
SetUniformScaling 266

Transform 267
IDirect3DRMwinDevice 269
　　　HandleActivate 269
　　　HandlePaint 270
IDirect3DRMWrap 271
　　　Apply 271
　　　ApplyRelative 272
　　　Init 272
Retained-Mode Structures 275
　　　D3DRMBOX 275
　　　D3DRMIMAGE 275
　　　D3DRMLOADMEMORY 277
　　　D3DRMLOADRESOURCE 277
　　　D3DRMPALETTEENTRY 278
　　　D3DRMPICKDESC 279
　　　D3DRMQUATERNION 280
　　　D3DRMVECTOR4D 280
　　　D3DRMVERTEX 281
Retained-Mode Enumerated and Other Types 283
　　　D3DRCOLORSOURCE 283
　　　D3DRMCOMBINETYPE 283
　　　D3DRMFILLMODE 284
　　　D3DRMFOGMODE 285
　　　D3DRMFRAMECONSTRAINT 286
　　　D3DRMLIGHTMODE 287
　　　D3DRMLIGHTTYPE 287
　　　D3DRMMATERIALMODE 288
　　　D3DRMPALETTEFLAGS 289
　　　D3DRMPROJECTIONTYPE 289
　　　D3DRMRENDERQUALITY 290
　　　D3DRMSHADEMODE 291
　　　D3DRMSORTMODE 292
　　　D3DRMTEXTUREQUALITY 292
　　　D3DRMUSERVISUALREASON 293
　　　D3DRMWRAPTYPE 294

D3DRMXOFFORMAT	294
D3DRMZBUFFERMODE	295
Retained-Mode Other Types	296
D3DRMANIMATIONOPTIONS	296
D3DRMCOLORMODEL	297
D3DRMLOADOPTIONS	297
D3DRMMAPPING	299
D3DRMMATRIX4D	300
D3DRMSAVEOPTIONS	300
Retained-Mode Data Types and Return Values	303

Part III: Immediate-Mode Function Reference

Immediate-Mode Functions   307

Immediate-Mode Macros	307
D3DDivide	308
D3DMultiply	308
D3DRGB	308
D3DRGBA	309
D3DSTATE_OVERRIDE	310
D3DVAL	311
D3DVALP	311
RGB_GETBLUE	312
RGB_GETGREEN	312
RGB_GETRED	313
RGB_MAKE	313
RGB_TORGBA	314
RGBA_GETALPHA	315
RGBA_GETBLUE	315
RGBA_GETGREEN	316
RGBA_GETRED	316
RGBA_MAKE	317
RGBA_SETALPHA	317
RGBA_TORGB	318
Immediate-Mode Callbacks	319
D3DENUMDEVICESCALLBACK	319

D3DENUMTEXTUREFORMATSCALLBACK 320
  D3DVALIDATECALLBACK 321
IDirect3D 323
  CreateLight 323
  CreateMaterial 324
  CreateViewport 325
  EnumDevices 325
  FindDevice 326
  Initialize 327
IDirect3DDevice 328
  AddViewport 328
  BeginScene 329
  CreateExecuteBuffer 330
  CreateMatrix 331
  DeleteMatrix 331
  DeleteViewport 332
  EndScene 333
  EnumTextureFormats 333
  Execute 334
  GetCaps 335
  GetDirect3D 336
  GetMatrix 336
  GetPickRecords 337
  GetStats 338
  Initialize 338
  NextViewport 339
  Pick 340
  SetMatrix 341
  SwapTextureHandles 342
IDirect3DExecuteBuffer 343
  GetExecuteData 343
  Initialize 344
  Lock 345
  Optimize 346
  SetExecuteData 346
  Unlock 347

20   Direct3D Professional Reference

    Validate 348
  IDirect3DLight 349
    GetLight 349
    Initialize 350
    SetLight 350
  IDirect3DMaterial 351
    GetHandle 351
    GetMaterial 352
    Initialize 353
    Reserve 353
    SetMaterial 354
    Unreserve 354
  IDirect3DTexture 355
    GetHandle 355
    Initialize 356
    Load 357
    PaletteChanged 357
    Unload 358
  IDirect3DViewport 359
    AddLight 360
    Clear 360
    DeleteLight 361
    GetBackground 362
    GetBackgroundDepth 363
    GetViewport 364
    Initialize 365
    LightElements 365
    NextLight 366
    SetBackground 367
    SetBackgroundDepth 367
    SetViewport 368
    TransformVertices 369

Immediate-Mode Function Reference   371

  Immediate-Mode Structures 371
    D3DBRANCH 371

D3DCOLORVALUE	372
D3DDEVICEDESC	373
D3DEXECUTEBUFFERDESC	376
D3DEXECUTEDATA	377
D3DFINDDEVICERESULT	378
D3DFINDDEVICESEARCH	379
D3DHVERTEX	382
D3DINSTRUCTION	383
D3DLIGHT	384
D3DLIGHTDATA	385
D3DLIGHTINGCAPS	386
D3DLIGHTINGELEMENT	387
D3DLINE	388
D3DLINEPATTERN	388
D3DLVERTEX	389
D3DMATERIAL	390
D3DMATRIX	392
D3DMATRIXLOAD	392
D3DMATRIXMULTIPLY	393
D3DPICKRECORD	394
D3DPOINT	394
D3DPRIMCAPS	395
D3DPROCESSVERTICES	404
D3DRECT	405
D3DSPAN	406
D3DSTATE	406
D3DSTATS	407
D3DSTATUS	408
D3DTEXTURELOAD	411
D3DTLVERTEX	412
D3DTRANSFORMCAPS	413
D3DTRANSFORMDATA	414
D3DTRIANGLE	416
D3DVECTOR	420
D3DVERTEX	420
D3DVIEWPORT	422

Immediate-Mode Enumerated Types 425
    D3DBLEND 425
    D3DCMPFUNC 427
    D3DCOLORMODEL 428
    D3DCULL 429
    D3DFILLMODE 429
    D3DFOGMODE 430
    D3DLIGHTSTATETYPE 431
    D3DLIGHTTYPE 433
    D3DOPCODE 434
    D3DRENDERSTATETYPE 436
    D3DSHADEMODE 442
    D3DTEXTUREADDRESS 443
    D3DTEXTUREBLEND 444
    D3DTEXTUREFILTER 445
    D3DTRANSFORMSTATETYPE 446
Immediate-Mode Other Values 448
    D3DCOLOR 448
    D3DVALUE 448
Immediate-Mode Data Types and Return Values 449

Part IV: Appendix

DirectX File Format   455

File Format Syntax 456
    Reserved Words 456
    Header 456
    Comments 457
    Templates 458
    Instances 461
Template Reference 463
    Header 463
    Vector 464
    Coords2d 464
    Quaternion 465
    Matrix4×4 466

ColorRGBA 466
Color RGB 467
IndexedColor 467
Boolean 468
Boolean2d 468
Material 469
TextureFilename 470
MeshFace 470
MeshFaceWraps 471
MeshTextureCoords 472
MeshNormals 472
MeshVertexColors 473
MeshMaterialList 473
Mesh 474
FrameTransformMatrix 475
Frame 476
FloatKeys 476
TimedFloatKeys 477
AnimationKey 478
AnimationOptions 478
Animation 479
AnimationSet 480
Binary Format Specification 480
   Header 480
   Templates 481
   Data 482
   Tokens 483
Record-Bearing Token Reference 484
   TOKEN_NAME 484
   TOKEN_STRING 484
   TOKEN_INTEGER 485
   TOKEN_GUID 485
   TOKEN_INTEGER_LIST 486
   TOKEN_REALNUM_LIST 486

Index   **487**

Part I

Principles of Direct 3D and DirectX

1   *Introduction to 3D* *3*

2   *Introduction to DirectX* *21*

3   *Introduction to Direct3D* *27*

INTRODUCTION 1

Introduction to 3D

This chapter provides a starting point for understanding the features and concepts of 3D graphics and animation necessary for using Direct3D. This chapter is not a comprehensive overview of 3D graphics and animation, nor does it completely cover each topic. It is intended to give the reader familiarity with 3D graphics animation, especially as they relate to Direct3D's set of features and capabilities. Most of the topics in this chapter are covered at a high level, except when referring to specific Direct3D features or functionality.

3D graphics exist for one reason: to represent three-dimensional objects on a two-dimensional image plane. This image plane, in the case of computer entertainment, usually refers to the monitor. As with any of the two-dimensional image planes, objects are not presented in three-dimensions, but are made to appear "three-dimensional" by utilizing methods for fooling the human eye into believing that three dimensions exist in the image. 3D animation exists to provide movement for the 3D objects, as computer entertainment generally requires something more than static objects arranged in a pretty image. *Animation* can be defined as a series of still images viewed quickly in succession to give the illusion of motion.

In order to represent a three-dimensional scene, a computer graphics system must provide two main sets of functionality. The first set encompasses the representation of a set of objects in a three-dimensional space. Before a 2D image can be created, an internal representation of the objects as they exist in three dimensions, including an object's shape, position, orientation, color, and texture, must exist. In addition, the lights of a scene must be described, as well as the point from which the scene is being viewed. The second set of functionality provides the conversion from three dimensions to two dimensions.

Coordinate Systems

To represent objects and motion in three-dimensional space, a system is needed to describe points. In 3D graphics, the *coordinate system* consists of three axes: x, y, and z. Each axis is oriented at 90 degrees relative to the other two.

Two types of coordinate systems used in computer graphics exist: right-handed and left-handed, which differ only in the orientation of the z-axis. A right-handed coordinate system points the positive z-axis toward the viewpoint of the scene (out of the screen), and a left-handed coordinate system points the positive z-axis away from the viewpoint (into the screen). Typically, the x-axis is along the horizontal edge of the screen and the y-axis is along the vertical edge of the screen. Direct3D uses a left-handed coordinate system, with the positive x-axis along the bottom edge of the screen and positive y-axis along the left edge of the screen. See figures 1.1a and 1.1b for an illustration.

Figure 1.1a

Left-handed coordinate system.

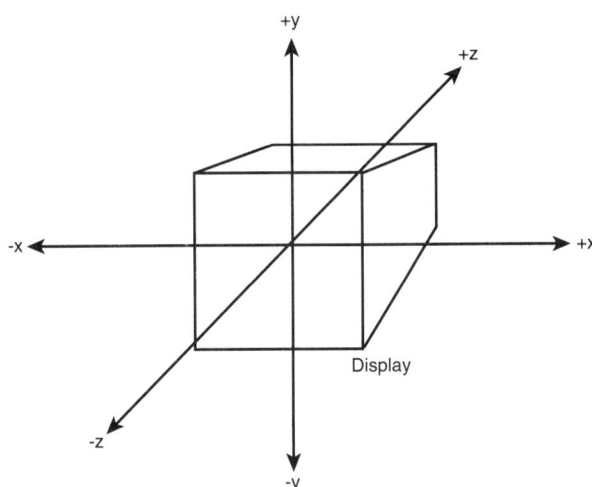

Another coordinate system is used in computer graphics for specifying locations of pixels in an image bitmap. This coordinate system consists of two axes, referred to as the u-axis (or s-axis) and v-axis (or t-axis). In Direct3D, the u-axis is along the bottom edge of the texture and the v-axis is along the left edge of the texture (see fig. 1.1c). Also in Direct3D, the bottom-left corner of a texture is (0.0, 0.0) and the top-right corner of the texture is (1.0, 1.0).

Figure 1.1b

Right-handed coordinate system.

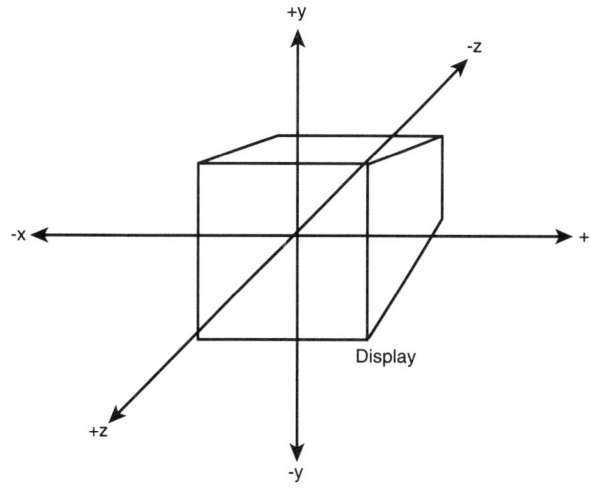

Figure 1.1c

Texture coordinate system.

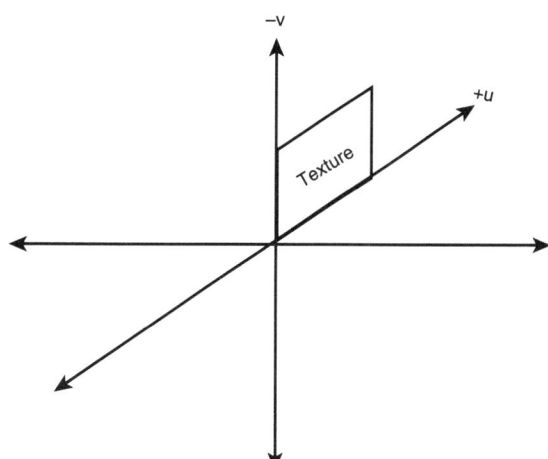

3D Geometry

Three-dimensional objects can have a wide variety of shapes and complexities. A simple method is needed to approximate an object's geometry in a three-dimensional coordinate system. One approach, *polygonal modeling*, represents an object as a set of polygons in three-dimensional space. Each polygon consists of a set of points connected in a specific order to form a closed geometrical shape, or *mesh*. This approach allows for a wide range of approximation and flexibility because more polygons can be added to achieve a higher degree of accuracy. Another approach, *spline-based modeling*, approximates an object using a set of curves defined by points in space. 3D objects represented with splines are still displayed by using polygons, generally triangles. Direct3D currently supports only polygonal representation of objects.

Vertices

Vertices usually refer to points that are used to define objects. They are the simplest building block in creating polygonal meshes, and much of the mathematics of computer graphics consists of operations on vertices. Each vertex can be represented by three values that represent the signed offsets from the three axes. Each vertex uniquely identifies a point, or coordinate, in a three-dimensional space. A special coordinate, the *origin*, is defined to be (0, 0, 0) and is the point at which all three axes of the coordinate system intersect (see fig. 1.2a). A single vertex can have different mathematical representations in different coordinate systems. One function of the computer graphics pipeline is to determine the representation of vertices in the screen coordinate system.

Figure 1.2a

Vertices and the origin.

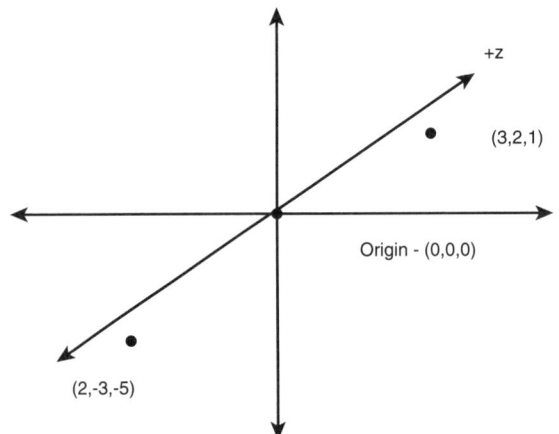

Lines

Each polygon consists of a series of line segments that form the boundary of the shape. Connecting two vertices can create a line segment (see fig. 1.2b). In computer graphics, these line segments are often referred to as lines, not to be confused with mathematical lines, which extend infinitely in both directions.

Faces

A *face*, or polygon, is a set of three or more vertices connected in a specific order to form a planar surface (see fig. 1.2b). The triangle is the simplest polygon and is popular in computer graphics for a variety of reasons. Triangles form easy-to-use building blocks for 3D objects and are guaranteed to be co-planar (all the points reside in a single plane), which prevents a computer graphics system from having to resolve complicated issues involving non-coplanar faces. Additionally, most rendering systems can only handle convex polygons, and concave polygons can always be decomposed into convex polygons. A triangle is guaranteed to be convex. Direct3D's low-level interface only accepts triangles, and although Direct3D's higher-level interface allows polygons with more than three vertices, internally, Direct3D triangulates all the faces.

Figure 1.2b

Lines and faces.

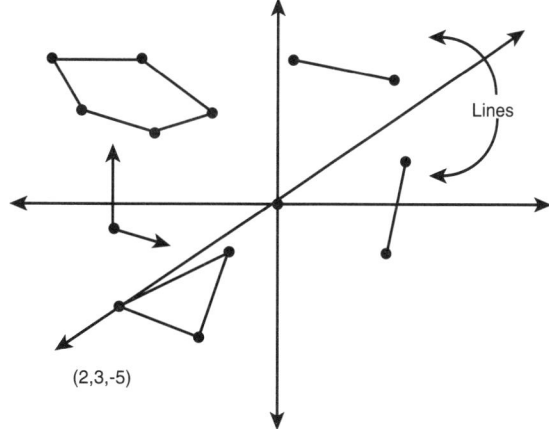

Vectors and Normals

A vector, like a vertex, is represented by three values that specify a point; however, a vector has a magnitude and a direction. The magnitude of a vector is the distance from the origin to the point and the direction points from the origin towards the point (see fig. 1.2c). Similar to a vertex, a vector can be represented as a set of three values corresponding to offsets from the three axes. However, these values form a line segment that starts at the origin, ends at the specified vertex, and points in the direction of the vertex. A vector has *magnitude*, defined as the length of the line segment. *Unit vectors* are vectors with a length of 1.0 and are a special subset of vectors. A variety of mathematical operations can be performed on vectors, including addition, subtraction, and multiplication of a scalar and a vector.

A *normal vector*, or normal, is a type of unit vector used extensively in lighting calculations (see fig. 1.2c). A *face normal* is a unit vector perpendicular (or normal) to a face and is most commonly associated with the flat shading model (see the Lights section under Shading Models). The direction of a face normal is determined by the order of the vertices and the handedness of the coordinate system. The face normal also denotes the front of the face. Many 3D systems (including Direct3D) do not display a face if it faces away from the viewpoint. A *vertex normal* is a unit vector associated with a vertex and is calculated by averaging the normals of the faces that share the vertex. Vertex normals are used to compute vertex colors; various shading schemes approximate the shading of a polygon based on its vertex colors.

Figure 1.2c
Vectors and normals.

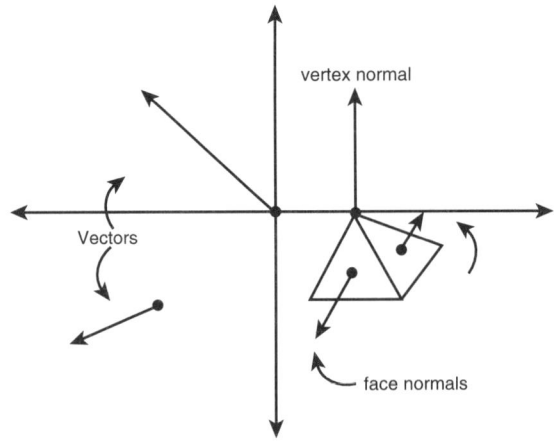

Meshes

A mesh consists of a set of vertices and a set of faces defined from those vertices to form a 3D object (see fig. 1.2d). Meshes can contain a single face or have complex geometries. Combining faces into a mesh enables easier manipulation of objects and object parts with respect to animation, materials, and textures. A set of meshes is generally combined to form a complete 3D object. Triangle strips and fans are two examples of meshes (see fig. 1.2e).

Figure 1.2d

An example of a mesh.

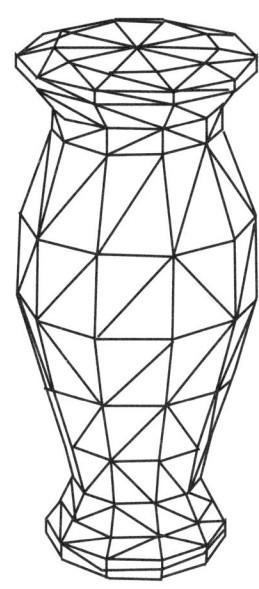

Figure 1.2e

A triangle strip and triangle fan.

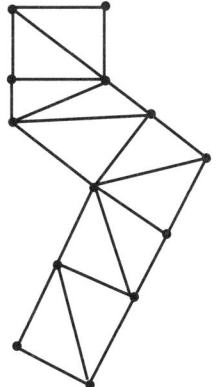
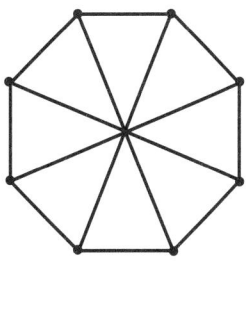

Visual Characteristics

A 3D object's basic visual characteristics are determined from the lights in a scene, the textures that are associated with an object, and how the objects in a scene reflect light. A *material* is a set of values that describe how light behaves when reflected by an object, usually an approximation of the way real-world objects reflect light. A *texture* is a 2D bitmap that can be applied to a face or set of faces of a 3D object. Textures are often used to provide more realism, adding richness to a polygon that would otherwise be smoothly shaded. A *light* is a 3D object that has no geometry (the actual light objects are not visible, just the light they generate). Lighting enables the scene to be viewed, much in the same way light works in the real world. When these three elements are combined during the drawing, or rendering, of a scene, they provide an object's geometry with a more realistic and viewable appearance.

Materials

Materials consist of a set of parameters that define how an object reflects light. *Ambient color* is the color of an object when viewed with ambient light only. *Diffuse color* is the reflection component that is scattered equally in all directions. *Specular color* defines the shiny component of a material, allowing for a complete range from dull objects (no specular reflection) to very shiny objects (metal). The *specular exponent* (or specular power) is a value that is used to define the sharpness of the specular highlights. *Emissive color* is color emitted from the object itself and can be used to make objects appear to glow. However, emissive color does not reflect off of other objects and does not represent a true light source.

Lights

Lights in a 3D scene are used to illuminate the objects in the scene. Five major types of lights (all of which exist in Direct3D) are as follows:

- Ambient
- Directional

- Point
- Parallel point
- Spot

Each light type serves a different purpose, and each has a different set of attributes and computational requirements.

Ambient Light

An ambient light source is reflected by all the objects in a scene equally, regardless of the object's position, orientation, and material characteristics. Ambient lights only have color attributes and do not need position or orientation. Although multiple ambient light sources can be created for a single scene, in general they are combined to form a single ambient light source value. The illumination of an object due to ambient light is based only on the ambient light color.

Directional Light

A directional light has a color and orientation, but no position. A directional light illuminates all faces with the same orientation equally. Directional lights are often utilized to simulate distant light sources, such as the sun, because directional lights produce parallel light rays. Directional lights often give the best trade off between realistic lighting and computational performance. The illumination of an object due to a directional light is based on the light's color and orientation.

Point Light

Point lights have color and position, but no orientation. Point lights radiate light equally in all directions from the point at which they are placed in the scene. Point lights can simulate the lighting effects of light bulbs or candles, but at a computational performance cost. The illumination of an object due to a point light is based on the light's color and position relative to the object.

Parallel Point Light

Parallel point lights combine the functionality of both directional and point lights. Like directional lights, parallel point lights radiate parallel rays of light. Like point lights, the orientation of the parallel rays is determined from the light's position relative to the object. Parallel point lights are also computationally expensive.

Spot Light

Spot lights produce rays of light that form a cone. Spot lights have color, position, and orientation, as well as two angle values that define two cones of light—the umbra and the penumbra. The cone defined by the umbra is the center cone of the spot light and radiates the full illumination of the light. The cone defined by the penumbra surrounds the inner umbra cone and radiates a dimmer light to blend with the scene. An attribute called *falloff* defines the decrease in illumination from the umbra to the outer edge of the penumbra.

Light Range and Attenuation

In addition to the attributes described for the various types of lights, point lights and spot lights have a range. The range defines the maximum distance at which objects can be lit. Any object farther than the specified range of a point or spot light will not be illuminated by the light. Some computer graphics systems also give lights attenuation values that define how a light's illumination should decrease the farther from the light a particular object is. Direct3D, for example, provides three attenuation values that form a quadratic equation defining a light's attenuation.

Textures

Textures are bitmaps, usually patterns or images, that can add realism to an object by simulating surface detail, enhanced geometry, or shading on the surface of an object's geometry. Single faces or groups of faces can be associated with a specific bitmap texture. There are various methods for mapping a two-dimensional bitmap to a three-dimensional object, depending on the desired appearance. *Mipmapping* is a technique by which a series of bitmaps of varying sizes is associated with a particular object. The smaller bitmaps are used for texture mapping the object at a distance, while the larger bitmaps are used when the object is close.

Texture Coordinates

Texture coordinates define the correspondence between the vertices of an object's face or group of faces and the pixels of the associated bitmap. Texture coordinates exist in a two-dimensional coordinate system.

Texture Mapping

Texture mapping is the process of applying a bitmap to a face or group of faces. The texture coordinates define which pixels of the texture are drawn on which parts of the face or faces. Direct3D provides a method called *wrapping* for generating texture coordinates for an object. The four major types of wraps are as follows:

- Flat wrap—This applies to a face as if projected directly onto the face.
- Cylindrical wrap—This wraps the texture map in a cylinder around the object.
- Spherical wrap—This wraps the texture map in a sphere around the object.
- Chrome wrap—This generates the texture coordinates so that the object appears to reflect the texture.

Additionally, texture coordinates can simply be assigned to vertices. This technique can be used when reading in objects from 3D modeling software packages.

Mipmapping

Although texture mapping can provide added realism to objects, the source textures are one size, regardless of the distance of the object from the viewpoint. Mipmapping is a technique that combines small textures for objects at a large distance with increasingly larger textures for objects as they approach the viewpoint of the scene. There are a variety of performance and appearance tradeoffs when using mipmapping. Direct3D currently does not implement mipmapping in software; however, certain 3D accelerator cards may support it.

Viewing a 3D Scene

After a 3D scene has been set up, the computer graphics system must translate the three-dimensional world to the two-dimensional screen. Mathematically, geometric transformations form the basis of this process. Transformations are also used to move, rotate, and scale object geometry.

Frames of Reference

A 3D scene generally refers to a set of objects that will be rendering for an image or rendered while moving for an animation. Each object in a scene will most likely occupy a different position in three-dimensional space and may be uniquely oriented and scaled. Additionally, objects usually exist in a *scene hierarchy*, an organizational construct that describes a parent and child relationship between all the objects in a scene. This organization enables complex description of the method in which objects move. For example, a modeled human character object might be defined with the left hand as a child of the left forearm. This would permit the hand to move and rotate independently, but would also cause the hand to move and rotate when the forearm moves, providing a simple abstraction of the complexity of human motion. At a higher level, each 3D scene exists within its own frame of reference, as do each of the several stages in the viewing process.

Transformations

The three most common geometric transformations utilized in 3D graphics are the following:

- Translation
- Rotation
- Scale

Each frame of reference in a scene can be described by a translation (specifying the frame's location), a rotation (specifying the frame's orientation), and a scale (specifying the frame's size).

A *translation* represents a change in position of an object. For example, if a cube centered at the origin was translated by (0, 2, −1), the cube would then be centered at (0, 2, −1). A *rotation* represents a change in orientation of an object. Object rotation can be specified in a number of ways, including matrix representation, Euler angles, or a quaternion (rotation angle around a specific axis). *Scale* gives an object a size in the three dimensions. Scale can also change an object's position, depending on the point from which scaling occurs.

Viewing Volume

The first step in viewing a three-dimensional scene is describing the viewing volume that defines which objects will appear in the scene.

The viewing volume, or frustum, is defined by four elements that describe a geometric volume:

- Viewpoint (or camera)
- Field of view
- Front clipping plane
- Back clipping plane

The *viewpoint* is the point from which the scene is being viewed, the *field of view* defines the width and height of the view, and the *front and back clipping planes* describe a range along the camera's positive z-axis that defines the bounding space for objects to be viewed. Any objects that exist outside the viewing frustum will not be visible in the view of the scene. There are two major types of scene viewing projection—perspective and orthographic (or parallel). In perspective projection, the center of projection is defined to be the position of the camera (see fig. 1.3a). Objects in the distance appear smaller in the 2D image than objects closer to the viewpoint in perspective projection. In orthographic (or parallel) projection, the center of projection is at infinity (see fig. 1.3b). Similar-sized objects in the distance appear the same size as their nearer counterparts.

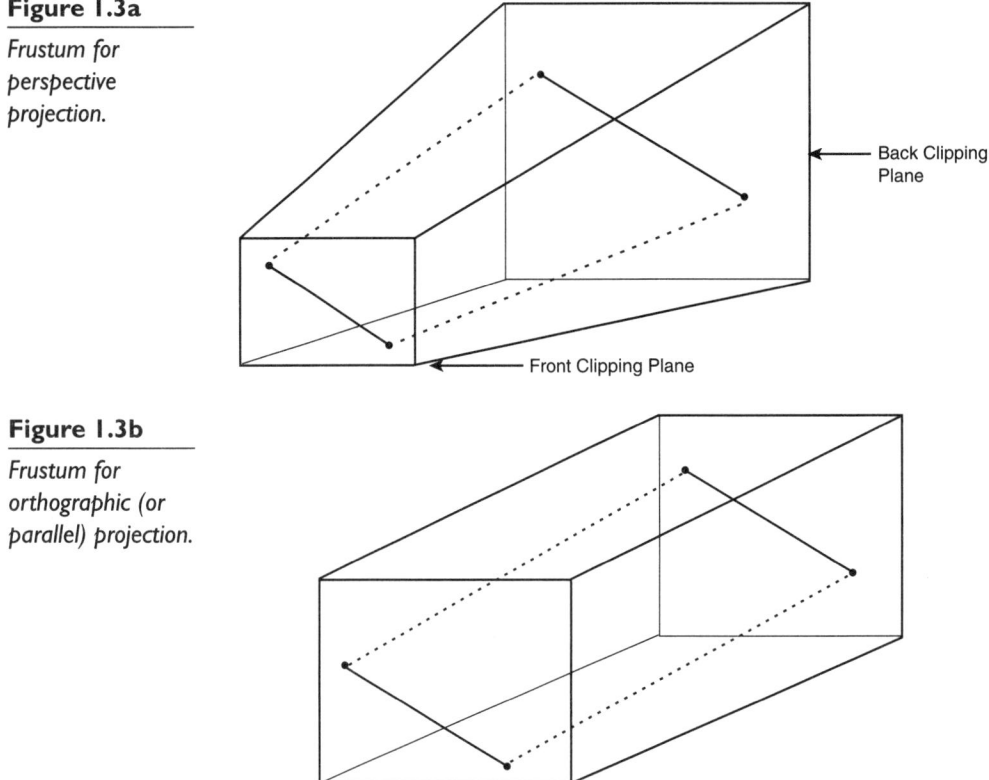

Figure 1.3a

Frustum for perspective projection.

Figure 1.3b

Frustum for orthographic (or parallel) projection.

Viewing in 3D

In Direct3D, there are several different phases in converting the geometry of a scene from its three-dimensional representation to a two-dimensional representation for display on a screen. The coordinates of an object enter the transformation pipeline in the model coordinate system. The world matrix transforms the coordinates into world coordinate system representation. The view matrix transforms the coordinates into camera coordinate system representation. The last transformation performed by the projection matrix puts the coordinates in canonical view volume coordinates. Visible coordinates exist in the range from (–1.0, –1.0, 0.0) to (1.0, 1.0, 1.0) where the x coordinate and y coordinate are canonical screen coordinates and the z coordinate is a z-buffer value. The canonical screen coordinates are then translated into screen pixel coordinates for display.

The associative property of matrix multiplication enables the transformation matrices to be multiplied together to create a single transformation matrix, which is then applied to the object coordinates. Direct3D takes advantage of this optimization.

Rasterization

Rasterization is the process by which transformed geometry is drawn and displayed on the screen. Rasterizing generally combines optimized removal and depth-sorting of geometry with rendering and its associated attributes.

Rendering Quality

When rendering a scene, a variety of different methods for displaying the scene exists. Various shading and lighting models define how the color values of the individual pixels of a face are calculated and displayed based on the lights and materials defined in a scene.

The four major rendering methods are as follows:

- Wireframe
- Flat
- Gouraud
- Phong

Wireframe

Wireframe rendering only displays the edges of a face. In some systems, the actual texture pixels that represent the face edges are drawn, and in some systems, just the material of a face is used. This method allows for very quick display or object analysis, but can be very confusing for complex objects if the capability to perform hidden-line removal does not exist.

Flat

Flat shading usually is used in one of two ways. Unlit flat shading doesn't use the lights of a scene in calculating a face's colors. This is a very quick method of viewing a scene, but objects tend to appear as silhouettes without any depth. Lit flat shading does make use of the lights in a scene and utilizes the face normal for lighting each face. This means that regardless of the face's relative position and orientation to the light, the entire face will have the same lighting and shading.

Gouraud

Gouraud shading represents an improvement from lit flat shading, as vertex normals are used instead of face normals in calculating the lighting and shading of a face. Specifically, a shading value is calculated at each vertex of a face, and then the shading values of the vertices are interpolated for each of the pixels in the face. Gouraud shading can create smoothly colored surfaces for objects, giving them a more realistic effect. Gouraud shading is more computationally expensive than flat shading, but provides somewhat more realistic shading.

Phong

Phong shading represents an improvement from Gouraud shading. As with Gouraud shading, vertex normals are used. However, instead of calculating shading values at each vertex and averaging, Phong shading interpolates the vertex normals over the entire face and calculates a new shading value at each pixel. Whereas Gouraud shading cannot render effects from specular lighting contained entirely inside a face properly, Phong shading can. Phong shading is more computationally expensive compared to any of the previously discussed lighting and shading techniques. Currently, Direct3D does not support Phong shading.

Visible-Surface Determination

In order to maintain the illusion of 3D, computer graphics systems must draw the faces of an object and the objects in a scene in the proper order. There are a variety of techniques for rendering a scene properly.

One technique that enables the faces of an object to be drawn properly is backface culling. Backface culling works on the principal that any polygon that faces away from the camera cannot be viewed. These faces can then be culled out of the rendering pipeline, so no computations are wasted.

Two common rendering techniques that properly display the objects in a scene are:

- painter's algorithm
- z-buffering

The painter's algorithm draws the objects of a scene in depth-sorted order from back-to-front. This means that in general, objects in the foreground of a scene when viewed will appear in front of objects in the background. However, the painter's algorithm has the potential to fail with objects that are intertwined. Another technique, z-buffering, provides pixel accurate scene rendering by utilizing a buffer with the same dimensions as the frame buffer. For each pixel to be displayed, the z-buffer algorithm compares its depth value with the value currently in the z-buffer. If the new pixel is closer to the camera, its color value is written into the frame buffer and the z-buffer. Otherwise its value is ignored. This algorithm provides decent performance, but requires additional memory for the z-buffer.

Animation

You can use a variety of techniques for animating objects in a 3D scene, but the most common system is key-frame animation. In key-frame animation, the positions of objects are described with keys, each which has a time value defining the time and a value that describes a new position, rotation, or scale for the object at the specified time. As the time of a particular animation progresses, the system interpolates between the keys to determine the new position, rotation, or scale at that time. Most computer graphics systems provide a variety of interpolation methods, including linear interpolation and spline-based interpolation (both of which Direct3D provides). Animations also have the option of playing through once or looping. In looped animation, when the time reaches the last key, the time is reset to the beginning.

INTRODUCTION 2

Introduction to DirectX

by John De Goes

Games and other multimedia-intensive applications require a wide variety of sound, video, and input capabilities. Because many original equipment manufacturers (OEMs) are producing these devices, it has been difficult in the past for developers to create truly hardware-independent software.

In DOS, no software layer existed, and thus, an application desiring to support all OEM devices had to write a tremendous amount of code or resort to third-party libraries. The Windows 3.1 operating system presented a device-independent solution to this situation, but for multimedia developers, whose applications demanded fast, direct access to hardware, the many software layers of the Windows API led to mediocre performance.

Windows 95 and NT both improved Windows in this respect by offering expanded support for graphics delivery, more robust sound drivers, and better networking, but the added features fell far short of the power level to which multimedia developers had become accustomed.

Before Windows 95 was released, Microsoft began working on a library that would extend the multimedia functionality of Windows while maintaining device-independence. Shortly after the release of Windows 95, Microsoft released the DirectX software development kit (SDK). From then on developers of high-performance applications had consistent and direct access to display, sound, and network hardware.

The DirectX SDK was a library of Component Object Model (COM) technologies that enabled developers to obtain access to device-dependent features in a device-independent way. This SDK maintained compatibility with the existing multimedia subsystems of Windows (the GDI, MCI, and so on) and provided a new level of performance for Windows-based applications.

DirectX Structure of Today

The DirectX SDK has evolved substantially since its first release. In its current version, it provides support for 3D sound devices, 2D and 3D accelerated display hardware, general-purpose network connections, and a wide range of input devices. The SDK will continue to expand in the future to provide support for new technologies (for example, the Talisman initiative) and devices, while maintaining compatibility with older DirectX applications.

The individual parts that make up DirectX include the following:

- DirectDraw
- DirectSound
- DirectPlay
- Direct3D
- DirectInput
- DirectSetup

> **Developer's Note** Documentation of AutoPlay, although not part of DirectX, but an extension of Windows 95, has been included in the reference set as a convenience for the reader. AutoPlay enables games to automatically install and run themselves when the user inserts a CD-ROM in the CD-ROM drive.

These components of DirectX are usually implemented in the form of COM objects, which bear more than a passing resemblance to C++ objects. This topic is covered in depth later in the Component Object Model section.

Many of the DirectX components have two software layers:

- Hardware abstraction layer
- Hardware emulation layer

The hardware abstraction layer, often referred to as the HAL, is a thin software layer that directly interfaces with the hardware to provide access to the hardware's features. The hardware emulation layer, usually abbreviated HEL, provides a set of emulated features for those that are not natively supported by the hardware. For example, in the case of

Direct3D, an application can access the interfaces without determining the capabilities of the user's machine. If the hardware does not natively support certain features, Direct3D will emulate them; however, it may be advantageous for an application to determine whether or not the user's machine is capable of emulating certain features with acceptable performance.

DirectX Components at a Glance

The DirectDraw component of the SDK provides applications with an interface to the display hardware. This SDK component is compatible with the GDI and presents developers with a wide range of functions to handle the most common hardware-implemented features, such as stretching and overlaying. For many of these features, if hardware support is unavailable, DirectDraw will emulate the missing functionality.

The DirectSound component of DirectX is the digital audio component, which interfaces to the audio hardware. This component enables developers to make use of 3D sound, multiple channels of streaming audio, and other special effects—many emulated if the hardware provides inadequate facilities.

DirectPlay is the network module of the SDK. It provides device-independent access to networking functions, handling the complexity of establishing a network connection and receiving and transmitting information. The new version of DirectPlay also supports guaranteed delivery of data packets and lobbying services—both features that are very helpful for many games.

The Direct3D module of DirectX is of great value to developers of 3D software. Direct3D comes in two layers: Retained-Mode and Immediate-Mode. *Retained-Mode* is a high-level 3D library that provides support for many 3D functions (such as z-buffering, texturing, fog, shading, transformations, and picking) and transparently takes advantage of 3D hardware. Retained-mode also boasts built-in support for geometry and hierarchical management, a feature usually found only in high-cost, third-party toolkits. *Immediate-Mode* is a low-level layer designed specifically for developers who want to port their existing 3D applications to Direct3D with minimal effort; or those developers who desire to write most of the 3D software themselves while still taking advantage of lighting, transformation, and rasterization hardware when it is available.

DirectInput is the component designed for input devices. It is divided into two sections: A set of Win32 (expanded) routines for dealing with joysticks, and a set of interfaces for more general-purpose input devices such as keyboards and mice.

This component provides developers with an easy way to support the latest input devices without worrying whether such devices are digital or analog or how they must be natively supported.

DirectSetup is designed to enable applications to support the installation of the DirectX drivers. Because the current versions of Windows do not ship with DirectX, this component will be temporarily needed by all applications that use DirectX.

DirectX and the Component Object Model

Because DirectX objects are COM objects, the way an application interfaces with them is based on the Component Object Model. What follows is a short primer on COM objects that will give readers the relevant information on using the COM features as they pertain to DirectX. For more information on COM, readers should look at the Win32 reference or any of Microsoft's COM/ActiveX tutorials.

COM Fundamentals

The Component Object Model lies at the heart of ActiveX technologies and is very much the foundation of DirectX objects. In COM terminology, an object is a "black box" that represents a set of capabilities. Objects communicate through a software interface via methods (methods are another term for functions), which are analogous to C++ member functions.

All COM objects have the IUnknown interface available on them. The "I" in IUnknown (and the other DirectX objects) stands for "interface" and is used to designate a set of methods that are available on a particular COM object. The IUnknown interface provides the virtual functionality for every COM object. This interface includes three functions that must be implemented in a consistent way for every COM object: AddRef, QueryInterface, and Release. For more information on these methods, see the COM Reference section located in the function reference section.

COM and C++

COM is a language-independent standard for accessing methods on objects. As currently implemented, COM methods are accessed in precisely the same way that C++ member functions are accessed. This is true for two main reasons: First, all COM methods require a pointer to an object, which is implemented as the *this* pointer in C++; second, all COM methods are called via a vtable, as is done with C++ objects.

This makes C++ a convenient choice for working with COM objects, but by no means essential choice. The architecture of COM is also supported in ActiveX and is very similar to the architecture of Java.

Accessing COM Objects via C

Although C++ is often the language used to access COM interfaces, it is possible to use the C language to interface with them as well.

Developers should take into account two differences between using C++ and C when using the C language with the DirectX SDK. First, C++ automatically passes the *this* pointer to every function; in C, this must be done manually. Second, because C does not directly support structures that have methods, each interface method must be called through the structure's vtable, which is defined as the member lpVtbl.

To illustrate the distinction between C++ and C, observe the following piece of C++ code (which assumes lpDD2 is a pointer to a DirectDraw2 object):

```
lpDD2->GetCaps ( &ddcapsDriver, &ddcapsHEL );
```
In C, this same call would look as follows:

```
lpDD2->lpVtbl->GetCaps ( lpDD2, &ddscapsDriver, &ddscapsHEL );
```
Note that this documentation assumes its readers are using C++, and therefore, does not list the lpDD2 pointer (the *this* pointer in C++) in the parameter list. Developers of C applications should remember this when reading the reference entries or studying any sample code.

INTRODUCTION 3

Introduction to Direct3D

This chapter provides a general overview of Direct3D's history, architecture, and relation to other parts of DirectX.

History

Before Windows, DOS was the most popular operating system for the PC, and games were programmed in DOS exclusively for many years. Despite the widespread acceptance of Windows, game developers resisted developing for it because of unacceptable graphics and audio performance. Under DOS, a game could virtually take over the machine, but under Windows, a game had to coexist with other applications and use an API that was intended to support primarily business applications. These constraints precluded low-level access to graphics and sound hardware and made high-performance games under Windows a virtual impossibility.

The direct access to hardware that DOS afforded came with its own complications, however. In particular, each DOS game had to support the full range of video and audio hardware, which forced developers to write complex code to support dozens of different configurations just to provide consistent graphics and audio across all PCs.

DirectX was created to provide low-level access to hardware features through a consistent, device-independent API. DirectX provides the performance previously available only through DOS, within Windows, and without the complexity of supporting each vendor's particular hardware solutions.

Direct3D is the part of DirectX for accessing the advanced graphics capabilities of 3D hardware accelerators. Like all of DirectX, Direct3D promotes device independence and hardware abstraction by providing a common interface to the various capabilities of 3D accelerator cards. Code written properly for Direct3D will work on Direct3D devices now and in the future.

What is now Direct3D was purchased by Microsoft in early 1995 from RenderMorphics, a British company founded in 1993 by Servan Keondjian, Kate Seekings, and Doub Rabson. Formerly called Reality Lab, Direct3D was modified to integrate with the rest of DirectX, and the first version was released to developers by Microsoft in late 1995.

Direct3D Architecture

Direct3D consists of two distinct APIs: Retained-Mode and Immediate-Mode. Retained-Mode is a high-level API that manages meshes, geometry, and hierarchical scenes. Immediate-Mode is a low-level API that is well-suited for sending batches of triangle primitives to a 3D accelerator card.

As is shown in figure 3.1, a Win32 application can make calls to the Retained-Mode interface or it can make calls directly to the Immediate-Mode interface. Regardless of which API is used, all graphic primitives are processed by the rendering engine for display.

Figure 3.1
Direct3D Architecture

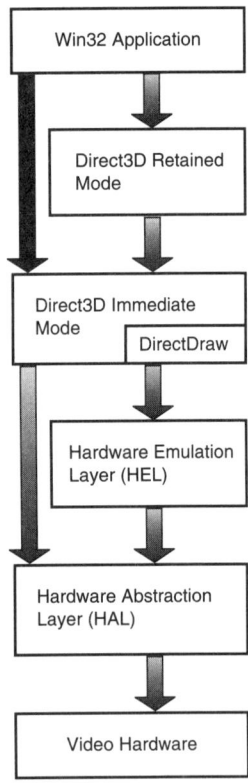

Immediate-Mode is implemented on top of the Hardware Abstraction Layer (HAL) and the Hardware Emulation Layer (HEL). These two layers combine to present a device-independent interface to hardware features and to provide emulation of those features not implemented in hardware.

The Retained-Mode API

Retained-Mode is a high-level interface designed for modeling and managing 3D scenes and their objects. Retained-Mode provides functionality to manage hierarchies of meshes, lights, textures, materials, viewports, mesh animations, and shadows. It also supports its own extensible file format (see Appendix A, "DirectX File Format"), which can store entire scenes in text or binary formats.

Besides providing high-level abstractions for managing scenes, Retained-Mode insulates an application from all aspects of supporting 3D hardware accelerators.

The Immediate-Mode API

Immediate-Mode is a low-level interface that provides a thin layer of abstraction between the application and 3D hardware accelerators. The Immediate-Mode interface does not provide scene management or functionality for loading 3D objects. Immediate-Mode does provide support for viewports, lights, materials, textures, matrices, and execute buffers. Meshes are rendered in Immediate-Mode by constructing execute buffers that set the renderer's state and provide vertex and face lists in large batches for efficient processing. Immediate-Mode also enables a developer to use only part of Direct3D's rendering engine in order to leverage legacy or highly-optimized transformation or lighting engines.

Unlike Retained-Mode, an Immediate-Mode application is not insulated completely from the details of a particular hardware accelerator. Typically the application must query a 3D hardware device for its capabilities and perform differently depending on which capabilities are present.

The Hardware Abstraction Layer

The Hardware Abstraction Layer (HAL) is an interface that abstracts 3D accelerator hardware. Hardware vendors write drivers for their accelerator cards that conform to the HAL's driver architecture. This shelters the application from the details of the underlying hardware. In general, the more services that are handled by the HAL, the better the performance.

The Hardware Emulation Layer

The Hardware Emulation Layer (HEL) is an interface that abstracts the software emulation of features not supported by a particular 3D accelerator device. When an application uses a feature of Direct3D that is not implemented in hardware, the HEL attempts to emulate that feature in software.

The Rendering Engine

The Direct3D rendering engine (see fig. 3.2) is that part of Immediate-Mode that takes information about the object data of a scene, the viewport parameters, the lighting data, and the operations to be performed on this data and renders the scene to the display surfaces. The data for the entire process reaches the rendering engine after it has been stored in execute buffers and passed to the engine. The rendering engine itself is composed of three modules that work together to generate the visual scene:

Figure 3.2

Direct3D Rendering Engine

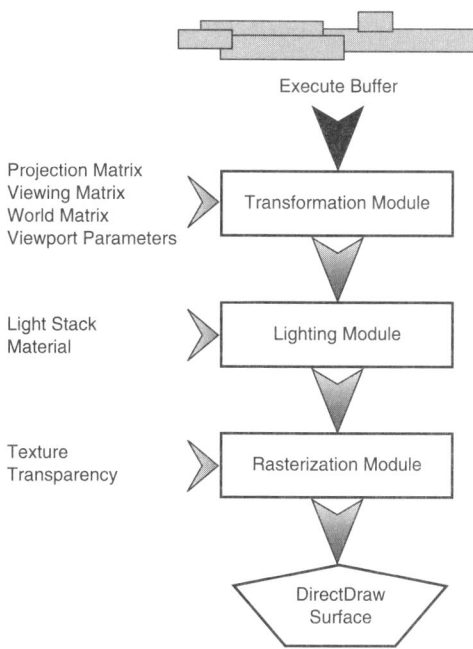

- The *Transformation Module* handles transforming vertices from model coordinates to screen coordinates. It maintains the world, view, and projection matrices. The world matrix transforms vertices from model coordinates to world coordinates. The view matrix transforms vertices from world coordinates to camera coordinates. The projection matrix transforms vertices from camera coordinates to screen coordinates. The Transformation Module composes these three matrices into a single matrix, which is used to convert vertices from their model coordinates to screen coordinates. The Transformation Module also handles clipping triangles to a particular viewport.

- The *Lighting Module* computes the color of each vertex based on the current lighting and material information. The Lighting Module supports two different lighting models: the monochromatic, or ramp, model and the RGB model. In the ramp model, lights are colorless, and vertex colors are computed as indices into a table of shade values, called a ramp. For each color in the scene, a ramp of colors is constructed ranging from black to that color. A vertex color is then computed as an index into the ramp. In the RGB model, a vertex color is computed by computing red, green, and blue components separately. The ramp model is typically used when no 3D accelerator hardware is present because it requires much less processing per vertex than the RGB model.

- The *Rasterization Module* takes the output of the Transformation and Lighting Modules and generates the actual pixels. The Rasterization Module performs shading and texture mapping. The Rasterization Module also performs triangle culling and z-buffer testing, if enabled. An application can bypass the Transformation Module and/or the Lighting Module and access the Rasterization Module directly. Currently, most 3D accelerator hardware implements only the Rasterization Module.

Execute Buffers

Execute buffers contain the data that is passed to the rendering engine. These buffers hold lists of vertices and lists of instructions, defined by their *opcodes*. The opcodes specify render states, triangles to be rendered, and can perform simple forward branches within the execute buffer's instruction stream based on various conditions, such as if all vertices are not visible.

DirectDraw

DirectDraw provides the highest performance access to video memory, and DirectDraw and Direct3D are tightly coupled as a result. DirectDraw provides an abstraction for the display device, as well as the screen, offscreen buffers, palettes, and clipper objects.

DirectDraw surfaces are used to represent the primary surface (the screen), all offscreen (back) buffers, z-buffers, and textures. DirectDraw provides the means to specify whether a particular buffer is in video memory or system memory and provides the blit or flip mechanism for getting rendered pixels on to the screen.

Part II

Retained-Mode Function Reference

4 Introduction to the Direct3D Reference Section..... 35

INTRODUCTION 4

Introduction to the Direct3D Reference Section

The Direct3D Reference is broken down into the following sections for your convenience:

- COM Methods
- Retained-Mode Functions
- Retained-Mode Callbacks
- Retained-Mode Structures
- Retained-Mode Enumerated and Other Types
- Retained-Mode Data Types and Return Values
- Immediate-Mode Functions
- Immediate-Mode Callbacks
- Immediate-Mode Structures
- Immediate-Mode Enumerated and Other Types
- Immediate-Mode Data Types and Return Values

Functions, structures, and types are listed at the top of each page in bold print.

Each function entry includes a description of the function; any notes related to the function; the function arguments, return types, and return values; and places to find information related to the function.

Each structure and type entry includes a definition of the structure or type; a description of the structure or type; member data elements, if appropriate; and places to find related information.

Retained-Mode Function Reference

COM Methods

The IUnknown interface forms the basis of the Component Object Model (COM). All COM objects (and therefore all DirectX objects) must implement the IUnknown interface. The AddRef() and Release() functions provide object reference counting, which the operating system uses to determine whether an object is being used or can be deallocated. The QueryInterface() method provides a mechanism for determining whether a COM object supports specific interfaces and for obtaining those interfaces.

AddRef

Interface:	IUnknown
Description:	This function increases a COM object's reference count by one.
Notes:	When an object is created, its reference count is set to one. When an interface to the object is obtained (through QueryInterface()), or AddRef() is called, the reference count is increased by one. The reference count is decreased by one with a call to Release(). When an object's reference count reaches zero, the operating system deallocates the object. Each AddRef() call (as well as every QueryInterface() call) should be accompanied by a matching Release() call so that the system can properly dispose of the object.
	Although the operating system creates and modifies an object's reference count, an application can modify the reference count for its own purposes, including object copying or object tracking. The operating system will not release the object until its object reference count is zero, regardless of who modified the count.

continues

continued

Arguments:	None
Return Type:	ULONG
Return Values:	Returns the updated reference count of the object.
See Also:	IUnknown::QueryInterface, IUnknown::Release

QueryInterface

Interface:	IUnknown
Description:	This function is used to retrieve a pointer to a particular COM interface from an existing COM object. If the particular interface is supported, QueryInterface() sets a pointer to the requested object.
Notes:	If the COM interface supports the specified interface, the first argument will point to the requested object, and the object's reference count will automatically be increased by one when the function returns. As with AddRef(), this call requires a matching Release() call to enable proper deallocation of the object. An object obtained from QueryInterface for a particular context must have its Release method called when the object is no longer in use within that context.
Arguments:	REFIID riid—Reference identifier of the COM interface requested, a GUID.
	LPVOID* obp—Pointer to the object type requested.
Return Type:	HRESULT
Return Values:	See Direct3D Retained-Mode Return Values.
See Also:	IUnknown::AddRef, IUnknown::Release

Release

Interface:	IUnknown
Description:	This function decreases an object's reference count by one. It is generally used in conjunction with AddRef() or QueryInterface().

Notes:	An object obtained from QueryInterface() must have its Release() method called when the application is done with the object. Release() should also be called once for each call to AddRef(). If Release() is called one too many times, the object will be destroyed although references to it still exist. If an object still has a reference when an application ends, memory leaks may result.
	When an object's reference reaches zero, the object is deallocated by the operating system automatically.
Arguments:	None
Return Type:	ULONG
Return Values:	Returns the object's new reference count.
See Also:	IUnknown::AddRef, IUnknown::QueryInterface

CoCreateInstance

Interface:	None
Description:	This function is used to create an instance of a COM object.
Notes:	This function can be called to create an uninitialized instance of a COM object whose reference identifier is known.
	An application must initialize COM by calling CoInitialize() before creating any COM objects.
Arguments:	REFCLSID rclsid—This specifies the reference class identifier (CLSID) of the object to be created.
	LPUNKNOWN PunkOuter—This specifies the controlling IUnknown object of the aggregate to use the newly created object instance. If this parameter is NULL, the instance will not be created as part of an aggregate.
	DWORD dwClsContext—This specifies the context in which the instance is to be run. This parameter can be one of the Win32 CLSCTX enumeration flags.

continues

continued

	REFIID riid—This specifies the interface used to communicate with the object.
	LPVOID *ppv—This specifies the address of a 32-bit pointer. If this function succeeds, this pointer will be set to the newly created object.
Return Type:	STDAPI
Return Values:	S_OK—An instance of the specified object class was successfully created.
	REGDB_E_CLASSNOTREG—The specified object class is not registered in the registration database. This value can also indicate that the type of server requested in the CLSCTX enumeration is not registered or that the values for the server types in the registry are corrupt.
	CLASS_E_NOAGGREGATION—This class cannot be created as part of an aggregate.
See Also:	CoInitialize

CoInitialize

Interface:	None
Description:	This function initializes the Component Object Model (COM) library for use.
Notes:	This function should be called to initialize the Component Object Model before an application uses any of the standard COM functions, such as CoCreateInstance.
Arguments:	LPVOID pvReserved—Reserve for future use. In the present implementation, this parameter must be set to 0.
Return Type:	HRESULT
Return Values:	S_OK—The library was initialized successfully.
	S_FALSE—The library was already initialized or default allocator could not be released.
	E_INVALIDARG—The pvReserved argument is not NULL.

	E_OUTOFMEMORY—There was insufficient memory to complete the operation.
See Also:	CoCreateInstance

CoUninitialize

Interface:	None
Description:	This function uninitializes the Component Object Model (COM) library.
Notes:	An application should call this function to uninitialize the Component Object Model (COM) library before the application terminates. Calls to CoInitialize() and CoUninitialize() must be paired.
Arguments:	None
Return Type:	Void
Return Values:	None
See Also:	CoInitialize
Type:	CLSCTX
| Definition: | ```
typedef enum tagCLSCTX
{
    CLSCTX_INPROC_SERVER  = 1,
    CLSCTX_INPROC_HANDLER = 2,
    CLSCTX_LOCAL_SERVER   = 4,
    CLSCTX_REMOTE_SERVER  = 16
} CLSCTX;
#define CLSCTX_SERVER    (CLSCTX_INPROC_SERVER |
CLSCTX_LOCAL_SERVER | CLSCTX_REMOTE_SERVER)
#define CLSCTX_ALL       (CLSCTX_INPROC_HANDLER | CLSCTX_SERVER)
``` |
| Notes: | Values from the CLSCTX enumeration are used in activation calls to indicate the execution contexts in which an object is to be run. These values are also used in calls to `CoRegisterClassObject` to indicate the set of execution contexts in which a class object is to be made available for requests to construct instances. |

continues
```

continued

Members: CLSCTX_INPROC_SERVER—The code that creates and manages objects of this class runs in the same process as the caller of the function specifying the class context.

CLSCTX_INPROC_HANDLER—The code that manages objects of this class is an in-process handler. This is a DLL that runs in the client process and implements client-side structures of this class when instances of the class are accessed remotely.

CLSCTX_LOCAL_SERVER—The EXE code that creates and manages objects of this class is loaded in a separate process space (runs on same machine but in a different process).

CLSCTX_REMOTE_SERVER—A remote machine context. The LocalServer32 or LocalService code that creates and manages objects of this class is run on a different machine.

Defined Terms: CLSCTX_SERVER—Indicates server code, whether in-process, local, or remote.

CLSCTX_ALL—Indicates all class contexts.

Retained-Mode Functions

The basic Direct3D Retained-Mode functions provide functionality for creating the Retained-Mode object and for the manipulation of colors, vectors, and quaternions. The Retained-Mode functions include:

Direct3DRMCreate

D3DRMColorGetAlpha

D3DRMColorGetBlue

D3DRMColorGetGreen

D3DRMColorGetRed

D3DRMCreateColorRGB

D3DRMCreateColorRGBA

D3DRMMatrixFromQuaternion

D3DRMQuaternionFromRotation

D3DRMQuaternionMultiply

D3DRMQuaternionSlerp

D3DRMVectorAdd

D3DRMVectorCrossProduct

D3DRMVectorDotProduct

D3DRMVectorModulus

D3DRMVectorNormalize

D3DRMVectorRandom

D3DRMVectorReflect

D3DRMVectorRotate

D3DRMVectorScale

D3DRMVectorSubtract

Direct3DRMCreate

Interface:	None
Declaration:	`HRESULT Direct3DRMCreate(LPDIRECT3DRM FAR * lplpD3DRM);`
Description:	This function creates an instance of a Direct3D Retained-Mode object.
Notes:	This function should only need to be called once per Retained-Mode application, but can be called multiple times without error.
Arguments:	LPDIRECT3DRM* lplpD3DRM—This points to a pointer that will be initialized with a Direct3DRM object if the call is successful or NULL if the call fails.
Return Type:	HRESULT
Return Values:	See Direct3D Retained-Mode Return Values.
See Also:	None

D3DRMColorGetAlpha
D3DRMColorGetBlue
D3DRMColorGetGreen
D3DRMColorGetRed

Interface:	None

Declaration:	`D3DVALUE D3DRMColorGetAlpha(D3DCOLOR d3drmc);`
	`D3DVALUE D3DRMColorGetBlue(D3DCOLOR d3drmc);`
	`D3DVALUE D3DRMColorGetGreen(D3DCOLOR d3drmc);`
	`D3DVALUE D3DRMColorGetRed(D3DCOLOR d3drmc);`

Description:	These functions return the components of a Direct3D RGB color.
Notes:	Color components should be within the range of 0.0 to 1.0.
Arguments:	D3DCOLOR d3drmc—The color from which the component is retrieved.
Return Type:	D3DVALUE
Return Values:	Returns the red, green, blue, or alpha value of the color.

See Also:	D3DRMCreateColorRGB, D3DRMCreateColorRGBA, IDirect3DRMFace::GetColor, IDirect3DRMFace::SetColor, IDirect3DRMFrame::GetColor, IDirect3DRMFrame::SetColor, IDirect3DRMLight::GetColor, IDirect3DRMLight::SetColor, D3DCOLOR

D3DRMCreateColorRGB
D3DRMCreateColorRGBA

Interface:	None
Declaration:	`D3DCOLOR D3DRMCreateColorRGB(D3DVALUE red, D3DVALUE green, D3DVALUE blue);` `D3DCOLOR D3DRMCreateColorRGBA(D3DVALUE red, D3DVALUE green, D3DVALUE blue, D3DVALUE alpha);`
Description:	These functions create a Direct3D color from the supplied color components.
Notes:	The color created with D3DRMCreateColorRGB has an alpha component value of 1.0.
Arguments:	D3DVALUE red—The red component of color. D3DVALUE green—The green component of color. D3DVALUE blue—The blue component of color. D3DVALUE alpha—The alpha component of color. (D3DRMCreateColorRGBA ONLY)
Return Type:	D3DCOLOR
Return Values:	If all the arguments are between 0.0 and 1.0, the resulting Direct3D color is returned. Otherwise, the color black is returned (100% transparent black if alpha blending or stippling).
See Also:	D3DRMColorGetAlpha, D3DRMColorGetBlue, D3DRMColorGetGreen, D3DRMColorGetRed, IDirect3DRMFace::GetColor, IDirect3DRMFace::SetColor, IDirect3DRMFrame::GetColor, IDirect3DRMFrame::SetColor, IDirect3DRMLight::GetColor, IDirect3DRMLight::SetColor, D3DCOLOR

D3DRMMatrixFromQuaternion

Interface:	None
Declaration:	`void D3DRMMatrixFromQuaternion (D3DRMMATRIX4D mat, LPD3DRMQUATERNION lpquat);`
Description:	This function calculates the rotation matrix for the unit quaternion specified.
Notes:	This function can be used in the calculation of rotation interpolations.
Arguments:	D3DRMMATRIX4D mat—The array that will contain the calculated rotation matrix. LPD3DRMQUATERNION lpquat—The pointer to the quaternion containing rotation.
Return Type:	Void
Return Values:	None
See Also:	D3DQuaternionFromRotation, D3DQuaternionMultiply, D3DQuaternionSlerp, D3DRMMATRIX4D, D3DRMQUATERNION

D3DRMQuaternionFromRotation

Interface:	None
Declaration:	`LPD3DRMQUATERNION D3DRMQuaternionFromRotation (LPD3DRMQUATERNION lpquat, LPD3DVECTOR lpv, D3DVALUE theta);`
Description:	This function computes a unit quaternion from a given rotation around a given axis.
Notes:	This function can be used in the calculation of rotation interpolations.
Arguments:	LPD3DRMQUATERNION lpquat—The pointer to quaternion that will be computed. LPD3DVECTOR lpv—The vector representing the axis of rotation. D3DVALUE theta—The rotation around a given axis in radians.
Return Type:	LPD3DRMQUATERNION

Return Values:	Returns the address of the quaternion that was passed as the first parameter.
See Also:	D3DRMMatrixFromQuaternion, D3DQuaternionMultiply, D3DQuaternionSlerp, D3DRMQUATERNION

D3DRMQuaternionMultiply

Interface:	None
Declaration:	`LPD3DRMQUATERNION D3DRMQuaternionMultiply(LPD3DRMQUATERNION lpq, LPD3DRMQUATERNION lpa, LPD3DRMQUATERNION lpb);`
Description:	This function multiplies two quaternions.
Notes:	When used in conjunction with D3DRMQuaternionSlerp(), this function can perform complex object rotations. D3DRMQuaternionMultiply() can composite multiple rotations represented as quaternions, and D3DRMQuaternionSlerp() can smoothly interpolate between two quaternion rotations.
	Quaternion multiplication is sometimes referred to as composition.
	If NULL is passed as any of the arguments, Retained-Mode will crash.
Arguments:	LPD3DRMQUATERNION lpq—The address where the result of the multiplication will be stored.
	LPD3DRMQUATERNION lpa—The pointer to the first quaternion to be multiplied.
	LPD3DRMQUATERNION lpb—The pointer to the first quaternion to be multiplied.
Return Type:	LPD3DRMQUATERNION
Return Values:	This function returns a pointer to the computed quaternion.
See Also:	D3DRMMatrixFromQuaternion, D3DRMMatrixQuaternionFromRotation, D3DQuaternionSlerp, D3DRMQUATERNION

D3DRMQuaternionSlerp

Interface:	None
Declaration:	`LPD3DRMQUATERNION D3DRMQuaternionSlerp(LPD3DRMQUATERNION lpq, LPD3DRMQUATERNION lpa, LPD3DRMQUATERNION lpb, D3DVALUE alpha);`
Description:	This function interpolates between two quaternions using spherical linear interpolation.
Notes:	When used in conjunction with D3DRMQuaternionMultiply(), this function can perform complex object rotations. D3DRMQuaternionMultiply() can composite multiple rotations represented as quaternions, and D3DRMQuaternionSlerp() can smoothly interpolate between two quaternion rotations. If NULL is passed as any of the arguments, Retained-Mode will crash.
Arguments:	LPD3DRMQUATERNION lpq—The address where the result of the interpolation will be stored. LPD3DRMQUATERNION lpa—The pointer to the first quaternion for interpolation. LPD3DRMQUATERNION lpb—The pointer to the second quaternion for interpolation. D3DVALUE alpha—The value of the parameter for interpolation, between 0.0 and 1.0.
Return Type:	LPD3DRMQUATERNION
Return Values:	This function returns a pointer to the computed quaternion.
See Also:	D3DRMMatrixFromQuaternion, D3DRMMatrixQuaternionFromRotation, D3DQuaternionMultiply, D3DRMQUATERNION

D3DRMVectorAdd

Interface:	None
Declaration:	`LPD3DVECTOR D3DRMVectorAdd(LPD3DVECTOR lpd, LPD3DVECTOR lps1, LPD3DVECTOR lps2);`
Description:	This function adds two vectors.
Notes:	If NULL is passed as any of the arguments, Retained-Mode will crash.
Arguments:	LPD3DVECTOR lpd—The pointer to the computed vector.
	LPD3DVECTOR lps1—The pointer to the first vector operand.
	LPD3DVECTOR lps2—The pointer to the second vector operand.
Return Type:	LPD3DVECTOR
Return Values:	The pointer to the computed vector.
See Also:	D3DVectorCrossProduct, D3DVectorDotProduct, D3DVectorModulus, D3DVectorNormalize, D3DVectorRandom, D3DVectorReflect, D3DVectorRotate, D3DRMVectorScale, D3DRMVectorSubtract, D3DVECTOR

D3DRMVectorCrossProduct

Interface:	None
Declaration:	`LPD3DVECTOR D3DRMVectorCrossProduct(LPD3DVECTOR lpd, LPD3DVECTOR lps1, LPD3DVECTOR lps2);`
Description:	This function computes the cross product of two vectors.
Notes:	The resulting vector from a cross product is perpendicular to both of the operand vectors.
	If NULL is passed as any of the arguments, Retained-Mode will crash.

continues

continued

Arguments:	LPD3DVECTOR lpd—The pointer to the computed vector.
	LPD3DVECTOR lps1—The pointer to the first vector operand.
	LPD3DVECTOR lps2—The pointer to the second vector operand.
Return Type:	LPD3DVECTOR
Return Values:	This function returns a pointer to the computed vector.
See Also:	D3DVectorAdd, D3DVectorDotProduct, D3DVectorModulus, D3DVectorNormalize, D3DVectorRandom, D3DVectorReflect, D3DVectorRotate, D3DRMVectorScale, D3DRMVectorSubtract, D3DVECTOR

D3DRMVectorDotProduct

Interface:	None
Declaration:	`D3DVALUE D3DRMVectorDotProduct(LPD3DVECTOR lps1, LPD3DVECTOR lps2);`
Description:	This function computes the dot product of two vectors.
Notes:	This function can be used to calculate the angle between two vectors using the formula:
	theta = arccos ((v·w) / (|v|·|w|))
	If NULL is passed as any of the arguments, Retained-Mode will crash.
Arguments:	LPD3DVECTOR lps1—The pointer to the first vector operand.
	LPD3DVECTOR lps2—The pointer to the second vector operand.
Return Type:	D3DVALUE
Return Values:	This function returns the computed dot product.
See Also:	D3DVectorAdd, D3DVectorCrossProduct, D3DVectorModulus, D3DVectorNormalize, D3DVectorRandom, D3DVectorReflect, D3DVectorRotate, D3DRMVectorScale, D3DRMVectorSubtract, D3DVECTOR

D3DRMVectorModulus

Interface:	None
Declaration:	D3DVALUE D3DRMVectorModulus(LPD3DVECTOR lpv);
Description:	This function calculates the length of a vector.
Notes:	The length of a vector is defined to be the square root of the sum of the squares of its components.
Arguments:	LPD3DVECTOR lpv—The pointer to the vector on which the length is calculated.
Return Type:	D3DVALUE
Return Values:	This function returns the length of the vector.
See Also:	D3DVectorAdd, D3DVectorCrossProduct, D3DVectorDotProduct, D3DVectorNormalize, D3DVectorRandom, D3DVectorReflect, D3DVectorRotate, D3DRMVectorScale, D3DRMVectorSubtract, D3DVECTOR

D3DRMVectorNormalize

Interface:	None
Declaration:	LPD3DVECTOR D3DRMVectorNormalize(LPD3DVECTOR lpv);
Description:	This function normalizes a vector.
Notes:	This function creates a unit vector (a vector of length one unit) from any source vector and normalizes the zero vector (0, 0, 0) to (1, 0, 0).
Arguments:	LPD3DVECTOR lpv—The pointer to the vector to be normalized.
Return Type:	LPD3DVECTOR
Return Values:	Returns the address of the vector passed in the lpv argument.
See Also:	D3DVectorAdd, D3DVectorCrossProduct, D3DVectorDotProduct, D3DVectorModulus, D3DVectorRandom, D3DVectorReflect, D3DVectorRotate, D3DRMVectorScale, D3DRMVectorSubtract, D3DVECTOR

D3DRMVectorRandom

Interface:	None
Declaration:	`LPD3DVECTOR D3DRMVectorRandom(LPD3DVECTOR lpd);`
Description:	This function returns a random vector of length 1.
Notes:	This function could be used to generate a random direction.
	If NULL is passed as the argument, Retained-Mode will crash.
Arguments:	LPD3DVECTOR lpd—The pointer to the vector to be filled with a random unit vector.
Return Type:	LPD3DVECTOR
Return Values:	Returns a pointer to the random vector.
See Also:	D3DVectorAdd, D3DVectorCrossProduct, D3DVectorDotProduct, D3DVectorModulus, D3DVectorNormalize, D3DVectorReflect, D3DVectorRotate, D3DRMVectorScale, D3DRMVectorSubtract, D3DVECTOR

D3DRMVectorReflect

Interface:	None
Declaration:	`LPD3DVECTOR D3DRMVectorReflect(LPD3DVECTOR lpd, LPD3DVECTOR lpRay, LPD3DVECTOR lpNorm);`
Description:	This function calculates the reflection of a ray about a normal.
Notes:	The function could be used for object collision computations.
	If NULL is passed as any of the arguments, Retained-Mode will crash.
Arguments:	LPD3DVECTOR lpd—The pointer to the reflected vector.
	LPD3DVECTOR lpRay—The pointer to the incident vector.
	LPD3DVECTOR lpNorm—The pointer to the normal vector.
Return Type:	LPD3DVECTOR

Return Values:	Returns a pointer to the calculated vector.
See Also:	D3DVectorAdd, D3DVectorCrossProduct, D3DVectorDotProduct, D3DVectorModulus, D3DVectorNormalize, D3DVectorRandom, D3DVectorRotate, D3DRMVectorScale, D3DRMVectorSubtract, D3DVECTOR

D3DRMVectorRotate

Interface:	None
Declaration:	`LPD3DVECTOR D3DRMVectorRotate(LPD3DVECTOR lpr, LPD3DVECTOR lpv, LPD3DVECTOR lpaxis, D3DVALUE theta);`
Description:	This function rotates a vector around an axis.
Notes:	The rotation of the vector is represented in radians. There are 2π radians in a circle. The conversion between degrees and radians is:
	AngleInDegrees = 57.295779513082323πAngleInRadians;
	AngleInRadians = 0.017453292519943295πAngleInDegrees;
	If NULL is passed as any of the arguments, Retained-Mode will crash.
Arguments:	LPD3DVECTOR lpr—The pointer to the rotated vector.
	LPD3DVECTOR lpv—The pointer to the source vector.
	LPD3DVECTOR lpaxis—The pointer to the incident vector.
	D3DVALUE theta—The number of radians to rotate the vector.
Return Type:	LPD3DVECTOR
Return Values:	Returns a pointer to the calculated vector.
See Also:	D3DVectorAdd, D3DVectorCrossProduct, D3DVectorDotProduct, D3DVectorModulus, D3DVectorNormalize, D3DVectorRandom, D3DVectorReflect, D3DRMVectorScale, D3DRMVectorSubtract, D3DVECTOR

D3DRMVectorScale

Interface:	None
Declaration:	`LPD3DVECTOR D3DRMVectorScale(LPD3DVECTOR lpd, LPD3DVECTOR lps, D3DVALUE factor);`
Description:	This function multiplies each component of a vector by a scalar value.
Notes:	This function has the same effect as scaling a vector uniformly in all axes. This function cannot be used for non-uniform scaling. A scale transformation matrix must be used for non-uniform scaling.
	If NULL is passed as any of the arguments, Retained-Mode will crash.
Arguments:	LPD3DVECTOR lpd—The pointer to the scaled vector.
	LPD3DVECTOR lps—The pointer to the source vector.
	D3DVALUE factor—The amount to uniformly scale the vector. A value of 1 does not change the vector, but a value of 2 doubles the length of the vector.
Return Type:	LPD3DVECTOR
Return Values:	Returns a pointer to the calculated vector.
See Also:	D3DVectorAdd, D3DVectorCrossProduct, D3DVectorDotProduct, D3DVectorModulus, D3DVectorNormalize, D3DVectorRandom, D3DVectorReflect, D3DVectorRotate, D3DRMVectorSubtract, D3DVECTOR

D3DRMVectorSubtract

Interface:	None
Declaration:	LPD3DVECTOR D3DRMVectorSubtract(LPD3DVECTOR lpd, LPD3DVECTOR lps1, LPD3DVECTOR lps2);
Description:	This function subtracts two vectors.
Notes:	The vector pointed to by lps2 is subtracted from the vector pointed to by lps1.
	If NULL is passed as any of the arguments, Retained-Mode will crash.
Arguments:	LPD3DVECTOR lpd—The pointer to the computed vector.
	LPD3DVECTOR lps1—The pointer to the first vector operand.
	LPD3DVECTOR lps2—The pointer to the second vector operand.
Return Type:	LPD3DVECTOR
Return Values:	Returns a pointer to the calculated vector.
See Also:	D3DVectorAdd, D3DVectorCrossProduct, D3DVectorDotProduct, D3DVectorModulus, D3DVectorNormalize, D3DVectorRandom, D3DVectorReflect, D3DVectorRotate, D3DRMVectorScale, D3DVECTOR

Retained-Mode Callbacks

The Direct3D Retained-Mode Callbacks enable communication between Direct3D and an application and provide a method for attaching application-specific behavior related to Direct3D events. The Retained-Mode Callbacks include:

D3DRMDEVICEPALETTECALLBACK

D3DRMFRAMEMOVECALLBACK

D3DRMLOADCALLBACK

D3DRMLOADTEXTURECALLBACK

D3DRMOBJECTCALLBACK

D3DRMUPDATECALLBACK

D3DRMUSERVISUALCALLBACK

D3DRMWRAPCALLBACK

D3DRMDEVICEPALETTECALLBACK

Interface:	None
Declaration:	`void (*D3DRMDEVICEPALETTECALLBACK) (LPDIRECT3DRMDEVICE lpDirect3DRMDev, LPVOID lpArg, DWORD dwIndex, LONG red, LONG green, LONG blue);`
Description:	This function prototype defines the Direct3D Retained-Mode device palette callback type.
Arguments:	LPDIRECT3DRMDEVICE lpDirect3DRMDev—The address of the IDirect3DRMDevice object for this device.
	LPVOID lpArg—The address of application-defined data passed to this callback function.
	DWORD dwIndex—The index of the palette entry being described.

LONG red—The red component of the color at the given index in the palette.

LONG green—The green component of the color at the given index in the palette.

LONG blue—The blue component of the color at the given index in the palette.

Return Type:	Void
Return Values:	None
See Also:	None

D3DRMFRAMEMOVECALLBACK

Interface:	None
Declaration:	`void (*D3DRMFRAMEMOVECALLBACK)(LPDIRECT3DRMFRAME lpD3DRMFrame, LPVOID lpArg, D3DVALUE delta);`
Description:	This function prototype defines the Direct3D Retained-Mode frame move callback type.
Notes:	This callback is used in conjunction with IDirect3DRMFrame::Move(). The callback function will be called every time IDirect3DRMFrame::Move() is executed. The callback is called before Retained-Mode executes its velocity and rotational physics.
Arguments:	LPDIRECT3DRMFRAME lpD3DRMFrame—The address of the Direct3D Retained-Mode frame object to be moved.
	LPVOID lpArg—The address of application-defined data passed to this callback.
	D3DVALUE delta—The amount of time that has passed. This value is passed from IDirect3DRMFrame::Move().
Return Type:	Void
Return Values:	None
See Also:	IDirect3DRMFrame::AddMoveCallback, IDirect3DRMFrame::DeleteMoveCallback, IDirect3DRMFrame::Move

D3DRMLOADCALLBACK

Interface:	None
Declaration:	`void (*D3DRMLOADCALLBACK) (LPDIRECT3DRMOBJECT lpObject, REFIID ObjectGuid, LPVOID lpArg);`
Description:	This function prototype defines the Direct3D Retained-Mode load callback type.
Notes:	This callback is used in conjunction with IDirect3DRM::Load(). The callback function will be called every time an object is loaded by IDirect3DRM::Load(). This function is useful for integrating application-specific file formats.
Arguments:	LPDIRECT3DRMOBJECT lpObject—The address of the Direct3D Retained-Mode object being loaded.
	REFIID ObjectGuid—Globally unique identifier (GUID) of the object being loaded.
	LPVOID lpArg—The address of application-defined data passed to this callback.
Return Type:	Void
Return Values:	None
See Also:	IDirect3DRM::Load

D3DRMLOADTEXTURECALLBACK

Interface:	None
Declaration:	`HRESULT (*D3DRMLOADTEXTURECALLBACK) (char *tex_name, void *lpArg, LPDIRECT3DRMTEXTURE *lpD3DRMTex);`
Description:	This function prototype defines the Direct3D Retained-Mode load texture callback type.
Notes:	This callback is used in conjunction with IDirect3DRM::Load(), IDirect3DRMAnimationSet::Load(), IDirect3DRMFrame::Load(), and IDirect3DRMMeshBuilder::Load(). The callback function will be

	called for each texture referred to by the object loaded. This function can be used to support application-specific texture file or resource file formats that Retained-Mode does not support.
Arguments:	char *tex_name—The address of a string containing the name of the texture.
	void *lpArg—The address of application-defined data passed to this callback.
	LPDIRECT3DRMTEXTURE *lpD3DRMTex—The address of the Direct3D Retained-Mode texture object.
Return Type:	HRESULT
Return Values:	See Direct3D Retained-Mode Return Values.
See Also:	IDirect3DRM::Load, IDirect3DRMAnimationSet::Load, IDirect3DRMFrame::Load, IDirect3DRMMeshBuilder::Load

D3DRMOBJECTCALLBACK

Interface:	None
Declaration:	`void (*D3DRMOBJECTCALLBACK)(LPDIRECT3DRMOBJECT lpD3DRMobj, LPVOID lpArg);`
Description:	This function prototype defines a generic Direct3D Retained-Mode object callback type.
Notes:	This callback can be used in conjunction with IDirect3DRM::EnumerateObjects(), where it will be called on the object specified for enumeration. This callback can also be registered to execute when an object is destroyed (using IDirect3DMObject::AddDestroyCallback()).
Arguments:	LPDIRECT3DRMOBJECT lpD3DRMobj—The address of a Direct3D Retained-Mode object interface for the object being enumerated or destroyed. The application must call the Release() function for each object if being enumerated.
	LPVOID lpArg—The address of application-defined data passed to this callback.

continues

continued

Return Type:	Void
Return Values:	None
See Also:	IDirect3DRMObject::AddDestroyCallback, IDirect3DRMObject::DeleteDestroyCallback IDirect3DRM::EnumerateObjects

D3DRMUPDATECALLBACK

Interface:	None
Declaration:	`void (*D3DRMUPDATECALLBACK)(LPDIRECT3DRMDEVICE lpobj, LPVOID lpArg, int iRectCount, LPD3DRECT d3dRectUpdate);`
Description:	This function prototype defines the Direct3D Retained-Mode update callback type.
Notes:	This callback is used in conjunction with IDirect3DRMDevice::Update(). After the callback has been installed with IDirect3DRMDevice::AddUpdateCallback(), the callback function will be called every time IDirect3DRMDevice::Update() executes.
Arguments:	LPDIRECT3DRMDEVICE lpobj—The address of the Direct3D device object to which this callback function applies.
	LPVOID lpArg—The address of application-defined data passed to this callback.
	int iRectCount—The number of rectangles specified in the d3dRectUpdate parameter.
	LPD3DRECT d3dRectUpdate—The array of one or more Direct3D rectangle structures that describe the area to be updated. The coordinates are specified in device units.
Return Type:	Void
Return Values:	None
See Also:	IDirect3DRMDevice::AddUpdateCallback, IDirect3DRMDevice::DeleteUpdateCallback, IDirect3DRMDevice::Update

D3DRMUSERVISUALCALLBACK

Interface: None

Declaration: `int (*D3DRMUSERVISUALCALLBACK)(LPDIRECT3DRMUSERVISUAL lpD3DRMUV, LPVOID lpArg, D3DRMUSERVISUALREASON lpD3DRMUVreason, LPDIRECT3DRMDEVICE lpD3DRMDev, LPDIRECT3DRMVIEWPORT lpD3DRMview);`

Description: This function prototype defines the Direct3D Retained-Mode user visual callback type.

Notes: The callback function will be called when the system needs an application to do one of the following:

- Determine if the user visual is visible (lpD3DRMUVreason parameter is D3DRMUSERVISUAL_CANSEE).
- Render the user visual (lpD3DRMUVreason parameter is D3DRMUSERVISUAL_RENDER).

User visuals are used mainly to mix Immediate-Mode and Retained-Mode functionality. In this situation, the callback could be used to execute Immediate-Mode execute buffers.

Arguments: LPDIRECT3DRMUSERVISUAL lpD3DRMUV—The address of the Direct3D Retained-Mode user visual object.

LPVOID lpArg—The address of application-defined data passed to this callback function.

D3DRMUSERVISUALREASON lpD3DRMUVreason—One of the members of the D3DRMUSERVISUALREASON enumerated type:

D3DRMUSERVISUAL_CANSEE—The application should return TRUE if the user-visual object is visible in the viewport. In this case, the application uses the device specified in the lpD3DRMview parameter.

D3DRMUSERVISUAL_RENDER—The application should render the user-visual element. In this case, the application uses the device specified in the lpD3DRMDev parameter.

continues

continued

	LPDIRECT3DRMDEVICE lpD3DRMDev—The address of a Direct3D Retained-Mode device object used to render the Direct3DRMUserVisual object.
	LPDIRECT3DRMVIEWPORT lpD3DRMview—The address of a Direct3D Retained-Mode viewport object used to determine whether the user visual object is visible.
Return Type:	int
Return Values:	If the lpD3DRMUVreason parameter is D3DRMUSERVISUAL_CANSEE, this function should return TRUE or FALSE depending on whether the object is visible in the specified viewport.
	If the lpD3DRMUVreason parameter is D3DRMUSERVISUAL_RENDER, the return value is application-defined.
	It is always safe to return TRUE.
See Also:	IDirect3DRM::CreateUserVisual, IDirect3DRMUserVisual::Init, IDirect3DRMViewport::Render

D3DRMWRAPCALLBACK

Interface:	None
Declaration:	`void (*D3DRMWRAPCALLBACK)(LPD3DVECTOR lpD3DVector, int* lpU, int* lpV, LPD3DVECTOR lpD3DRMVA, LPD3DVECTOR lpD3DRMVB, LPVOID lpArg);`
Description:	This callback function is not implemented.

ARRAY

The various Retained-Mode array interfaces enable easy manipulation of groups of objects. The array interfaces provide functionality for retrieving a member (or element) of the array as well as the array size. The array interfaces are as follows:

IDirect3DRMArray

IDirect3DRMDeviceArray

IDirect3DRMFaceArray

IDirect3DRMFrameArray

IDirect3DRMLightArray

IDirect3DRMPickedArray

IDirect3DRMViewportArray

IDirect3DRMVisualArray

The array interfaces, as with all COM interfaces, are derived from IUnknown and inherit its methods. The array interfaces also inherit the methods of IDirect3DRMObject. The following table describes the methods from which the various array objects can be obtained:

Direct3DRMDeviceArray	Direct3DRMLightArray
IDirect3DRM::GetDevices()	IDirect3DRMFrame::GetLights()
Direct3DRMFaceArray	Direct3DRMPickedArray
IDirect3DRMMeshBuilder::GetFaces()	IDirect3DRMViewport::Pick()
Direct3DRMFrameArray	Direct3DRMViewportArray
IDirect3DRMPickedArray::GetPick()	IDirect3DRM::CreateFrame()
or	Direct3DRMVisualArray
IDirect3DRMFrame::GetChildren()	IDirect3DRMFrame::GetVisuals()

continues

continued

All the array interfaces implement GetSize(). All the array interfaces implement GetElement() except for IDirect3DRMPickedArray, which implements GetPick().

GetSize

Interface:	IDirect3DRMArray, IDirect3DRMDeviceArray, IDirect3DRMFaceArray, IDirect3DRMFrameArray, IDirect3DRMLightArray, IDirect3DRMPickedArray, IDirect3DRMViewportArray, IDirect3DRMVisualArray
Declaration:	`DWORD GetSize();`
Description:	This method retrieves the number of elements in an array object.
Arguments:	None
Return Type:	DWORD
Return Values:	Returns the number of elements in an array object.
See Also:	GetElement

GetElement

Interface:	IDirect3DRMDeviceArray, IDirect3DRMFaceArray, IDirect3DRMFrameArray, IDirect3DRMLightArray, IDirect3DRMViewportArray, IDirect3DRMVisualArray

Declaration:	`HRESULT GetElement(DWORD index, LPDIRECT3DRMDEVICE *lplpD3DRMDevice);`
	`HRESULT GetElement(DWORD index, LPDIRECT3DRMFACE *lplpD3DRMFace);`
	`HRESULT GetElement(DWORD index, LPDIRECT3DRMFRAME *lplpD3DRMFrame);`
	`HRESULT GetElement(DWORD index, LPDIRECT3DRMLIGHT *lplpD3DRMLight);`
	`HRESULT GetElement(DWORD index, LPDIRECT3DRMVIEWPORT *lplpD3DRMViewport);`
	`HRESULT GetElement(DWORD index, LPDIRECT3DRMVISUAL *lplpD3DRMVisual);`

Description:	This method retrieves a specific element from an array object.

Notes:	The generic array object, IDirect3DRMArray, does not have a GetElement method, due to overloading and COM.
Arguments:	DWORD index—The index of the element in the array to be retrieved.
	The second argument is one of the following based on the type of array object being called:
	LPDIRECT3DRMDEVICE *lplpD3DRMDevice—The address that will be filled with a pointer to an IDirect3DRMDevice interface.
	LPDIRECT3DRMFACE *lplpD3DRMFace—The address that will be filled with a pointer to an IDirect3DRMFace interface.
	LPDIRECT3DRMFRAME *lplpD3DRMFrame—The address that will be filled with a pointer to an IDirect3DRMFrame interface.
	LPDIRECT3DRMLIGHT *lplpD3DRMLight—The address that will be filled with a pointer to an IDirect3DRMLight interface.
	LPDIRECT3DRMVIEWPORT *lplpD3DRMViewport—The address that will be filled with a pointer to an IDirect3DRMViewport interface.
	LPDIRECT3DRMVISUAL *lplpD3DRMVisual—The address that will be filled with a pointer to an IDirect3DRMVisual interface.
Return Type:	HRESULT
Return Values:	See Direct3D Retained-Mode Return Values.
See Also:	GetSize

GetPick

Interface:	IDirect3DRMPickedArray
Declaration:	`HRESULT GetPick(DWORD index, LPDIRECT3DRMVISUAL * lplpVisual, LPDIRECT3DRMFRAMEARRAY * lplpFrameArray, LPD3DRMPICKDESC lpD3DRMPickDesc);`
Description:	This method retrieves a pick record from an array of picked objects.
Notes:	Pick records are generated with IDirect3DRMViewport::Pick() which is used to select an object in a scene through screen coordinates. If the

continues

continued

screen coordinates are within an object's rendered viewport representation, the scene hierarchy containing the object is placed into the pick array, with the root of the scene in the first pick array element and the object's frame in the last.

Arguments: DWORD index—The index specifying the element of the array to be retrieved.

LPDIRECT3DRMVISUAL *lplpVisual—The address that will contain a pointer to the Direct3D Retained-Mode visual object associated with the specified pick array element.

LPDIRECT3DRMFRAMEARRAY *lplpFrameArray—The address that will contain a pointer to the Direct3D Retained-Mode frame array object associated with the specified pick array element.

LPD3DRMPICKDESC lpD3DRMPickDesc—The address of a D3DRMPICKDESC structure specifying the pick position, face, and group identifiers of the specified pick array element.

Return Type: HRESULT

Return Values: See Direct3D Retained-Mode Return Values.

See Also: IDirect3DRMViewport::Pick(), D3DRMPICKDESC, GetSize

IDirect3DRM

The IDirect3DRM interface provides the functionality to create Retained-Mode objects, load objects and textures, work with the Retained-Mode scene graph, and set several Retained-Mode variables. The IDirect3DRM interface can be used to create animation, animation set, device, face, frame, light, material, mesh, mesh builder, shadow, texture, user visual, viewport, and wrap objects as well as uninitialized Retained-Mode objects. An application can retrieve a named object and call a function for every object in the scene graph.

IDirect3DRM, as with all COM interfaces, is derived from IUnknown and inherits its methods. A Direct3DRM object can be obtained by calling Direct3DRMCreate(). IDirect3DRM implements the following methods:

- AddSearchPath
- CreateAnimation
- CreateAnimationSet
- CreateDevice
- CreateDeviceFromClipper
- CreateDeviceFromD3D
- CreateDeviceFromSurface
- CreateFace
- CreateFrame
- CreateLight
- CreateLightRGB
- CreateMaterial
- CreateMesh
- CreateMeshBuilder
- CreateObject
- CreateShadow
- CreateTexture
- CreateTextureFromSurface
- CreateUserVisual
- CreateViewport
- CreateWrap
- EnumerateObjects
- GetDevices
- GetNamedObject
- GetSearchPath
- Load
- LoadTexture
- LoadTextureFromResource
- SetDefaultTextureColors
- SetDefaultTextureShades
- SetSearchPath
- Tick

AddSearchPath

Interface:	IDirect3DRM
Declaration:	`HRESULT AddSearchPath(LPCSTR lpPath);`
Description:	Adds a directory or directories to the current search path.
Notes:	Retained-Mode keeps an environment variable holding a list of directories to search when asked to load a mesh, frame, animation, or texture from a file. Directories can be appended to this list by using AddSearchPath().
Arguments:	LPCSTR lpPath—The pointer to a NULL-terminated C string containing a single directory name or several directory names separated by semicolons.
Return Type:	HRESULT
Return Values:	See Direct3D Retained-Mode Return Values.
See Also:	IDirect3DRM::SetSearchPath, IDirect3DRM::GetSearchPath, IDirect3DRM::Load, IDirect3DRMAnimationSet::Load, IDirect3DRMFrame::Load, IDirect3DRMMeshBuilder::Load, IDirect3DRM::LoadTexture

CreateAnimation

Interface:	IDirect3DRM
Declaration:	`HRESULT CreateAnimation(LPDIRECT3DRMANIMATION* lplpD3DRMAnimation);`
Description:	Creates a new, empty IDirect3DRMAnimation object.
Notes:	Once created, an Animation object is usually attached to an IDirect3DRMFrame object.
Arguments:	LPDIRECT3DRMANIMATION *lplpD3DRMAnimation—The address of a pointer that will point to the new IDirect3DRMAnimation object, or NULL if the call fails.

Return Type:	HRESULT
Return Values:	See Direct3D Retained-Mode Return Values.
See Also:	IDirect3DRM::CreateAnimationSet, IDirect3DAnimation

CreateAnimationSet

Interface:	IDirect3DRM
Declaration:	`HRESULT CreateAnimationSet (LPDIRECT3DRMANIMATIONSET* lplpD3DRMAnimationSet);`
Description:	Creates a new IDirect3DRMAnimationSet object.
Notes:	An AnimationSet object can contain IDirect3DRMAnimation objects, which in turn can animate various IDirect3DRMFrame objects. An AnimationSet object can then be used to animate a number of different frames at once.
Arguments:	LPDIRECT3DRMANIMATIONSET* lplpD3DRMAnimationSet— The address of a pointer that will point to the new IDirect3DRMAnimationSet object, or NULL if the call fails.
Return Type:	HRESULT
Return Values:	See Direct3D Retained-Mode Return Values.
See Also:	IDirect3DRM::CreateAnimation, IDirect3DRMAnimationSet

CreateDevice

Interface:	IDirect3DRM
Declaration:	`HRESULT CreateDevice(DWORD dwWidth, DWORD dwHeight, LPDIRECT3DRMDEVICE* lplpD3DRMDevice);`
Description:	This method is not implemented.

CreateDeviceFromClipper

Interface:	IDirect3DRM
Declaration:	`HRESULT CreateDeviceFromClipper(LPDIRECTDRAWCLIPPER lpDDClipper, LPGUID lpGUID, int width, int height, LPDIRECT3DRMDEVICE * lplpD3DRMDevice);`
Description:	Creates an IDirect3DRMDevice suitable for use with an IDirectDrawClipper object.
Notes:	CreateDeviceFromClipper() is used to create an IDirect3DRMDevice object suitable for use in windowed mode. The IDirectDrawClipper object is used by Direct3D to clip appropriately—when the device's window is obscured by other windows—at the expense of drawing speed.
	Because some hardware devices cannot work with IDirectDrawClipper objects, full-screen apps should generally use IDirect3DRM::CreateDeviceFromD3D.
	If NULL is passed in the lpGUID parameter, CreateDeviceFromClipper() searches for a hardware device that supports the minimum set of capabilities Retained-Mode needs in order to function. Otherwise the ramp software driver is chosen.
	To be chosen, a hardware driver must support the settings described by the following flags from the D3DPRIMCAPS Immediate-Mode structure:
	D3DPCMPCAPS_LESSEQUAL—Less-than-or-equal z-buffer model.
	D3DPMISCCAPS_CULLCCW—Counter-clockwise culling of triangle faces.
	D3DPRASTERCAPS_FOGVERTEX —Vertex fogging.
	D3DPSHADECAPS_ALPHAFLATSTIPPLED—Alpha flat blending and alpha stippled transparency.
	D3DPTADDRESSCAPS_WRAP—Texture wrapping.
	D3DPTBLENDCAPS_COPY	

	D3DPTBLENDCAPS_MODULATE—Copy or modulate mode texture blending.
	D3DPTEXTURECAPS_PERSPECTIVE | D3DPTEXTURECAPS_TRANSPARENCY—Perspective texture mapping or transparent textures.
	D3DPTFILTERCAPS_NEAREST—Nearest-texel texture mapping.
Arguments:	LPDIRECTDRAWCLIPPER lpDDClipper—The pointer to an IDirectDrawClipper object.
	LPGUID lpGUID—The pointer to a device GUID, or NULL for the default device.
	int width—The desired width of the device in pixels.
	int height—The desired height of the device in pixels.
	LPDIRECT3DRMDEVICE * lplpD3DRMDevice—The address of a pointer that will point to the new IDirect3DRMDevice object, or NULL if the call fails.
Return Type:	HRESULT
Return Values:	See Direct3D Retained-Mode Return Values.
See Also:	IDirect3DRMDevice, IDirect3DRM::CreateDeviceFromD3D, IDirect3DRM::CreateDeviceFromSurface, IDirect3DDevice::GetCaps, D3DPRIMCAPS

CreateDeviceFromD3D

Interface:	IDirect3DRM

Declaration:	`HRESULT CreateDeviceFromD3D(LPDIRECT3D lpD3D,`
	`LPDIRECT3DDEVICE lpD3DDev,`
	`LPDIRECT3DRMDEVICE * lplpD3DRMDevice);`

Description:	Creates an IDirect3DRMDevice from an IDirect3D object.
Notes:	CreateDeviceFromD3D() is used often to create an IDirect3DRMDevice object suitable for use in full-screen mode.

continues

continued

If NULL is passed in the lpD3DDev parameter, CreateDeviceFromD3D() searches for a hardware device that supports the minimum set of capabilities Retained-Mode needs to function. Otherwise, the ramp software driver is chosen.

To be chosen, a hardware driver must support the settings described by the following flags from the D3DPRIMCAPS Immediate-Mode structure:

D3DPCMPCAPS_LESSEQUAL—Less-than-or-equal z-buffer model.

D3DPMISCCAPS_CULLCCW—Counter-clockwise culling of triangle faces.

D3DPRASTERCAPS_FOGVERTEX—Vertex fogging.

D3DPSHADECAPS_ALPHAFLATSTIPPLED—Alpha flat blending and alpha stippled transparency.

D3DPTADDRESSCAPS_WRAP—Texture wrapping.

D3DPTBLENDCAPS_COPY | D3DPTBLENDCAPS_MODULATE—Copy or modulate mode texture blending.

D3DPTEXTURECAPS_PERSPECTIVE | D3DPTEXTURECAPS_TRANSPARENCY—Perspective texture mapping or transparent textures.

D3DPTFILTERCAPS_NEAREST—Nearest-texel texture mapping.

Arguments: LPDIRECT3D lpD3D—The pointer to an IDirect3D object.

LPDIRECT3DDEVICE lpD3DDev—The pointer to a particular IDirect3DDevice object, or NULL for the default.

LPDIRECT3DRMDEVICE * lplpD3DRMDevice—The address of a pointer that will point to the new IDirect3DRMDevice object, or NULL if the call fails.

Return Type: HRESULT

Return Values: See Direct3D Retained-Mode Return Values.

See Also: IDirect3DRMDevice, IDirect3DRM::CreateDeviceFromClipper, IDirect3DRM::CreateDeviceFromSurface, IDirect3DRMDevice::GetCaps, D3DPRIMCAPS

CreateDeviceFromSurface

Interface:	IDirect3DRM
Declaration:	`HRESULT CreateDeviceFromSurface(LPGUID lpGUID, LPDIRECTDRAW lpDD, LPDIRECTDRAWSURFACE lpDDSBack, LPDIRECT3DRMDEVICE * lplpD3DRMDevice);`
Description:	Creates an IDirect3DRMDevice object from a DirectDraw surface.
Notes:	The primary DirectDraw surface must be created with the DDSCAPS_3DDEVICE flag set for CreateDeviceFromSurface() to succeed.

If NULL is passed in the lpGUID parameter, CreateDeviceFromSurface() searches for a hardware device that supports the minimum set of capabilities Retained-Mode needs to function. Otherwise, the ramp software driver is chosen.

To be chosen, a hardware driver must support the settings described by the following flags from the D3DPRIMCAPS Immediate-Mode structure:

D3DPCMPCAPS_LESSEQUAL—Less-than-or-equal z-buffer model.

D3DPMISCCAPS_CULLCCW—Counter-clockwise culling of triangle faces.

D3DPRASTERCAPS_FOGVERTEX—Vertex fogging.

D3DPSHADECAPS_ALPHAFLATSTIPPLED—Alpha flat blending and alpha stippled transparency.

D3DPTADDRESSCAPS_WRAP—Texture wrapping.

D3DPTBLENDCAPS_COPY | D3DPTBLENDCAPS_MODULATE—Copy or modulate mode texture blending.

D3DPTEXTURECAPS_PERSPECTIVE | D3DPTEXTURECAPS_TRANSPARENCY—Perspective texture mapping or transparent textures.

D3DPTFILTERCAPS_NEAREST—Nearest-texel texture mapping.

continues

continued

Arguments:	LPGUID lpGUID—The pointer to the GUID of the desired device, or NULL for the default.
	LPDIRECTDRAW lpDD—The pointer to the IDirectDraw object that created the lpDDSBack parameter.
	LPDIRECTDRAWSURFACE lpDDSBack—The pointer to an IDirectDrawSurface object, into which Retained-Mode will render.
	LPDIRECT3DRMDEVICE * lplpD3DRMDevice—The address of a pointer that will point to the new IDirect3DRMDevice object, or NULL if the call fails.
Return Type:	HRESULT
Return Values:	See Direct3D Retained-Mode Return Values.
See Also:	IDirect3DRMDevice, IDirect3DRM::CreateDeviceFromD3D, IDirect3DDevice::GetCaps, PRIMCAPS

CreateFace

Interface:	IDirect3DRM
Declaration:	`HRESULT CreateFace(LPDIRECT3DRMFACE * lplpd3drmFace);`
Description:	Creates an IDirect3DRMFace object.
Notes:	If you're creating an IDirect3DRMFace object to use with an IDirect3DRMMeshBuilder object, you can use IDirect3DRMMeshBuilder::CreateFace() to create faces that are automatically added to the mesh builder.
Arguments:	LPDIRECT3DRMFACE * lplpd3drmFace—The address of a pointer that will point to the new IDirect3DRMFace object, or NULL if the call fails.
Return Type:	HRESULT
Return Values:	See Direct3D Retained-Mode Return Values.
See Also:	IDirect3DRMFace, IDirect3DRMMeshBuilder::CreateFace

CreateFrame

Interface:	IDirect3DRM
Declaration:	`HRESULT CreateFrame(LPDIRECT3DRMFRAME lpD3DRMFrame,` `LPDIRECT3DRMFRAME* lplpD3DRMFrame);`
Description:	Creates a new IDirect3DRMFrame object.
Notes:	Frames that have no parent are called scenes and can be created by calling CreateFrame() and specifying NULL as the parent frame. A frame with no parent can be associated with a parent frame later by using IDirect3DRMFrame::AddChild().
Arguments:	LPDIRECT3DRMFRAME lpd3drmParentFrame—The pointer to the parent frame, or NULL.
	LPDIRECT3DRMFRAME* lplpD3DRMFrame—The address of a pointer that will point to the new IDirect3DRMFrame object, or NULL if the call fails.
Return Type:	HRESULT
Return Values:	See Direct3D Retained-Mode Return Values.
See Also:	IDirect3DRMFrame

CreateLight

Interface:	IDirect3DRM
Declaration:	`HRESULT CreateLight(D3DRMLIGHTTYPE d3drmltLightType,` `D3DCOLOR cColor, LPDIRECT3DRMLIGHT* lplpD3DRMLight);`
Description:	Creates a new IDirect3DRMLight object.
Notes:	The light's color is specified as R, G, and B values within the range 0 to 255. Alpha values are ignored.
Arguments:	D3DRMLIGHTTYPE d3drmltLightType—One of the D3DRMLIGHTTYPE enumerated types: D3DRMLIGHT_AMBIENT, D3DRMLIGHT_POINT, D3DRMLIGHT_SPOT,

continues

continued

	D3DRMLIGHT_DIRECTIONAL, or D3DRMLIGHT_PARALLELPOINT.
	D3DCOLOR cColor—The color of the light.
	LPDIRECT3DRMLIGHT* lplpD3DRMLight—The address of a pointer that will point to the new IDirect3DRMLight object, or NULL if the call fails.
Return Type:	HRESULT
Return Values:	See Direct3D Retained-Mode Return Values.
See Also:	IDirect3DRMLight, IDirect3DRM::CreateLightRGB, D3DRMLIGHTTYPE, D3DCOLOR, RGB_MAKE

CreateLightRGB

Interface:	IDirect3DRM
Declaration:	`HRESULT CreateLightRGB(D3DRMLIGHTTYPE ltLightType, D3DVALUE vRed, D3DVALUE vGreen, D3DVALUE vBlue, LPDIRECT3DRMLIGHT* lplpD3DRMLight);`
Description:	Creates a new IDirect3DRMLight object.
Notes:	Individual R, G, and B components are specified by using D3DVALUE's, typically between 0 and 1.
Arguments:	D3DRMLIGHTTYPE d3drmltLightType—One of the D3DRMLIGHTTYPE enumerated types: D3DRMLIGHT_AMBIENT, D3DRMLIGHT_POINT, D3DRMLIGHT_SPOT, D3DRMLIGHT_DIRECTIONAL, or D3DRMLIGHT_PARALLELPOINT.
	D3DVALUE vRed—The red component of light's color, typically in the range 0 through 1.
	D3DVALUE vGreen—The green component of light's color, typically in the range 0 through 1.

D3DVALUE vBlue—The blue component of light's color, typically in the range 0 through 1.

LPDIRECT3DRMLIGHT* lplpD3DRMLight—The address of a pointer that will point to the new IDirect3DRMLight object, or NULL if the call fails.

Return Type:	HRESULT
Return Values:	See Direct3D Retained-Mode Return Values.
See Also:	IDirect3DRMLight, IDirect3DRM::CreateLight, D3DRMLIGHTTYPE

CreateMaterial

Interface:	IDirect3DRM
Declaration:	`HRESULT CreateMaterial(D3DVALUE vPower, LPDIRECT3DRMMATERIAL * lplpD3DRMMaterial);`
Description:	Creates a new IDirect3DRMMaterial object with a given specular property.
Notes:	vPower is the sharpness of the reflected highlights. Five causes a metallic look, and higher values create a more plastic look.
Arguments:	D3DVALUE vPower—The parameter specifying the power of the specular exponent of the material.
	LPDIRECT3DRMMATERIAL * lplpD3DRMMaterial—The address of a pointer that will point to the new IDirect3DRMMaterial object, or NULL if the call fails.
Return Type:	HRESULT
Return Values:	See Direct3D Retained-Mode Return Values.
See Also:	IDirect3DRMMaterial

CreateMesh

Interface:	IDirect3DRM
Declaration:	`HRESULT CreateMesh(LPDIRECT3DRMMESH* lplpD3DRMMesh);`
Description:	Creates a new IDirect3DRMMesh object.
Notes:	Creates an empty mesh object. The mesh object must be added to an IDirect3DRMFrame object before it can be rendered.
Arguments:	LPDIRECT3DRMMESH* lplpD3DRMMesh—The address of a pointer that will point to the new IDirect3DRMMaterial object, or NULL if the call fails.
Return Type:	HRESULT
Return Values:	See Direct3D Retained-Mode Return Values.
See Also:	IDirect3DRMMesh

CreateMeshBuilder

Interface:	IDirect3DRM
Declaration:	`HRESULT CreateMeshBuilder(LPDIRECT3DRMMESHBUILDER* lplpD3DRMMeshBuilder);`
Description:	Creates a new IDirect3DRMMeshBuilder object.
Notes:	A mesh builder provides a convenient interface for building a mesh and retrieving information about the mesh.
Arguments:	LPDIRECT3DRMMESHBUILDER* lplpD3DRMMeshBuilder—The address of a pointer that will point to the new IDirect3DRMMeshBuilder object, or NULL if the call fails.
Return Type:	HRESULT
Return Values:	See Direct3D Retained-Mode Return Values.
See Also:	IDirect3DRMMeshBuilder

CreateObject

Interface:	IDirect3DRM
Declaration:	`HRESULT CreateObject(REFCLSID rclsid, LPUNKNOWN pUnkOuter, REFIID riid, LPVOID FAR* ppv);`
Description:	Creates a new, uninitialized object.
Notes:	This method is used internally by the various other Create() methods in the IDirect3DRM interface. Any object created with this method must have its Init() method called before it can be safely used.
Arguments:	REFCLSID rclsid—Class identifier GUID.
	LPUNKNOWN pUnkOuter—The pointer to the aggregate outer IUnknown object if COM aggregation is being used. Usually NULL. Use this parameter to implement aggregation in a Direct3DRM object.
	REFIID riid—Interface identifier GUID.
	LPVOID FAR* ppv—The address of a pointer that will point to the new object, or NULL if the call fails.
Return Type:	HRESULT
Return Values:	See Direct3D Retained-Mode Return Values.
See Also:	IDirect3DRM::CreateAnimation, IDirect3DRM::CreateAnimationSet, IDirect3DRM::CreateFace, IDirect3DRM::CreateFrame, IDirect3DRM::CreateLight, IDirect3DRM::CreateLightRGB, IDirect3DRM::CreateMaterial, IDirect3DRM::CreateMesh, IDirect3DRM::CreateMeshBuilder, IDirect3DRM::CreateShadow, IDirect3DRM::CreateTexture, IDirect3DRM::CreateTextureFromSurface, IDirect3DRM::CreateUserVisual, IDirect3DRM::CreateViewport, IDirect3DRM::CreateWrap

CreateShadow

Interface:	IDirect3DRM
Declaration:	HRESULT CreateShadow(LPDIRECT3DRMVISUAL lpVisual, LPDIRECT3DRMLIGHT lpLight, D3DVALUE px, D3DVALUE py, D3DVALUE pz, D3DVALUE nx,D3DVALUE ny, D3DVALUE nz, LPDIRECT3DRMVISUAL* lplpShadow);
Description:	Creates a shadow on a plane from a specified visual object and light source.
Notes:	Creates an IDirect3DRMVisual object that is the shadow cast onto the specified plane by the specified IDirect3DRMVisual object in the presence of the specified IDirect3DRMLight object. The IDirect3DRMVisual object presenting the shadow must be added to the same IDirect3DRMFrame object that contains the visual casting the shadow. A point on the plane and a vector normal to the plane define the shadow plane.
Arguments:	LPDIRECT3DRMVISUAL lpVisual—The pointer to IDirect3DRMVisual object casting the shadow.
	LPDIRECT3DRMLIGHT lpLight—The pointer to IDirect3DRMLight object that is the light source.
	D3DVALUE px—X coordinate of a point on the plane onto which the shadow is cast.
	D3DVALUE py—Y coordinate of a point on the plane onto which the shadow is cast.
	D3DVALUE pz—Z coordinate of a point on the plane onto which the shadow is cast.
	D3DVALUE nx—X coordinate of a vector normal to the surface onto which the shadow is cast.
	D3DVALUE ny—Y coordinate of a vector normal to the surface onto which the shadow is cast.
	D3DVALUE nz—Z coordinate of a vector normal to the surface onto which the shadow is cast.

	LPDIRECT3DRMVISUAL* lplpShadow—The address of a pointer that will point to the new IDirect3DRMVisual object representing the shadow, or NULL if the call fails.
Return Type:	HRESULT
Return Values:	See Direct3D Retained-Mode Return Values.
See Also:	IDirect3DRMShadow

CreateTexture

Interface:	IDirect3DRM
Declaration:	`HRESULT CreateTexture(LPD3DRMIMAGE lpImage,` `LPDIRECT3DRMTEXTURE* lplpD3DRMTexture);`
Description:	Creates a new IDirect3DRMTexture object.
Notes:	The memory associated with the image is used each time the texture is rendered, rather than being copied into Direct3DRM's buffers. This allows the image to be used both as a rendering target and as a texture.
Arguments:	LPD3DRMIMAGE lpImage—The pointer to a D3DRMIMAGE struct, containing a description of the source of the texture.
	LPDIRECT3DRMTEXTURE* lplpD3DRMTexture—The address of a pointer that will point to the new IDirect3DRMTexture object, or NULL if the call fails.
Return Type:	HRESULT
Return Values:	See Direct3D Retained-Mode Return Values.
See Also:	IDirect3DRM::CreateTextureFromSurface, IDirect3DRMTexture

CreateTextureFromSurface

Interface:	IDirect3DRM
Declaration:	`HRESULT CreateTextureFromSurface(LPDIRECTDRAWSURFACE lpDDS,` `LPDIRECT3DRMTEXTURE* lplpD3DRMTexture);`

continues

continued

Description:	Creates a texture from an IDirectDrawSurface object.
Notes:	This method enables DirectDraw surfaces to be used as textures for 3D objects. This includes movies that are rendered into DirectDraw surfaces.
Arguments:	LPDIRECTDRAWSURFACE lpDDS—The pointer to IDirectDrawSurface object from which a texture is to be made.
	LPDIRECT3DRMTEXTURE* lplpD3DRMTexture—The address of a pointer that will point to the new IDirect3DRMTexture object, or NULL if the call fails.
Return Type:	HRESULT
Return Values:	See Direct3D Retained-Mode Return Values.
See Also:	IDirect3DRM::CreateTexture, IDirect3DRMTexture

CreateUserVisual

Interface:	IDirect3DRM
Declaration:	`HRESULT CreateUserVisual(D3DRMUSERVISUALCALLBACK fn, LPVOID lpArg, LPDIRECT3DRMUSERVISUAL* lplpD3DRMUV);`
Description:	Creates a new IDirect3DRMUserVisual object.
Notes:	UserVisual objects provide a mechanism to use Immediate-Mode execute buffers from within the Retained-Mode or perform application-defined render functions.
Arguments:	D3DRMUSERVISUALCALLBACK fn—The address of the callback function Retained-Mode will call to signal the UserVisual object to render itself.
	LPVOID lpArg—The value Retained-Mode will pass as the lpArg parameter to the callback function.
	LPDIRECT3DRMUSERVISUAL* lplpD3DRMUV—The address of a pointer that will point to the new IDirect3DRMTexture object, or NULL if the call fails.
Return Type:	HRESULT

Return Values:	See Direct3D Retained-Mode Return Values.
See Also:	IDirect3DRMUserVisual

CreateViewport

Interface:	IDirect3DRM

Declaration:	`HRESULT CreateViewport(LPDIRECT3DRMDEVICE lpDev,`
	`LPDIRECT3DRMFRAME lpCamera, DWORD dwXPos, DWORD dwYPos,`
	`DWORD dwWidth, DWORD dwHeight,`
	`LPDIRECT3DRMVIEWPORT* lplpD3DRMViewport);`

Description:	Creates a new IDirect3DRMViewport object.
Notes:	The viewport object defines how the 3D scene is viewed on the 2D screen.
Arguments:	LPDIRECT3DRMDEVICE lpDev—The pointer to the IDirect3DRMDevice object the viewport will use. LPDIRECT3DRMFRAME lpCamera—The pointer to an IDirect3DRMFrame object describing the camera position and orientation. DWORD dwXPos—The left-most pixel coordinate of the viewport within the device's back buffer. DWORD dwYPos—The top-most pixel coordinate of the viewport within the device's back buffer. DWORD dwWidth—The width of the viewport in pixels. DWORD dwHeight—The height of the viewport in pixels. LPDIRECT3DRMVIEWPORT* lplpD3DRMViewport—The address of a pointer that will point to the new IDirect3DRMViewport object, or NULL if the call fails.
Return Type:	HRESULT
Return Values:	See Direct3D Retained-Mode Return Values.
See Also:	IDirect3DRMViewport

CreateWrap

Interface:	IDirect3DRM
Declaration:	HRESULT CreateWrap(D3DRMWRAPTYPE type, LPDIRECT3DRMFRAME lpRef, D3DVALUE ox, D3DVALUE oy, D3DVALUE oz, D3DVALUE dx, D3DVALUE dy, D3DVALUE dz, D3DVALUE ux, D3DVALUE uy, D3DVALUE uz, D3DVALUE ou, D3DVALUE ov, D3DVALUE su, D3DVALUE sv, LPDIRECT3DRMWRAP* lplpD3DRMWrap);
Description:	Creates a new IDirect3DRMWrap object.
Notes:	A wrap object is used to generate the texture coordinates for a face or mesh.
Arguments:	D3DRMWRAPTYPE type—Flag specifying the type of wrap. One of D3DRMWRAP_FLAT, D3DRMWRAP_CYLINDER, D3DRMWRAP_SPHERE, or D3DRMWRAP_CHROME.
	LPDIRECT3DRMFRAME lpRef—The pointer to the IDirect3DRMFrame object that defines the reference frame for the wrap.
	D3DVALUE ox, oy, oz—Together specify the origin of the wrap in the reference frame.
	D3DVALUE dx, dy, dz—Together specify the z-axis for the wrap in the reference frame.
	D3DVALUE ux, uy, uz—Together specify the y-axis for the wrap in the reference frame.
	D3DVALUE ou, ov—Specify the origin of the texture for wrapping purposes, in texture coordinates.
	D3DVALUE su—The scale factor for the horizontal component of the texture.
	D3DVALUE sv—The scale factor for the vertical component of the texture.
	LPDIRECT3DRMWRAP* lplpD3DRMWrap—The address of a pointer that will point to the new IDirect3DRMWrap object, or NULL if the call fails.

Return Type:	HRESULT
Return Values:	See Direct3D Retained-Mode Return Values.
See Also:	IDirect3DRMWrap, IDirect3DRMTexture

EnumerateObjects

Interface:	IDirect3DRM
Declaration:	`HRESULT EnumerateObjects(D3DRMOBJECTCALLBACK func, LPVOID lpArg);`
Description:	This method enumerates all Retained-Mode objects, calling the user-supplied D3DRMOBJECTCALLBACK callback function for each object.
Notes:	This method could be used to count objects in the scene or to perform a specific task for each object in the scene hierarchy.
Arguments:	D3DRMOBJECTCALLBACK func—The address of the callback function that will be called for each Retained-Mode object.
	LPVOID lpArg—The value Retained-Mode will pass as the lpArg parameter to the callback function.
Return Type:	HRESULT
Return Values:	See Direct3D Retained-Mode Return Values.
See Also:	D3DRMOBJECTCALLBACK

GetDevices

Interface:	IDirect3DRM
Declaration:	`HRESULT GetDevices(LPDIRECT3DRMDEVICEARRAY* lplpDevArray);`
Description:	Creates an IDirect3DRMDeviceArray object and fills it with references to all IDirect3DRMDevice objects created.
Arguments:	LPDIRECT3DRMDEVICEARRAY* lplpDevArray—The address of a pointer that will point to the new IDirect3DRMDeviceArray object, or NULL if the call fails.

continues

continued

Return Type:	HRESULT
Return Values:	See Direct3D Retained-Mode Return Values.
See Also:	IDirect3DRMDeviceArray, IDirect3DRMDevice

GetNamedObject

Interface:	IDirect3DRM
Declaration:	`HRESULT GetNamedObject(const char * lpName, LPDIRECT3DRMOBJECT* lplpD3DRMObject);`
Description:	Finds an IDirect3DRMObject by name.
Notes:	Objects that have been loaded in the .X file format are named. GetNamedObject() can be used to retrieve an object previously loaded, given its name. Objects can be given names with IDirect3DRMObject::SetName().
Arguments:	const char * lpName—The pointer to a NULL-terminated C string containing the name of the object.
	LPDIRECT3DRMOBJECT* lplpD3DRMObject—The address of a pointer that will point to the IDirect3DRMObject with the given name, or NULL if no such object exists.
Return Type:	HRESULT
Return Values:	See Direct3D Retained-Mode Return Values.
See Also:	IDirect3DRM::Load, IDirect3DRMAnimationSet::Load, IDirect3DRMFrame::Load, IDirect3DRMMeshBuilder::Load, IDirect3DRMObject::SetName, IDirect3DRMObject::GetName

GetSearchPath

Interface:	IDirect3DRM
Declaration:	`HRESULT GetSearchPath(DWORD * lpdwSize, LPSTR lpszPath);`
Description:	Returns a string containing the current search path.

Notes:	If the lpszPath parameter is NULL, GetSearchPath() stores the number of bytes in the string holding the complete search path in the DWORD pointed to by lpdwSize.
	If lpszPath is the address of a string, lpdwSize must point to a DWORD holding the size of the string lpszPath points to. If the string isn't big enough to hold the complete string, GetSearchPath() returns D3DRMERR_BADVALUE.
Arguments:	DWORD * lpdwSize—The pointer to DWORD holding the length of the string pointed to lpszPath. If lpszPath is NULL, the DWORD pointed to by lpdwSize will hold the required size of the string.
	LPSTR lpszPath—The pointer to an array of chars that will hold the string containing the search path, or NULL to retrieve the necessary size of the array.
Return Type:	HRESULT
Return Values:	See Direct3D Retained-Mode Return Values.
See Also:	IDirect3DRM::SetSearchPath, IDirect3DRM::AddSearchPath

Load

Interface:	IDirect3DRM
Declaration:	```HRESULT Load(LPVOID lpvObjSource, LPVOID lpvObjID,
LPIID * lplpGUIDs, DWORD dwcGUIDs, D3DRMLOADOPTIONS d3drmLOFlags,
D3DRMLOADCALLBACK d3drmLoadProc, LPVOID lpArgLP,
D3DRMLOADTEXTURECALLBACK d3drmLoadTextureProc,
LPVOID lpArgLTP, LPDIRECT3DRMFRAME lpParentFrame);```
Description:	Loads an IDirect3DRMObject from file, resource, or memory.
Notes:	This method would typically be used to load objects stored in Retained-Mode formats.
Arguments:	LPVOID lpvObjSource—This parameter is a pointer to data indicating the source of the object data, or NULL. If d3drmLOFlags includes D3DRMLOAD_FROMFILE, this parameter must point to a NULL-terminated string holding the file name to load. If d3drmLOFlags

continues

continued

includes D3DRMLOAD_FROMRESOURCE, this parameter must point to a D3DRMLOADRESOURCE struct containing the relevant resource information. If d3drmLOFlags includes D3DRMLOAD_FROMMEMORY, this parameter must point to a D3DRMLOADMEMORY struct containing a pointer to the memory, and the size of the memory block.

LPVOID lpvObjID—This parameter is either NULL or a pointer to an object name or position, depending on which load options are selected in the d3drmLOFlags parameter. If d3drmLOFlags includes D3DRMLOAD_BYNAME, this parameter must point to a NULL-terminated string holding the name of the object. If d3drmLOFlags includes D3DRMLOAD_BYPOSITION, lpvObjID must point to a DWORD holding the index of the desired animation set (from 0 to $n-1$ if there are n objects sets in the file). If d3drmLOFlags includes D3DRMLOAD_FIRST, or none of D3DRMLOAD_BYPOSITION, or D3DRMLOAD_BYNAME is specified, lpvObjID should be NULL.

LPIID * lplpGUIDs—The pointer to an array of pointers to GUIDs specifying object types to be loaded. For example, if one of the values in the array points to a GUID with the value IID_IDirect3DRMAnimationSet, all IDirect3DAnimationSet objects will be loaded.

DWORD dwcGUIDs—The number of GUIDs in the array pointed to by the lplpGUIDs parameter.

D3DRMLOADOPTIONS d3drmLOFlags—This parameter consists of flags specifying the source type of the animation (file, resource, or memory) and which object is loaded (the first, by index, by name). If 0 is passed as d3drmLOFlags, Retained-Mode assumes D3DRMLOAD_FROMFILE|D3DRMLOAD_FIRST.

The source should be specified using exactly one of D3DRMLOAD_FROMFILE, D3DRMLOAD_FROMRESOURCE, D3DRMLOAD_FROMMEMORY. The D3DRMLOAD_FROMSTREAM option is not allowed in DirectX 3.

To load a specific animation from a file, it can be selected by using either D3DRMLOAD_BYNAME if it is named within the source, D3DRMLOAD_BYPOSITION to specify it by its order among other objects in the file, or D3DRMLOAD_FIRST to just load the first object encountered in the file. D3DRMLOAD_FIRST is implied if none of these options is chosen.

D3DRMLOAD_INSTANCEBYREFERENCE is implied in DirectX 3. Passing D3DRMLOAD_INSTANCEBYCOPYING generates an error; only instances by reference capabilities are implemented in DirectX 3.

D3DRMLOADCALLBACK d3drmLoadProc—The address of the callback function Retained-Mode will call to actually load each object.

LPVOID lpArgLP—The value Retained-Mode will pass as the lpArg parameter to the callback function.

D3DRMLOADTEXTURECALLBACK d3drmLoadTextureProc—This parameter is a callback that Load will call to load textures. If NULL, Retained-Mode will do its best to load the texture files specified in the file, resource, or memory block. In DirectX 3, only BMP and PPM files are supported, so a callback must be supplied to load textures from any other format.

LPVOID lpArgLTP—The pointer to the application-defined data that Load will pass to the texture callback passed via d3drmLTP, if any.

LPDIRECT3DRMFRAME lpParentFrame—The pointer to an existing parent frame, into which Retained-Mode will load the object or objects.

Return Type:	HRESULT
Return Values:	See Direct3D Retained-Mode Return Values.
See Also:	IDirect3DAnimationSet::Load, IDirect3DRMMeshBuilder::Load, IDirect3DRMFrame::Load

LoadTexture

Interface:	IDirect3DRM
Declaration:	`HRESULT LoadTexture(const char * lpFileName, LPDIRECT3DRMTEXTURE* lplpD3DRMTexture);`
Description:	Loads the specified texture from a file, creating an IDirect3DRMTexture object to hold it.
Notes:	The texture can have 8, 24, or 32 bits-per-pixel, and it should be in either the Windows bitmap (.bmp) or Portable Pixmap (.ppm) P6 format.
Arguments:	const char * lpFileName—The pointer to the NULL-terminated string holding the file name of the texture.
	LPDIRECT3DRMTEXTURE * lplpD3DRMTexture—The address of a pointer that will point to the new IDirect3DRMTexture object, or NULL if the call fails.
Return Type:	HRESULT
Return Values:	See Direct3D Retained-Mode Return Values.
See Also:	IDirect3DRM::LoadTextureFromResource, IDirect3DRMTexture

LoadTextureFromResource

Interface:	IDirect3DRM
Declaration:	`HRESULT LoadTextureFromResource(HRSRC rs, LPDIRECT3DRMTEXTURE * lplpD3DRMTexture);`
Description:	Loads the specified texture from a resource, creating an IDirect3DRMTexture object to hold it.
Notes:	The texture can have 8, 24, or 32 bits-per-pixel, and it should be in either the Windows bitmap (.bmp) or Portable Pixmap (.ppm) P6 format.

Arguments:	HRSRC rs—The resource handle of the resource to load from.
	LPDIRECT3DRMTEXTURE * lplpD3DRMTexture—The address of a pointer that will point to the new IDirect3DRMTexture object, or NULL if the call fails.
Return Type:	HRESULT
Return Values:	See Direct3D Retained-Mode Return Values.
See Also:	IDirect3DRM::LoadTexture

SetDefaultTextureColors

Interface:	IDirect3DRM
Declaration:	`HRESULT SetDefaultTextureColors(DWORD dwColors);`
Description:	Sets the number of colors each texture may use.
Notes:	This method affects the texture colors only when it is called before IDirect3DRM::CreateTexture(). It has no effect on textures that have already been created. This method is usually called before IDirect3DRM::CreateTexture(), IDirect3DRM::LoadTexture(), or IDirect3DRM::LoadTextureFromResource(). When the texture is loaded, if it has more colors than the number last passed to this method, it will be reduced on the fly.
	The total number of colors needed to represent the texture is the number of texture colors times the number of texture shades. In an 8-bit color environment, care must be taken to make best use of the available 256 colors. Note that this method only sets the number of colors, not the number of shades.
	The default number of texture colors can be overridden on a texture-by-texture basis using IDirect3DRMTexture::SetColors().
Arguments:	DWORD dwColors—The number of colors allowed per texture
Return Type:	HRESULT
Return Values:	See Direct3D Retained-Mode Return Values.
See Also:	IDirect3DRM::SetDefaultTextureShades, IDirect3DRMTexture::SetColors

SetDefaultTextureShades

Interface:	IDirect3DRM
Declaration:	`HRESULT SetDefaultTextureShades(DWORD dwShades);`
Description:	Sets the number of shades each texture may use.
Notes:	SetDefaultTextureShades() sets the size of the "ramp" of colors created for each color in a texture. The ramp ranges from a dark to a light version of the color and is used when Direct3D lights the object.
	In 8-bit color mode, for each color in a texture, Retained-Mode tries to allocate a ramp of values in the palette, so in a scene with many different textures and colors, care must be taken to make best use of the limited palette.
	This method affects the texture shades only when it is called before IDirect3DRM::CreateTexture(). It has no effect on textures that have already been created. This method is usually called before IDirect3DRM::CreateTexture(), IDirect3DRM::LoadTexture(), or IDirect3DRM::LoadTextureFromResource().
	The default number of texture shades can be overridden on a texture-by-texture basis by using IDirect3DRMTexture::SetShades().
Arguments:	DWORD dwShades—The number of shades for each color in a texture.
Return Type:	HRESULT
Return Values:	See Direct3D Retained-Mode Return Values.
See Also:	IDirect3DRM::SetDefaultTextureColors, IDirect3DRMTexture::SetShades, IDirect3DRMDevice::SetShades

SetSearchPath

Interface:	IDirect3DRM
Declaration:	`HRESULT SetSearchPath(LPCSTR lpPath);`
Description:	Sets the search path Retained-Mode will use when opening files.
Notes:	By default, the search path is specified by the environment variable D3DPATH. When attempting to open a file, Retained-Mode first looks for the file in the current working directory, then in each directory in the search path.
	Multiple directories separated by a semicolon can be included in the string parameter to SetSearchPath().
Arguments:	LPCSTR lpPath—The pointer to a NULL-terminated C string containing one or more directory paths (separated by semicolons) to be set as the new search path.
Return Type:	HRESULT
Return Values:	See Direct3D Retained-Mode Return Values.
See Also:	IDirect3DRM::GetSearchPath, IDirect3DRM::AddSearchPath

Tick

Interface:	IDirect3DRM
Declaration:	`HRESULT Tick(D3DVALUE d3dvalTick);`
Description:	Advances the Retained-Mode system heartbeat.
Notes:	Tick updates moving frame positions and rotations, the scene is rendered into the current device, and various callback functions are called as appropriate.
	Tick() is a synchronous method, which may take considerable time to execute for a complex scene.

continues

continued

An application can implement the functionality of this method by using other Retained-Mode methods to allow more flexibility in rendering a scene.

Arguments: D3DVALUE d3dvalTick—Velocity and rotation step for IDirect3DRMFrame::SetRotation() and IDirect3DRMFrame::SetVelocity().

Return Type: HRESULT

Return Values: See Direct3D Retained-Mode Return Values.

See Also: IDirect3DFrame::SetVelocity, IDirect3DRMFrame::SetRotation, D3DRMFRAMEMOVECALLBACK, D3DRMUPDATECALLBACK, D3DRMUSERVISUALCALLBACK

IDirect3DRMAnimation

The IDirect3DRMAnimation interface provides the functionality to animate the position, orientation, or scale of a Retained-Mode frame, enable animation of Retained-Mode visual, light, and viewport objects. A Retained-Mode animation is specified by a set of keys, each containing a time and a value. Applications can use the methods of IDirect3DRMAnimation to add and delete keys, set the frame to animate and current time of the animation, and change the animation options.

IDirect3DRMAnimation, as with all COM interfaces, is derived from IUnknown and inherits its methods. IDirect3DRMAnimation also inherits the methods of IDirect3DRMObject. A Direct3DRMAnimation object can be obtained by calling IDirect3DRM::CreateAnimation(). IDirect3DRMAnimation implements the following methods:

- AddPositionKey
- AddRotateKey
- AddScaleKey
- DeleteKey
- GetOptions
- SetFrame
- SetOptions
- SetTime

AddPositionKey

Interface: IDirect3DAnimation

Declaration:
```
HRESULT AddPositionKey(D3DVALUE rvTime, D3DVALUE rvX,
D3DVALUE rvY, D3DVALUE rvZ);
```

continues

continued

Description: Adds a new position key to the Animation object at the specified time.

Notes: Position keys form control points of smoothly interpolated paths. Paths are either straight lines or splines, depending on whether D3DRMANIMATION_LINEARPOSITION or D3DRMANIMATION_SPLINEPOSITION is passed to IDirect3DRMAnimation::SetOptions().

Animations are like splines that can be interpolated linearly—a straight line between control points, or as smoothly interpolated splines.

Adding multiple keys with the same time value causes the position keys to be "executed" in order at the particular time. This can be used to replace smooth interpolation between points with discrete jumps.

Keys added with AddPositionKey() only take effect if the D3DRMANIMATION_POSITION option is set for the Animation object with IDirect3DRMAnimation::SetOptions().

The position vector passed to AddPositionKey() is in the parent frame of the Animation's frame, if any. If this frame doesn't have a parent (in other words, is at the root level), the position is in world coordinates.

The time units are arbitrary and zero-based; a key whose rvTime value is 50 occurs exactly in the middle of an animation whose last key has an rvTime value of 100.

Arguments: D3DVALUE rvTime—Time value this key will be played.

D3DVALUE rvX—X coordinate in the parent or world coordinates.

D3DVALUE rvY—Y coordinate in the parent or world coordinates.

D3DVALUE rvZ—Z coordinate in the parent or world coordinates.

Return Type: HRESULT

Return Values: See Direct3D Retained-Mode Return Values.

See Also: IDirect3DRMAnimation::AddRotateKey,
IDirect3DRMAnimation::AddScaleKey,
IDirect3DRMAnimation::SetTime,
IDirect3DRMAnimation::GetOptions,
IDirect3DRMAnimation::SetOptions

AddRotateKey

Interface:	IDirect3DAnimation
Declaration:	`HRESULT AddRotateKey(D3DVALUE rvTime, D3DRMQUATERNION *rqQuat);`
Description:	Adds a new rotation key to the Animation object at the specified time. Each entry is the key.
Notes:	Rotations are represented as quaternions. Each quaternion is a control point between which the rotation of the frame is interpolated by using spherical linear interpolation (SLERP).
	Keys added with AddRotateKey() only take effect if the D3DRMANIMATION_SCALEANDROTATION option is set for the Animation object with IDirect3DRMAnimation::SetOptions().
Arguments:	D3DVALUE rvTime—Time value for this key to be played.
	D3DRMQUATERNION *rqQuat—Quaternion containing the desired rotation at time rvTime.
Return Type:	HRESULT
Return Values:	See Direct3D Retained-Mode Return Values.
See Also:	IDirect3DRMAnimation::AddPositionKey, IDirect3DRMAnimation::AddScaleKey, IDirect3DRMAnimation::SetTime, D3DRMQUATERNION, D3DRMQuaternionFromRotation.

AddScaleKey

Interface:	IDirect3DAnimation
Declaration:	`HRESULT AddScaleKey(D3DVALUE rvTime, D3DVALUE rvX, D3DVALUE rvY, D3DVALUE rvZ);`
Description:	Adds a new scale key to the Animation object at the specified time key.
Notes:	Scale keys are used as control points for linearly interpolated scaling over time.

continues

continued

Adding multiple keys with the same time value causes the position keys to be "executed" in order at the particular time. This can be used to replace smooth interpolation between scales with discrete jumps.

Keys added with AddScaleKey() only take effect if the D3DRMANIMATION_SCALEANDROTATION option is set for the Animation object with IDirect3DRMAnimation::SetOptions().

Arguments: D3DVALUE rvTime—Time value for this key to be played.

D3DVALUE rvX—The scale factor along the x-axis.

D3DVALUE rvY—The scale factor along the y-axis.

D3DVALUE rvZ—The scale factor along the z-axis.

Return Type: HRESULT

Return Values: See Direct3D Retained-Mode Return Values.

See Also: IDirect3DRMAnimation::AddPositionKey,
IDirect3DRMAnimation::AddRotationKey,
IDirect3DRMAnimation::SetTime

DeleteKey

Interface: IDirect3DAnimation

Declaration: `HRESULT DeleteKey(D3DVALUE rvTime);`

Description: Deletes all keys with the specified time value from the Animation object.

Notes: Unfortunately, DirectX 3 doesn't provide a way to remove a particular key at a particular time; instead it removes all keys at that particular time.

All position keys can be disabled by clearing the D3DRMANIMATION_POSITION flag with IDirect3DRMAnimation::SetOptions(), and all scale and rotate keys can be disabled by clearing the D3DRMANIMATION_SCALEROTATION flags with IDirect3DRMAnimation::SetOptions().

Arguments:	D3DVALUE rvTime—Time value of keys to delete.
Return Type:	HRESULT
Return Values:	See Direct3D Retained-Mode Return Values.
See Also:	None

GetOptions

Interface:	IDirect3DAnimation
Declaration:	`D3DRMANIMATIONOPTIONS GetOptions();`
Description:	Returns the options for the Animation object.
Notes:	The options for an Animation object are: whether or not it loops, whether the animation is allowed to modify the frames position or scale and rotation, or both, and whether positions are interpolated linearly or with splines.
	See D3DRMANIMATIONOPTIONS for a description of the various flags you can logically test for the return result.
Arguments:	None
Return Type:	D3DRMANIMATIONOPTIONS
Return Values:	See Direct3D Retained-Mode Return Values.
See Also:	IDirect3DRMAnimation::SetOptions, D3DRMANIMATIONOPTIONS

SetFrame

Interface:	IDirect3DAnimation
Declaration:	`HRESULT SetFrame(LPDIRECT3DRMFRAME lpD3DRMFrame);`
Description:	Sets the Frame object that the Animation object will act upon.
Notes:	SetFrame() will also accept NULL, which has the effect of disabling the Animation. Calling SetTime() on an Animation object with a NULL frame does not generate an error.

continues

continued

Arguments:	LPDIRECT3DRMFRAME lpD3DRMFrame
Return Type:	HRESULT
Return Values:	See Direct3D Retained-Mode Return Values.
See Also:	IDirect3DRMAnimation::SetTime, IDirect3DRMFrame

SetOptions

Interface:	IDirect3DAnimation
Declaration:	`HRESULT SetOptions(D3DRMANIMATIONOPTIONS d3drmanimFlags);`
Description:	Used to enable or disable the various Animation options, such as whether the animation will loop, whether it is allowed to change its frame's position or scale and rotation, and whether positions are interpolated linearly or with a spline.
Notes:	For position keys to take effect, the D3DRMANIMATION_POSITION option must be set, as well as D3DRMANIMATION_LINEARPOSITION or D3DRMANIMATION_SPLINEPOSITION, depending on whether positions should be interpolated linearly or by a spline. Passing D3DRMANIMATION_POSITON without passing one of the two interpolation options will return an error from SetOptions().
	For scale and rotate keys to take effect, the D3DRMANIMATION_SCALEANDROTATION option must be set.
	Note that the position keys can be temporarily disabled within an Animation object calling SetOptions() without the D3DRMANIMATION_POSITION flag. Rotations and scalings both can be temporarily disabled by calling SetOptions() without the D3DRMANIMATION_SCALEANDROTATION flag.
	For an animation to loop, the D3DRMANIMATION_CLOSED option must be set. Animations with this option set will loop by repeating all keys between the highest and lowest time valued keys at the right times. Internally, RM takes the modulus of the time passed to

SetTime() with the highest key value. Unpredictable behavior may result if you use SetTime() with a time smaller than the time value of the smallest keys with the D3DRMANIMATION_CLOSED option set.

Setting the D3DRMANIMATION_OPEN option causes the Animation to animate once. Any time value passed to SetTime() that is greater than the largest time value of any key in the Animation will cause the largest existing time value to be used.

Arguments:	D3DRMANIMATIONOPTIONS d3drmanimFlags
Return Type:	HRESULT
Return Values:	See Direct3D Retained-Mode Return Values.
See Also:	IDirect3DRMAnimation::GetOptions, D3DRMANIMATIONOPTIONS, IDirect3DRMAnimation::SetTime

SetTime

Interface:	IDirect3DAnimation
Declaration:	`HRESULT SetTime(D3DVALUE rvTime);`
Description:	Sets the current time of the Animation object.
Notes:	SetTime() drives the animation. Typically you would call SetTime() on an animation during the rendering of each frame. The animation then updates the position, scale, and rotation of its frame depending on what options are set with IDirect3DRMAnimation::SetOptions(), and when the frame is rendered, it exhibits the latest stage of the animation.
Arguments:	D3DVALUE rvTime—Current time to set for the animation.
Return Type:	HRESULT
Return Values:	See Direct3D Retained-Mode Return Values.
See Also:	IDirect3DRMAnimationSet::SetTime

IDirect3DRMAnimationSet

The IDirect3DRMAnimationSet interface enables applications to group multiple Retained-Mode animations together. The animations can then be driven by the same clock—providing easy synchronization of complex animations. IDirect3DRMAnimationSet contains methods for adding and deleting animations, loading animation sets, and setting the time parameter.

IDirect3DRMAnimationSet, as with all COM interfaces, is derived from IUnknown and inherits its methods. IDirect3DRMAnimationSet also inherits the methods of IDirect3DRMObject. A Direct3DRMAnimationSet object can be obtained by calling IDirect3DRM::CreateAnimationSet(). IDirect3DRMAnimationSet implements the following methods:

    AddAnimation

    DeleteAnimation

    Load

    SetTime

AddAnimation

Interface:	IDirect3DRMAnimationSet
Declaration:	`HRESULT AddAnimation(LPDIRECT3DRMANIMATION lpD3DRMAnimation);`
Description:	This method adds an Animation object to an AnimationSet.
Notes:	AddAnimation() is used to add an animation object into an animation set.
Arguments:	LPDIRECT3DRMANIMATION lpD3DRMAnimation—The pointer to IDirect3DRMAnimation object.
Return Type:	HRESULT
Return Values:	See Direct3D Retained-Mode Return Values.
See Also:	IDirect3DRMAnimationSet::DeleteAnimation

DeleteAnimation

Interface:	IDirect3DRMAnimationSet
Declaration:	`HRESULT DeleteAnimation(LPDIRECT3DRMANIMATION lpD3DRMAnimation);`
Description:	This method removes the specified animation object from the animation set.
Notes:	DeleteAnimation() removes the specified animation object from the animation "mix."
Arguments:	LPDIRECT3DRMANIMATION lpD3DRMAnimation—The pointer to IDirect3DRMAnimation object previously added to the set with AddAnimation.
Return Type:	HRESULT
Return Values:	See Direct3D Retained-Mode Return Values.
See Also:	IDirect3DRMAnimationSet::AddAnimation

Load

Interface:	IDirect3DRMAnimationSet
Declaration:	`HRESULT Load(LPVOID lpvObjSource, LPVOID lpvObjID, D3DRMLOADOPTIONS d3drmLOFlags, D3DRMLOADTEXTURECALLBACK d3drmLoadTextureProc, LPVOID lpArgLTP, LPDIRECT3DRMFRAME lpParentFrame);`
Description:	This method loads an animation set from a file, memory, or resource.
Notes:	Load() can be used to load an animation set from a file, a resource, raw memory, or a stream. Loading through files and resources is documented; loading from memory or a stream is not.
	To Load an animation set from a file, lpvObjSource should point to the name of the file to be loaded.
Arguments:	LPVOID lpvObjSource—The pointer to the data indicating the source of the animation data. What lpvObjSource points to depends on the contents of the d3drmLOFlags parameter.

continues

continued

LPVOID lpvObjID—The pointer to an object name or position from which the animation set is to be loaded. What lpvObjID points to depends on the contents of the d3drmLOFlags parameters. This parameter may be NULL.

D3DRMLOADOPTIONS d3drmLOFlags—The flags specifying the source of the animation set (file, resource, memory, or stream), whether the animation set is being specified by name, position in the file, or GUID, and whether or not the animation set should be shared or duplicated if it's already been loaded. There are three different groups of D3DRMLOADOPTIONS flags; you may specify zero or one flag from each group, but no more than one from each group.

Specify the source of the animation by using a flag from this group. If none of these flags is used, D3DRMLOAD_FROMFILE is supplied implicitly:

D3DRMLOAD_FROMFILE, D3DRMLOAD_FROMRESOURCE, D3DRMLOAD_FROMMEMORY, D3DRMLOAD_FROMSTREAM

Indicate how it is specified using a flag from this group:

D3DRMLOAD_BYNAME, D3DRMLOAD_BYPOSITION, D3DRMLOAD_BYGUID, D3DRMLOAD_FIRST

Specify whether or not this animation may be shared across multiple Loads, or enforce a distinct copy from every load by using a flag from this group:

D3DRMLOAD_INSTANCEBYREFERENCE, D3DRMLOAD_INSTANCEBYCOPYING

D3DRMLOADTEXTURECALLBACK d3drmLoadTextureProc—A D3DRMLOADTEXTURECALLBACK callback function called to load any textures used by the object that require special formatting. This parameter can be NULL.

LPVOID lpArgLTP—The address of application-defined data passed to the D3DRMLOADTEXTURECALLBACK callback function.

	LPDirect3DRMFrame lpParentFrame—The address of a parent Direct3DRMFrame object. This prevents the frames referred to by the animation set from being created with a NULL parent.
Return Type:	HRESULT
Return Values:	See Direct3D Retained-Mode Return Values.
See Also:	IDirect3DRMAnimationSet::AddAnimation

SetTime

Interface:	IDirect3DRMAnimationSet
Declaration:	`HRESULT SetTime(D3DVALUE rvTime);`
Description:	This method sets the current time for the animation set. This has the effect of setting each of the component Animation objects to that time.
Notes:	The SetTime() method is used to drive the animation set. Typically, you would call SetTime() once per frame to advance the animation to the next frame.
Arguments:	D3DVALUE rvTime—This parameter specifies the time the animation set should be set to. The meaning of rvTime depends on the key frame times set in the individual animations or the tool used to generate the animations.
Return Type:	HRESULT
Return Values:	See Direct3D Retained-Mode Return Values.
See Also:	IDirect3DRMAnimationSet::AddAnimation

IDirect3DRMDevice

The IDirect3DRMDevice interface provides functionality for control of the display location for rendered output. Through this interface, an application can adjust rendering and display characteristics such as render quality, number of render buffers, dithering, levels of shading, and texture quality. Additionally, applications can retrieve information about the output device such as supported color model, height and width, wireframe options, and viewports associated with the device. IDirect3DRMDevice can also be used to obtain the associated Immediate-Mode device object (IDirect3DDevice).

IDirect3DRMDevice, as with all COM interfaces, is derived from IUnknown and inherits its methods. IDirect3DRMDevice also inherits the methods of IDirect3DRMObject. A Direct3DRMDevice object can be obtained by calling IDirect3DRM::CreateDeviceFromClipper(), IDirect3DRM::CreateDeviceFromD3D(), or IDirect3DRM::CreateDeviceFromSurface(). IDirect3DRMDevice implements the following methods:

AddUpdateCallback	GetWidth
DeleteUpdateCallback	GetWireframeOptions
GetBufferCount	Init
GetColorModel	InitFromClipper
GetDirect3DDevice	InitFromD3D
GetDither	SetBufferCount
GetHeight	SetDither
GetTrianglesDrawn	SetQuality
GetQuality	SetShades
GetShades	SetTextureQuality
GetTextureQuality	Update
GetViewports	

AddUpdateCallback

Interface:	IDirect3DRMDevice
Declaration:	`HRESULT AddUpdateCallback(D3DRMUPDATECALLBACK d3drmUpdateProc, LPVOID arg);`
Description:	This method registers a function callback that is called every time IDirect3DRMDevice::Update() is called on this device.
Notes:	This method could be used to override the device update behavior. For example, the callback could be passed the rectangles for drawing (blitting) through the lpArg argument. The callback could then do custom blitting and update the blit rectangles accordingly. If everything were custom blitted using the callback, Retained-Mode would not do any drawing.
Arguments:	D3DRMUPDATECALLBACK d3drmUpdateProc—The pointer to the application-defined callback function.
	LPVOID lpArg—The pointer to the data structure to be passed to the callback function as an argument.
Return Type:	HRESULT
Return Values:	See Direct3D Retained-Mode Return Values.
See Also:	IDirect3DRMDevice::DeleteUpdateCallback, D3DRMUPDATECALLBACK

DeleteUpdateCallback

Interface:	IDirect3DRMDevice
Declaration:	`HRESULT DeleteUpdateCallback(D3DRMUPDATECALLBACK d3drmUpdateProc, LPVOID arg);`
Description:	This method removes a previously registered update callback function from an object.
Notes:	Update callbacks are registered with IDirect3DDevice::AddUpdateCallback().

continues

continued

Arguments:	D3DRMUPDATECALLBACK d3drmUpdateProc—The pointer to the application-defined callback function.
	LPVOID lpArg—The pointer to the data structure passed as the argument to IDirect3DDevice::AddUpdateCallback().
Return Type:	HRESULT
Return Values:	See Direct3D Retained-Mode Return Values.
See Also:	IDirect3DRMDevice::AddUpdateCallBack, D3DRMUPDATECALLBACK

GetBufferCount

Interface:	IDirect3DRMDevice
Declaration:	`DWORD GetBufferCount();`
Description:	This method returns the number of buffers being used for device updates.
Notes:	The default value is one (single-buffering).
Arguments:	None
Return Type:	DWORD
Return Values:	Returns the number of buffers.
See Also:	IDirect3DRMDevice::SetBufferCount

GetColorModel

Interface:	IDirect3DRMDevice
Declaration:	`D3DCOLORMODEL GetColorModel();`
Description:	This method returns the current color model of a device.

Notes:	The color model desired by an application is usually specified when enumerating the available Direct3D devices. Because a device may support either, however, this function can be useful in determining the current model if an application has not specified one on device creation.
Arguments:	None
Return Type:	D3DCOLORMODEL
Return Values:	Returns the current color model of a device. The possible values are:
	D3DCOLOR_MONO—The current color model is the monochromatic (ramp) model.
	D3DCOLOR_RGB—The current color model is the RGB model.
See Also:	IDirect3D::EnumDevices, IDirect3D::FindDevice, D3DCOLORMODEL

GetDirect3DDevice

Interface:	IDirect3DRMDevice
Declaration:	`HRESULT GetDirect3DDevice(LPDIRECT3DDEVICE * lplpD3DDevice);`
Description:	This method retrieves a pointer to the current Immediate-Mode device.
Notes:	This method can be used in conjunction with IDirect3DDevice::GetDirect3D() to obtain a pointer to the current Direct3D Immediate-Mode object.
Arguments:	LPDIRECT3DDEVICE * D3DDevice—The pointer to the Immediate-Mode device object that will be initialized by this method.
Return Type:	HRESULT
Return Values:	See Direct3D Retained-Mode Return Values.
See Also:	IDirect3DDevice::GetDirect3D

GetDither

Interface:	IDirect3DRMDevice
Declaration:	`BOOL GetDither();`
Description:	This method returns TRUE or FALSE, depending on whether or not the current device is dithered.
Notes:	Dithering is enabled by default.
Arguments:	None
Return Type:	BOOL
Return Values:	TRUE or FALSE.
See Also:	IDirect3DRMDevice::SetDither

GetHeight

Interface:	IDirect3DRMDevice
Declaration:	`DWORD GetHeight();`
Description:	This method returns the height of a device in pixels.
Arguments:	None
Return Type:	DWORD
Return Values:	Returns the height of the device in pixels.
See Also:	IDirect3DRMDevice::GetWidth

GetTrianglesDrawn

Interface:	IDirect3DRMDevice
Declaration:	`DWORD GetTrianglesDrawn();`
Description:	This method returns the number of triangles that have been drawn to a device since it was created.

Notes:	This count includes triangles that were culled but not triangles that were completely outside the viewing frustum.
Arguments:	None
Return Type:	DWORD
Return Values:	Returns the number of triangles drawn.
See Also:	None

GetQuality

Interface:	IDirect3DRMDevice
Declaration:	`D3DRMRENDERQUALITY GetQuality();`
Description:	This method returns the rendering quality of a device.
Notes:	The default render quality setting for a device is D3DRMRENDER_FLAT. The render quality of a device consists of a shade mode, a light mode, and a fill mode. Direct3D provides a convenient method for setting render quality (see Direct3D Render Quality Enumerated Types).
	Retained-Mode Mesh and MeshBuilder objects also have a render quality associated with them, but meshes may not be rendered at a higher quality than the render quality of the Device object.
	Phong shading is not currently supported in Direct3D.
Arguments:	None
Return Type:	D3DRMRENDERQUALITY
Return Values:	Returns the render quality of the device. See Direct3D Render Quality Enumerated Types for the complete list. The most commonly used values represent a combination of a shade mode, a fill mode, and a light mode combined with a logical OR:
	D3DRMRENDER_WIREFRAME—Wireframe model, renders the outlines of triangles.
	D3DRMRENDER_UNLITFLAT—Triangles are rendered with flat shading and no lighting.

continues

continued	
	D3DRMRENDER_FLAT—Triangles are rendered with flat shading and lighting.
	D3DRMRENDER_GOURAUD—Triangles are Gouraud shaded.
	D3DRMRENDER_PHONG—Triangles are Phong shaded (not currently supported).
See Also:	IDirect3DRMDevice::SetQuality, IDirect3DMeshBuilder::GetQuality, IDirect3DMeshBuilder::SetQuality, IDirect3DMesh::GetGroupQuality, IDirect3DMesh::SetGroupQuality, D3DRMRENDERQUALITY

GetShades

Interface:	IDirect3DRMDevice
Declaration:	`DWORD GetShades();`
Description:	This method retrieves the number of shades used in each color's ramp.
Notes:	The default number of shades for a color is 32. The number of shades is relevant only if the device is using the ramp (monochromatic) color model.
Arguments:	None
Return Type:	DWORD
Return Values:	Returns the number of ramp model shades.
See Also:	IDirect3DRMDevice::SetShades, IDirect3DRMDevice::GetColorModel

GetTextureQuality

Interface:	IDirect3DRMDevice
Declaration:	`D3DRMTEXTUREQUALITY GetTextureQuality();`
Description:	This method retrieves the texture quality of a device.
Notes:	The default device texture quality is D3DRMTEXTURE_NEAREST.
Arguments:	None

Return Type: D3DRMTEXTUREQUALITY

Return Values: Returns the texture quality of the device. Possible values for the texture quality are:

D3DRMTEXTURE_NEAREST—Choose the nearest pixel in the texture.

D3DRMTEXTURE_LINEAR—Linearly interpolate between the four nearest pixels.

D3DRMTEXTURE_MIPNEAREST—Choose the nearest pixel in the appropriate mipmap.

D3DRMTEXTURE_MIPLINEAR—Linearly interpolate between the four nearest pixels in the appropriate mipmap.

MIPLINEAR is a linear interpolation between 2 pixels, each a point sample of a mipmap.

D3DRMTEXTURE_LINEARMIPNEAREST—Linearly interpolate between the two nearest mipmaps and then choose the nearest pixel in the resulting mipmap.

LINEARMIPNEAREST is bi-linear filtering on the nearest mipmap.

D3DRMTEXTURE_LINEARMIPLINEAR—Linearly interpolate between the two nearest mipmaps, then linearly interpolate between the four nearest pixels in the resulting mipmap.

Each mipmap is bi-linearly filtered, and the resulting texel values are then linearly interpolated.

See Also: IDirect3DRMDevice::SetTextureQuality, D3DRMTEXTUREQUALITY

GetViewports

Interface: IDirect3DRMDevice

Declaration: `HRESULT GetViewports(LPDIRECT3DRMVIEWPORTARRAY* lplpViewports);`

Description: This method returns a viewport array object that contains all the viewports currently associated with a device.

continues

continued

Notes:	This method can be used to inform all the viewports of a change such as a new viewport size.
Arguments:	LPDIRECT3DRMVIEWPORTARRAY* lplpViewports—This pointer will point at the viewport array if the call is successful.
Return Type:	HRESULT
Return Values:	See Direct3D Retained-Mode Return Values.
See Also:	None

GetWidth

Interface:	IDirect3DRMDevice
Declaration:	`DWORD GetWidth();`
Description:	This method returns the width of a device in pixels.
Arguments:	None
Return Type:	DWORD
Return Values:	Returns the width of the device in pixels.
See Also:	IDirect3DRMDevice::GetHeight

GetWireframeOptions

Interface:	IDirect3DRMDevice
Declaration:	`DWORD GetWireframeOptions();`
Description:	This method returns the wireframe options of a device.
Arguments:	None
Return Type:	DWORD
Return Values:	Returns the wireframe options as a bitwise, or of zero or more of the following values:
	D3DRMWIREFRAME_CULL—If set, the backfacing polygons are not drawn (culled).

D3DRMWIREFRAME_HIDDENLINE—If set, wireframe-rendered lines are obscured by objects nearer to the camera.

See Also: IDirect3DRMDevice::GetQuality, IDirect3DRMDevice::GetQuality

Init

Interface: IDirect3DRMDevice

Declaration: `HRESULT Init(ULONG width, ULONG height);`

Description: This method is not implemented.

InitFromClipper

Interface: IDirect3DRMDevice

Declaration: `HRESULT InitFromClipper(LPDIRECTDRAWCLIPPER lpDDClipper, LPGUID lpGUID, int width, int height);`

Description: This method initializes a Retained-Mode Device object from a DirectDraw Clipper object.

Notes: Most applications will not utilize this method. The recommended method of initializing a Retained-Mode Device from a DirectDraw Clipper object is to use IDirect3DRM::CreateDeviceFromClipper(), which encapsulates the functionality of creating a Device object and its surface, and attaching a clipper object to the primary surface. The advantage to IDirect3DRM::CreateDeviceFromClipper() is that the operating system can automatically find a device with default capabilities. This method should be used in conjunction with a call to IDirect3DRM::CreateObject() to create an empty object as well as functionality to determine the GUID of a valid Direct3D device.

Arguments: LPDIRECTDRAWCLIPPER lpDDClipper—The pointer to DirectDrawClipper object to be used for initialization.

continues

continued

	LPGUID lpGUID—The pointer to the GUID of the valid device.
	int width—The width of the device in pixels.
	int height—The height of the device in pixels.
Return Type:	HRESULT
Return Values:	See Direct3D Retained-Mode Return Values.
See Also:	IDirect3DRMDevice::InitFromD3D, IDirectDraw2::DirectDrawCreateClipper, IDirectDraw2::CreateClipper, IDirect3DRM::CreateDeviceFromClipper

InitFromD3D

Interface:	IDirect3DRMDevice
Declaration:	`HRESULT InitFromD3D(LPDIRECT3D lpD3D, LPDIRECT3DDEVICE lpD3DIMDev);`
Description:	This method initializes a device object from an Immediate-Mode object and an Immediate-Mode Device object.
Notes:	Most applications will not utilize this method. The recommended method of initializing a Retained-Mode Device from an Immediate-Mode object and Device object is to use IDirect3DRM::CreateDeviceFromD3D(), which encapsulates the functionality of creating a Device object and initializing it from the Immediate-Mode objects. IDirect3DRMDevice::InitFromD3D() should be used in conjunction with a call to IDirect3DRM::CreateObject() to create an empty object, IDirectDraw2::QueryInterface() to obtain an Immediate-Mode object, calls to either IDirect3D::EnumDevices() or IDirect3D::FindDevice() to obtain a valid Direct3D device GUID, and a call IDirect3DDevice::QueryInterface() to obtain an Immediate-Mode Device object.
Arguments:	LPDIRECT3D lpD3D—The pointer to an Immediate-Mode object used for initialization.

	LPDIRECT3DDEVICE lpD3DIMDev—The pointer to an Immediate-Mode Device object used for initialization.
Return Type:	HRESULT
Return Values:	See Direct3D Retained-Mode Return Values.
See Also:	IDirect3DRMDevice::InitFromClipper, IDirect3DRM::CreateDeviceFromD3D

SetBufferCount

Interface:	IDirect3DRMDevice
Declaration:	`HRESULT SetBufferCount(DWORD dwCount);`
Description:	This method sets the number of buffers used for device updates.
Notes:	The default value is one (single-buffering).
Arguments:	DWORD dwCount—The number of buffers to be used for device updates.
Return Type:	HRESULT
Return Values:	See Direct3D Retained-Mode Return Values.
See Also:	IDirect3DRMDevice::GetBufferCount

SetDither

Interface:	IDirect3DRMDevice
Declaration:	`HRESULT SetDither(BOOL bDither);`
Description:	This method enables or disables dithering for a device.
Notes:	Dithering is enabled by default.
Arguments:	BOOL bDither—TRUE to enable dithering or FALSE to disable dithering.
Return Type:	HRESULT
Return Values:	See Direct3D Retained-Mode Return Values.
See Also:	IDirect3DRMDevice::GetDither

SetQuality

Interface:	IDirect3DRMDevice
Declaration:	`HRESULT SetQuality (D3DRMRENDERQUALITY rqQuality);`
Description:	This method sets the rendering quality of a device.
Notes:	The default render quality setting for a device is D3DRMRENDER_FLAT. The render quality of a device consists of a shade mode, a light mode, and a fill mode. Direct3D provides a convenient method for setting render quality. Retained-Mode Mesh and MeshBuilder objects also have a render quality associated with them, but meshes cannot be rendered at a higher quality than the render quality of the Device object. Phong shading is not currently supported in Direct3D.
Arguments:	D3DRMRENDERQUALITY rqQuality—Render quality for a device. The most commonly used values represent a combination of a shade mode, a fill mode, and a light mode combined with a logical OR: D3DRMRENDER_WIREFRAME—Wireframe model, renders the outlines of triangles. D3DRMRENDER_UNLITFLAT—Triangles are rendered with flat shading and no lighting. D3DRMRENDER_FLAT—Triangles are rendered with flat shading and lighting D3DRMRENDER_GOURAUD—Triangles are Gouraud shaded. D3DRMRENDER_PHONG—Triangles are Phong shaded (not currently supported).
Return Type:	HRESULT
Return Values:	See Direct3D Retained-Mode Return Values.
See Also:	IDirect3DRMDevice::GetQuality, IDirect3DMeshBuilder::GetQuality, IDirect3DMeshBuilder::SetQuality, IDirect3DMesh::GetGroupQuality, IDirect3DMesh::SetGroupQuality, D3DRMRENDERQUALITY

SetShades

Interface:	IDirect3DRMDevice
Declaration:	`HRESULT SetShades(DWORD ulShades);`
Description:	Sets the number of shades per color ramp.
Notes:	The default number of shades for a color ramp is 32. The number of shades is relevant only if the device is using the ramp (monochromatic) color model.
Arguments:	DWORD ulShades—The number of shades for each color ramp.
Return Type:	HRESULT
Return Values:	See Direct3D Retained-Mode Return Values.
See Also:	IDirect3DRMDevice::GetShades, IDirect3DRMDevice::GetColorModel

SetTextureQuality

Interface:	IDirect3DRMDevice
Declaration:	`HRESULT SetTextureQuality(D3DRMTEXTUREQUALITY tqTextureQuality);`
Description:	Sets the texture quality for a device.
Notes:	The default device texture quality is D3DRMTEXTURE_NEAREST. See Direct3D Texture Quality Enumerated Types for the complete list of possible texture qualities and descriptions.
Arguments:	D3DRMTEXTUREQUALITY tqTextureQuality—The texture quality for a device. Possible values for the texture quality are: D3DRMTEXTURE_NEAREST—Choose the nearest pixel in the texture. D3DRMTEXTURE_LINEAR—Linearly interpolate between the four nearest pixels. D3DRMTEXTURE_MIPNEAREST—Choose the nearest pixel in the appropriate mipmap.

continues

continued

> D3DRMTEXTURE_MIPLINEAR—Linearly interpolate between the four nearest pixels in the appropriate mipmap.
>
> D3DRMTEXTURE_LINEARMIPNEAREST—Linearly interpolate between the two nearest mipmaps and then choose the nearest pixel in the resulting mipmap.
>
> LINEARMIPNEAREST is bi-linear filtering on the nearest mipmap.
>
> D3DRMTEXTURE_LINEARMIPLINEAR—Linearly interpolate between the two nearest mipmaps and then linearly interpolate between the four nearest pixels in the resulting mipmap.
>
> Each mipmap is bi-linearly filtered. The resulting texel values are then linearly interpolated.

Return Type: HRESULT

Return Values: See Direct3D Retained-Mode Return Values.

See Also: IDirect3DRMDevice::GetTextureQuality, D3DRMTEXTUREQUALITY

Update

Interface: IDirect3DRMDevice

Declaration: `HRESULT Update();`

Description: This method copies the image that has been rendered in a viewport to a device, usually for display on the screen.

Notes: If the device supports page-flipping, this function flips the back buffer to the screen and the previous screen becomes the new back buffer. If the device does not support page-flipping, this function blits the back buffer to the front buffer.

Each call to this method causes the operating system to call an application-defined callback function, D3DRMUPDATECALLBACK. The update callback can be registered with IDirect3DDevice::AddUpdateCallback().

IDirect3DDevice::DeleteUpdateCallback is used to unregister the update callback. The callback can be used to override the default behavior of the application.

Arguments:	None
Return Type:	HRESULT
Return Values:	See Direct3D Retained-Mode Return Values.
See Also:	IDirect3DRMDevice::AddUpdateCallback, IDirect3DRMDevice::DeleteUpdateCallback

IDirect3DRMFace

The IDirect3DRMFace interface provides the functionality to represent a polygonal surface. IDirect3DRMFace enables applications to retrieve and adjust information associated with the polygon, including vertices, normals, color, materials, and textures.

IDirect3DRMFace, as with all COM interfaces, is derived from IUnknown and inherits its methods. IDirect3DRMFace also inherits the methods of IDirect3DRMObject. A Direct3DRMFace object can be obtained by calling IDirect3DRM::CreateFace(). IDirect3DRMFace implements the following methods:

- AddVertex
- AddVertexAndNormalIndexed
- GetColor
- GetMaterial
- GetNormal
- GetTexture
- GetTextureCoordinateIndex
- GetTextureCoordinates
- GetTextureTopology
- GetVertex
- GetVertexCount
- GetVertexIndex
- GetVertices
- SetColor
- SetColorRGB
- SetMaterial

SetTexture

SetTextureCoordinates

SetTextureTopology

AddVertex

Interface:	IDirect3DRMFace
Declaration:	HRESULT AddVertex(D3DVALUE x, D3DVALUE y, D3DVALUE z);
Description:	Adds a new vertex to an IDirect3DRMFace object.
Notes:	The vertex is in world coordinate space until the face object is added to a mesh builder. Once added, the vertex is in model coordinate space.
Arguments:	D3DVALUE x, y, z—Coordinates of the vertex within the face's frame.
Return Type:	HRESULT
Return Values:	See Direct3D Retained-Mode Return Values.
See Also:	IDirect3DRMFace::AddVertexAndNormalIndexed

AddVertexAndNormalIndexed

Interface:	IDirect3DRMFace
Declaration:	HRESULT AddVertexAndNormalIndexed(DWORD vertex, DWORD normal);
Description:	Adds a vertex and normal to an IDirect3DRMFace object using an index for the vertex and an index for the normal in the mesh builder containing the face.
Notes:	The face, vertex, and normal must already have been added to an IDirect3DRMMeshBuilder object.
Arguments:	DWORD vertex—The vertex index returned from IDirect3DRMMeshBuilder::AddVertex.
	DWORD normal—The normal index returned from IDirect34RMMeshBuilder::AddNormal.

continues

continued

Return Type:	HRESULT
Return Values:	See Direct3D Retained-Mode Return Values.
See Also:	IDirect3DRMFace::AddVertex, IDirect3DRMMeshBuilder::AddVertex, IDirect3DRMMeshBuilder::AddNormal

GetColor

Interface:	IDirect3DRMFace
Declaration:	`D3DCOLOR GetColor();`
Description:	Returns the color of the face.
Notes:	The color returned is both the ambient and the diffuse color of the face.
Arguments:	None
Return Type:	D3DCOLOR
Return Values:	Color of the face.
See Also:	IDirect3DRMFace::SetColor, D3DCOLOR

GetMaterial

Interface:	IDirect3DRMFace
Declaration:	`HRESULT GetMaterial(LPDIRECT3DRMMATERIAL* lplpMaterial);`
Description:	Retrieves the IDirect3DRMMaterial object associated with the face.
Notes:	The IDirect3DRMMaterial object should have its Release() method called when it is no longer in use.
Arguments:	LPDIRECT3DRMMATERIAL* lplpMaterial—The address of a pointer that will point to the IDirect3DRMMaterial object, or NULL if the call fails.
Return Type:	HRESULT

Return Values:	See Direct3D Retained-Mode Return Values.
See Also:	IDirect3DRMFace::SetMaterial, IDirect3DRMMaterial

GetNormal

Interface:	IDirect3DRMFace
Declaration:	`HRESULT GetNormal(D3DVECTOR *lpNormal);`
Description:	Retrieves the normal vector of the face.
Notes:	The vertex is in world coordinate space until the face object is added to a mesh builder. Once added, the vertex is in model coordinate space.
Arguments:	D3DVECTOR *lpNormal—The pointer to D3DVECTOR that is assigned the normal vector of the face.
Return Type:	HRESULT
Return Values:	See Direct3D Retained-Mode Return Values.
See Also:	None

GetTexture

Interface:	IDirect3DRMFace
Declaration:	`HRESULT GetTexture(LPDIRECT3DRMTEXTURE* lplpTexture);`
Description:	Retrieves the IDirect3DRMTexture object associated with the face, if any.
Notes:	If the face doesn't have a texture associated with it, GetTexture sets the lplpTexture argument to NULL and returns D3D_OK.
Arguments:	LPDIRECT3DRMTEXTURE* lplpTexture—The address of a pointer that will point to the IDirect3DRMTexture object, or NULL if no texture is assigned to the face.
Return Type:	HRESULT
Return Values:	See Direct3D Retained-Mode Return Values.
See Also:	IDirect3DRMFace::SetTexture, IDirect3DRMTexture

GetTextureCoordinateIndex

Interface:	IDirect3DRMFace
Declaration:	`int GetTextureCoordinateIndex(DWORD dwIndex);`
Description:	Converts an index into the face's table of texture coordinates into an index into its mesh builder's table of texture coordinates.
Notes:	The return value of this method would typically be passed as the first parameter to IDirect3DRMMeshBuilder::GetTextureCoordinates.
Arguments:	DWORD dwIndex—The index into the face's table of texture coordinates.
Return Type:	int
Return Values:	Returns an index into mesh builder's table of texture coordinates.
See Also:	IDirect3DRMFace::GetTextureCoordinates, IDirect3DRMMeshBuilder::GetTextureCoordinates

GetTextureCoordinates

Interface:	IDirect3DRMFace
Declaration:	`HRESULT GetTextureCoordinates(DWORD index, D3DVALUE *lpU, D3DVALUE *lpV);`
Description:	Retrieves the texture coordinates for a particular vertex.
Notes:	The index parameter to this method can be converted to an index to pass to IDirect3DRMMeshBuilder::GetTextureCoordinates by the IDirect3DRMFace::GetTextureCoordinateIndex method.
Arguments:	DWORD index—The index of the vertex for which to retrieve texture coordinates.
	D3DVALUE *lpU—The pointer to D3DVALUE that will hold the horizontal texture coordinate.
	D3DVALUE *lpV—The pointer to D3DVALUE that will hold the vertical texture coordinate.

Return Type:	HRESULT
Return Values:	See Direct3D Retained-Mode Return Values.
See Also:	SetTextureCoordinates, IDirect3DRMTexture

GetTextureTopology

Interface:	IDirect3DRMFace
Declaration:	`HRESULT GetTextureTopology(BOOL *lpU, BOOL *lpV);`
Description:	Retrieves the texture topology of the IDirect3DRMFace object.
Notes:	This method sets the BOOLs pointed to by the parameters lpU and lpV to TRUE or FALSE, depending on whether textures are wrapped in the horizontal and vertical direction. If both are FALSE, the topology is flat. If both are TRUE, the topology is spherical. If only one is TRUE, the topology is cylindrical in that direction.
Arguments:	BOOL *lpU—The pointer to BOOL that will be set to TRUE if the texture is wrapped in the horizontal direction.
	BOOL *lpV—The pointer to BOOL that will be set to TRUE if the texture is wrapped in the vertical direction.
Return Type:	HRESULT
Return Values:	See Direct3D Retained-Mode Return Values.
See Also:	IDirect3DRMFace::SetTextureTopology, IDirect3DRMTexture

GetVertex

Interface:	IDirect3DRMFace
Declaration:	`HRESULT GetVertex(DWORD index, D3DVECTOR *lpPosition, D3DVECTOR *lpNormal);`
Description:	Retrieves the position and normal vectors for a vertex in the face.

continues

continued

Notes:	The index parameter passed to this method can be converted into an index to pass to IDirect3DRMMeshBuilder::GetVertex by the IDirect3DRMFace::GetVertexIndex method.
Arguments:	DWORD index—The vertex index.
	D3DVECTOR *lpPosition—The pointer to D3DVECTOR that will hold the position vector of the vertex.
	D3DVECTOR *lpNormal—The pointer to D3DVECTOR that will hold the normal vector of the vertex.
Return Type:	HRESULT
Return Values:	See Direct3D Retained-Mode Return Values.
See Also:	IDirect3DRMFace::AddVertex, IDirect3DRMFace::AddVertexAndNormalIndex, IDirect3DRMFace::GetVertexIndex, IDirect3DRMMeshBuilder::GetVertex

GetVertexCount

Interface:	IDirect3DRMFace
Declaration:	`int GetVertexCount();`
Description:	Returns the number of vertices in a face object.
Arguments:	None
Return Type:	int
Return Values:	Number of vertices in the face.
See Also:	IDirect3DRMFace::GetVertices

GetVertexIndex

Interface:	IDirect3DRMFace
Declaration:	`int GetVertexIndex (DWORD dwIndex);`

Description:	Converts an index into the face's table of vertices, into an index into its mesh builder's table of vertices.
Notes:	The return value of this method would typically be passed as the first parameter to IDirect3DRMMeshBuilder::SetVertex, or to find a face's vertices in the array of vertices returned by IDirect3DRMMeshBuilder::GetVertices.
Arguments:	DWORD dwIndex—The index into the face's table of vertices.
Return Type:	HRESULT
Return Values:	See Direct3D Retained-Mode Return Values.
See Also:	IDirect3DRMMeshBuilder::GetVertices, IDirect3DRMMeshBuilder::SetVertex

GetVertices

Interface:	IDirect3DRMFace
Declaration:	`HRESULT GetVertices(DWORD *lpdwVertexCount, D3DVECTOR *lpPosition, D3DVECTOR *lpNormal);`
Description:	Retrieves the position and normal vectors for each vertex in an IDirect3DRMFace object.
Notes:	This method is used to get both the vertices and the vertex count. Passing NULL for the lpPosition and lpNormal arguments results in the DWORD pointed to by the lpdwVertexCount argument to be set to the number of vertices, which is the same value returned by IDirect3DRMFace::GetVertexCount.
	If lpPosition and lpNormal are not NULL, and the DWORD pointed to by lpdwVertexCount is smaller than the number of vertices, this method will return an error code and the contents of the arrays remains unchanged.
Arguments:	DWORD *lpdwVertexCount—The pointer to a DWORD that holds the number of D3DVECTORs the arrays pointed to by the lpPosition and

continues

continued

	lpNormal arguments can hold. If those arguments are NULL, the DWORD will be set to the number of vertices in the IDirect3DRMFace object.
	D3DVECTOR *lpPosition—The pointer to an array of D3DVECTORs that will hold the position vectors for the vertices of the IDirect3DRMFace object, or NULL.
	D3DVECTOR *lpNormal—The pointer to an array of D3DVECTORs that will hold the normal vectors for the vertices of the IDirect3DRMFace object, or NULL.
Return Type:	HRESULT
Return Values:	See Direct3D Retained-Mode Return Values.
See Also:	IDirect3DRMFace::GetVertexCount

SetColor

Interface:	IDirect3DRMFace
Declaration:	`HRESULT SetColor(D3DCOLOR color);`
Description:	Sets the ambient and diffuse color of the IDirect3DRMFace object to the specified color.
Notes:	The color parameter is usually constructed by using the RGB_MAKE macro, which converts three RGB values, each between 0 and 255, into a D3DCOLOR with the maximum alpha value. To vary the alpha component, use the RGBA_MAKE macro.
	To specify the RGB components as values between 0.0 and 1.0, use IDirect3DRMFace::SetColorRGB.
Arguments:	D3DCOLOR color—Color of the face.
Return Type:	HRESULT
Return Values:	See Direct3D Retained-Mode Return Values.
See Also:	IDirect3DRMFace::SetColorRGB, RGB_MAKE, IDirect3DRMFace::GetColor

SetColorRGB

Interface:	IDirect3DRMFace
Declaration:	`HRESULT SetColorRGB(D3DVALUE red, D3DVALUE green, D3DVALUE blue);`
Description:	Sets the ambient and diffuse color of the IDirect3DRMFace object to the specified color with the maximum alpha value.
Notes:	The values for the R, G, and B components should be between 0.0 and 1.0. To specify the RGB components as values between 0 and 255, or to specify a different alpha value, use IDirect3DRMFace::SetColor.
Arguments:	D3DVALUE red, green, blue—The red, green, and blue components of the face's color. Values should be between 0 and 1.
Return Type:	HRESULT
Return Values:	See Direct3D Retained-Mode Return Values.
See Also:	IDirect3DRMFace::SetColor, IDirect3DRMFace::GetColor

SetMaterial

Interface:	IDirect3DRMFace
Declaration:	`HRESULT SetMaterial(LPDIRECT3DRMMATERIAL lpD3DRMMaterial);`
Description:	Sets the material of an IDirect3DRMFace object to be the specified IDirect3DRMMaterial object.
Notes:	SetMaterial can be used instead of IDirect3DRMFace::SetColor or IDirect3DRMFace::SetColorRGB to change the color and alpha value of the face. It also allows changing the spectral and emissive colors of the face and the power of the spectral exponent.
Arguments:	LPDIRECT3DRMMATERIAL lpD3DRMMaterial—Pointer to an IDirect3DRMMaterial object.
Return Type:	HRESULT
Return Values:	See Direct3D Retained-Mode Return Values.
See Also:	IDirect3DRMFace::GetMaterial, IDirect3DRMMaterial

SetTexture

Interface:	IDirect3DRMFace
Declaration:	`HRESULT SetTexture(LPDIRECT3DRMTEXTURE lpD3DRMTexture);`
Description:	Sets the texture of the IDirect3DRMFace object to be the specified IDirect3DTexture object.
Notes:	The texture is mapped to the face based on the texture coordinates of the vertices, the texture topology of the face, and the device's current texture quality mode.
Arguments:	LPDIRECT3DRMTEXTURE lpD3DRMTexture—Pointer to an IDirect3DRMTexture object.
Return Type:	HRESULT
Return Values:	See Direct3D Retained-Mode Return Values.
See Also:	IDirect3DRMFace::GetTexture, IDirect3DRMTexture, IDirect3DRMFace::SetTextureCoordinates, IDirect3DRMFace::SetTextureTopology, IDirect3DRMDevice::SetTextureQuality

SetTextureCoordinates

Interface:	IDirect3DRMFace
Declaration:	`HRESULT SetTextureCoordinates(DWORD vertex, D3DVALUE u, D3DVALUE v);`
Description:	Assigns new texture coordinates to the specified vertex within the IDirect3DRMFace object.
Notes:	Changing the texture coordinates of all the vertices of a face can be used to create various effects, such as animated texture.
Arguments:	DWORD vertex—The vertex index. D3DVALUE u, v—The new texture coordinates for the vertex.

Return Type:	HRESULT
Return Values:	See Direct3D Retained-Mode Return Values.
See Also:	IDirect3DRMFace::GetTextureCoordinates, IDirect3DRMTexture

SetTextureTopology

Interface:	IDirect3DRMFace
Declaration:	`HRESULT SetTextureTopology(BOOL cylU, BOOL cylV);`
Description:	Sets the texture topology of the IDirect3DRMFace object.
Notes:	This method is used to set the texture topology to flat, cylindrical, or spherical. If both arguments are FALSE, the topology is flat. If both arguments are TRUE, the topology is spherical. If only one is TRUE, the topology is cylindrical in that direction.
Arguments:	BOOL cylU—TRUE to enable horizontal wrapping, FALSE to disable horizontal wrapping.
	BOOL cylV—TRUE to enable vertical wrapping, FALSE to disable vertical wrapping.
Return Type:	HRESULT
Return Values:	See Direct3D Retained-Mode Return Values.
See Also:	IDirect3DRMFace::GetTextureTopology, IDirect3DRMTexture

IDirect3DRMFrame

The IDirect3DRMFrame interface provides control of an object frame of reference and its associated scene graph. IDirect3DRMFrame enables applications to add and delete child frames, add and delete visuals, and adjust lights, colors, materials, textures, fog, sorting, and transformations, including position, orientation, and scale. Additionally, applications can perform basic animation on an object's frame through this interface.

IDirect3DRMFrame, as with all COM interfaces, is derived from IUnknown and inherits its methods. IDirect3DRMFrame also inherits the methods of IDirect3DRMObject. A Direct3DRMFrame object can be obtained by calling IDirect3DRM::CreateFrame(). IDirect3DRMFrame implements the following methods:

AddChild	GetOrientation
AddLight	GetParent
AddMoveCallback	GetPosition
AddRotation	GetRotation
AddScale	GetScene
AddTransform	GetSceneBackground
AddTranslation	GetSceneBackgroundDepth
AddVisual	GetSceneFogColor
DeleteChild	GetSceneFogEnable
DeleteLight	GetSceneFogMode
DeleteMoveCallback	GetSceneFogParams
DeleteVisual	GetSortMode
GetChildren	GetTexture
GetColor	GetTextureTopology
GetLights	GetTransform

continues

continued

GetMaterialMode	SetSceneBackground
GetVelocity	SetSceneBackgroundDepth
GetVisuals	SetSceneBackgroundImage
GetZbufferMode	SetSceneBackgroundRGB
InverseTransform	SetSceneFogColor
Load	SetSceneFogEnable
LookAt	SetSceneFogMode
Move	SetSceneFogParams
SetColor	SetSortMode
SetColorRGB	SetTexture
SetMaterialMode	SetTextureTopology
SetOrientation	SetVelocity
SetPosition	SetZbufferMode
SetRotation	Transform

AddChild

Interface:	IDirect3DRMFrame
Declaration:	`HRESULT AddChild(LPDIRECT3DRMFRAME lpD3DRMFrameChild);`
Description:	This method adds an IDirect3DRMFrame object as a child frame of this frame.
Notes:	When a frame is added as a child, its transform is modified so the frame has the same orientation and position in world coordinates as it did before being added.

	If the frame being added is already a child frame of another frame, it is removed from the other frame's child hierarchy before it is added as a child of the new parent frame.
Arguments:	LPDIRECT3DRMFRAME lpD3DRMFrameChild—The IDirect3DRMFrame object to be added as a child frame.
Return Type:	HRESULT
Return Values:	See Direct3D Retained-Mode Return Values.
See Also:	IDirect3DRMFrame::DeleteChild, IDirect3DRMFrame::GetTransform

AddLight

Interface:	IDirect3DRMFrame
Declaration:	`HRESULT AddLight(LPDIRECT3DRMLIGHT lpD3DRMLight);`
Description:	This method adds an IDirect3DRMLight object to the frame.
Notes:	All lights added to a frame are used in calculating the lighting for all objects in this frame and any of its child frames.
Arguments:	LPDIRECT3DRMLIGHT lpD3DRMLight—The IDirect3DRMLight object to be added.
Return Type:	HRESULT
Return Values:	See Direct3D Retained-Mode Return Values.
See Also:	IDirect3DRMFrame::DeleteLight, IDirect3DRMLight

AddMoveCallback

Interface:	IDirect3DRMFrame
Declaration:	`HRESULT AddMoveCallback(D3DRMFRAMEMOVECALLBACK d3drmFMC, VOID* lpArg);`
Description:	This method adds a move callback function to the frame.

continues

	continued
Notes:	A move callback lets an application do special processing to override or enhance Retained-Mode's frame dynamics or to perform other specialized processing, such as adjusting the sound with DirectSound.
	The same callback function may be used with different lpArg values.
Arguments:	D3DRMFRAMEMOVECALLBACK d3drmFMC—The address of the callback function.
	VOID* lpArg—The application-defined parameter that will be passed to the callback function.
Return Type:	HRESULT
Return Values:	See Direct3D Retained-Mode Return Values.
See Also:	IDirect3DRMFrame::DeleteMoveCallback, D3DRMFRAMEMOVECALLBACK

AddRotation

Interface:	IDirect3DRMFrame
Declaration:	`HRESULT AddRotation(D3DRMCOMBINETYPE rctCombine, D3DVALUE rvX, D3DVALUE rvY, D3DVALUE rvZ, D3DVALUE rvTheta);`
Description:	This method adds a rotation to the IDirect3DRMFrame object's transform.
Notes:	The rctCombine argument is used to specify how the rotation will affect the frame's transform. If its value is D3DRMCOMBINE_REPLACE, the frame's transform is replaced by a rotation transform. If its value is D3DRMCOMBINE_BEFORE or D3DRMCOMBINE_AFTER, it is composed by using pre-multiplication or post-multiplication, respectively.
Arguments:	D3DRMCOMBINETYPE rctCombine—One of D3DRMCOMBINE_REPLACE, D3DRMCOMBINE_BEFORE, or D3DRMCOMBINE_AFTER.

	D3DVALUE rvX, rvY, rvZ—The three coordinates specifying a direction axis around which rotation is to occur.
	D3DVALUE rvTheta—The rotation amount, in radians.
Return Type:	HRESULT
Return Values:	See Direct3D Retained-Mode Return Values.
See Also:	IDirect3DRMFrame::AddScale, IDirect3DRMFrame::AddTranslation, IDirect3DRMFrame::AddTransform, D3DRMCOMBINETYPE

AddScale

Interface:	IDirect3DRMFrame
Declaration:	`HRESULT AddScale(D3DRMCOMBINETYPE rctCombine, D3DVALUE rvX, D3DVALUE rvY, D3DVALUE rvZ);`
Description:	Adds a scale to the IDirect3DRMFrame object's transform.
Notes:	The rctCombine argument is used to specify how the scaling will affect the frame's transform. If its value is D3DRMCOMBINE_REPLACE, the frame's transform is replaced by a rotation transform. The values D3DRMCOMBINE_BEFORE and D3DRMCOMBINE_AFTER both produce the same effect (because a scaling transform commutes with other transforms) of composing a scaling transform constructed from the arguments with the frame's current transform.
Arguments:	D3DRMCOMBINETYPE rctCombine—One of D3DRMCOMBINE_REPLACE, D3DRMCOMBINE_BEFORE, or D3DRMCOMBINE_AFTER.
	D3DVALUE rvX—The scale factor in the x direction.
	D3DVALUE rvY—The scale factor in the y direction.
	D3DVALUE rvZ—The scale factor in the z direction.
Return Type:	HRESULT
Return Values:	See Direct3D Retained-Mode Return Values.

continues

continued

See Also:	IDirect3DRMFrame::AddRotation, IDirect3DRMFrame::AddTransform, IDirect3DRMFrame::AddTranslation, D3DRMCOMBINETYPE

AddTransform

Interface:	IDirect3DRMFrame
Declaration:	`HRESULT AddTransform(D3DRMCOMBINETYPE rctCombine, D3DRMMATRIX4D rmMatrix);`
Description:	Transforms or replaces the IDirect3DRMFrame's current transform.
Notes:	The rctCombine argument is used to specify how the transform is composed with the frame's current transform. If its value is D3DRMCOMBINE_REPLACE, the frame's transform is replaced by a new transform. If its value is D3DRMCOMBINE_BEFORE or D3DRMCOMBINE_AFTER, it is composed using pre-multiplication or post-multiplication, respectively.
Arguments:	D3DRMCOMBINETYPE rctCombine—One of D3DRMCOMBINE_REPLACE, D3DRMCOMBINE_BEFORE, or D3DRMCOMBINE_AFTER.
	D3DRMMATRIX4D rmMatrix—The transform to combine with or replace the frame's current transform.
Return Type:	HRESULT
Return Values:	See Direct3D Retained-Mode Return Values.
See Also:	IDirect3DRMFrame::AddRotation, IDirect3DRMFrame::AddScale, IDirect3DRMFrame::AddTranslation, D3DRMCOMBINETYPE

AddTranslation

Interface:	IDirect3DRMFrame
Declaration:	`HRESULT AddTranslation(D3DRMCOMBINETYPE rctCombine, D3DVALUE rvX, D3DVALUE rvY, D3DVALUE rvZ);`

Description:	Adds a translation to the IDirect3DRMFrame object's transform.
Notes:	The rctCombine argument is used to specify how the translation is composed with the frame's current transform. If its value is D3DRMCOMBINE_REPLACE, the frame's transform is replaced by a translation transform. If its value is D3DRMCOMBINE_BEFORE or D3DRMCOMBINE_AFTER, it is composed using pre-multiplication or post-multiplication, respectively, with a translation transform.
Arguments:	D3DRMCOMBINETYPE rctCombine—One of D3DRMCOMBINE_REPLACE, D3DRMCOMBINE_BEFORE, D3DRMCOMBINE_AFTER.
	D3DVALUE rvX—The x coordinate of translation vector.
	D3DVALUE rvY—The y coordinate of translation vector.
	D3DVALUE rvZ—The z coordinate of translation vector.
Return Type:	HRESULT
Return Values:	See Direct3D Retained-Mode Return Values.
See Also:	IDirect3DFrame::AddRotation, IDirect3DRMFrame::AddScale, IDirect3DRMFrame::AddTransform

AddVisual

Interface:	IDirect3DRMFrame
Declaration:	`HRESULT AddVisual(LPDIRECT3DRMVISUAL lpD3DRMVisual);`
Description:	Adds a new IDirect3DRMVisual object to the IDirect3DRMFrame object.
Notes:	The visuals of a frame comprise the parts of a frame that can be rendered. Retained-Mode frame, mesh, shadow, mesh builder, texture, and user visual objects can be added to a frame as visuals.
Arguments:	LPDIRECT3DRMVISUAL lpD3DRMVisual—Pointer to an IDirect3DRMVisual object.
Return Type:	HRESULT
Return Values:	See Direct3D Retained-Mode Return Values.

continues

continued

See Also:	IDirect3DRMFrame, IDirect3DRMMesh, IDirect3DRMShadow, IDirect3DRMMeshBuilder, IDirect3DRMTexture, IDirect3DRMUserVisual

DeleteChild

Interface:	IDirect3DRMFrame
Declaration:	HRESULT DeleteChild(LPDIRECT3DRMFRAME lpChild);
Description:	Remove the specified IDirect3DRMFrame object from this IDirect3DRMFrame object's hierarchy.
Notes:	The lpChild argument must have been added to this frame's hierarchy with IDirect3DRMFrame::AddChild().
	DeleteChild() calls the child frame's Release() method.
Arguments:	LPDIRECT3DRMFRAME lpChild—The pointer to an IDirect3DRMFrame object to remove from the hierarchy.
Return Type:	HRESULT
Return Values:	See Direct3D Retained-Mode Return Values.
See Also:	IDirect3DRMFrame::AddChild, IUnknown::Release

DeleteLight

Interface:	IDirect3DRMFrame
Declaration:	HRESULT DeleteLight(LPDIRECT3DRMLIGHT lpD3DRMLight);
Description:	Removes an IDirect3DRMLight object from this IDirect3DRMFrame object.
Notes:	The light object must have been added previously to the frame with IDirect3DRMFrame::AddLight().
	DeleteLight() calls the light object's Release() method.
Arguments:	LPDIRECT3DRMLIGHT lpD3DRMLight—The pointer to IDirect3DRMLight object to be removed.

Return Type:	HRESULT
Return Values:	See Direct3D Retained-Mode Return Values.
See Also:	IDirect3DRMFrame::AddLight, IDirect3DRMLight, IUnknown::Release

DeleteMoveCallback

Interface:	IDirect3DRMFrame
Declaration:	`HRESULT DeleteMoveCallback(D3DRMFRAMEMOVECALLBACK d3drmFMC, VOID* lpArg);`
Description:	Disables a move callback function that was earlier added with IDirect3DRMFrame::AddMoveCallback().
Notes:	A particular callback is specified both by the address of the callback function and the value of lpArg. To remove a particular callback, the value passed to IDirect3DRMFrame::AddMoveCallback() as lpArg must be used as lpArg in the call to DeleteMoveCallback().
Arguments:	D3DRMFRAMEMOVECALLBACK d3drmFMC—The address of callback function earlier passed to IDirect3DRMFrame::AddMoveCallback.
	VOID * lpArg—The user value earlier passed to IDirect3DRMFrame::AddMoveCallback.
Return Type:	HRESULT
Return Values:	See Direct3D Retained-Mode Return Values.
See Also:	IDirect3DRMFrame::AddMoveCallback, D3DRMFRAMEMOVECALLBACK

DeleteVisual

Interface:	IDirect3DRMFrame
Declaration:	`HRESULT DeleteVisual(LPDIRECT3DRMVISUAL lpD3DRMVisual);`

continues

continued

Description:	Removes an IDirect3DRMVisual object from the IDirect3DRMFrame's hierarchy.
Notes:	The IDirect3DRMVisual object must have been added to the hierarchy previously with IDirect3DRMFrame::AddVisual().
	The visuals of a frame comprise the parts of a frame that can be rendered. Retained-Mode frame, mesh, shadow, mesh builder, texture, and user visual objects can be added to a frame as visuals.
Arguments:	LPDIRECT3DRMVISUAL lpD3DRMVisual—The pointer to an IDirect3DRMVisual object.
Return Type:	HRESULT
Return Values:	See Direct3D Retained-Mode Return Values.
See Also:	IDirect3DRMFrame::AddVisual, IDirect3DRMFrame, IDirect3DRMMesh, IDirect3DRMShadow, IDirect3DRMMeshBuilder, IDirect3DRMTexture, IDirect3DRMUserVisual

GetChildren

Interface:	IDirect3DRMFrame
Declaration:	`HRESULT GetChildren(LPDIRECT3DRMFRAMEARRAY* lplpChildren);`
Description:	Constructs an IDirect3DRMFrameArray object and fills it with references to the IDirect3DRMFrame object's child frames.
Notes:	A frame can have any number of children, but only one parent.
Arguments:	LPDIRECT3DRMFRAMEARRAY* lplpChildren—The address of a pointer that will point to the IDirect3DRMFrameArray object, or NULL if the call fails.
Return Type:	HRESULT
Return Values:	See Direct3D Retained-Mode Return Values.
See Also:	IDirect3DRMFrame::AddChild, IDirect3DRMFrameArray

GetColor

Interface:	IDirect3DRMFrame
Declaration:	`D3DCOLOR GetColor();`
Description:	Retrieves the IDirect3DRMFrame object's color.
Notes:	The frame's material mode must be set to D3DRMMATERIAL_FROMFRAME for the color to be applied to objects in the frame.
Arguments:	None
Return Type:	D3DCOLOR
Return Values:	Returns the color of the frame object.
See Also:	IDirect3DRMFrame::SetColor, IDirect3DRMFrame::SetColorRGB, IDirect3DRMFrame::SetMaterialMode

GetLights

Interface:	IDirect3DRMFrame
Declaration:	`HRESULT GetLights(LPDIRECT3DRMLIGHTARRAY* lplpLights);`
Description:	Constructs an IDirect3DRMLightArray object and fills it with references to all IDirect3DRMLight objects in this frame.
Notes:	Lights enable the objects in the scene to be visible. A scene with no lights would appear to be an empty scene.
Arguments:	LPDIRECT3DRMLIGHTARRAY* lplpLights—The address of a pointer that will point to the IDirect3DRMLightArray object, or NULL if the call fails.
Return Type:	HRESULT
Return Values:	See Direct3D Retained-Mode Return Values.
See Also:	IDirect3DRMFrame::AddLight, IDirect3DRMLight

GetMaterialMode

Interface:	IDirect3DRMFrame
Declaration:	`D3DRMMATERIALMODE GetMaterialMode();`
Description:	Returns the IDirect3DRMFrame object's material mode.
Notes:	The material mode determines the location from which information about the material is retrieved.
Arguments:	None
Return Type:	D3DRMMATERIALMODE
Return Values:	D3DRMMATERIAL_FROMMESH—The material information is retrieved from the visual object (the mesh) itself. This is the default setting.
	D3DRMMATERIAL_FROMPARENT—The material information, along with color or texture information, is inherited from the parent frame.
	D3DRMMATERIAL_FROMFRAME—The material information is retrieved from the frame, overriding any previous material information that the visual object may have possessed.
See Also:	IDirect3DRMFrame::SetMaterialMode, IDirect3DRMFrame::SetColor, IDirect3DRMFrame::SetColorRGB, D3DRMMATERIALMODE

GetOrientation

Interface:	IDirect3DRMFrame
Declaration:	`HRESULT GetOrientation(LPDIRECT3DRMFRAME lpRef, LPD3DVECTOR lprvDir, LPD3DVECTOR lprvUp);`
Description:	Retrieves the orientation of this IDirect3DRMFrame object relative to another IDirect3DRMFrame.

Notes:	This method can be used to determine a frame's orientation in world coordinates by passing the root node as the reference frame.
Arguments:	LPDIRECT3DRMFRAME lpRef—The pointer to an IDirect3DRMFrame object. This frame is used as the reference frame. This parameter may not be NULL.
	LPD3DVECTOR lprvDir—The pointer to a D3DVECTOR that will hold the direction of this frame's z-axis in the reference frame's coordinate system.
	LPD3DVECTOR lprvUp—The pointer to a D3DVECTOR that will hold the direction of this frame's y-axis in the reference frame's coordinate system.
Return Type:	HRESULT
Return Values:	See Direct3D Retained-Mode Return Values.
See Also:	IDirect3DRMFrame::SetOrientation

GetParent

Interface:	IDirect3DRMFrame
Declaration:	`HRESULT GetParent(LPDIRECT3DRMFRAME* lplpParent);`
Description:	Retrieves the IDirect3DRMFrame object that is this IDirect3DRMFrame object's parent, if any.
Notes:	A frame without a parent is the root frame, also refered to as the scene.
Arguments:	LPDIRECT3DRMFRAME* lplpParent—The address of a pointer that will point to an IDirect3DRMFrame object, or NULL if this frame has no parent.
Return Type:	HRESULT
Return Values:	See Direct3D Retained-Mode Return Values.
See Also:	IDirect3DRMFrame::AddChild, IDirect3DRMFrame::GetScene

GetPosition

Interface:	IDirect3DRMFrame
Declaration:	`HRESULT GetPosition(LPDIRECT3DRMFRAME lpRef, LPD3DVECTOR lprvPos);`
Description:	Retrieves the position of the IDirect3DRMFrame with respect to a reference IDirect3DRMFrame object.
Notes:	If lpRef is NULL, this method retrieves the position of the frame in world or scene coordinates.
Arguments:	LPDIRECT3DRMFRAME lpRef—The pointer to an IDirect3DRMFrame object that is the reference frame.
	LPD3DVECTOR lprvPos—The pointer to D3DVECTOR that will hold the position of this frame in the reference frame's coordinate system.
Return Type:	HRESULT
Return Values:	See Direct3D Retained-Mode Return Values.
See Also:	SetPosition

GetRotation

Interface:	IDirect3DRMFrame
Declaration:	`HRESULT GetRotation(LPDIRECT3DRMFRAME lpRef, LPD3DVECTOR lprvAxis, LPD3DVALUE lprvTheta);`
Description:	Retrieves the rotation of the IDirect3DRMFrame with respect to a reference IDirect3DRMFrame object.
Notes:	If lpRef is NULL, this method retrieves the rotation of the frame with respect to the scene frame.
Arguments:	LPDIRECT3DRMFRAME lpRef—The pointer to an IDirect3DRMFrame object that is the reference frame.
	LPD3DVECTOR lprvAxis—The pointer to a D3DVECTOR that will hold the axis around which this frame is rotated in the reference frame.

GetScene/GetSceneBackground

	LPD3DVALUE lprvTheta—The pointer to a D3DVALUE that will hold the size of the rotation, in radians.
Return Type:	HRESULT
Return Values:	See Direct3D Retained-Mode Return Values.
See Also:	SetRotation

GetScene

Interface:	IDirect3DRMFrame
Declaration:	`HRESULT GetScene(LPDIRECT3DRMFRAME* lplpRoot);`
Description:	Retrieves the root IDirect3DRMFrame object that contains this IDirect3DRMFrame object.
Notes:	If this IDirect3DRMFrame object is the root frame, GetScene() will retrieve this object.
Arguments:	LPDIRECT3DRMFRAME* lplpRoot—The address of a pointer that will point to root the IDirect3DRMFrame object, or NULL if the call fails.
Return Type:	HRESULT
Return Values:	See Direct3D Retained-Mode Return Values.
See Also:	IDirect3DRMFrame::GetParent

GetSceneBackground

Interface:	IDirect3DRMFrame
Declaration:	`D3DCOLOR GetSceneBackground();`
Description:	Returns the background color of the scene.
Notes:	This method has undefined behavior if the IDirect3DRMFrame object isn't a scene; that is, if it has a parent frame.
Arguments:	None

continues

continued

Return Type:	D3DCOLOR
Return Values:	See Direct3D Retained-Mode Return Values.
See Also:	IDirect3DRMFrame::SetSceneBackground, IDirect3DRMFrame::GetScene

GetSceneBackgroundDepth

Interface:	IDirect3DRMFrame
Declaration:	`HRESULT GetSceneBackgroundDepth(LPDIRECTDRAWSURFACE* lplpDDSurface);`
Description:	Retrieves the background z-buffer of the scene.
Notes:	The z-buffer is an IDirectDrawSurface object. The format of the z-buffer is not documented by Microsoft and may vary between hardware drivers.
	If a scene has a background depth, IDirect3DRMViewport::Clear() sets the IDirect3DRMDevice's z-buffer to the contents of the scene's background depth IDirectDraw surface. Then all rendering takes place with respect to that z-buffer.
Arguments:	LPDIRECTDRAWSURFACE *lplpDDSurface—The address of a pointer that will point to the IDirectDrawSurface object, or NULL if there is none.
Return Type:	HRESULT
Return Values:	See Direct3D Retained-Mode Return Values.
See Also:	IDirect3DRMFrame::SetBackgroundDepth, IDirect3DRMViewport::Clear

GetSceneFogColor

Interface:	IDirect3DRMFrame
Declaration:	`D3DCOLOR GetSceneFogColor();`

Description:	Retrieves the fog color of the scene.
Notes:	This method's behavior is undefined if the IDirect3DRMFrame object is not a root frame.
Arguments:	None
Return Type:	D3DCOLOR
Return Values:	Returns the color of the scene fog (provided the frame is a root frame).
See Also:	IDirect3DRMFrame::SetSceneFogColor, IDirect3DRMFrame::GetScene

GetSceneFogEnable

Interface:	IDirect3DRMFrame
Declaration:	`BOOL GetSceneFogEnable();`
Description:	Returns a BOOL indicating whether fog is enabled for this scene.
Notes:	Returns TRUE if fog is enabled for the scene, otherwise FALSE.
	The behavior of this method is undefined if the IDirect3DRMFrame object is not a root frame.
Arguments:	None
Return Type:	BOOL
Return Values:	Returns TRUE or FALSE, depending on whether fog is enabled or disabled (provided the frame is a root frame).
See Also:	IDirect3DRMFrame::SetSceneFogEnable, IDirect3DRMFrame::GetScene

GetSceneFogMode

Interface:	IDirect3DRMFrame
Declaration:	`D3DRMFOGMODE GetSceneFogMode();`
Description:	Retrieves the fog mode for the scene.

continues

continued

Notes:	DirectX 3 only supports the linear fog mode, so D3DRMFOG_LINEAR is always returned from this method.
	The behavior of this method is undefined if the IDirect3DRMFrame object is not a root frame.
Arguments:	None
Return Type:	D3DRMFOGMODE
Return Values:	Always returns D3DRMFOG_LINEAR.
See Also:	IDirect3DRMFrame::SetSceneFogMode, D3DRMFOGMODE

GetSceneFogParams

Interface:	IDirect3DRMFrame
Declaration:	HRESULT GetSceneFogParams(D3DVALUE* lprvStart, D3DVALUE* lprvEnd, D3DVALUE* lprvDensity);
Description:	Retrieves the fog parameters from the IDirect3DRMFrame object.
Notes:	The density parameter only applies to the exponential fog modes, which DirectX 3 doesn't currently support.
	The behavior of this method is undefined if the IDirect3DRMFrame object is not a root frame.
Arguments:	D3DVALUE* lprvStart—The pointer to a D3DVALUE that will hold the distance from the camera the fog will start.
	D3DVALUE* lprvEnd—The pointer to a D3DVALUE that will hold the distance from the camera at which and beyond the fog will be at its full intensity.
	D3DVALUE* lprvDensity—The pointer to a D3DVALUE that will hold the fog density parameter, a value between 0 and 1.
Return Type:	HRESULT
Return Values:	See Direct3D Retained-Mode Return Values.
See Also:	IDirect3DRMFrame::SetFogParams, IDirect3DRMFrame::GetScene

GetSortMode

Interface:	IDirect3DRMFrame
Declaration:	`D3DRMSORTMODE GetSortMode();`
Description:	Retrieves the sort mode of the IDirect3DRMFrame object.
Notes:	In DirectX 3, Retained-Mode does not support face sorting, relying instead on z-buffering and culling for hidden surface removal. It does sort meshes within a frame, however.
	The default value is D3DRMSORT_FROMPARENT.
Arguments:	None
Return Type:	D3DRMSORTMODE
Return Values:	D3DRMSORT_FROMPARENT—The child frames inherit the sorting order of their parents.
	D3DRMSORT_NONE—The child frames are not sorted.
	D3DRMSORT_FRONTTOBACK—The child frames are sorted front-to-back.
	D3DRMSORT_BACKTOFRONT—The child frames are sorted back-to-front.
See Also:	IDirect3DRMFrame::SetSortMode, D3DRMSORTMODE

GetTexture

Interface:	IDirect3DRMFrame
Declaration:	`HRESULT GetTexture(LPDIRECT3DRMTEXTURE* lplpTexture);`
Description:	Retrieves the IDirect3DRMTexture object associated with the IDirect3DRMFrame object, if any.
Notes:	The frame's material mode must be set to D3DRMMATERIAL_FROMFRAME for the texture to be applied to objects in the frame.

continues

	continued
Arguments:	LPDIRECT3DRMTEXTURE* lplpTexture—The address of a pointer that will point to the IDirect3DRMTexture object, or NULL if there is none.
Return Type:	HRESULT
Return Values:	See Direct3D Retained-Mode Return Values.
See Also:	IDirect3DRMFrame::SetTexture, IDirect3DRMFrame::GetMaterialMode

GetTextureTopology

Interface:	IDirect3DRMFrame
Declaration:	`HRESULT GetTextureTopology(BOOL* lpbWrap_u, BOOL* lpbWrap_v);`
Description:	Retrieves the texture topology of the IDirect3DRMFrame object.
Notes:	This method sets the BOOLs pointed to by the parameters lpU and lpV to TRUE or FALSE, depending on whether textures are wrapped in the horizontal (texture u-axis) and vertical (texture v-axis) direction. If both are FALSE, the topology is flat, if both are TRUE the topology is toroidal, and if only one is TRUE, the topology is cylindrical in that direction.
	The frame's material mode must be set to D3DRMMATERIAL_FROMFRAME for the texture topology to be applied when texture mapping.
Arguments:	BOOL* lpbWrapU—The pointer to BOOL that will be set to TRUE if the texture is wrapped in the horizontal direction (along the u-axis).
	BOOL* lpbWrapV—The pointer to BOOL that will be set to TRUE if the texture is wrapped in the vertical direction (along the v-axis).
Return Type:	HRESULT
Return Values:	See Direct3D Retained-Mode Return Values.
See Also:	IDirect3DRMFrame::SetTextureTopology, IDirect3DRMFrame::GetMaterialMode

GetTransform

Interface:	IDirect3DRMFrame
Declaration:	`HRESULT GetTransform(D3DRMMATRIX4D rmMatrix);`
Description:	Retrieves the transform of the IDirect3DRMFrame object.
Notes:	The D3DRMMATRIX4D retrieved from this method is the matrix that converts the coordinates of the frame (in model coordinate space) to world coordinate space.
Arguments:	D3DRMMATRIX4D rmMatrix—A D3DRMMATRIX4D array that will hold the IDirect3DRMFrame's transform.
Return Type:	HRESULT
Return Values:	See Direct3D Retained-Mode Return Values.
See Also:	IDirect3DRMFrame::SetTransform, IDirect3DRMFrame::AddTransform, IDirect3DRMFrame::Transform, IDirect3DRMFrame::InverseTransform

GetVelocity

Interface:	IDirect3DRMFrame
Declaration:	`HRESULT GetVelocity(LPDIRECT3DRMFRAME lpRef, LPD3DVECTOR lprvVel, BOOL fRotVel);`
Description:	Retrieves the IDirect3DRMFrame object's velocity relative to a particular IDirect3DRMFrame object.
Notes:	When IDirect3DRMFrame::Move() is called, the object is moved an amount equal to its speed times the parameter passed to IDirect3DRMFrame::Move(), in the direction of its velocity vector.
Arguments:	LPDIRECT3DRMFRAME lpRef—The pointer to reference IDirect3DRMFrame object. LPD3DVECTOR lprvVel—The pointer to a D3DVECTOR that will hold the frame's velocity.

continues

continued

	BOOL fRotVel—Set to TRUE to include contributions to the IDirect3DRMFrame's velocity due to rotation, or FALSE to return only the linear velocity.
Return Type:	HRESULT
Return Values:	See Direct3D Retained-Mode Return Values.
See Also:	IDirect3DRMFrame::SetVelocity, IDirect3DRMFrame::SetRotation, IDirect3DRMFrame::Move

GetVisuals

Interface:	IDirect3DRMFrame
Declaration:	`HRESULT GetVisuals(LPDIRECT3DRMVISUALARRAY* lplpVisuals);`
Description:	Constructs an IDirect3DRMVisualArray object and fills it with references to all the IDirect3DRMVisual objects in this frame.
Notes:	The visuals of a frame comprise the parts of a frame that can be rendered. Retained-Mode frame, mesh, shadow, mesh builder, texture, and user visual objects can be added to a frame as visuals.
Arguments:	LPDIRECT3DRMVISUALARRAY *lplpVisuals—The address of a pointer that will point to the IDirect3DRMVisualArray object, or NULL if the call fails.
Return Type:	HRESULT
Return Values:	See Direct3D Retained-Mode Return Values.
See Also:	IDirect3DRMFrame, IDirect3DRMMesh, IDirect3DRMShadow, IDirect3DRMMeshBuilder, IDirect3DRMTexture, IDirect3DRMUserVisual.

GetZbufferMode

Interface:	IDirect3DRMFrame
Declaration:	`D3DRMZBUFFERMODE GetZbufferMode();`

Description:	Retrieves the z-buffer mode of the IDirect3DRMFrame object.
Notes:	The mode returned will be one of D3DRMZBUFFER_FROMPARENT, D3DRMZBUFFER_ENABLE, or D3DRMZBUFFER_DISABLE. IDirect3DRMFrame objects are in the D3DRMZBUFFER_FROMPARENT mode by default.
Arguments:	None
Return Type:	D3DRMZBUFFERMODE
Return Values:	D3DRMZBUFFER_FROMPARENT—The frame inherits the z-buffer setting from its parent frame. This is the default setting. D3DRMZBUFFER_ENABLE—Z-buffering is enabled. D3DRMZBUFFER_DISABLE—Z-buffering is disabled.
See Also:	IDirect3DRMFrame::SetZbufferMode, D3DRMZBUFFERMODE

InverseTransform

Interface:	IDirect3DRMFrame
Declaration:	`HRESULT InverseTransform(D3DVECTOR *lprvDst, D3DVECTOR *lprvSrc);`
Description:	Transforms a D3DVECTOR in scene coordinates into the IDirect3DRMFrame object's local coordinate system.
Notes:	This is usually thought of as transforming from world to model coordinates.
Arguments:	D3DVECTOR *lprvDst—The pointer to a D3DVECTOR that will hold the transformed vector. D3DVECTOR *lprvSrc—The pointer to a D3DVECTOR that is to be transformed.
Return Type:	HRESULT
Return Values:	See Direct3D Retained-Mode Return Values.
See Also:	IDirect3DRMFrame::Transform, IDirect3DRMFrame::GetTransform, IDirect3DRMFrame::GetScene

Load

Interface:	IDirect3DRMFrame
Declaration:	HRESULT Load(LPVOID lpvObjSource, LPVOID lpvObjID, D3DRMLOADOPTIONS d3drmLOFlags, D3DRMLOADTEXTURECALLBACK d3drmLoadTextureProc, LPVOID lpArgLTP);
Description:	Loads an IDirect3DRMFrame hierarchy from a file, resource, or from memory.
Notes:	This method is used to load frames stored in Retained-Mode format.
Arguments:	LPVOID lpvObjSource—This parameter is a pointer to data indicating the source of the object data, or NULL. If d3drmLOFlags includes D3DRMLOAD_FROMFILE, this parameter must point to a NULL-terminated string holding the file name to load. If d3drmLOFlags includes D3DRMLOAD_FROMRESOURCE, this parameter must point to a D3DRMLOADRESOURCE structure containing the relevant resource information. If d3drmLOFlags includes D3DRMLOAD_FROMMEMORY, this parameter must point to a D3DRMLOADMEMORY structure containing a pointer to the memory, and the size of the memory block.
	LPVOID lpvObjID—This parameter is either NULL or a pointer to an object name or position, depending on which load options are selected in the d3drmLOFlags parameter. If d3drmLOFlags includes D3DRMLOAD_BYNAME, this parameter must point to a NULL-terminated string holding the name of the object. If d3drmLOFlags includes D3DRMLOAD_BYPOSITION, lpvObjID must point to a DWORD holding the index of the desired animation set (from 0 to $n-1$ if there are n objects sets in the file). If d3drmLOFlags includes D3DRMLOAD_FIRST, or neither D3DRMLOAD_BYPOSITION or D3DRMLOAD_BYNAME is specified, lpvObjID should be NULL.
	D3DRMLOADOPTIONS d3drmLOFlags—This parameter consists of flags specifying the source type of the animation (file, resource, or memory), and which object is loaded (the first, by index, or by name).

If 0 is passed as d3drmLOFlags, Retained-Mode assumes D3DRMLOAD_FROMFILE|D3DRMLOAD_FIRST.

To load a specific frame from a file, it can be selected by using either D3DRMLOAD_BYNAME if it is named within the source, D3DRMLOAD_BYPOSITION to specify it by its order among other objects in the file, or D3DRMLOAD_FIRST to just load the first object encountered in the file. D3DRMLOAD_FIRST is implied if none of these options is chosen.

D3DRMLOAD_INSTANCEBYREFERENCE is implied in DirectX 3. Passing D3DRMLOAD_INSTANCEBYCOPYING generates an error; only instance by reference capabilities are implemented in DirectX 3.

D3DRMLOADTEXTURECALLBACK d3drmLoadTextureProc—This parameter is a callback that Load will call to load textures. If NULL, Retained-Mode will do its best to load the texture files specified in the file, resource, or memory block. In DirectX 3, only BMP and PPM files are supported, so a callback must be supplied to load textures from any other format.

LPVOID lpArgLTP—The pointer to application-defined data that Load will pass to the texture callback passed via d3drmLTP, if any.

Return Type: HRESULT

Return Values: See Direct3D Retained-Mode Return Values.

See Also: IDirect3DRMAnimationSet::Load, IDirect3DRMMeshBuilder::Load, IDirect3DRM::Load

LookAt

Interface: IDirect3DRMFrame

Declaration: `HRESULT LookAt(LPDIRECT3DRMFRAME lpTarget, LPDIRECT3DRMFRAME lpRef, D3DRMFRAMECONSTRAINT rfcConstraint);`

Description: Orients the IDirect3DRMFrame object so that its positive z-axis is pointing toward the specified IDirect3DRMFrame.

continues

continued	
Notes:	This method often is used to orient an IDirect3DRMLight or IDirect3DRMViewport object's IDirect3DRMFrame to point at another frame.
Arguments:	LPDIRECT3DRMFRAME lpTarget—The IDirect3DRMFrame object to look at.
	LPDIRECT3DRMFRAME lpRef—The IDirect3DRMFrame object that's the reference frame for the rotation. This is almost always the scene or root frame.
	D3DRMFRAMECONSTRAINT rfcConstraint—One of D3DRMCONSTRAIN_Z, D3DRMCONSTRAIN_Y, or D3DRMCONSTRAIN_X to prevent rotations around the z-, y-, or x-axes, respectively.
Return Type:	HRESULT
Return Values:	See Direct3D Retained-Mode Return Values.
See Also:	IDirect3DRMFrame::SetOrientation

Move

Interface:	IDirect3DRMFrame
Declaration:	`HRESULT Move(D3DVALUE delta);`
Description:	Moves and rotates all IDirect3DRMFrame objects within this IDirect3DRMFrame object's hierarchy.
Notes:	The delta parameter can be varied to accommodate fluctuating frame rates. Typically delta is 1, though it might be increased or decreased to speed up or slow down the motion, respectively.
	If a frame has velocity, it is moved through a distance equal to its speed times delta, in the direction of the velocity vector. If a frame has rotation, it is rotated through an angle equal to its rotational speed times delta, around the rotational axis.
Arguments:	D3DVALUE delta—The number of ticks to move.
Return Type:	HRESULT

Return Values: See Direct3D Retained-Mode Return Values.

See Also: IDirect3DRMFrame::SetRotation, IDirect3DRMFrame::SetVelocity, IDirect3DRM::Tick

SetColor

Interface:	IDirect3DRMFrame
Declaration:	`HRESULT SetColor(D3DCOLOR rcColor);`
Description:	Sets the IDirect3DRMFrame object's color.
Notes:	The frame's material mode must be set to D3DRMMATERIAL_FROMFRAME for the color to be applied to objects in the frame.
	The alpha value of the color is not ignored, so typically an application would use the RGBA_MAKE macro instead of RGB_MAKE. RGB_MAKE gives the color an alpha value of zero, which makes it completely transparent.
Arguments:	D3DCOLOR rcColor—The color value for the frame.
Return Type:	HRESULT
Return Values:	See Direct3D Retained-Mode Return Values.
See Also:	IDirect3DRMFrame::SetColorRGB, IDirect3DRMFrame::GetColor, IDirect3DRMFrame::SetMaterialMode

SetColorRGB

Interface:	IDirect3DRMFrame
Declaration:	`HRESULT SetColorRGB(D3DVALUE rvRed, D3DVALUE rvGreen, D3DVALUE rvBlue);`
Description:	Sets the color for the frame.

continues

	continued
Notes:	SetColorRGB forces the alpha component to 1. To use a different alpha value for the color, (to make a mesh transparent, for instance) use IDirect3DRM::SetColor.
	SetColorRGB has no effect unless the frame's material mode is set to D3DRMMATERIAL_FROMFRAME.
Arguments:	D3DVALUE rvRed—The red component of the color, between 0.0 and 1.0.
	D3DVALUE rvGreen—The green component of the color, between 0.0 and 1.0.
	D3DVALUE rvBlue—The blue component of the color, between 0.0 and 1.0.
Return Type:	HRESULT
Return Values:	See Direct3D Retained-Mode Return Values.
See Also:	IDirect3DRMFrame::SetColor, IDirect3DRMFrame::GetColor, D3DRMMATERIALMODE

SetMaterialMode

Interface:	IDirect3DRMFrame
Declaration:	`HRESULT SetMaterialMode(D3DRMMATERIALMODE rmmMode);`
Description:	Sets the material mode of the IDirect3DRMFrame object.
Notes:	The material mode of an IDirect3DRMFrame object determines from where visuals in the frame get their material information. The default mode is D3DRMMATERIAL_FROMMESH, which causes the material information to come from the mesh itself.
Arguments:	D3DRMMATERIALMODE rmmMode—One of D3DRMMATERIAL_FROMMESH, D3DRMMATERIAL_FROMPARENT, or D3DRMMATERIAL_FROMFRAME.

Return Type:	HRESULT
Return Values:	See Direct3D Retained-Mode Return Values.
See Also:	IDirect3DRMFrame::GetMaterialMode, IDirect3DRMFrame::SetColor, IDirect3DRMFrame::SetColorRGB, IDirect3DRMFrame::SetTexture

SetOrientation

Interface:	IDirect3DRMFrame
Declaration:	`HRESULT SetOrientation(LPDIRECT3DRMFRAME lpRef, D3DVALUE rvDx, D3DVALUE rvDy, D3DVALUE rvDz, D3DVALUE rvUx, D3DVALUE rvUy, D3DVALUE rvUz);`
Description:	Sets the orientation of the IDirect3DRMFrame object with respect to some other IDirect3DRMFrame object.
Notes:	The orientation of an IDirect3DRMFrame object is specified by providing direction vectors in a reference frame that are to become the frame's z- and y-axes.
	If lpRef is NULL, the frame is oriented relative to the scene, or root, frame.
Arguments:	LPDIRECT3DRMFRAME lpRef—The reference IDirect3DRMFrame object.
	D3DVALUE rvDx, rvDy, rvDz—The coordinates of a vector in lpRef's coordinate system that points in the direction of the frame's new z-axis.
	D3DVALUE rvUx, rvUy, rvUz—The coordinates of a vector in lpRef's coordinate system that point in the direction of the frame's new y-axis.
Return Type:	HRESULT
Return Values:	See Direct3D Retained-Mode Return Values.
See Also:	IDirect3DRMFrame::GetOrientation, IDirect3DRMFrame::SetPosition

SetPosition

Interface:	IDirect3DRMFrame
Declaration:	`HRESULT SetPosition(LPDIRECT3DRMFRAME lpRef, D3DVALUE rvX, D3DVALUE rvY, D3DVALUE rvZ);`
Description:	Sets the position of the origin of the IDirect3DRMFrame object in a reference IDirect3DRMFrame object's coordinate system.
Notes:	If lpRef is NULL, the scene, or root, frame is used as the reference frame.
Arguments:	LPDIRECT3DRMFRAME lpRef—The reference frame in which coordinates rvX, rvY, and rvZ are located.
	D3DVALUE rvX, rvY, rvZ—The coordinates of the position of the origin of the IDirect3DRMFrame object in lpRef's coordinate system.
Return Type:	HRESULT
Return Values:	See Direct3D Retained-Mode Return Values.
See Also:	IDirect3DRMFrame::GetPosition, IDirect3DRMFrame::SetOrientation

SetRotation

Interface:	IDirect3DRMFrame
Declaration:	`HRESULT SetRotation(LPDIRECT3DRMFRAME lpRef, D3DVALUE rvX, D3DVALUE rvY, D3DVALUE rvZ, D3DVALUE rvTheta);`
Description:	Sets the rotational velocity to the frame.
Notes:	When IDirect3DRMFrame::Move() or IDirect3DRM::Tick() is called, this frame is rotated around the specified axis by vTheta × delta, where delta is the D3DVALUE argument passed to Move() or Tick().
	SetRotation() replaces the previous rotational velocity of the frame rather than combining with it because the rotational velocity is expressed as a vector and a rotation, not a matrix. For more complex rotations, use a move callback function.
	If lpRef is NULL, the scene is used as the reference frame.

Arguments:	LPDIRECT3DRMFRAME lpRef—The reference frame in which rvX, rvY, and rvZ are specified.
	D3DVALUE rvX, rvY, rvZ—The axis in lpRef's coordinate system around which rotation will take place.
	D3DVALUE rvTheta—The angular speed, in radians/delta.
Return Type:	HRESULT
Return Values:	See Direct3D Retained-Mode Return Values.
See Also:	IDirect3DRMFrame::SetVelocity, IDirect3DRMFrame::Move, IDirect3DRM::Tick, IDirect3DRMFrame::AddMoveCallback

SetSceneBackground

Interface:	IDirect3DRMFrame
Declaration:	`HRESULT SetSceneBackground(D3DCOLOR rcColor);`
Description:	Sets the background color of an IDirect3DRMFrame object that is a root frame.
Notes:	The behavior of this method is undefined if the IDirect3DRMFrame object isn't a scene, or root, frame.
	The alpha value of the color is ignored.
Arguments:	D3DCOLOR rcColor—The new background color.
Return Type:	HRESULT
Return Values:	See Direct3D Retained-Mode Return Values.
See Also:	IDirect3DRMFrame::GetSceneBackground, IDirect3DRMFrame::GetScene

SetSceneBackgroundDepth

Interface:	IDirect3DRMFrame
Declaration:	`HRESULT SetSceneBackgroundDepth(LPDIRECTDRAWSURFACE lpImage);`

continues

continued

Description:	Sets the background z-buffer of the scene.
Notes:	The z-buffer is an IDirectDrawSurface object. The format of the z-buffer is not documented by Microsoft and may vary between hardware drivers. It is always safe to use a z-buffer created by the current driver.
	If a scene has a background depth, IDirect3DRMViewport::Clear() sets the IDirect3DRMDevice's z-buffer to the contents of the scene's background depth IDirectDraw surface. Then all rendering takes place with respect to that z-buffer.
	The behavior of this method is undefined if the IDirect3DRMFrame object isn't a scene, or root, frame.
Arguments:	LPDIRECTDRAWSURFACE lpImage—The IDirectDrawSurface object holding the z-buffer.
Return Type:	HRESULT
Return Values:	See Direct3D Retained-Mode Return Values.
See Also:	IDirect3DRMFrame::GetBackgroundDepth, IDirect3DRMViewport::Clear, IDirect3DRMFrame::Scene

SetSceneBackgroundImage

Interface:	IDirect3DRMFrame
Declaration:	`HRESULT SetSceneBackgroundImage(LPDIRECT3DRMTEXTURE lpTexture);`
Description:	Sets the background image of the scene.
Notes:	If a scene has a background image, IDirect3DRMViewport::Clear() sets the IDirect3DRMDevice's back buffer to the contents of the background image. Then all rendering is on top of the image.
	The behavior of this method is undefined if the IDirect3DRMFrame object isn't a scene, or root, frame.

	Some hardware devices restrict texture sizes to 64×64, 128×128, or 256×256 pixels.
Arguments:	LPDIRECT3DRMTEXTURE lpTexture—The pointer to an IDirect3DRMTexture object to be used for the scene background.
Return Type:	HRESULT
Return Values:	See Direct3D Retained-Mode Return Values.
See Also:	IDirect3DRMFrame::SetScene, IDirect3DRMTexture

SetSceneBackgroundRGB

Interface:	IDirect3DRMFrame
Declaration:	`HRESULT SetSceneBackgroundRGB(D3DVALUE rvRed, D3DVALUE rvGreen, D3DVALUE rvBlue);`
Description:	Sets the background color of an IDirect3DRMFrame object that is a root frame.
Notes:	The behavior of this method is undefined if the IDirect3DRMFrame object isn't a scene, or root, frame.
Arguments:	D3DVALUE rvRed—The red component of the background color, between 0.0 and 1.0.
	D3DVALUE rvGreen—The green component of the background color, between 0.0 and 1.0.
	D3DVALUE rvBlue—The blue component of the background color, between 0.0 and 1.0.
Return Type:	HRESULT
Return Values:	See Direct3D Retained-Mode Return Values.
See Also:	IDirect3DRMFrame::SetSceneBackground, IDirect3DRMFrame::GetScene

SetSceneFogColor

Interface:	IDirect3DRMFrame
Declaration:	`HRESULT SetSceneFogColor(D3DCOLOR rcColor);`
Description:	Sets the fog color of the scene.
Notes:	This method's behavior is undefined if the IDirect3DRMFrame object is not a root frame.
	The alpha value of the fog color is ignored.
Arguments:	D3DCOLOR rcColor—The color of the fog.
Return Type:	HRESULT
Return Values:	See Direct3D Retained-Mode Return Values.
See Also:	IDirect3DRMFrame::GetSceneFogColor, IDirect3DRMFrame::SetSceneFogParams, IDirect3DRMFrame::SetSceneFogEnable, IDirect3DRMFrame::GetScene

SetSceneFogEnable

Interface:	IDirect3DRMFrame
Declaration:	`HRESULT SetSceneFogEnable(BOOL bEnable);`
Description:	Enables or disables fog within the scene.
Notes:	Fog is either entirely on or entirely off for a given pixel in ramp mode.
	This method's behavior is undefined if the IDirect3DRMFrame object is not a root frame.
Arguments:	BOOL bEnable—A BOOL value indicating whether fog should be enabled or disabled. Use TRUE to enable, FALSE to disable.
Return Type:	HRESULT
Return Values:	See Direct3D Retained-Mode Return Values.
See Also:	IDirect3DRMFrame::GetSceneFogEnable, IDirect3DRMFrame::GetScene

SetSceneFogMode

Interface:	IDirect3DRMFrame
Declaration:	`HRESULT SetSceneFogMode(D3DRMFOGMODE rfMode);`
Description:	Sets the fog mode for the scene.
Notes:	DirectX 3 only supports the linear fog mode, so D3DRMFOG_LINEAR should always be passed to this method.
	The behavior of this method is undefined if the IDirect3DRMFrame object is not a root frame.
Arguments:	D3DRMFOGMODE rfMode—The fog mode, one of D3DRMFOG_LINEAR, D3DRMFOG_EXPONENTIAL, or D3DRMFOG_EXPONENTIALSQUARED.
Return Type:	HRESULT
Return Values:	See Direct3D Retained-Mode Return Values.
See Also:	IDirect3DRMFrame::GetSceneFogMode, IDirect3DRMFrame::GetScene, D3DRMFOGMODE

SetSceneFogParams

Interface:	IDirect3DRMFrame
Declaration:	`HRESULT SetSceneFogParams(D3DVALUE rvStart, D3DVALUE rvEnd, D3DVALUE rvDensity);`
Description:	Sets the fog parameters for the scene.
Notes:	The behavior of this method is undefined if the IDirect3DRMFrame object is not a root frame.
Arguments:	D3DVALUE rvStart—The distance from the camera the fog will start.
	D3DVALUE rvEnd—The distance from the camera at which, and beyond, the fog will be at its full intensity.
	D3DVALUE rvDensity—The maximum fog density, between 0.0 and 1.0.

continues

continued

Return Type:	HRESULT
Return Values:	See Direct3D Retained-Mode Return Values.
See Also:	IDirect3DRMFrame::GetSceneFogParams, IDirect3DRMFrame::GetScene

SetSortMode

Interface:	IDirect3DRMFrame
Declaration:	`HRESULT SetSortMode(D3DRMSORTMODE d3drmSM);`
Description:	Sets the sort mode of the IDirect3DRMFrame object.
Notes:	In DirectX 3, Retained-Mode does not support face sorting, relying instead on z-buffering and culling for hidden surface removal. It does sort meshes within a frame, however.
	The default value is D3DRMSORT_FROMPARENT.
Arguments:	D3DRMSORTMODE d3drmSM—In sort mode, one of D3DRMSORT_FROMPARENT, D3DRMSORT_NONE, D3DRMSORT_FRONTTOBACK, or D3DRMSORT_BACKTOFRONT.
Return Type:	HRESULT
Return Values:	See Direct3D Retained-Mode Return Values.
See Also:	IDirect3DRMFrame::GetSortMode, D3DRMSORTMODE

SetTexture

Interface:	IDirect3DRMFrame
Declaration:	`HRESULT SetTexture(LPDIRECT3DRMTEXTURE lpD3DRMTexture);`
Description:	Associates an IDirect3DRMTexture object with the IDirect3DRMFrame object.

Notes:	This method is useful for setting up various frames with different textures, so that the same mesh can be shared, but with different textures applied to it in different frames.
	The frame's material mode must be set to D3DRMMATERIAL_FROMFRAME for the texture to be applied to objects in the frame.
Arguments:	LPDIRECT3DRMTEXTURE lpD3DRMTexture—The pointer to an IDirect3DRMTexture object.
Return Type:	HRESULT
Return Values:	See Direct3D Retained-Mode Return Values.
See Also:	IDirect3DRMFrame::GetTexture, IDirect3DRMFrame::SetMaterialMode, IDirect3DRMTexture

SetTextureTopology

Interface:	IDirect3DRMFrame
Declaration:	`HRESULT SetTextureTopology(BOOL bWrap_u, BOOL bWrap_v);`
Description:	Sets the texture topology of the IDirect3DRMFrame object.
Notes:	This method is used to set the texture topology to flat, cylindrical, or spherical. If both arguments are FALSE, the topology is flat. If both arguments are TRUE, the topology is spherical. If only one is TRUE, the topology is cylindrical in that direction.
Arguments:	BOOL bWrapU—Is TRUE to enable horizontal wrapping, FALSE to disable horizontal wrapping.
	BOOL bWrapV—Is TRUE to enable vertical wrapping, FALSE to disable vertical wrapping.
Return Type:	HRESULT
Return Values:	See Direct3D Retained-Mode Return Values.
See Also:	IDirect3DRMFrame::GetTextureTopology

SetVelocity

Interface:	IDirect3DRMFrame
Declaration:	HRESULT SetVelocity(LPDIRECT3DRMFRAME lpRef, D3DVALUE rvX, D3DVALUE rvY, D3DVALUE rvZ, BOOL fRotVel);
Description:	Assigns the frame a constant velocity with respect to some reference frame.
Notes:	When IDirect3DRMFrame::Tick() is called, the frame is moved by an amount equal to its speed times the delta argument to Tick() in the direction of its velocity vector in the reference frame pointed to by lpRef.
Arguments:	LPDIRECT3DRMFRAME lpRef—The pointer to IDirect3DRMFrame object that is the reference frame.
	D3DVALUE rvX, rvY, rvZ—The components of a velocity vector in the reference frame.
	BOOL fRotVel—If TRUE, the frame's rotational velocity, if any, will be included when it computes the frame's linear velocity. If FALSE, any rotational velocity is ignored when setting the frame's linear velocity.
Return Type:	HRESULT
Return Values:	See Direct3D Retained-Mode Return Values.
See Also:	IDirect3DRMFrame::GetVelocity, IDirect3DRMFrame::SetRotation

SetZbufferMode

Interface:	IDirect3DRMFrame
Declaration:	HRESULT SetZbufferMode(D3DRMZBUFFERMODE d3drmZBM);
Description:	Sets the z-buffer mode for the IDirect3DRMFrame object.

Notes:	In DirectX 3, Retained-Mode will always create a z-buffer and use it by default. Retained-Mode does allow enabling and disabling the z-buffer on a frame-by-frame basis, however.
	The default mode is D3DRMZBUFFER_FROMPARENT.
Arguments:	D3DRMZBUFFERMODE d3drmZBM—One of D3DRMZBUFFER_FROMPARENT, D3DRMZBUFFER_ENABLE, or D3DRMZBUFFER_DISABLE.
Return Type:	HRESULT
Return Values:	See Direct3D Retained-Mode Return Values.
See Also:	IDirect3DRMFrame::GetZbufferMode, D3DRMZBUFFERMODE

Transform

Interface:	IDirect3DRMFrame
Declaration:	`HRESULT Transform(D3DVECTOR *lpd3dVDst, D3DVECTOR *lpd3dVSrc);`
Description:	Transforms a vector in this IDirect3DRMFrame's coordinate system into scene coordinates.
Notes:	This is usually thought of as transforming from model to world coordinates.
Arguments:	D3DVECTOR *lpd3dVDst—The pointer to a D3DVECTOR that will hold the transformed vector.
	D3DVECTOR *lpd3dVSrc—The pointer to a D3DVECTOR that holds the vector to be transformed.
Return Type:	HRESULT
Return Values:	See Direct3D Retained-Mode Return Values.
See Also:	IDirect3DRMFrame::InverseTransform, IDirect3DRMFrame::GetScene

IDirect3DRMLight

The IDirect3DRMLight interface provides functionality for controlling the attributes of a Retained-Mode light object. Through this interface, applications can adjust the type, color, range, and attenuation of a light as well as the frame in which the light is enabled. Various options for spotlights can also be changed with IDirect3DRMLight.

IDirect3DRMLight, as with all COM interfaces, is derived from IUnknown and inherits its methods. IDirect3DRMLight also inherits the methods of IDirect3DRMObject. A Direct3DRMLight object can be obtained by calling IDirect3DRM::CreateLight(). IDirect3DRMLight implements the following methods:

GetColor	SetConstantAttenuation
GetConstantAttenuation	SetEnableFrame
GetEnableFrame	SetLinearAttenuation
GetLinearAttenuation	SetPenumbra
GetPenumbra	SetQuadraticAttenuation
GetQuadraticAttenuation	SetRange
GetRange	SetType
GetType	SetUmbra
SetColorRGB	

GetColor

Interface: IDirect3DRMLight
Declaration: `D3DCOLOR GetColor();`
Description: Returns the color of the light.

Notes:	Lights are used to view objects in a scene. A scene without lights appears as an empty scene.
Arguments:	None
Return Type:	D3DCOLOR
Return Values:	See Direct3D Retained-Mode Return Values.
See Also:	IDirect3DRMLight::SetColor, IDirect3DRMLight::SetColorRGB

GetConstantAttenuation

Interface:	IDirect3DRMLight
Declaration:	`D3DVALUE GetConstantAttenuation();`
Description:	Returns the constant attenuation factor of the light.
Notes:	The constant attenuation attenuates the light without regard for the distance of the vertex being lit. The default value is 1.
	The total attenuation of the light at a particular vertex is computed from the constant, linear, and quadratic attenuation by using the following formula:
	$\text{attenuation}_{Total} = \text{attenuation}_{Constant} + r \times \text{attenuation}_{Linear} + r^2 \times \text{attenuation}_{Quadratic}$
	where r is the distance from the light to the vertex being lit.
	The total attenuation affects the intensity of the light at a particular vertex as an inverse proportion, that is:
	$I_{Vertex} = I_{Light} / \text{attenuation}_{Total}$
Arguments:	None
Return Type:	D3DVALUE
Return Values:	Returns the constant attenuation of the light.
See Also:	IDirect3DRMLight::SetConstantAttenuation, IDirect3DRMLight::GetLinearAttenuation, IDirect3DRMLight::GetQuadraticAttenuation

GetEnableFrame

Interface:	IDirect3DRMLight
Declaration:	`HRESULT GetEnableFrame(LPDIRECT3DRMFRAME * lplpEnableFrame);`
Description:	Retrieves the enable frame for the light.
Notes:	If the enable frame is non-NULL, the light will illuminate only those objects in the enable frame and its children.
Arguments:	LPDIRECT3DRMFRAME *lplpEnableFrame—The address of a pointer that will point to the IDirect3DRMFrame object, or NULL if the call fails.
Return Type:	HRESULT
Return Values:	See Direct3D Retained-Mode Return Values.
See Also:	IDirect3DRMLight::SetEnableFrame, IDirect3DRMFrame

GetLinearAttenuation

Interface:	IDirect3DRMLight
Declaration:	`D3DVALUE GetLinearAttenuation();`
Description:	Retrieves the linear attenuation of the IDirect3DRMLight object.
Notes:	By default, the linear attenuation is 0.

The total attenuation of the light at a particular vertex is computed from the constant, linear, and quadratic attenuation by using the following formula:

$$\text{attenuation}_{Total} = \text{attenuation}_{Constant} + r \times \text{attenuation}_{Linear} + r^2 \times \text{attenuation}_{Quadratic}$$

where r is the distance from the light to the vertex being lit.

The total attenuation affects the intensity of the light at a particular vertex as an inverse proportion, that is:

$$I_{Vertex} = I_{Light} / \text{attenuation}_{Total}$$

Arguments:	None
Return Type:	D3DVALUE
Return Values:	Returns the linear attenuation of the light.
See Also:	IDirect3DRMLight::SetLinearAttenuation, IDirect3DRMLight::GetConstantAttenuation, IDirect3DRM::GetQuadraticAttenuation

GetPenumbra

Interface:	IDirect3DRMLight
Declaration:	`D3DVALUE GetPenumbra();`
Description:	Returns the angle of the penumbra, in radians.
Notes:	The penumbra is the outer, dimmer cone of light emitting from a spotlight, which surrounds the umbra.
	This method is only meaningful for IDirect3DRMLight objects whose type is D3DRMLIGHT_SPOT.
Arguments:	None
Return Type:	D3DVALUE
Return Values:	Returns the angle of the penumbra of the light.
See Also:	IDirect3DRMLight::SetPenumbra, IDirect3DRMLight::GetUmbra, IDirect3DRMLight::GetType

GetQuadraticAttenuation

Interface:	IDirect3DRMLight
Declaration:	`D3DVALUE GetQuadraticAttenuation();`
Description:	Retrieves the quadratic attenuation of the IDirect3DRMLight object.
Notes:	By default, the quadratic attenuation is 0. If the quadratic attenuation is not zero, the light is attenuated quadratically in the distance between the light and a vertex being lit, in world coordinates.

continues

continued

The total attenuation affects the intensity of the light at a particular vertex as an inverse proportion, that is,

$\text{attenuation}_{\text{Total}} = \text{attenuation}_{\text{Constant}} + r \times \text{attenuation}_{\text{Linear}} + r^2 \times \text{attenuation}_{\text{Quadratic}}$

where r is the distance from the light to the vertex being lit.

The total attenuation affects the intensity of the light at a particular vertex as an inverse proportion, that is:

$I_{\text{Vertex}} = I_{\text{Light}} / \text{attenuation}_{\text{Total}}$

Arguments: None
Return Type: D3DVALUE
Return Values: Retrieves the quadratic attenuation of the light.
See Also: IDirect3DRMLight::SetQuadraticAttenuation, IDirect3DRMLight::GetConstantAttenuation, IDirect3DRMLight::GetLinearAttenuation

GetRange

Interface: IDirect3DRMLight
Declaration: `D3DVALUE GetRange();`
Description: Returns the range of the IDirect3DRMLight object, in world coordinate space units.
Notes: The default range of lights is 256.
Arguments: None
Return Type: D3DVALUE
Return Values: Returns the range of the light.
See Also: IDirect3DRMLight::SetRange

GetType

Interface:	IDirect3DRMLight
Declaration:	D3DRMLIGHTTYPE GetType();
Description:	Returns the type of the IDirect3DRMLight object.
Notes:	Ambient and directional lights are not as computationally expensive as point and spot lights.
Arguments:	None
Return Type:	D3DRMLIGHTTYPE
Return Values:	D3DRMLIGHT_AMBIENT—The light is an ambient source. D3DRMLIGHT_POINT—The light is a point source. D3DRMLIGHT_SPOT—The light is a spotlight source. D3DRMLIGHT_DIRECTIONAL—The light is a directional source. D3DRMLIGHT_PARALLELPOINT—The light is a parallel point source.
See Also:	IDirect3DRMLight::SetType, D3DRMLIGHTTYPE

GetUmbra

Interface:	IDirect3DRMLight
Declaration:	D3DVALUE GetUmbra();
Description:	Returns the angle of the umbra, in radians.
Notes:	The umbra is the inner, brighter cone of light emitting from a spotlight, which is surrounded by the penumbra. This method is only meaningful for IDirect3DRMLight objects whose type is D3DRMLIGHT_SPOT.
Arguments:	None
Return Type:	D3DVALUE

continues

continued

Return Values: Returns the angle of the umbraUflf the light.

See Also: IDirect3DRMLight::SetUmbra, IDirect3DRMLight::GetPenumbra, IDirect3DRMLight::GetType

SetColor

Interface: IDirect3DRMLight

Declaration: `HRESULT SetColor(D3DCOLOR rcColor);`

Description: Sets the color of the IDirect3DRMLight object.

Notes: The alpha color value of the light is always set to 1.0 regardless of the alpha component in the rcColor argument.

Arguments: D3DCOLOR rcColor—The color of the light.

Return Type: HRESULT

Return Values: See Direct3D Retained-Mode Return Values.

See Also: IDirect3DRMLight::SetColorRGB, RGB_MAKE

SetColorRGB

Interface: IDirect3DRMLight

Declaration: `HRESULT SetColorRGB(D3DVALUE rvRed, D3DVALUE rvGreen, D3DVALUE rvBlue);`

Description: Sets the color of the IDirect3DRMLight object.

Notes: The alpha color value of a light is always set to 1.0.

Arguments: D3DVALUE rvRed—The red component of light's color. Typically in the range 0.0 through 1.0.

D3DVALUE rvGreen—The green component of light's color. Typically in the range 0.0 through 1.0.

D3DVALUE rvBlue—The blue component of light's color. Typically in the range 0.0 through 1.0.

Return Type: HRESULT

Return Values: See Direct3D Retained-Mode Return Values.

See Also: IDirect3DRMLight::SetColor

SetConstantAttenuation

Interface: IDirect3DRMLight

Declaration: `HRESULT SetConstantAttenuation(D3DVALUE rvAtt);`

Description: Sets the constant attenuation of the IDirect3DRMLight object.

Notes: By default, the constant attenuation value is 1, and the other attenuation values are 0.

The total attenuation affects the intensity of the light at a particular vertex as an inverse proportion, that is:

$$\text{attenuation}_{Total} = \text{attenuation}_{Constant} + r \times \text{attenuation}_{Linear} + r^2 \times \text{attenuation}_{Quadratic}$$

where r is the distance from the light to the vertex being lit.

The total attenuation affects the intensity of the light at a particular vertex as an inverse proportion, that is:

$$I_{Vertex} = I_{Light} / \text{attenuation}_{Total}$$

Arguments: D3DVALUE rvAtt—Constant attenuation value.

Return Type: HRESULT

Return Values: See Direct3D Retained-Mode Return Values.

See Also: IDirect3DRMLight::GetConstantAttenuation,
IDirect3DRMLight::SetLinearAttenuation,
IDirect3DRMLight::SetQuadraticAttenuation

SetEnableFrame

Interface:	IDirect3DRMLight
Declaration:	HRESULT SetEnableFrame(LPDIRECT3DRMFRAME lpEnableFrame);
Description:	Sets the enable frame for the IDirect3DRMLight object.
Notes:	If the enable frame is non-NULL, the light will illuminate only those objects in the enable frame and its children. Otherwise, the light will illuminate all objects in the scene.
Arguments:	LPDIRECT3DRMFRAME lpEnableFrame—The pointer to IDirect3DRMFrame object to be lit, or NULL.
Return Type:	HRESULT
Return Values:	See Direct3D Retained-Mode Return Values.
See Also:	IDirect3DRMLight::GetEnableFrame

SetLinearAttenuation

Interface:	IDirect3DRMLight
Declaration:	HRESULT SetLinearAttenuation(D3DVALUE rvAtt);
Description:	Sets the linear attenuation of the IDirect3DRMLight object.
Notes:	By default, the linear attenuation value is 0, the constant attenuation value is 1, and the quadratic attenuation value is 0.

The total attenuation affects the intensity of the light at a particular vertex as an inverse proportion, that is:

$$\text{attenuation}_{Total} = \text{attenuation}_{Constant} + r \times \text{attenuation}_{Linear} + r^2 \times \text{attenuation}_{Quadratic}$$

where r is the distance from the light to the vertex being lit.

The total attenuation affects the intensity of the light at a particular vertex as an inverse proportion, that is:

$$I_{Vertex} = I_{Light} / \text{attenuation}_{Total}$$

Arguments:	D3DVALUE rvAtt—Linear attenuation value.
Return Type:	HRESULT
Return Values:	See Direct3D Retained-Mode Return Values.
See Also:	IDirect3DRMLight::GetLinearAttenuation, IDirect3DRMLight::SetConstantAttenuation, IDirect3DRMLight::GetQuadraticAttenuation

SetPenumbra

Interface:	IDirect3DRMLight
Declaration:	`HRESULT SetPenumbra(D3DVALUE rvAngle);`
Description:	Sets the penumbra angle.
Notes:	The penumbra is the outer, dimmer cone of light emitting from a spotlight, which surrounds the umbra.
	This method is only meaningful for IDirect3DRMLight objects whose type is D3DRMLIGHT_SPOT.
Arguments:	D3DVALUE rvAngle—The angle of penumbra, in radians.
Return Type:	HRESULT
Return Values:	See Direct3D Retained-Mode Return Values.
See Also:	IDirect3DRMLight::GetPenumbra, IDirect3DRMLight::SetUmbra

SetQuadraticAttenuation

Interface:	IDirect3DRMLight
Declaration:	`HRESULT SetQuadraticAttenuation(D3DVALUE rvAtt);`
Description:	Sets the quadratic attenuation of the IDirect3DRMLight object.
Notes:	By default, the quadratic attenuation value is 0, the constant attenuation value is 1, and the linear attenuation value is 0.

continues

continued

The total attenuation affects the intensity of the light at a particular vertex as an inverse proportion, that is:

$\text{attenuation}_{\text{Total}} = \text{attenuation}_{\text{Constant}} + r \times \text{attenuation}_{\text{Linear}} + r^2 \times \text{attenuation}_{\text{Quadratic}}$

where r is the distance from the light to the vertex being lit.

The total attenuation affects the intensity of the light at a particular vertex as an inverse proportion, that is:

$I_{\text{Vertex}} = I_{\text{Light}} / \text{attenuation}_{\text{Total}}$

Arguments:	D3DVALUE rvAtt—The quadratic attenuation value.
Return Type:	HRESULT
Return Values:	See Direct3D Retained-Mode Return Values.
See Also:	IDirect3DRMLight::GetQuadraticAttenuation, IDirect3DRMLight::SetConstantAttenuation, IDirect3DRMLight::SetLinearAttenuation

SetRange

Interface:	IDirect3DRMLight
Declaration:	`HRESULT SetRange(D3DVALUE rvRange);`
Description:	Sets the range of the IDirect3DRMLight object.
Notes:	The default range is 256.
Arguments:	D3DVALUE rvRange—The range of the light, in world coordinates.
Return Type:	HRESULT
Return Values:	See Direct3D Retained-Mode Return Values.
See Also:	IDirect3DRMLight::GetRange

SetType

Interface:	IDirect3DRMLight
Declaration:	`HRESULT SetType(D3DRMLIGHTTYPE d3drmtType);`
Description:	Sets the type of the light.
Notes:	The type of light must be one of the D3DRMLIGHTTYPE values, D3DRMLIGHT_AMBIENT, D3DRMLIGHT_POINT, D3DRMLIGHT_SPOT, D3DRMLIGHT_DIRECTIONAL, or D3DRMLIGHT_PARALLELPOINT.
Arguments:	D3DRMLIGHTTYPE d3drmtType—The new type for the light.
Return Type:	HRESULT
Return Values:	See Direct3D Retained-Mode Return Values.
See Also:	IDirect3DRMLight::GetType, D3DRMLIGHTTYPE

SetUmbra

Interface:	IDirect3DRMLight
Declaration:	`HRESULT SetUmbra(D3DVALUE rvAngle);`
Description:	Sets the umbra angle.
Notes:	The penumbra is the outer, dimmer cone of light emitting from a spotlight, which surrounds the umbra.
	This method is only meaningful for IDirect3DRMLight objects whose type is D3DRMLIGHT_SPOT.
Arguments:	D3DVALUE rvAngle—The new angle for the umbra, in radians.
Return Type:	HRESULT
Return Values:	See Direct3D Retained-Mode Return Values.
See Also:	IDirect3DRMLight::GetUmbra, IDirect3DRMLight::SetPenumbra, D3DRMLIGHTTYPE

IDirect3DRMMaterial

The IDirect3DRMMaterial interface provides functionality for controlling the attributes of a Retained-Mode material object, which defines how a polygonal surface reflects light. Through this interface, applications can adjust the specular and emissive component of the material as well as the power for the specular exponent.

IDirect3DRMMaterial, as with all COM interfaces, is derived from IUnknown and inherits its methods. IDirect3DRMMaterial also inherits the methods of IDirect3DRMObject. A Direct3DRMMaterial object can be obtained by calling IDirect3DRM::CreateMaterial(). IDirect3DRMMaterial implements the following methods:

GetEmissive

GetPower

GetSpecular

SetEmissive

SetPower

SetSpecular

GetEmissive

Interface:	IDirect3DRMMaterial
Declaration:	`HRESULT GetEmissive(D3DVALUE *lpr, D3DVALUE *lpg, D3DVALUE *lpb);`
Description:	Retrieves the emissive color of the IDirect3DRMMaterial object.
Notes:	An object with non-black emissive color appears to radiate or glow light of that color. This light is not used by the lighting module, however, and therefore is not reflected off other objects.
Arguments:	D3DVALUE *lpr—The pointer to a D3DVALUE that will be set with the value of the red component, between 0.0 and 1.0.

GetPower/GetSpecular

	D3DVALUE *lpg—The pointer to a D3DVALUE that will be set with the value of the green component, between 0.0 and 1.0.
	D3DVALUE *lpb—The pointer to a D3DVALUE that will be set with the value of the blue component, between 0.0 and 1.0.
Return Type:	HRESULT
Return Values:	See Direct3D Retained-Mode Return Values.
See Also:	IDirect3DRMMaterial::SetEmissive

GetPower

Interface:	IDirect3DRMMaterial
Declaration:	`D3DVALUE GetPower();`
Description:	Returns the specular exponent of the IDirect3DRMMaterial object.
Notes:	The specular exponent affects the sharpness of specular highlights. A value near 5 gives a metallic look, and higher values give a smooth, plastic look. A perfect mirror has an infinite specular exponent.
Arguments:	None
Return Type:	D3DVALUE
Return Values:	Returns the specular exponent of the material.
See Also:	IDirect3DRMMaterial::SetPower

GetSpecular

Interface:	IDirect3DRMMaterial
Declaration:	`HRESULT GetSpecular(D3DVALUE *lpr, D3DVALUE *lpg, D3DVALUE *lpb);`
Description:	Retrieves the color used for specular highlights from the IDirect3DRMMaterial.
Notes:	The specular color is the shiny component of a material and defines the color when light reflects off a surface directly toward the camera.

continues

continued

Arguments:	D3DVALUE *lpr—The pointer to a D3DVALUE that will be set with the value of the red component, between 0.0 and 1.0.
	D3DVALUE *lpg—The pointer to a D3DVALUE that will be set with the value of the green component, between 0.0 and 1.0.
	D3DVALUE *lpb—The pointer to a D3DVALUE that will be set with the value of the blue component, between 0.0 and 1.0.
Return Type:	HRESULT
Return Values:	See Direct3D Retained-Mode Return Values.
See Also:	IDirect3DRMMaterial::SetSpecular

SetEmissive

Interface:	IDirect3DRMMaterial
Declaration:	`HRESULT SetEmissive(D3DVALUE r, D3DVALUE g, D3DVALUE b);`
Description:	Sets the emissive color of the IDirect3DRMMaterial.
Notes:	An object with a non-black emissive color appears to radiate or glow light of that color. This light is not used by the lighting module, however, and therefore is not reflected off other objects.
Arguments:	D3DVALUE r—The red component of the emissive color, between 0.0 and 1.0.
	D3DVALUE g—The green component of the emissive color, between 0.0 and 1.0.
	D3DVALUE b—The blue component of the emissive color, between 0.0 and 1.0.
Return Type:	HRESULT
Return Values:	See Direct3D Retained-Mode Return Values.
See Also:	IDirect3DRM::GetEmissive

SetPower

Interface:	IDirect3DRMMaterial
Declaration:	`HRESULT SetPower(D3DVALUE rvPower);`
Description:	Sets the specular exponent of the IDirect3DRMMaterial object.
Notes:	The specular exponent affects the sharpness of specular highlights. A value near 5 gives a metallic look, and higher values give a smooth, plastic look. A perfect mirror has an infinite specular exponent.
Arguments:	D3DVALUE rvPower—The new value for the power.
Return Type:	HRESULT
Return Values:	See Direct3D Retained-Mode Return Values.
See Also:	IDirect3DRMMaterial::GetPower

SetSpecular

Interface:	IDirect3DRMMaterial
Declaration:	`HRESULT SetSpecular(D3DVALUE r, D3DVALUE g, D3DVALUE b);`
Description:	Sets the color used for specular highlights when lighting faces that have this IDirect3DRMMaterial.
Notes:	The specular color is the shiny component of a material and defines the color when light reflects off a surface directly toward the camera.
Arguments:	D3DVALUE r—The red component of the specular color, between 0.0 and 1.0.
	D3DVALUE g—The green component of the specular color, between 0.0 and 1.0.
	D3DVALUE b—The blue component of the specular color, between 0.0 and 1.0.
Return Type:	HRESULT
Return Values:	See Direct3D Retained-Mode Return Values.
See Also:	IDirect3DRMMaterial::GetSpecular

IDirect3DRMMesh

The IDirect3DRMMesh interface provides functionality for grouping polygonal faces into more complex 3D objects, which enables easier manipulation and adjustment of the object's attributes. IDirect3DRMMesh provides methods for adjusting the vertices, colors, materials, textures, and rendering quality of the mesh. Additionally, an application can add a group of faces and obtain group information with the IDirect3DRMMesh interface.

IDirect3DRMMesh, as with all COM interfaces, is derived from IUnknown and inherits its methods. IDirect3DRMMesh also inherits the methods of IDirect3DRMObject. A Direct3DRMMesh object can be obtained by calling IDirect3DRM::CreateMesh(). IDirect3DRMMesh implements the following methods:

AddGroup	Scale
GetBox	SetGroupColor
GetGroup	SetGroupColorRGB
GetGroupColor	SetGroupMapping
GetGroupCount	SetGroupMaterial
GetGroupMapping	SetGroupQuality
GetGroupMaterial	SetGroupTexture
GetGroupQuality	SetVertices
GetGroupTexture	Translate
GetVertices	

AddGroup

Interface:	IDirect3DRMMesh
Declaration:	HRESULT AddGroup(unsigned vCount, unsigned fCount, unsigned vPerFace,unsigned *fData, D3DRMGROUPINDEX *returnId);
Description:	Groups a collection of faces together and assigns the group a unique identifier.
Notes:	A group is a collection of faces that can be manipulated as a separate entity within a mesh. When a new group is added, it has no texture or specular reflection (it defaults to a color of white), and the position and normal of each vertex in the group will be zero.
	Groups are used to control properties of a set of faces.
Arguments:	unsigned vCount—The number of vertices in the group.
	unsigned fCount—The number of faces in the group.
	unsigned vPerFace—The number of vertices per face in the group. If faces have varying number of vertices, this parameter must be zero.
	unsigned *fData—The address of the structure that contains the face data. If the *vPerFace* parameter specifies a value, this data is simply a list of indices into the group's vertex array. If *vPerFace* is zero, the vertex indices should be preceded by an integer giving the number of vertices in that face. For example, if *vPerFace* is zero and the group is made up of triangular and quadrilateral faces, the data might be in the following form: 3 *index index index* 4 *index index index index* 3 *index index index* ...
	D3DRMGROUPINDEX *returnId—The address of the index variable returned from the method that will be used to uniquely identify the group.
Return Type:	HRESULT
Return Values:	See Direct3D Retained-Mode Return Values.
See Also:	IDirect3DRMMesh::SetVertices, IDirect3DRMMesh::GetGroup

GetBox

Interface:	IDirect3DRMMesh
Declaration:	`HRESULT GetBox(D3DRMBOX * lpD3DRMBox);`
Description:	Retrieves the bounding box structure for a Direct3DRMMesh object. The bounding box contains the minimum and maximum coordinates for the mesh object in each dimension.
Notes:	GetBox() is typically used in collision detection routines. Note that this box may not be appropriate depending on the mesh objects extremities. For example, an object with a large protrusion in the x-axis direction will cause the returned bounding box to be particularly large in the x-axis direction, causing large amounts of space in the box where there is actually no object.
Arguments:	D3DRMBOX lpD3DRMBox—The address of a D3DRMBOX structure, which will contain the objects bounding box.
Return Type:	HRESULT
Return Values:	See Direct3D Retained-Mode Return Values.
See Also:	IDirect3DRMMeshBuilder::GetBox, D3DRMBOX

GetGroup

Interface:	IDirect3DRMMesh
Declaration:	`HRESULT GetGroup(D3DRMGROUPINDEX id, unsigned *vCount, unsigned *fCount,unsigned *vPerFace, DWORD *fDataSize, unsigned *fData);`
Description:	Returns the unique identifier and data for a group created by using IDirect3DRMMesh::AddGroup().
Notes:	If you are unsure of the size of a group, call IDirect3DRMMesh::GetGroup() passing NULL for the fData argument. The unsigned pointed to by fDataSize will then be filled with the required buffer size.

Arguments:	D3DRMGROUPINDEX id—The identifier for the group whose data you wish to obtain. This identifier must have been created by using IDirect3DRMMesh::AddGroup().
	unsigned *vCount—The address of the variable that will contain the number of vertices in the group.
	unsigned *fCount—The address of the variable that will contain the number of faces in the group.
	unsigned *vPerFace—The address of the variable that will contain the number of vertices per face in the group.
	DWORD *fDataSize—The address of the variable that will contain the number of unsigned variables contained in the buffer. This parameter must not be NULL.
	unsigned *fData—The address of a structure that will contain the face data for the group. This parameter can be NULL, resulting in a return of the required buffer size in the fDataSize parameter.
Return Type:	HRESULT
Return Values:	See Direct3D Retained-Mode Return Values.
See Also:	IDirect3DRMMesh::AddGroup

GetGroupColor

Interface:	IDirect3DRMMesh
Declaration:	`D3DCOLOR GetGroupColor(D3DRMGROUPINDEX id);`
Description:	Retrieves the D3DCOLOR for a given group.
Notes:	None.
Arguments:	D3DRMGROUPINDEX id—The identifier for the group for which data is sought.
Return Type:	D3DCOLOR
Return Values:	Returns the color of a group.
See Also:	IDirect3DRMMesh::AddGroup, IDirect3DRMMesh::SetGroupColor, IDirect3DRMMesh::SetGroupColorRGB, D3DCOLOR

GetGroupCount

Interface:	IDirect3DRMMesh
Declaration:	`unsigned GetGroupCount();`
Description:	Returns the number of groups that have been defined for an IDirect3DRMMesh object.
Notes:	Each group must have been created by a call to IDirect3DRMMesh::AddGroup().
Arguments:	None
Return Type:	unsigned int
Return Values:	Returns the number of groups.
See Also:	IDirect3DRMMesh::AddGroup

GetGroupMapping

Interface:	IDirect3DRMMesh
Declaration:	`D3DRMMAPPING GetGroupMapping(D3DRMGROUPINDEX id);`
Description:	Returns a D3DRMMAPPING description of how textures are mapped to a group on a mesh object.
Notes:	This method returns whether textures are wrapped in the horizontal (texture u-axis) and vertical (texture v-axis) direction. If both are FALSE, the texture topology is flat. If both are TRUE, the texture topology is toroidal. If only one is TRUE, the texture topology is cylindrical in that direction.
	This method also returns whether perspective-correct texture mapping is enabled or disabled.
Arguments:	D3DRMGROUPINDEX id—The identifier for the group for which data is sought.

Return Type:	D3DRMMAPPING
Return Values:	Zero or more of the following values, combined with a logical OR: D3DRMMAP_WRAPU—The texture wraps in the u direction. D3DRMMAP_WRAPV—The texture wraps in the v direction. D3DRMMAP_PERSPCORRECT—The texture wrapping is perspective-corrected.
See Also:	IDirect3DRMMesh::AddGroup, IDirect3DRM::SetGroupMapping, D3DRMMAPPING

GetGroupMaterial

Interface:	IDirect3DRMMesh
Declaration:	`HRESULT GetGroupMaterial(D3DRMGROUPINDEX id, LPDIRECT3DRMMATERIAL *returnPtr);`
Description:	Returns a pointer to the material associated with a group.
Notes:	The IDirect3DRMMesh interface provides grouping as a mechanism for applications to assign the same characteristics (such as material or texture) to several vertices or faces.
Arguments:	D3DRMGROUPINDEX id—The identifier for the group for which data is sought. LPDIRECT3DRMMATERIAL *returnPtr—The address of the pointer to the variable that will contain the IDirect3DRMMaterial for the group.
Return Type:	HRESULT
Return Values:	See Direct3D Retained-Mode Return Values.
See Also:	IDirect3DRMMesh::AddGroup, IDirect3DRMMesh::SetGroupMaterial, D3DRMGROUPINDEX

GetGroupQuality

Interface:	IDirect3DRMMesh
Declaration:	`D3DRMRENDERQUALITY GetGroupQuality(D3DRMGROUPINDEX id);`
Description:	Returns the D3DRMRENDERQUALITY for a group.
Notes:	If a mesh object is composed of several groups of faces with different render qualities, this method can be used to determine the qualities of the different groups.
Arguments:	D3DRMGROUPINDEX id—The identifier for the group for which data is sought.
Return Type:	D3DRMRENDERQUALITY
Return Values:	This should be a list of the actual return values. See D3DRMRENDERQUALITY for details.
See Also:	IDirect3DRMMesh::AddGroup, IDirect3DRMMesh::SetGroupQuality, D3DRMRENDERQUALITY

GetGroupTexture

Interface:	IDirect3DRMMesh
Declaration:	`HRESULT GetGroupTexture(D3DRMGROUPINDEX id, LPDIRECT3DRMTEXTURE *returnPtr);`
Description:	Returns the address of the texture for a group.
Notes:	If no texture is associated with the mesh, *returnPtr will be NULL.
Arguments:	D3DRMGROUPINDEX id—The identifier for the group for which data is sought.
	LPDIRECT3DRMTEXTURE *returnPtr—The address of a pointer to the variable that will contain the IDirect3DRMTexture for a group.
Return Type:	HRESULT
Return Values:	See Direct3D Retained-Mode Return Values.
See Also:	IDirect3DRMMesh::AddGroup, IDirect3DRMMesh::SetGroupTexture

GetVertices

Interface:	IDirect3DRMMesh
Declaration:	HRESULT GetVertices(D3DRMGROUPINDEX id, DWORD index, DWORD count, D3DRMVERTEX *returnPtr);
Description:	Returns the vertices for a group.
Notes:	The vertices returned are in the form of an array of D3DRMVERTEX structures.
Arguments:	D3DRMGROUPINDEX id—The identifier for the group for which data is sought.
	DWORD index—The starting position in the array of D3DRMVERTEX structures. For example, if you have three D3DRMVERTEX structures and only want to return vertex information starting with the second vertex structure, pass in an index value corresponding to the second D3DRMVERTEX structure.
	DWORD count—The number of D3DRMVERTEX structures to retrieve beyond the initial read at the index. For example, if you have five D3DRMVERTEX structures and want to return vertex information starting with the second structure but ending with the fourth, pass in an index value corresponding to the second D3DRMVERTEX structure and a count value of two. This value cannot be NULL.
	D3DRMVERTEX *returnPtr—The array of D3DRMVERTEX structures that will be filled with the information returned from the method. If this value is NULL, the number of required D3DRMVERTEX structures will be returned in the count argument.
Return Type:	HRESULT
Return Values:	See Direct3D Retained-Mode Return Values.
See Also:	IDirect3DRMMesh::AddGroup, IDirect3DRMMesh::SetVertices

Scale

Interface:	IDirect3DRMMesh
Declaration:	`HRESULT Scale(D3DVALUE sx, D3DVALUE sy, D3DVALUE sz);`
Description:	Performs a scaling operation on an IDirect3DRMMesh object given the scale amounts parallel to the x, y, and z-axis.
Notes:	*Scale* is a quick way to change an object's size or otherwise distort its appearance. When performing a scale operation on less than three axes, an argument value of 1.0 indicates no change along that axis.
Arguments:	D3DVALUE sx—The factor by which the mesh is to be scaled along the x-axis.
	D3DVALUE sy—The factor by which the mesh is to be scaled along the y-axis.
	D3DVALUE sz—The factor by which the mesh is to be scaled along the z-axis.
Return Type:	HRESULT
Return Values:	See Direct3D Retained-Mode Return Values.
See Also:	None

SetGroupColor

Interface:	IDirect3DRMMesh
Declaration:	`HRESULT SetGroupColor(D3DRMGROUPINDEX id, D3DCOLOR value);`
Description:	Sets the color of a group.
Notes:	The IDirect3DRMMesh interface provides grouping as a mechanism for applications to assign the same characteristics (such as material or texture) to several vertices or faces.
Arguments:	D3DRMGROUPINDEX id—The identifier of the group for which data is to be set.
	D3DCOLOR value—The new color of the group.

Return Type:	HRESULT
Return Values:	See Direct3D Retained-Mode Return Values.
See Also:	IDirect3DRMMesh::AddGroup, IDirect3DRMMesh::GetGroupColor, IDirect3DRMMesh::SetGroupColorRGB, D3DCOLOR

SetGroupColorRGB

Interface:	IDirect3DRMMesh
Declaration:	`HRESULT SetGroupColorRGB(D3DRMGROUPINDEX id, D3DVALUE red, D3DVALUE green, D3DVALUE blue);`
Description:	Sets the color value of a group.
Notes:	This method can be used to set color of a group by using an RGB value. In 8-bit ramp mode, setting the color of a group to a color not in the palette will cause undesired results.
Arguments:	D3DRMGROUPINDEX id—The identifier of the group for which data is to be set.
	D3DVALUE red—The red component of the color.
	D3DVALUE green—The green component of the color.
	D3DVALUE blue—The blue component of the color.
Return Type:	HRESULT
Return Values:	See Direct3D Retained-Mode Return Values.
See Also:	IDirect3DRMMesh::AddGroup, IDirect3DRMMesh::SetGroupColor, IDirect3DRMMesh::GetGroupColor

SetGroupMapping

Interface:	IDirect3DRMMesh
Declaration:	`HRESULT SetGroupMapping(D3DRMGROUPINDEX id, D3DRMMAPPING value);`
Description:	Sets the D3DRMMAPPING type for the group.

continues

continued	
Notes:	This method sets whether or not textures are wrapped in the horizontal (texture u-axis) and vertical (texture v-axis) direction. If both are FALSE, the texture topology is flat. If both are TRUE the texture topology is toroidal. If only one is TRUE, the texture topology is cylindrical in that direction.
	This method also sets whether perspective-correct texture mapping is enabled or disabled. Perspective-correct texture mapping is computationally expensive; however, many 3D chipsets support this feature.
Arguments:	D3DRMGROUPINDEX id—The identifier of the group for which data is to be set.
	D3DRMMAPPING value—The D3DRMMAPPING type that describes how textures will be mapped to the faces in this group. Zero or more of the following values, combined with a logical OR:
	D3DRMMAP_WRAPU—The texture wraps in the u direction.
	D3DRMMAP_WRAPV—The texture wraps in the v direction.
	D3DRMMAP_PERSPCORRECT—The texture wrapping is perspective-corrected.
Return Type:	HRESULT
Return Values:	See Direct3D Retained-Mode Return Values.
See Also:	IDirect3DRMMesh::GetGroupMapping

SetGroupMaterial

Interface:	IDirect3DRMMesh
Declaration:	`HRESULT SetGroupMaterial(D3DRMGROUPINDEX id, LPDIRECT3DRMMATERIAL value);`
Description:	Sets the material of a group.
Notes:	None
Arguments:	D3DRMGROUPINDEX id—The identifier of the group for which data is to be set.

	LPDIRECT3DRMMATERIAL value—The address of the IDirect3DRMMaterial to apply to the group.
Return Type:	HRESULT
Return Values:	See Direct3D Retained-Mode Return Values.
See Also:	IDirect3DRMMesh::GetGroupMaterial, IDirect3DRMMaterial

SetGroupQuality

Interface:	IDirect3DRMMesh
Declaration:	`HRESULT SetGroupQuality(D3DRMGROUPINDEX id, D3DRMRENDERQUALITY value);`
Description:	Sets the rendering quality of a group.
Notes:	Different parts of a mesh can be rendered with different qualities.
Arguments:	D3DRMGROUPINDEX id—The identifier of the group for which data is to be set.
	D3DRMRENDERQUALITY value—The render quality that will be applied to all faces in the group.
Return Type:	HRESULT
Return Values:	See Direct3D Retained-Mode Return Values.
See Also:	IDirect3DRMMesh::AddGroup, IDirect3DRMMesh::GetGroupQuality

SetGroupTexture

Interface:	IDirect3DRMMesh
Declaration:	`HRESULT SetGroupTexture(D3DRMGROUPINDEX id, LPDIRECT3DRMTEXTURE value);`
Description:	Assigns a texture to a group.
Notes:	The IDirect3DRMMesh interface provides grouping as a mechanism for applications to assign the same characteristics (such as material or texture) to several vertices or faces.

continues

continued

Arguments:	D3DRMGROUPINDEX id—The identifier of the group for which data is to be set and produced by invoking the IDirect3DRMMesh::AddGroup method.
	LPDIRECT3DRMTEXTURE value—The address of the texture that will be applied to all faces in the group.
Return Type:	HRESULT
Return Values:	See Direct3D Retained-Mode Return Values.
See Also:	IDirect3DRMMesh::AddGroup, IDirect3DRMMesh::GetGroupTexture

SetVertices

Interface:	IDirect3DRMMesh
Declaration:	`HRESULT SetVertices(D3DRMGROUPINDEX id, unsigned index, unsigned count, D3DRMVERTEX *values);`
Description:	Sets the positions of the vertices of a group.
Notes:	Groups cannot share vertices.
	Because the faces of a group index into the table of vertices, reordering the vertices can have a significant impact on the mesh.
Arguments:	D3DRMGROUPINDEX id—The identifier for the group for which data is to be set.
	unsigned index—The index into the array of D3DRMVERTEX structures at which to begin setting the vertices.
	unsigned count—The number of vertices to set beyond and including the specified index.
	D3DRMVERTEX *values—The array of D3DRMVERTEX structures specifying the vertex positions to be set.
Return Type:	HRESULT
Return Values:	See Direct3D Retained-Mode Return Values.
See Also:	IDirect3DRMMesh::AddGroup, IDirect3DRMMesh::GetVertices

Translate

Interface:	IDirect3DRMMesh
Declaration:	`HRESULT Translate(D3DVALUE tx, D3DVALUE ty, D3DVALUE tz);`
Description:	This method changes the position of all vertices in a mesh by the specified offsets.
Notes:	This method can be used to move the mesh specified by offsets in x, y, and z in the model coordinate system.
Arguments:	D3DVALUE tx—The vertices offset along the x-axis.
	D3DVALUE ty—The vertices offset along the y-axis.
	D3DVALUE tz—The vertices offset along the z-axis.
Return Type:	HRESULT
Return Values:	See Direct3D Retained-Mode Return Values.
See Also:	IDirect3DRMMesh::Scale

IDirect3DRMMeshBuilder

The IDirect3DRMMeshBuilder interface is built on top of the IDirect3DRMMesh interface and provides easier manipulation of the individual faces and vertices of a mesh. IDirect3DRMMeshBuilder enables an application to add and delete vertices, faces, and normals to a mesh as well as adjust the colors, textures, and rendering quality of the mesh.

IDirect3DRMMeshBuilder, as with all COM interfaces, is derived from IUnknown and inherits its methods. IDirect3DRMMeshBuilder also inherits the methods of IDirect3DRMObject. A Direct3DRMMeshBuilder object can be obtained by calling IDirect3DRM::CreateMeshBuilder(). IDirect3DRMMeshBuilder implements the following methods:

AddFace	GetQuality
AddFaces	GetTextureCoordinates
AddFrame	GetVertexColor
AddMesh	GetVertexCount
AddMeshBuilder	GetVertices
AddNormal	Load
AddVertex	ReserveSpace
CreateFace	Save
CreateMesh	Scale
GenerateNormals	SetColor
GetBox	SetColorRGB
GetColorSource	SetColorSource
GetFaceCount	SetMaterial
GetFaces	SetNormal
GetPerspective	SetPerspective

SetQuality   SetVertex
SetTexture   SetVertexColor
SetTextureCoordinates   SetVertexColorRGB
SetTextureTopology   Translate

AddFace

Interface:	IDirect3DRMMeshBuilder
Declaration:	`HRESULT AddFace(LPDIRECT3DRMFACE lpD3DRMFace);`
Description:	Adds a face object to an IDirect3DRMMeshBuilder object.
Notes:	A face can only exist in one Direct3DRMMeshBuilder object at a time. If the same face data is needed on more than one MeshBuilder object, it must be cloned and added to each separately. Faces can be created with IDirect3DRMMeshBuilder::CreateFace().
Arguments:	LPDIRECT3DRMFACE lpD3DRMFACE—The address of the face to be added to the MeshBuilder object.
Return Type:	HRESULT
Return Values:	See Direct3D Retained-Mode Return Values.
See Also:	IDirect3DRMMeshBuilder::AddFaces, IDirect3DRMMeshBuilder::CreateFace, IDirect3DRMMeshBuilder::GetFaceCount, IDirect3DRMMeshBuilder::GetFaces, IDirect3DRMFace

AddFaces

Interface:	IDirect3DRMMeshBuilder
Declaration:	`HRESULT AddFaces(DWORD dwVertexCount, D3DVECTOR* lpD3DVertices, DWORD normalCount, D3DVECTOR *lpNormals, DWORD *lpFaceData, LPDIRECT3DRMFACEARRAY* lplpD3DRMFaceArray);`
Description:	Adds faces to an IDirect3DRMMeshBuilder object.

continues

continued

Notes: If the normalCount parameter is zero, signifying that normals are not specified, the face data must contain for each face the number of vertices in the face and the vertex indices for the face. For example:

```
unsigned long faceData[] =
{
    8, 7, 6, 5, 4, 3, 2, 1, 0, /* This face has 8 vertices. */
    4, 0, 1, 9, 8,             /* This face has 4 vertices. */
    3, 1, 2, 4,                /* This face has 3 vertices. */
    0,                         /* Face data must end with a zero. */
};
```

If the normalCount parameter is not zero, normals are specified, and the face data must contain for each face the number of vertices in the face followed by pairs of indices for the vertex and normal indices. For example:

```
unsigned long faceData[] =
{
    /* This face has 8 vertices (0—7) and 8 normals (0—7). */
    8, 7, 7, 6, 6, 5, 5, 4, 4, 3, 3, 2, 2, 1, 1, 0, 0,
    /* This face has 4 vertices (0, 1, 9, 8) and 4 normals (0, 6, 1, 0). */
    4, 0, 0, 1, 6, 9, 1, 8, 0,
    /* This face has 3 vertices (1, 2, 4) and 3 normals (6, 2, 3). */
    3, 1, 6, 2, 2, 4, 3,
    0,                         /* Face data must end with a zero. */
};
```

In either case, a zero signifies the end of the face data.

Arguments: DWORD dwVertexCount—The total number of vertices

D3DVECTOR lpD3DVertices—Address of an array of D3DVECTOR structures that hold the information for the vertices to be added to the IDirect3DRMMeshBuilder object.

DWORD normalCount—The total number of normals.

D3DVECTOR lpNormals—The base address of an array of D3DVECTOR structures that stores the normal positions.

DWORD lpFaceData—Pointer to a buffer containing face data. If normalCount is zero, the face data contains the number of vertices and the vertex indices for each face. If normalCount is not zero, the face data contains the number of vertices and the vertex and normal indices for each face.

AddFrame/AddMesh 207

	LPDIRECT3DRMFACEARRAY lplpD3DRMFaceArray—The address of a pointer to an IDirect3DRMFaceArray interface that will be filled with a pointer to the newly created faces.
Return Type:	HRESULT
Return Values:	See Direct3D Retained-Mode Return Values.
See Also:	IDirect3DRMMeshBuilder::AddFace, IDirect3DRMMeshBuilder::CreateFace, IDirect3DRMMeshBuilder::GetFaceCount, IDirect3DRMMeshBuilder::GetFaces, IDirect3DRMFace

AddFrame

Interface:	IDirect3DRMMeshBuilder
Declaration:	`HRESULT AddFrame(LPDIRECT3DRMFRAME lpD3DRMFrame);`
Description:	Adds the contents of an IDirect3DRMFrame object to an IDirect3DRMMeshBuilder object.
Notes:	Frame objects can be created with IDirect3DRM::CreateFrame().
Arguments:	LPDIRECT3DRMFRAME lpD3DRMFrame—The address of the frame whose data will be added to the IDirect3DRMMeshBuilder object.
Return Type:	HRESULT
Return Values:	See Direct3D Retained-Mode Return Values.
See Also:	IDirect3DRMFrame

AddMesh

Interface:	IDirect3DRMMeshBuilder
Declaration:	`HRESULT AddMesh(LPDIRECT3DRMMESH lpD3DRMMesh);`
Description:	Adds the contents of an IDirect3DRMMesh object to an IDirect3DRMMeshBuilder object.

continues

continued

Notes:	The Direct3DRMMesh object being added is not modified by this operation.
Arguments:	LPDIRECT3DRMMESH lpD3DRMMesh—The address of the IDirect3DRMMesh object whose data will be added.
Return Type:	HRESULT
Return Values:	See Direct3D Retained-Mode Return Values.
See Also:	IDirect3DRMMeshBuilder::CreateMesh, IDirect3DRM::CreateMesh, IDirect3DRMMesh

AddMeshBuilder

Interface:	IDirect3DRMMeshBuilder
Declaration:	`HRESULT AddMeshBuilder(LPDIRECT3DRMMESHBUILDER lpD3DRMMeshBuild);`
Description:	Adds the contents of an existing IDirect3DRMMeshBuilder object to the current IDirect3DRMMeshBuilder object.
Notes:	The Direct3DRMMeshBuilder object being added is not modified by this operation.
Arguments:	LPDIRECT3DRMMESHBUILDER lpD3DRMMeshBuild—The address of the IDirect3DRMMeshBuilder object whose data will be added.
Return Type:	HRESULT
Return Values:	See Direct3D Retained-Mode Return Values.
See Also:	IDirect3DRM::CreateMeshBuilder, IDirect3DRMMeshBuilder

AddNormal

Interface:	IDirect3DRMMeshBuilder
Declaration:	`int AddNormal(D3DVALUE x, D3DVALUE y, D3DVALUE z);`
Description:	Adds a new normal to an existing IDirect3DRMMeshBuilder object.
Notes:	None

Arguments:	D3DVALUE x—The x component of the direction of the normal.
	D3DVALUE y—The y component of the direction of the normal.
	D3DVALUE z—The z component of the direction of the normal.
Return Type:	int
Return Values:	The index of the normal in the MeshBuilder.
See Also:	IDirect3DRMMeshBuilder::GenerateNormals,
	IDirect3DRMMeshBuilder::SetNormal

AddVertex

Interface:	IDirect3DRMMeshBuilder
Declaration:	`int AddVertex(D3DVALUE x, D3DVALUE y, D3DVALUE z);`
Description:	Adds a vertex to an IDirect3DRMMeshBuilder object.
Notes:	The int value returned is the index of the new vertex. It is important to keep track of this index for use with IDirect3DRMMeshBuilder::GetTextureCoordinates(), IDirect3DRMMeshBuilder::GetVertexColor(), IDirect3DRMMeshBuilder::SetVertex(), IDirect3DRMMeshBuilder::SetVertexColor(), and IDirect3DRMMeshBuilder::SetVertexColorRGB().
Arguments:	D3DVALUE x—The x component of the position of the new vertex.
	D3DVALUE y—The y component of the position of the new vertex.
	D3DVALUE z—The z component of the position of the new vertex.
Return Type:	int
Return Values:	Returns the index of the new vertex.
See Also:	IDirect3DRMMeshBuilder::GetVertexColor,
	IDirect3DRMMeshBuilder::GetVertexCount,
	IDirect3DRMMeshBuilder::GetVertices,
	IDirect3DRMMeshBuilder::SetVertex,
	IDirect3DRMMeshBuilder::SetVertexColor,
	IDirect3DRMMeshBuilder::SetVertexCount

CreateFace

Interface:	IDirect3DRMMeshBuilder
Declaration:	HRESULT CreateFace(LPDIRECT3DRMFACE* lplpD3DRMFace);
Description:	Creates a new IDirect3DRMFace object in the IDirect3DRMMeshBuilder object.
Notes:	The newly created face has no vertices. The vertices must be added by using either IDirect3DRMFace::AddVertex() or IDirect3DRMFace::AddVertexAndNormalIndexed().
Arguments:	LPDIRECT3DRMFACE lplpD3DRMFace—The address of a pointer to an IDirect3DRMFace object that will contain the pointer to the newly created face after the method is completed.
Return Type:	HRESULT
Return Values:	See Direct3D Retained-Mode Return Values.
See Also:	IDirect3DRMMeshBuilder::AddFace, IDirect3DRMMeshBuilder::AddFaces, IDirect3DRMMeshBuilder::GetFaceCount, IDirect3DRMMeshBuilder::GetFaces

CreateMesh

Interface:	IDirect3DRMMeshBuilder
Declaration:	HRESULT CreateMesh(LPDIRECT3DRMMESH* lplpD3DRMMesh);
Description:	Creates an IDirect3DRMMesh object that is equivalent to the IDirect3DRMMeshBuilder object.
Notes:	A mesh builder object is a higher-level abstraction for creating a mesh. After a mesh is created through the mesh builder interface, it is more efficient to work with the mesh created by this method for certain modifications, such as vertex positions.

GenerateNormals/GetBox

Arguments: LPDIRECT3DRMMESH lplpD3DRM Mesh—The address of a pointer that will be filled with the pointer to the new IDirect3DRMMesh object.

Return Type: HRESULT

Return Values: See Direct3D Retained-Mode Return Values.

See Also: IDirect3DRMMeshBuilder::AddMesh, IDirect3DRM::CreateMesh, IDirect3DRMMesh

GenerateNormals

Interface: IDirect3DRMMeshBuilder

Declaration: `HRESULT GenerateNormals();`

Description: Processes the data in an IDirect3DRMMeshBuilder object and generates the normals for the object.

Notes: This computes the vertex normals from the face data and face normals. The vertex normals are the low-level normals used for lighting.

Arguments: None

Return Type: HRESULT

Return Values: See Direct3D Retained-Mode Return Values.

See Also: IDirect3DRMMeshBuilder::AddNormal, IDirect3DRMMeshBuilder::SetNormal

GetBox

Interface: IDirect3DRMMeshBuilder

Declaration: `HRESULT GetBox(D3DRMBOX *lpD3DRMBox);`

Description: Returns the bounding box for an IDirect3DRMMeshBuilder object.

Notes: Beware the effects of irregular-shaped objects as they will cause your bounding boxes to be filled with more empty space than object. This

continues

continued

	D3DRMBOX will return the minimum and maximum model coordinates in each dimension.
Arguments:	D3DRMBOX lpD3DRMBox—The address of a D3DRMBOX structure that will be filled with the bounding box of the IDirect3DRMMeshBuilder object.
Return Type:	HRESULT
Return Values:	See Direct3D Retained-Mode Return Values.
See Also:	IDirect3DRMMesh::GetBox, D3DRMBOX

GetColorSource

Interface:	IDirect3DRMMeshBuilder
Declaration:	`D3DRMCOLORSOURCE GetColorSource();`
Description:	Returns the color source of the mesh builder object.
Notes:	If the color source is D3DRMCOLOR_FROMFACE, the colors of the faces of an object are retrieved from the face colors. If the color source is D3DRMCOLOR_FROMVERTEX, the colors of the faces of an object are retrieved from the individual vertices of the faces.
Arguments:	None
Return Type:	D3DRMCOLORSOURCE
Return Values:	D3DRMCOLOR_FROMFACE—The object's color source is a face.
	D3DRMCOLOR_FROMVERTEX—The object's color source is a vertex.
See Also:	IDirect3DRMMeshBuilder::SetColorSource

GetFaceCount

Interface:	IDirect3DRMMeshBuilder
Declaration:	`int GetFaceCount();`

Description:	Returns the total number of faces in an IDirect3DRMMeshBuilder object.
Notes:	None
Arguments:	None
Return Type:	int
Return Values:	Returns the number of faces.
See Also:	IDirect3DRMMeshBuilder::AddFace, IDirect3DRMMeshBuilder::AddFaces, IDirect3DRMMeshBuilder::CreateFace, IDirect3DRMMeshBuilder::GetFaces, IDirect3DRMFace

GetFaces

Interface:	IDirect3DRMMeshBuilder
Declaration:	`HRESULT GetFaces(LPDIRECT3DRMFACEARRAY* lplpD3DRMFaceArray);`
Description:	This method retrieves the faces of a Direct3DRMMeshBuilder object.
Notes:	This method creates a face array and fills it with face data. The face array pointed to by the lplpD3DRMFaceArray argument does not need to be initialized.
Arguments:	LPDIRECT3DRMFACEARRAY lplpD3DRMFaceArray—The address of a pointer to a face array (IDirect3DRMFaceArray).
Return Type:	HRESULT
Return Values:	See Direct3D Retained-Mode Return Values.
See Also:	IDirect3DRMMeshBuilder::AddFace, IDirect3DRMMeshBuilder::AddFaces, IDirect3DRMMeshBuilder::CreateFace, IDirect3DRMMeshBuilder::GetFaceCount, IDirect3DRMFace

GetPerspective

Interface:	IDirect3DRMMeshBuilder
Declaration:	`BOOL GetPerspective();`
Description:	This method returns whether perspective correct texture mapping is enabled or disabled.
Notes:	Perspective-correct texture mapping is computationally expensive for the software renderer (HEL). Many 3D cards, however, support perspective-correct texture mapping in hardware.
Arguments:	None
Return Type:	BOOL
Return Values:	Returns TRUE or FALSE depending on whether perspective correct texture mapping is enabled or disabled.
See Also:	IDirect3DRMMeshBuilder::SetPerspective

GetQuality

Interface:	IDirect3DRMMeshBuilder
Declaration:	`D3DRMRENDERQUALITY GetQuality();`
Description:	Returns the D3DRMRENDERQUALITY associated with the current IDirect3DRMMeshBuilder object.
Notes:	The default render quality setting is D3DRMRENDER_FLAT. The render quality consists of a shade mode, a light mode, and a fill mode. Direct3D provides a convenient method for setting render quality (see Direct3D Render Quality Enumerated Types).
	Retained–Mode Device objects also have a render quality associated with them, and meshes (through IDirect3DRMMesh or IDirect3DRMMeshBuilder) may not be rendered at a higher quality than the render quality of the Device object.
	Phong shading is not currently supported in Direct3D.
Arguments:	None

Return Type:	D3DRMRENDERQUALITY
Return Values:	Returns the render quality of the device. See Direct3D Render Quality Enumerated Types for the complete list. The most commonly used values represent a combination of a shade mode, a fill mode, and a light mode combined with a logical OR:

> D3DRMRENDER_WIREFRAME—Wireframe model, renders the outlines of triangles.
>
> D3DRMRENDER_UNLITFLAT—Triangles are rendered with flat shading and no lighting.
>
> D3DRMRENDER_FLAT—Triangles are rendered with flat shading and lighting.
>
> D3DRMRENDER_GOURAUD—Triangles are Gouraud shaded.
>
> D3DRMRENDER_PHONG—Triangles are Phong shaded (not currently supported).

See Also:	IDirect3DRMMeshBuilder::SetQuality, IDirect3DRMMesh::GetGroupQuality, IDirect3DRMMesh::SetGroupQuality

GetTextureCoordinates

Interface:	IDirect3DRMMeshBuilder
Declaration:	`HRESULT GetTextureCoordinates(DWORD index, D3DVALUE *lpU, D3DVALUE *lpV);`
Description:	Returns the texture coordinates of the specified vertex.
Notes:	Texture coordinates describe how the pixels of a texture map correspond to the pixels in a face.
Arguments:	DWORD index—The index of the vertex for which data is sought. This index is generated with IDirect3DRMMeshBuilder::AddVertex().
	D3DVALUE lpU—The address of the variable that will contain the horizontal (u-axis) texture coordinate of the vertex.

continues

continued

	D3DVALUE lpV—The address of the variable that will contain the vertical (v-axis) texture coordinate of the vertex.
Return Type:	HRESULT
Return Values:	See Direct3D Retained-Mode Return Values.
See Also:	IDirect3DRMMeshBuilder::SetTextureCoordinates

GetVertexColor

Interface:	IDirect3DRMMeshBuilder
Declaration:	`D3DCOLOR GetVertexColor(DWORD index);`
Description:	Returns the D3DCOLOR value of a vertex within a Direct3DRMMeshBuilder object.
Notes:	None
Arguments:	DWORD index—The index of the vertex for which data is sought.
Return Type:	D3DCOLOR
Return Values:	See Direct3D Retained-Mode Return Values.
See Also:	IDirect3DRMMeshBuilder::AddVertex, IDirect3DRMMeshBuilder::GetVertexCount, IDirect3DRMMeshBuilder::GetVertices, IDirect3DRMMeshBuilder::SetVertex, IDirect3DRMMeshBuilder::SetVertexColor, IDirect3DRMMeshBuilder::SetVertexColorRGB

GetVertexCount

Interface:	IDirect3DRMMeshBuilder
Declaration:	`int GetVertexCount();`
Description:	Returns the total number of vertices in the IDirect3DRMMeshBuilder object.
Notes:	None

Arguments:	None
Return Type:	int
Return Values:	Returns the number of vertices.
See Also:	IDirect3DRMMeshBuilder::AddVertex,
	IDirect3DRMMeshBuilder::GetVertexColor,
	IDirect3DRMMeshBuilder::GetVertices,
	IDirect3DRMMeshBuilder::SetVertex,
	IDirect3DRMMeshBuilder::SetVertexColor,
	IDirect3DRMMeshBuilder::SetVertexColorRGB

GetVertices

Interface:	IDirect3DRMMeshBuilder
Declaration:	`HRESULT GetVertices(DWORD *vcount, D3DVECTOR *vertices, DWORD *ncount, D3DVECTOR *normals, DWORD *face_data_size, DWORD *face_data);`
Description:	Retrieves arrays of vertex, normal, and face information from an IDirect3DRMMeshBuilder object.
Notes:	Passing a value of NULL into the face_data parameter will return the required face buffer size in the face_data_size.
	The format of the face_data argument is the same as for IDirect3DRMMeshBuilder::AddFaces(), except that the data is NULL-terminated instead of zero-terminated.
Arguments:	DWORD *vcount—The address of a variable that will contain the number of vertices in the object.
	D3DVECTOR *vertices—The address of an array of D3DVECTOR structures that will be filled with vertex information.
	DWORD *ncount—The address of a variable that will contain the number of normals in the object.
	D3DVECTOR *normals—The address of an array of D3DVECTOR structures that will be filled with normal information.

continues

continued

        DWORD *face_data_size—The address of a variable that specifies the size of the face data buffer.

        DWORD *face_data—The address of the structure that will contain NULL-terminated face data.

Return Type: HRESULT

Return Values: See Direct3D Retained-Mode Return Values.

See Also: IDirect3DRMMeshBuilder::AddVertex,
IDirect3DRMMeshBuilder::GetVertexColor,
IDirect3DRMMeshBuilder::GetVertexCount,
IDirect3DRMMeshBuilder::SetVertex,
IDirect3DRMMeshBuilder::SetVertexColor,
IDirect3DRMMeshBuilder::SetVertexCount

Load

Interface: IDirect3DRMMeshBuilder

Declaration:
```
HRESULT Load(LPVOID lpvObjSource, LPVOID lpvObjID,
    D3DRMLOADOPTIONS d3drmLOFlags, D3DRMLOADTEXTURECALLBACK
    d3drmLoadTextureProc,
    LPVOID lpvArg);
```

Description: Loads the data for an IDirect3DRMMeshBuilder object from a file, resource, memory block, or data stream.

Notes: None

Arguments: LPVOID lpvObjSource—The pointer to data indicating the source of the IDirect3DRMMeshBuilder data, or NULL.

        LPVOID lpvObjID—The pointer to an object name, or position, depending on which load options are selected in the d3drmLOFlags parameter.

        D3DRMLOADOPTIONS d3drmLOFlags—The flags specifying the source of the IDirect3DRMMeshBuilder. A logical OR of one of each of the following sets of flags:

Source Flags:

D3DRMLOAD_FROMFILE—Load from a file. This is the default setting.

D3DRMLOAD_FROMRESOURCE—Load from a resource. If this flag is specified, the lpvObjSource parameter of the calling Load method must point to a D3DRMLOADRESOURCE structure.

D3DRMLOAD_FROMMEMORY—Load from memory. If this flag is specified, the lpvObjSource parameter of the calling Load method must point to a D3DRMLOADMEMORY structure.

D3DRMLOAD_FROMSTREAM—Load from a stream.

Identifier Flags:

D3DRMLOAD_BYNAME—Load any object by using a specified name.

D3DRMLOAD_BYPOSITION—Load a stand-alone object based on a given zero-based position (that is, the nth object in the file). Stand-alone objects can contain other objects, but are not contained by any other objects.

D3DRMLOAD_BYGUID—Load any object by using a specified globally unique identifier (GUID).

D3DRMLOAD_FIRST—This is the default setting. Load the first stand-alone object of the given type (for example, a mesh if the application calls IDirect3DRMMeshBuilder::Load). Stand-alone objects can contain other objects, but are not contained by any other objects.

Instance Flags:

D3DRMLOAD_INSTANCEBYREFERENCE—Check whether an object already exists with the same name as specified and, if so, use an instance of that object instead of creating a new one.

D3DRMLOAD_INSTANCEBYCOPYING—Check whether an object already exists with the same name as specified and, if so, copy that object.

D3DRMLOADTEXTURECALLBACK d3drmLoadTextureProc—This is the callback function that Load will call to load textures.

continues

continued

	DirectX currently only supports loads of BMP or PPM bitmaps. Thus, if you wish to load any file format other than BMP or PPM as textures, a callback must be supplied to load those textures.
	LPVOID lpvArg—This is a pointer to application-defined data that Load will pass to the texture callback passed via d3drmLoadTextureProc, if any.
Return Type:	HRESULT
Return Values:	See Direct3D Retained-Mode Return Values.
See Also:	IDirect3DRMMeshBuilder::Save

ReserveSpace

Interface:	IDirect3DRMMeshBuilder
Declaration:	`HRESULT ReserveSpace(DWORD vertexCount, DWORD normalCount, DWORD faceCount);`
Description:	Reserves space for a specified number of vertices, normals, and faces within an IDirect3DRMMeshBuilder object.
Notes:	This method allocates the precise memory requirement for the specified arguments allowing for better memory efficiency.
Arguments:	DWORD vertexCount—The number of vertices to allocate space for.
	DWORD normalCount—The number of normals to allocate space for.
	DWORD faceCount—The number of faces to allocate space for.
Return Type:	HRESULT
Return Values:	See Direct3D Retained-Mode Return Values.
See Also:	None

Save

Interface:	IDirect3DRMMeshBuilder
Declaration:	`HRESULT Save(const char* lpFilename, D3DRMXOFFORMAT d3drmXOFFormat, D3DRMSAVEOPTIONS d3drmSOContents);`
Description:	Saves the IDirect3DRMMeshBuilder to permanent storage.
Notes:	The data is saved in the DirectX file format.
Arguments:	const char* lpFilename—The address of the character string specifying the file name.
	D3DRMXOFFORMAT d3drmXOFFormat—The file format to which the object will be saved.
	D3DRMSAVEOPTIONS d3drmSOContents—The type of information you wish to save about the object (that is, face data only, face and texture data, etc.).
Return Type:	HRESULT
Return Values:	See Direct3D Retained-Mode Return Values.
See Also:	IDirect3DRMMeshBuilder::Load

Scale

Interface:	IDirect3DRMMeshBuilder
Declaration:	`HRESULT Scale(D3DVALUE sx, D3DVALUE sy, D3DVALUE sz);`
Description:	Performs a scaling operation on the IDirect3DRMMeshBuilder object along the x-, y-, and z-axes.
Notes:	If you do not wish to scale an object along a particular axis, pass in a one for the argument corresponding to that dimension.
Arguments:	D3DVALUE sx—The scaling factor of the object along the x-axis.
	D3DVALUE sy—The scaling factor of the object along the y-axis.
	D3DVALUE sz—The scaling factor of the object along the z-axis.
Return Type:	HRESULT
Return Values:	See Direct3D Retained-Mode Return Values.
See Also:	IDirect3DRMMesh::Scale, IDirect3DRMMeshBuilder::Translate

SetColor

Interface:	IDirect3DRMMeshBuilder
Declaration:	`HRESULT SetColor(D3DCOLOR color);`
Description:	Sets the color of all the faces in an IDirect3DRMMeshBuilder object to a specified D3DCOLOR.
Notes:	To manipulate groups of faces within a mesh builder, it must be converted to an IDirect3DRMMesh, which enables groups of one or more faces to be manipulated individually.
	This method enables the alpha component of color to be set.
Arguments:	D3DCOLOR color—The color to which all the faces will be set.
Return Type:	HRESULT
Return Values:	See Direct3D Retained-Mode Return Values.
See Also:	IDirect3DRMMeshBuilder::GetColor

SetColorRGB

Interface:	IDirect3DRMMeshBuilder
Declaration:	`HRESULT SetColorRGB(D3DVALUE red, D3DVALUE green, D3DVALUE blue);`
Description:	Sets the color of all faces in the object to a specified RGB triple.
Notes:	To manipulate groups of faces within a mesh builder, it must be converted to an IDirect3DRMMesh, which allows groups of one or more faces to be manipulated individually.
	This method does not enable the alpha component of color to be set. The alpha component is automatically set to 1.0.
Arguments:	D3DVALUE red—The red component of the color that will be applied to the object.

	D3DVALUE green—The green component of the color that will be applied to the object.
	D3DVALUE blue—The blue component of the color that will be applied to the object.
Return Type:	HRESULT
Return Values:	See Direct3D Retained-Mode Return Values.
See Also:	IDirect3DRMMeshBuilder::GetColor, IDirect3DRMMeshBuilder::SetColor

SetColorSource

Interface:	IDirect3DRMMeshBuilder
Declaration:	`HRESULT SetColorSource(D3DRMCOLORSOURCE source);`
Description:	Sets the D3DRMCOLORSOURCE for an IDirect3DRMMeshBuilder object.
Notes:	If the color source is D3DRMCOLOR_FROMFACE, the colors of the faces of an object are retrieved from the face colors. If the color source is D3DRMCOLOR_FROMVERTEX, the colors of the faces of an object are retrieved from the individual vertices of the faces.
Arguments:	D3DRMCOLORSOURCE source—The new color source of the object. One of the following:
	D3DRMCOLOR_FROMFACE—The object's color source is a face.
	D3DRMCOLOR_FROMVERTEX—The object's color source is a vertex.
Return Type:	HRESULT
Return Values:	See Direct3D Retained-Mode Return Values.
See Also:	IDirect3DRMMeshBuilder::GetColorSource

SetMaterial

Interface:	IDirect3DRMMeshBuilder
Declaration:	`HRESULT SetMaterial(LPDIRECT3DRMMATERIAL lpIDirect3DRMMaterial);`
Description:	Sets the IDirect3DRMMaterial of all the faces of the IDirect3DRMMeshBuilder object.
Notes:	To manipulate groups of faces of an object, it is better to work from an IDirect3DRMMesh object, as groups of faces on the IDirect3DRMMesh can be manipulated individually.
Arguments:	LPDIRECT3DRMMATERIAL lpIDirect3DRMMaterial—The address of an IDirect3DRMMaterial that will be applied to all faces of the object.
Return Type:	HRESULT
Return Values:	See Direct3D Retained-Mode Return Values.
See Also:	IDirect3DRMMesh::SetGroupMaterial

SetNormal

Interface:	IDirect3DRMMeshBuilder
Declaration:	`HRESULT SetNormal(DWORD index, D3DVALUE x, D3DVALUE y, D3DVALUE z);`
Description:	Sets the normal vector of the specified vertex.
Notes:	Vertex normals are used in lighting.
Arguments:	DWORD index—The index of the vertex for which data will be set. This index is generated by IDirect3DRMMeshBuilder::AddVertex().
	D3DVALUE x—The x component of the normal.
	D3DVALUE y—The y component of the normal.
	D3DVALUE z—The z component of the normal.
Return Type:	HRESULT
Return Values:	See Direct3D Retained-Mode Return Values.
See Also:	IDirect3DRMMeshBuilder::GenerateNormals, IDirect3DRMMeshBuilder::AddVertex

SetPerspective

Interface:	IDirect3DRMMeshBuilder
Declaration:	`HRESULT SetPerspective(BOOL perspective);`
Description:	This method enables or disables perspective correct texture mapping for a Direct3DRMMeshBuilder object.
Notes:	Perspective correct texture mapping is computationally expensive for the software renderer (HEL). Many 3D cards, however, support perspective correct texture mapping in hardware.
	To manipulate groups of faces of an object, it is better to work from an IDirect3DRMMesh object as groups of faces on the IDirect3DRMMesh can be manipulated individually.
Arguments:	BOOL perspective—The current setting of perspective correct texture mapping for the IDirect3DRMMeshBuilder object.
Return Type:	HRESULT
Return Values:	See Direct3D Retained-Mode Return Values.
See Also:	IDirect3DRMMeshBuilder::GetPerspective

SetQuality

Interface:	IDirect3DRMMeshBuilder
Declaration:	`HRESULT SetQuality(D3DRMRENDERQUALITY quality);`
Description:	Sets the D3DRMRENDERQUALITY for the IDirect3DRMMeshBuilder object.
Notes:	The default render quality setting is D3DRMRENDER_FLAT. The render quality consists of a shade mode, a light mode, and a fill mode. Direct3D provides a convenient method for setting render quality (see Direct3D Render Quality Enumerated Types).
	Retained–Mode Device objects also have a render quality associated with them, and meshes (through IDirect3DRMMesh or

continues

continued

	IDirect3DRMMeshBuilder) may not be rendered at a higher quality than the render quality of the Device object.
	Phong shading is not currently supported in Direct3D.
Arguments:	D3DRMRENDERQUALITY quality—The rendering quality that will be applied to the object.
Return Type:	HRESULT
Return Values:	See Direct3D Retained-Mode Return Values.
See Also:	IDirect3DRMMeshBuilder::GetQuality, D3DRMRENDERQUALITY

SetTexture

Interface:	IDirect3DRMMeshBuilder
Declaration:	`HRESULT SetTexture(LPDIRECT3DRMTEXTURE lpD3DRMTexture);`
Description:	Sets all the faces of an IDirect3DRMMeshBuilder object to an IDirect3DRMTexture.
Notes:	To manipulate groups of faces of an object, it is better to work from an IDirect3DRMMesh object, as groups of faces on the IDirect3DRMMesh can be manipulated individually.
	As there is no IDirect3DRMMeshBuilder::GetTexture(), an application should keep a reference to textures that must be regularly referenced.
Arguments:	LPDIRECT3DRMTEXTURE lpD3DRMTexture—The address of the texture object that will be applied to all the faces of the object.
Return Type:	HRESULT
Return Values:	See Direct3D Retained-Mode Return Values.
See Also:	IDirect3DRMMesh::GetGroupTexture, IDirect3DRMFace::GetTexture, IDirect3DRMFrame::GetTexture, IDirect3DRMTexture

SetTextureCoordinates

Interface:	IDirect3DRMMeshBuilder
Declaration:	HRESULT SetTextureCoordinates(DWORD index, D3DVALUE u, D3DVALUE v);
Description:	Sets the texture coordinates of a vertex in an IDirect3DRMMeshBuilder object.
Notes:	Texture coordinates describe how the pixels of a texture map correspond to the pixels in a face.
Arguments:	DWORD index—The index of the vertex for which data will be set.
	D3DVALUE u—The horizontal texture coordinate (u-axis) assigned to the mesh vertex.
	D3DVALUE v—The vertical texture coordinate (v-axis) assigned to the mesh vertex.
Return Type:	HRESULT
Return Values:	See Direct3D Retained-Mode Return Values.
See Also:	IDirect3DRMMeshBuilder::GetTextureCoordinates, IDirect3DRMMeshBuilder::AddVertex

SetTextureTopology

Interface:	IDirect3DRMMeshBuilder
Declaration:	HRESULT SetTextureTopology(BOOL cylU, BOOL cylV);
Description:	Sets the cylindrical texture topology of an entire IDirect3DRMMeshBuilder object.
Notes:	This method sets the arguments lpU and lpV to TRUE or FALSE, depending on whether textures should be wrapped in the horizontal (texture u-axis) and vertical (texture v-axis) direction. If both are FALSE, the topology is flat, if both are TRUE the topology is toroidal, and if only one is TRUE, the topology is cylindrical in that direction.

continues

continued

Arguments:	BOOL cylU—The flag indicating the status of texture topology along the horizontal texture axis (u-axis).
	BOOL cylV—The flag indicating the status of texture topology along the vertical texture axis (v-axis).
Return Type:	HRESULT
Return Values:	See Direct3D Retained-Mode Return Values.
See Also:	IDirect3DRMMeshBuilder::SetTexture, IDirect3DRMMeshBuilder::SetTextureCoordinates

SetVertex

Interface:	IDirect3DRMMeshBuilder
Declaration:	`HRESULT SetVertex(DWORD index, D3DVALUE x, D3DVALUE y, D3DVALUE z);`
Description:	Sets the position of a vertex in an IDirect3DRMMeshBuilder object.
Notes:	The position is in model coordinate space.
Arguments:	DWORD index—The index of the vertex for which data will be set.
	D3DVALUE x—The x position to be assigned to the vertex.
	D3DVALUE y—The y position to be assigned to the vertex.
	D3DVALUE z—The z position to be assigned to the vertex.
Return Type:	HRESULT
Return Values:	See Direct3D Retained-Mode Return Values.
See Also:	IDirect3DRMMeshBuilder::AddVertex, IDirect3DRMMeshBuilder::GetVertexColor, IDirect3DRMMeshBuilder::GetVertexCount, IDirect3DRMMeshBuilder::GetVertices, IDirect3DRMMeshBuilder::SetVertexColor, IDirect3DRMMeshBuilder::SetVertexCount

SetVertexColor

Interface:	IDirect3DRMMeshBuilder
Declaration:	`HRESULT SetVertexColor(DWORD index, D3DCOLOR color);`
Description:	Sets the color of a specified vertex in a Direct3DRMMeshBuilder object.
Notes:	Changing a vertex color may change how a face looks depending on the type of shading. This method enables the alpha component of the color to be set.
Arguments:	DWORD index—The index of the vertex for which data will be set.
	D3DCOLOR color—The color value that will be applied to the vertex.
Return Type:	HRESULT
Return Values:	See Direct3D Retained-Mode Return Values.
See Also:	IDirect3DRMMeshBuilder::AddVertex, IDirect3DRMMeshBuilder::GetVertexColor, IDirect3DRMMeshBuilder::GetVertexCount, IDirect3DRMMeshBuilder::GetVertices, IDirect3DRMMeshBuilder::SetVertices, IDirect3DRMMeshBuilder::SetVertexColorRGB

SetVertexColorRGB

Interface:	IDirect3DRMMeshBuilder
Declaration:	`HRESULT SetVertexColorRGB(DWORD index, D3DVALUE red, D3DVALUE green, D3DVALUE blue);`
Description:	Sets the color of the specified vertex to an RGB triple.
Notes:	This method does not enable the alpha component of the color to be set. The alpha component is always set to 1.0.

continues

continued

Arguments:	DWORD index—The index of the vertex for which data will be set.
	D3DVALUE red—The red component of the color that will be applied to the vertex.
	D3DVALUE green—The green component of the color that will be applied to the vertex.
	D3DVALUE blue—The blue component of the color that will be applied to the vertex.
Return Type:	HRESULT
Return Values:	See Direct3D Retained-Mode Return Values.
See Also:	IDirect3DRMMeshBuilder::AddVertex, IDirect3DRMMeshBuilder::GetVertexColor, IDirect3DRMMeshBuilder::GetVertexCount, IDirect3DRMMeshBuilder::GetVertices, IDirect3DRMMeshBuilder::SetVertices, IDirect3DRMMeshBuilder::SetVertexColor

Translate

Interface:	IDirect3DRMMeshBuilder
Declaration:	`HRESULT Translate(D3DVALUE tx, D3DVALUE ty, D3DVALUE tz);`
Description:	Applies the specified offsets to the vertices of the IDirect3DRMMeshBuilder object.
Notes:	This method can be used to move the mesh specified by the mesh builder object by offsets in x, y, and z in the model coordinate system.
Arguments:	D3DVALUE tx—The vertex change along the x-axis.
	D3DVALUE ty—The vertex change along the y-axis.
	D3DVALUE tz—The vertex change along the z-axis.
Return Type:	HRESULT
Return Values:	See Direct3D Retained-Mode Return Values.
See Also:	IDirect3DRMMeshBuilder::Scale

IDirect3DRMObject

The IDirect3DRMObject interface provides the general functionality for interacting with an object. IDirect3DRMObject enables an application to set and get an object's name, retrieve an object's class name, attach application-specific data to an object, clone an object, and register function callbacks to be executed when an object is destroyed. All the Retained-Mode interfaces, except for IDirect3DRM and the array interfaces, inherit methods from IDirect3DRMObject.

IDirect3DRMObject, as with all COM interfaces, is derived from IUnknown and inherits its methods. A Direct3DRMObject object can be obtained through the appropriate call to QueryInterface() from any Retained-Mode object. IDirect3DRMObject implements the following methods:

AddDestroyCallback

Clone

DeleteDestroyCallback

GetAppData

GetClassName

GetName

SetAppData

SetName

AddDestroyCallback

Interface: IDirect3DRMObject

Declaration: `HRESULT AddDestroyCallback(D3DRMOBJECTCALLBACK lpCallback, LPVOID lpArg);`

continues

continued

Description:	AddDestroyCallback registers a function to be executed when the object is destroyed.
Notes:	An object's destroy callback is executed when the object's reference count becomes zero (after a call to the object's Release() method). Application-specific information can be passed to the destroy callback using the lpArg argument. Because the destroy callback function will be called after the object is destroyed, you should not use the object as an argument to the callback.
	The lpArg argument can contain four bytes of data or a pointer to a data structure.
Arguments:	D3DRMOBJECTCALLBACK lpCallback—The pointer to the application-defined function.
	LPVOID lpArg—The data to be passed to callback function as argument.
Return Type:	HRESULT
Return Values:	See Direct3D Retained-Mode Return Values.
See Also:	IDirect3DRMObject::DeleteDestroyCallback, D3DRMOBJECTCALLBACK

Clone

Interface:	IDirect3DRMObject
Declaration:	`HRESULT Clone(LPUNKNOWN pUnkOuter, REFIID riid, LPVOID *ppvObj);`
Description:	This method creates a copy of an object.
Notes:	This method does not increase the reference count of the calling object.
Arguments:	LPUNKNOWN pUnkOuter—This enables COM aggregration features.
	REFIID riid—The reference identifier (GUID) of the object being copied.
	LPVOID *ppvObj—The pointer that will point to the copy of the object if the method is successful.

Return Type: HRESULT
Return Values: See Direct3D Retained-Mode Return Values.
See Also: IUnknown::QueryInterface

DeleteDestroyCallback

Interface: IDirect3DRMObject
Declaration: `HRESULT DeleteDestroyCallback(D3DRMOBJECTCALLBACK d3drmObjProc, LPVOID lpArg);`
Description: This method removes a previously registered destroy callback function from an object.
Notes: The lpArg argument must be the same data passed to IDirect3DRMObject::AddDestroyCallback() for the callback to be removed.

The lpArg argument can contain four bytes of data or a pointer to a data structure.
Arguments: D3DRMOBJECTCALLBACK d3drmObjProc—The pointer to the application-defined callback function.

LPVOID lpArg—The data passed as the destroy callback argument.
Return Type: HRESULT
Return Values: See Direct3D Retained-Mode Return Values.
See Also: IDirect3DRMObject::AddDestroyCallBack, D3DRMOBJECTCALLBACK

GetAppData

Interface: IDirect3DRMObject
Declaration: `DWORD GetAppData();`
Description: This method returns an object's application-specific data value.

continues

continued

Notes:	Every object can store 32 bits of data that are guaranteed to remain unmodified by Direct3D. The default value is zero.
Arguments:	None
Return Type:	DWORD
Return Values:	Returns the application-specific data associated with the object. This can be four bytes of data or a pointer to a data structure.
See Also:	IDirect3DRMObject::SetAppData

GetClassName

Interface:	IDirect3DRMObject
Declaration:	`HRESULT GetClassName(LPDWORD lpdwSize, LPSTR lpName);`
Description:	This method retrieves the name of the object class.
Notes:	This method can also be used to find out the size of the buffer required to contain the object class name string. This is done by calling GetClassName() with lpName equal to NULL. The class name is not to be confused with an object's user-defined name.
	Possible Direct3D object names are: Animation, AnimationSet, Device, Face, Frame, Light, Material, Mesh, MeshBuilder, Shadow, Texture, UserVisual, Viewport, and Wrap.
Arguments:	LPDWORD lpdwSize—The pointer to the variable containing the size of the buffer to the lpName parameter.
	LPSTR lpName—The pointer to the buffer that will be filled with name of the object class.
Return Type:	HRESULT
Return Values:	See Direct3D Retained-Mode Return Values.
See Also:	IDirect3DRMObject::GetName

GetName

Interface:	IDirect3DRMObject
Declaration:	HRESULT GetName(LPDWORD lpdwSize, LPSTR lpName);
Description:	This method retrieves the user-defined name of the object.
Notes:	This method should not be confused with IDirect3DRMObject::GetClassName(), which returns the Direct3D name for the object (for instance, "MeshBuilder").
	The user-defined name is assigned using IDirect3DRMObject::SetName().
Arguments:	LPDWORD lpdwSize—The pointer to the variable that contains the size of lpName buffer.
	LPSTR lpName—The pointer to the buffer that will be filled with the object's user-defined class.
Return Type:	HRESULT
Return Values:	See Direct3D Retained-Mode Return Values.
See Also:	IDirect3DRMObject::SetName

SetAppData

Interface:	IDirect3DRMObject
Declaration:	HRESULT SetAppData(DWORD ulData);
Description:	This method sets an object's application-specific data.
Notes:	Every object can store 32 bits of data that are guaranteed to remain unmodified by Direct3D. The default value is zero.
	The ulData argument can contain four bytes of data or a pointer to a data structure.
Arguments:	DWORD ulData—The user-defined data to be stored with the object.
Return Type:	HRESULT

continues

continued

Return Values: See Direct3D Retained-Mode Return Values.
See Also: IDirect3DRMObject::GetAppData

SetName

Interface:	IDirect3DRMObject
Declaration:	`HRESULT SetName(const char* lpName);`
Description:	This method assigns an object's user-defined name.
Notes:	Be careful not to confuse an object's class name with its user-defined name.
Arguments:	const char* lpName—The pointer to a string to be used for the name of the object.
Return Type:	HRESULT
Return Values:	See Direct3D Retained-Mode Return Values.
See Also:	IDirect3DRMObject::GetName, IDirect3DRMObject::GetClassName

IDirect3DRMShadow

The IDirect3DRMShadow interface provides only one method (in addition to those it inherits) that initializes a shadow object. A Retained-Mode shadow provides a quick and easy way to represent the shadow that a polygonal mesh would cast. Typically, an application will call IDirect3DRM::CreateShadow() to initialize a shadow object and set up the appropriate shadow attributes as opposed to calling IDirect3DRM::CreateObject() to create an object and IDirect3DRMShadow::Init() to initialize and set up the object.

IDirect3DRMShadow, as with all COM interfaces, is derived from IUnknown and inherits its methods. IDirect3DRMShadow also inherits the methods of IDirect3DRMObject. An IDirect3DRMShadow object can be obtained by calling IDirect3DRM::CreateShadow(). IDirect3DRMShadow implements the following method:

    Init

Init

Interface:	IDirect3DRMShadow
Declaration:	`HRESULT Init(LPDIRECT3DRMVISUAL lpD3DRMVisual, LPDIRECT3DRMLIGHT lpD3DRMLight, D3DVALUE px, D3DVALUE py, D3DVALUE pz, D3DVALUE nx, D3DVALUE ny, D3DVALUE nz);`
Description:	This method initializes a Direct3D shadow object.
Notes:	This method is used in conjunction with IDirect3DRM::CreateObject(). Alternatively, an application could use IDirect3DRM::CreateShadow() method, which both creates and initializes a Direct3D shadow object.
Arguments:	LPDIRECT3DRMVISUAL lpD3DRMVisual—The address of the Direct3D Retained-Mode visual object casting the shadow.

continues

continued

> LPDIRECT3DRMLIGHT lpD3DRMLight—The address of the Direct3D Retained-Mode light object that provides the light that defines the shadow.
>
> D3DVALUE px—The x coordinate of a point on the plane on which the shadow is cast.
>
> D3DVALUE py—The y coordinate of a point on the plane on which the shadow is cast.
>
> D3DVALUE pz—The z coordinate of a point on the plane on which the shadow is cast.
>
> D3DVALUE nx—The x coordinate of the normal vector of the plane on which the shadow is cast.
>
> D3DVALUE ny—The y coordinate of the normal vector of the plane on which the shadow is cast.
>
> D3DVALUE nz—The z coordinate of the normal vector of the plane on which the shadow is cast.

Return Type: HRESULT

Return Values: See Direct3D Retained-Mode Return Values.

See Also: IDirect3DRM::CreateShadow

IDirect3DRMTexture

The IDirect3DRMTexture interface is actually an interface to a DirectDraw surface object and provides functionality for manipulating the color, shading, and decal information of a texture object.

IDirect3DRMTexture, as with all COM interfaces, is derived from IUnknown and inherits its methods. IDirect3DRMTexture also inherits the methods of IDirect3DRMObject. A Direct3DRMTexture object can be obtained by calling IDirect3DRM::CreateTexture() or IDirect3DRM::CreateTextureFromSurface(). IDirect3DRMTexture implements the following methods:

Changed	InitFromResource
GetColors	InitFromSurface
GetDecalOrigin	SetColors
GetDecalScale	SetDecalOrigin
GetDecalSize	SetDecalScale
GetDecalTransparency	SetDecalSize
GetDecalTransparentColor	SetDecalTransparency
GetImage	SetDecalTransparentColor
GetShades	SetShades
InitFromFile	

Changed

Interface:	IDirect3DRMTexture
Declaration:	`HRESULT Changed(BOOL bPixels, BOOL bPalette);`
Description:	This method informs Direct3D that the application has changed the pixels or the palette of a Direct3D Retained-Mode texture.

continues

continued

Notes:	This method may force a reload of the texture from system memory (if the texture is stored there).
Arguments:	BOOL bPixels—If this parameter is TRUE, the pixels have changed.
	BOOL bPalette—If this parameter is TRUE, the palette has changed.
Return Type:	HRESULT
Return Values:	See Direct3D Retained-Mode Return Values.
See Also:	None

GetColors

Interface:	IDirect3DRMTexture
Declaration:	`DWORD GetColors();`
Description:	This method retrieves the maximum number of colors used in rendering a Direct3D Retained-Mode texture.
Notes:	IDirect3DRMTexture::GetColors() returns the number of colors to which the texture has been quantized, not the number of colors in the image from which the texture was created. Consequently, the number of colors returned usually matches the colors set by calling IDirect3DRM::SetDefaultTextureColors(), unless IDirect3DRMTexture::SetColors() was used explicitly to change the colors for the texture.
Arguments:	None
Return Type:	DWORD
Return Values:	Returns the number of colors. The default value is 8.
See Also:	IDirect3DRMTexture::SetColors, IDirect3DRM::SetDefaultTextureColors

GetDecalOrigin

Interface:	IDirect3DRMTexture
Declaration:	HRESULT GetDecalOrigin(LONG * lplX, LONG * lplY);
Description:	This method retrieves the current coordinates of a Direct3D Retained-Mode texture decal's origin.
Notes:	The default coordinates of a decal's origin are (0, 0).
Arguments:	LONG * lplX—The address of the variable that will be filled with the x coordinate of the decal origin.
	LONG * lplY—The address of the variable that will be filled with the y coordinate of the decal origin.
Return Type:	HRESULT
Return Values:	See Direct3D Retained-Mode Return Values.
See Also:	IDirect3DRMTexture::SetDecalOrigin

GetDecalScale

Interface:	IDirect3DRMTexture
Declaration:	DWORD GetDecalScale();
Description:	This method retrieves the scaling property of a Direct3D Retained-Mode texture decal.
Notes:	If the scaling property of a decal is TRUE, the decal is scaled according to its depth in the scene. If the scaling property of a decal is FALSE, the decal is not scaled.
Arguments:	None
Return Type:	DWORD
Return Values:	Returns the scaling factor if successful or –1 otherwise. The default value is TRUE.
See Also:	IDirect3DRMTexture::SetDecalScale

GetDecalSize

Interface:	IDirect3DRMTexture
Declaration:	`HRESULT GetDecalSize(D3DVALUE *lprvWidth, D3DVALUE *lprvHeight);`
Description:	This method retrieves the size of a Direct3D Retained-Mode texture decal.
Notes:	The size is used only if the decal is being scaled according to its depth in the scene.
Arguments:	D3DVALUE *lprvWidth—The addresses of the variable that will be filled with the width of a Direct3D Retained-Mode texture decal.
	D3DVALUE *lprvHeight—The addresses of the variable that will be filled with the height of a Direct3D Retained-Mode texture decal.
Return Type:	HRESULT
Return Values:	See Direct3D Retained-Mode Return Values.
See Also:	IDirect3DRMTexture::SetDecalSize

GetDecalTransparency

Interface:	IDirect3DRMTexture
Declaration:	`BOOL GetDecalTransparency();`
Description:	This method retrieves the transparency property of a Direct3D Retained-Mode texture decal.
Notes:	If the transparency property is TRUE, the decal has transparency and makes use of a texture's transparent color. The default transparency property is FALSE, and the default transparent color is black (0, 0, 0).
Arguments:	None
Return Type:	BOOL
Return Values:	Returns TRUE if the decal has transparency, FALSE otherwise.
See Also:	IDirect3DRMTexture::SetDecalTransparency, IDirect3DRMTexture::GetDecalTransparentColor, IDirect3DRMTexture::SetDecalTransparentColor

GetDecalTransparentColor

Interface:	IDirect3DRMTexture
Declaration:	`D3DCOLOR GetDecalTransparentColor();`
Description:	This method retrieves the transparent color of a Direct3D Retained-Mode texture decal.
Notes:	This method applies only when a decal's transparency property is TRUE. The default transparency property is FALSE.
Arguments:	None
Return Type:	D3DCOLOR
Return Values:	Returns the value of the transparent color. The default transparent color is black (0, 0, 0).
See Also:	IDirect3DRMTexture::SetDecalTransparentColor, IDirect3DRMTexture::GetDecalTransparency, IDirect3DRMTexture::SetDecalTransparency

GetImage

Interface:	IDirect3DRMTexture
Declaration:	`D3DRMIMAGE* GetImage();`
Description:	This method returns the address of the D3DRMIMAGE structure with which a Direct3D Retained-Mode texture has been created.
Notes:	D3DRMIMAGE is an outdated structure. The preferred method of representing a texture is with a DirectDraw surface.
Arguments:	None
Return Type:	D3DRMIMAGE
Return Values:	Returns a pointer to a D3DRMIMAGE structure.
See Also:	IDirect3DRM::CreateTexture

GetShades

Interface:	IDirect3DRMTexture
Declaration:	`DWORD GetShades();`
Description:	This method retrieves the maximum number of shades used for each color in a Direct3D Retained-Mode texture when rendering.
Notes:	This method applies only when using the Direct3D ramp (monochromatic) color model. The number of shades is a power of 2. The default value is 16.
Arguments:	None
Return Type:	DWORD
Return Values:	Returns the number of shades used for each color.
See Also:	IDirect3DRMTexture::SetShades, IDirect3DRMDevice::GetShades, IDirect3DRMDevice::SetShades

InitFromFile

Interface:	IDirect3DRMTexture
Declaration:	`HRESULT InitFromFile(const char *filename);`
Description:	This method initializes a Direct3D Retained-Mode texture by using information from a stored file.
Notes:	This method is only used in conjunction with IDirect3DRM::CreateObject(). IDirect3DRM::LoadTexture() encapsulates the functionality of both IDirect3DRM::CreateObject() and IDirect3DRMTexture::InitFromFile().
	The texture in the file can have 8, 24, or 32 bits-per-pixel, and it must be in either the Windows bitmap (.bmp) or Portable Pixmap (.ppm) P6 format.
Arguments:	const char *filename—The address of a string specifying the file from which initialization information is retrieved.

Return Type:	HRESULT
Return Values:	See Direct3D Retained-Mode Return Values.
See Also:	IDirect3DRM::LoadTexture, IDirect3DRMTexture::InitFromResource, IDirect3DRMTexture::InitFromSurface

InitFromResource

Interface:	IDirect3DRMTexture
Declaration:	`HRESULT InitFromResource(HRSRC rs);`
Description:	This method initializes a Direct3D Retained-Mode texture by using information from a specified resource.
Notes:	This method is only used in conjunction with IDirect3DRM::CreateObject(). IDirect3DRM::LoadTextureFromResource() encapsulates the functionality of both IDirect3DRM::CreateObject() and IDirect3DRMTexture::InitFromResource().
Arguments:	HRSRC rs—The handle of a resource from which initialization information is retrieved.
Return Type:	HRESULT
Return Values:	See Direct3D Retained-Mode Return Values.
See Also:	IDirect3DRM::LoadTextureFromResource, IDirect3DRMTexture::InitFromFile, IDirect3DRMTexture::InitFromSurface

InitFromSurface

Interface:	IDirect3DRMTexture
Declaration:	`HRESULT InitFromSurface(LPDIRECTDRAWSURFACE lpDDS);`
Description:	This method initializes a Direct3D Retained-Mode texture by using information from a DirectDraw surface.

continues

continued

Notes:	This method is only used in conjunction with IDirect3DRM::CreateObject(). IDirect3DRM::CreateTextureFromSurface() encapsulates the functionality of both IDirect3DRM::CreateObject() and IDirect3DRMTexture::InitFromSurface().
Arguments:	LPDIRECTDRAWSURFACE lpDDS—The address of a DirectDraw surface from which initialization information is drawn.
Return Type:	HRESULT
Return Values:	See Direct3D Retained-Mode Return Values.
See Also:	IDirect3DRM::CreateTextureFromSurface, IDirect3DRMTexture::InitFromFile, IDirect3DRMTexture::InitFromResource

SetColors

Interface:	IDirect3DRMTexture
Declaration:	`HRESULT SetColors(DWORD ulColors);`
Description:	This method sets the maximum number of colors used for rendering a Direct3D Retained-Mode texture.
Notes:	The argument specifies the number of colors for quantization of the Direct3D Retained-Mode texture, not the number of colors in the source image from which the texture was created.
Arguments:	DWORD ulColors—The number of colors. The default value is 8.
Return Type:	HRESULT
Return Values:	See Direct3D Retained-Mode Return Values.
See Also:	IDirect3DRMTexture::GetColors, IDirect3DRM::SetDefaultTextureColors

SetDecalOrigin

Interface:	IDirect3DRMTexture
Declaration:	`HRESULT SetDecalOrigin(LONG lX, LONG lY);`
Description:	This method sets a Direct3D Retained-Mode texture decal's origin.
Notes:	A decal's origin represents an offset from the top-left corner of the decal. The origin of a decal is used for depth-based decal scaling.
Arguments:	LONG lX—The new x coordinate of the decal origin. The default x coordinate is 0.
	LONG lY—The new y coordinate of the decal origin. The default y coordinate is 0.
Return Type:	HRESULT
Return Values:	See Direct3D Retained-Mode Return Values.
See Also:	IDirect3DRMTexture::GetDecalOrigin

SetDecalScale

Interface:	IDirect3DRMTexture
Declaration:	`HRESULT SetDecalScale(DWORD dwScale);`
Description:	This method sets the scaling property of a Direct3D Retained-Mode texture decal.
Notes:	If the scaling property of a decal is TRUE, depth is taken into account when the decal is scaled. If the scaling property is FALSE, depth information is ignored. The default value is TRUE.
Arguments:	DWORD dwScale—The new value for the decal's scaling property.
Return Type:	HRESULT
Return Values:	See Direct3D Retained-Mode Return Values.
See Also:	IDirect3DRMTexture::GetDecalScale

SetDecalSize

Interface:	IDirect3DRMTexture
Declaration:	`HRESULT SetDecalSize(D3DVALUE rvWidth, D3DVALUE rvHeight);`
Description:	This method sets the size of a Direct3D Retained-Mode texture decal.
Notes:	The size is used only if the decal is being scaled according to its depth in the scene.
Arguments:	rvWidth—The new width, in model coordinates, for the decal. The default width is 1.
	rvHeight—The new height, in model coordinates, for the decal. The default height is 1.
Return Type:	HRESULT
Return Values:	See Direct3D Retained-Mode Return Values.
See Also:	IDirect3DRMTexture::SetDecalSize

SetDecalTransparency

Interface:	IDirect3DRMTexture
Declaration:	`HRESULT SetDecalTransparency(BOOL bTransp);`
Description:	This method sets the transparency property of a Direct3D Retained-Mode texture decal.
Notes:	If the transparency property is TRUE, the decal has transparency and makes use of a texture's transparent color. The default transparency property is FALSE, and the default transparent color is black (0, 0, 0).
Arguments:	bTransp—The new transparency property for the decal.
Return Type:	HRESULT
Return Values:	See Direct3D Retained-Mode Return Values.
See Also:	IDirect3DRMTexture::GetDecalTransparency, IDirect3DRMTexture::GetDecalTransparentColor, IDirect3DRMTexture::SetDecalTransparentColor

SetDecalTransparentColor

Interface:	IDirect3DRMTexture
Declaration:	`HRESULT SetDecalTransparentColor(D3DCOLOR rcTransp);`
Description:	This method sets the transparent color for a Direct3D Retained-Mode texture decal.
Notes:	This method applies only when a decal's transparency property is TRUE. The default transparency property is FALSE, and the default transparent color is black (0, 0, 0).
Arguments:	D3DCOLOR rcTransp—The new transparent color for the decal.
Return Type:	HRESULT
Return Values:	See Direct3D Retained-Mode Return Values.
See Also:	IDirect3DRMTexture::GetDecalTransparentColor, IDirect3DRMTexture::GetDecalTransparency, IDirect3DRMTexture::SetDecalTransparency

SetShades

Interface:	IDirect3DRMTexture
Declaration:	`HRESULT SetShades(DWORD ulShades);`
Description:	This method sets the maximum number of shades to use for each color in a texture when rendering.
Notes:	This method applies only when using the Direct3D ramp (monochromatic) color model. The number of shades must be a power of 2. The default value is 16.
Arguments:	DWORD ulShades—The new number of shades. This value must be a power of 2.
Return Type:	HRESULT
Return Values:	See Direct3D Retained-Mode Return Values.
See Also:	IDirect3DRMTexture::GetShades, IDirect3DRMDevice::GetShades, IDirect3DRMDevice::SetShades

IDirect3DRMUserVisual

The IDirect3DRMUserVisual interface provides only one method (in addition to those it inherits) that initializes a user visual object. A user visual object enables application-specific visuals to be defined. Typically, an application will call IDirect3DRM::CreateUserVisual() to initialize and set up a user visual object as opposed to calling IDirect3DRM::CreateObject() to create an object and IDirect3DRMUserVisual::Init() to initialize and set up the object.

IDirect3DRMUserVisual, as with all COM interfaces, is derived from IUnknown and inherits its methods. IDirect3DRMUserVisual also inherits the methods of IDirect3DRMObject. An IDirect3DRMUserVisual object can be obtained by calling IDirect3DRM::CreateUserVisual(). IDirect3DRMUserVisual implements the following method:

   Init

Init

Interface:	IDirect3DRMUserVisual
Declaration:	`HRESULT Init(D3DRMUSERVISUALCALLBACK d3drmUVProc, void * lpArg);`
Description:	This method initializes a Direct3D Retained-Mode user visual object.
Notes:	This method is only used in conjunction with IDirect3DRM::CreateObject(). IDirect3DRM::CreateUserVisual() encapsulates the functionality of both IDirect3DRM::CreateObject() and IDirect3DRMUserVisual::Init().
Arguments:	D3DRMUSERVISUALCALLBACK d3drmUVProc—The application-defined D3DRMUSERVISUALCALLBACK callback function.
	void * lpArg—The application-defined data to be passed to the callback function.
Return Type:	HRESULT
Return Values:	See Direct3D Retained-Mode Return Values.
See Also:	IDirect3DRM::CreateUserVisual

IDirect3DRMViewport

The IDirect3DRMViewport interface enables an application to describe how a 3D scene should be mapped to a 2D viewport. Through this interface, an application can adjust the clipping planes, field of view, dimensions, projection type, scaling, and offsets of a viewport as well as set the camera and render a scene into the viewport.

IDirect3DRMViewport, as with all COM interfaces, is derived from IUnknown and inherits its methods. IDirect3DRMViewport also inherits the methods of IDirect3DRMObject. A Direct3DRMViewport object can be obtained by calling IDirect3DRM::CreateViewport(). IDirect3DRMViewport implements the following methods:

Clear	GetX
Configure	GetY
ForceUpdate	Init
GetBack	InverseTransform
GetCamera	Pick
GetDevice	Render
GetDirect3DViewport	SetBack
GetField	SetCamera
GetFront	SetField
GetHeight	SetFront
GetPlane	SetPlane
GetProjection	SetProjection
GetUniformScaling	SetUniformScaling
GetWidth	Transform

Clear

Interface:	IDirect3DRMViewport
Declaration:	`HRESULT Clear();`
Description:	This method clears a Direct3D Retained-Mode viewport to the current background color.
Notes:	None
Arguments:	None
Return Type:	HRESULT
Return Values:	See Direct3D Retained-Mode Return Values.
See Also:	None

Configure

Interface:	IDirect3DRMViewport
Declaration:	`HRESULT Configure(LONG lX, LONG lY, DWORD dwWidth, DWORD dwHeight);`
Description:	This method configures the origin and dimensions of a Direct3D Retained-Mode viewport.
Notes:	This method returns D3DRMERR_BADVALUE if lX + dwWidth or lY + dwHeight are greater than the width or height of the device, or if any of lX, lY, dwWidth, or dwHeight is less than zero.
Arguments:	LONG lX—The new x coordinate of the viewport.
	LONG lY—The new y coordinate of the viewport.
	DWORD dwWidth—The new width of the viewport.
	DWORD dwHeight—The new height of the viewport.
Return Type:	HRESULT
Return Values:	See Direct3D Retained-Mode Return Values.
See Also:	None

ForceUpdate

Interface:	IDirect3DRMViewport
Declaration:	`HRESULT ForceUpdate(DWORD dwX1, DWORD dwY1, DWORD dwX2, DWORD dwY2);`
Description:	The method forces an area of a Direct3D Retained-Mode viewport to be updated. The specified area will be copied to the screen during the next call to IDirect3DRMDevice::Update().
Notes:	The system might update any region that is larger than the specified rectangle, including possibly the entire window.
Arguments:	DWORD dwX1—The x coordinate of the upper-left corner of the area to be updated.
	DWORD dwY1—The y coordinate of the upper-left corner of the area to be updated.
	DWORD dwX2—The x coordinate of the lower-right corner of the area to be updated.
	DWORD dwY2—The y coordinate of the lower-right corner of the area to be updated.
Return Type:	HRESULT
Return Values:	See Direct3D Retained-Mode Return Values.
See Also:	IDirect3DRMDevice::Update

GetBack

Interface:	IDirect3DRMViewport
Declaration:	`D3DVALUE GetBack();`
Description:	This method retrieves the position of the back clipping plane for a Direct3D Retained-Mode viewport.
Notes:	The position of the back clipping plane is represented by the z coordinate of the plane (relative to the camera).

continues

continued

Arguments:	None
Return Type:	D3DVALUE
Return Values:	Returns the z coordinate representing the position of the back clipping plane. The default value is 100.
See Also:	IDirect3DRMViewport::SetBack, IDirect3DRMViewport::GetFront, IDirect3DRMViewport::SetFront

GetCamera

Interface:	IDirect3DRMViewport
Declaration:	`HRESULT GetCamera(LPDIRECT3DRMFRAME *lpCamera);`
Description:	This method retrieves the viewport's current camera frame.
Notes:	None.
Arguments:	LPDIRECT3DRMFRAME *lpCamera—The pointer to the Direct3DRMFrame object representing the camera.
Return Type:	HRESULT
Return Values:	See Direct3D Retained-Mode Return Values.
See Also:	IDirect3DRMViewport::SetCamera, IDirect3DRMFrame::LookAt

GetDevice

Interface:	IDirect3DRMViewport
Declaration:	`HRESULT GetDevice(LPDIRECT3DRMDEVICE *lpD3DRMDevice);`
Description:	This method retrieves the Direct3D Retained-Mode device associated with a Direct3D Retained-Mode viewport.
Notes:	Viewports are associated with a device when created.
Arguments:	LPDIRECT3DRMDEVICE *lpD3DRMDevice—The pointer that will point to the associated device if the call is successful.
Return Type:	HRESULT

Return Values:	See Direct3D Retained-Mode Return Values.
See Also:	None

GetDirect3DViewport

Interface:	IDirect3DRMViewport
Declaration:	`HRESULT GetDirect3DViewport(LPDIRECT3DVIEWPORT* lplpD3DViewport);`
Description:	This method retrieves the Direct3D Immediate-Mode viewport corresponding to a Direct3D Retained-Mode viewport.
Notes:	This method can be used in conjunction with a user visual to gain added functionality. For example, a Retained-Mode application could create an Immediate-Mode user visual that rendered execute buffers. The execute buffers must be rendered into an Immediate-Mode viewport.
Arguments:	LPDIRECT3DVIEWPORT* lplpD3DViewport—The address of a pointer that is initialized with a pointer to the Direct3D Immediate-Mode viewport.
Return Type:	HRESULT
Return Values:	See Direct3D Retained-Mode Return Values.
See Also:	None

GetField

Interface:	IDirect3DRMViewport
Declaration:	`D3DVALUE GetField();`
Description:	This method retrieves the field of view for a Direct3D Retained-Mode viewport.
Notes:	The field of view is an angle of view, defined by the following equation: $A = 2 \times \arctan(h / D)$

continues

continued

	where A is the angle of view, in radians, h is half the height of the front clipping plane, and D is the distance from the camera to the clipping plane.
	The default value is 0.5.
Arguments:	None
Return Type:	D3DVALUE
Return Values:	Returns the field of view of a viewport. The default value is 0.5.
See Also:	IDirect3DRMViewport::SetField

GetFront

Interface:	IDirect3DRMViewport
Declaration:	`D3DVALUE GetFront();`
Description:	This method retrieves the position of the front clipping plane for a Direct3D Retained-Mode viewport.
Notes:	The camera looks toward positive z from the origin in camera coordinates, with positive y up. The clipping plane is always normal to this z-axis, GetFront() returns the distance along the z-axis from the camera to the clipping plane.
Arguments:	None
Return Type:	D3DVALUE
Return Values:	Returns the position of the front clipping plane. The default value is 1.0
See Also:	IDirect3DRMViewport::SetFront, IDirect3DRMViewport::GetBack, IDirect3DRMViewport::SetBack

GetHeight

Interface:	IDirect3DRMViewport
Declaration:	`DWORD GetHeight();`
Description:	This method retrieves the height, in pixels, of the viewport.

Notes:	The height of the viewport is set when the viewport is created. To change the height of a viewport, the viewport must be destroyed and re-created with the new height.
Arguments:	None
Return Type:	DWORD
Return Values:	Returns the height of the viewport.
See Also:	IDirect3DRMViewport::GetWidth

GetPlane

Interface:	IDirect3DRMViewport
Declaration:	HRESULT GetPlane(D3DVALUE *lpd3dvLeft, D3DVALUE *lpd3dvRight, D3DVALUE *lpd3dvBottom, D3DVALUE *lpd3dvTop);
Description:	This method retrieves the dimensions, relative to the camera's z-axis, of a Direct3D Retained-Mode viewport on the front clipping plane.
Notes:	Setting the values for the viewport plane enables a viewport of arbitrary proportion and position.
Arguments:	D3DVALUE *lpd3dvLeft—The pointer to the variable that will contain minimum x coordinate of the left of the viewport.
	D3DVALUE *lpd3dvRight—The pointer to the variable that will contain maximum x coordinate of the right of the viewport.
	D3DVALUE *lpd3dvBottom—The pointer to the variable that will contain minimum y coordinate of the bottom of the viewport.
	D3DVALUE *lpd3dvTop—The pointer to the variable that will contain maximum y coordinate of the top of the viewport.
Return Type:	HRESULT
Return Values:	See Direct3D Retained-Mode Return Values.
See Also:	IDirect3DRMViewport::SetPlane

GetProjection

Interface:	IDirect3DRMViewport
Declaration:	`D3DRMPROJECTIONTYPE GetProjection();`
Description:	This method retrieves the viewport's projection type.
Notes:	A viewport can use either orthographic or perspective projection. Perspective projection means that objects are smaller the farther from the camera they are. Orthographic projection means that objects do not change in scale the farther from the camera they are. Perspective projection is the default value.
Arguments:	None
Return Type:	D3DRMPROJECTIONTYPE
Return Values:	D3DRMPROJECT_PERSPECTIVE—The viewport is using a perspective projection. D3DRMPROJECT_ORTHOGRAPHIC—The viewport is using an orthographic projection.
See Also:	IDirect3DRMViewport::SetProjection

GetUniformScaling

Interface:	IDirect3DRMViewport
Declaration:	`BOOL GetUniformScaling();`
Description:	This method retrieves the scaling property for scaling the viewing volume into the larger dimension of the window.
Notes:	If the scaling property of a viewport is TRUE, the same horizontal and vertical scaling factor is used to scale the viewing volume. Otherwise, different scaling factors are used to scale the viewing volume exactly into the window. For square viewports, the scaling property is usually set to TRUE. For non-square viewports, the scaling property is usually set to FALSE.

Arguments:	None
Return Type:	BOOL
Return Values:	Returns TRUE if the viewport scales uniformly or FALSE otherwise. The default setting is TRUE.
See Also:	IDirect3DViewport::SetUniformScaling

GetWidth

Interface:	IDirect3DRMViewport
Declaration:	`DWORD GetWidth();`
Description:	This method retrieves the width, in pixels, of the viewport.
Notes:	The width of the viewport is set when the viewport is created. To change the width of a viewport, the viewport must be destroyed and re-created with the new width.
Arguments:	None
Return Type:	DWORD
Return Values:	Returns the width of the viewport.
See Also:	IDirect3DRMViewport::GetHeight

GetX

Interface:	IDirect3DRMViewport
Declaration:	`LONG GetX();`
Description:	This method retrieves the x-offset of the start of a Direct3D Retained-Mode viewport on a Direct3D Retained-Mode device.
Notes:	The x-offset of the viewport is set when the viewport is created. To change the x-offset of a viewport, the viewport must be destroyed and re-created with the new x-offset.
Arguments:	None

continues

continued

Return Type:	LONG
Return Values:	Returns the x-offset of the start of a viewport on a device.
See Also:	IDirect3DRMViewport::GetY

GetY

Interface:	IDirect3DRMViewport
Declaration:	`LONG GetY();`
Description:	This method retrieves the y-offset of the start of a Direct3D Retained-Mode viewport on a Direct3D Retained-Mode device.
Notes:	The y-offset of the viewport is set when the viewport is created. To change the y-offset of a viewport, the viewport must be destroyed and re-created with the new y-offset.
Arguments:	None
Return Type:	LONG
Return Values:	Returns the y-offset of the start of a viewport on a device.
See Also:	IDirect3DRMViewport::GetX

Init

Interface:	IDirect3DRMViewport
Declaration:	`HRESULT Init(LPDIRECT3DRMDEVICE lpD3DRMDevice, LPDIRECT3DRMFRAME lpD3DRMFrameCamera, DWORD xpos, DWORD ypos, DWORD width, DWORD height);`
Description:	This method initializes a Direct3D Retained-Mode viewport object.
Notes:	This method is only used in conjunction with IDirect3DRM::CreateObject(). IDirect3DRM::CreateViewport() encapsulates the functionality of both IDirect3DRM::CreateObject() and IDirect3DRMViewport::Init().

Arguments:	LPDIRECT3DRMDEVICE lpD3DRMDevice—The address of the Direct3D Retained-Mode device associated with this viewport.
	LPDIRECT3DRMFRAME lpD3DRMFrameCamera—The address of the camera frame associated with this viewport.
	DWORD xpos—The x coordinate of the upper-left corner of the viewport.
	DWORD ypos—The y coordinate of the upper-left corner of the viewport.
	DWORD width—The width of the viewport.
	DWORD height—The height of the viewport.
Return Type:	HRESULT
Return Values:	See Direct3D Retained-Mode Return Values.
See Also:	IDirect3DRM::CreateViewport

InverseTransform

Interface:	IDirect3DRMViewport
Declaration:	`HRESULT InverseTransform(D3DVECTOR* lprvDst, D3DRMVECTOR4D* lprvSrc);`
Description:	This method transforms a vector in homogenous screen coordinates to world coordinates.
Notes:	None
Arguments:	D3DVECTOR* lprvDst—The address of a D3DVECTOR structure to be filled with the resultant vector in world coordinates.
	D3DRMVECTOR4D* lprvSrc—The address of a D3DRMVECTOR4D structure containing the source vector.
Return Type:	HRESULT
Return Values:	See Direct3D Retained-Mode Return Values.
See Also:	IDirect3DViewport::Transform

Pick

Interface:	IDirect3DRMViewport
Declaration:	HRESULT Pick(LONG lX, LONG lY, LPDIRECT3DRMPICKEDARRAY* lplpVisuals);
Description:	This method selects an object in a scene through the use of screen coordinates.
Notes:	If the screen coordinates represented by the lX and lY arguments are within an object's rendered viewport representation, the scene hierarchy containing the object is placed into the picked array argument, with the root of the scene in the first picked array element, and the object's frame in the last.
Arguments:	LONG lX—The x-coordinate of pick location.
	LONG lY – The y-coordinate of pick location.
	LPDIRECT3DRMPICKEDARRAY* lplpVisuals—The pointer to the variable that will contain a valid Direct3D Retained-Mode picked array, if the call succeeds.
Return Type:	HRESULT
Return Values:	See Direct3D Retained-Mode Return Values.
See Also:	IDirect3DRMPickArray::GetPick

Render

Interface:	IDirect3DRMViewport
Declaration:	HRESULT Render(LPDIRECT3DRMFRAME lpD3DRMFrame);
Description:	Renders a frame hierarchy to the given viewport.
Notes:	All visuals in the frame and the frame's children are rendered.
Arguments:	LPDIRECT3DRMFRAME lpD3DRMFrame—The pointer to the Direct3D Retained-Mode frame at the top of the hierarchy to be rendered.

Return Type: HRESULT
Return Values: See Direct3D Retained-Mode Return Values.
See Also: None

SetBack

Interface:	IDirect3DRMViewport
Declaration:	`HRESULT SetBack(D3DVALUE rvBack);`
Description:	This method sets the distance of the back clipping plane from the camera for a Direct3D Retained-Mode viewport.
Notes:	The distance of the back clipping plane is computed along the camera frame's positive z-axis. The default value is 100.
Arguments:	D3DVALUE rvBack—The new position of the back clipping plane.
Return Type:	HRESULT
Return Values:	See Direct3D Retained-Mode Return Values.
See Also:	IDirect3DRMViewport::GetBack, IDirect3DRMViewport::GetFront, IDirect3DRMViewport::SetFront

SetCamera

Interface:	IDirect3DRMViewport
Declaration:	`HRESULT SetCamera(LPDIRECT3DRMFRAME lpCamera);`
Description:	This method sets the current camera from the viewport.
Notes:	The viewport sets the camera to the specified frame's location and orientation. This causes a recomputation of the view matrix.
Arguments:	LPDIRECT3DRMFRAME lpCamera—The pointer to a Direct3D Retained-Mode frame that represents the camera.
Return Type:	HRESULT
Return Values:	See Direct3D Retained-Mode Return Values.
See Also:	IDirect3DRMViewport::GetCamera

SetField

Interface:	IDirect3DRMViewport
Declaration:	`HRESULT SetField(D3DVALUE rvField);`
Description:	This method sets the field of view for a Direct3D Retained-Mode viewport.
Notes:	The field of view is an angle of view, defined by the following equation:

$$A = 2 \times \arctan (h / D)$$

where A is the angle of view, in radians, h is half the height of the front clipping plane, and D is the distance from the camera to the clipping plane.

The default value is 0.5.

Arguments:	D3DVALUE rvField—The new field of view. This value must be greater than zero.
Return Type:	HRESULT
Return Values:	See Direct3D Retained-Mode Return Values.
See Also:	IDirect3DRMViewport::SetField

SetFront

Interface:	IDirect3DRMViewport
Declaration:	`HRESULT SetFront(D3DVALUE rvFront);`
Description:	This method sets the distance from the camera of the front clipping plane for a Direct3D Retained-Mode viewport.
Notes:	The distance of the front clipping plane is computed along the camera frame's positive z-axis. The default value is 1.0.
Arguments:	D3DVALUE rvFront—The new position of the front clipping plane.
Return Type:	HRESULT

Return Values: See Direct3D Retained-Mode Return Values.
See Also: IDirect3DRMViewport::GetFront, IDirect3DRMViewport::GetBack, IDirect3DRMViewport::SetBack

SetPlane

Interface: IDirect3DRMViewport

Declaration: HRESULT SetPlane(D3DVALUE rvLeft, D3DVALUE rvRight, D3DVALUE rvBottom, D3DVALUE rvTop);

Description: This method sets the dimensions, relative to the camera's z-axis, of a Direct3D Retained-Mode viewport on the front clipping plane.

Notes: Setting the values for the viewport plane enables a viewport of arbitrary proportion and position.

Arguments: D3DVALUE rvLeft—The minimum x coordinate of the left of the viewport.

D3DVALUE rvRight—The maximum x coordinate of the right of the viewport.

D3DVALUE rvBottom—The minimum y coordinate of bottom of the viewport.

D3DVALUE rvTop—The maximum y coordinate of the of the viewport.

Return Type: HRESULT

Return Values: See Direct3D Retained-Mode Return Values

See Also: IDirect3DRMViewport::GetPlane

SetProjection

Interface:	IDirect3DRMViewport
Declaration:	`HRESULT SetProjection(D3DRMPROJECTIONTYPE rptType);`
Description:	This method sets the projection type for a Direct3D Retained-Mode viewport.
Notes:	A viewport can use either orthographic or perspective projection. Perspective projection means that objects are smaller the farther from the camera they are. Orthographic projection means that objects do not change in scale the farther from the camera they are. Perspective projection is the default value.
Arguments:	D3DRMPROJECTIONTYPE rptType—One of the members of the D3DRMPROJECTIONTYPE enumerated type (D3DRMPROJECT_PERSPECTIVE or D3DRMPROJECT_ORTHOGRAPHIC).
Return Type:	HRESULT
Return Values:	See Direct3D Retained-Mode Return Values.
See Also:	IDirect3DRMViewport::GetProjection

SetUniformScaling

Interface:	IDirect3DRMViewport
Declaration:	`HRESULT SetUniformScaling(BOOL bScale);`
Description:	This method sets the scaling property for scaling the viewing volume into the larger dimension of the window.
Notes:	If the scaling property of a viewport is TRUE, the same horizontal and vertical scaling factor is used to scale the viewing volume. Otherwise, different scaling factors are used to scale the viewing volume exactly into the window. The default setting is TRUE.

For square viewports, the scaling property is usually set to TRUE. For non-square viewports, the scaling property is usually set to FALSE.

Arguments: BOOL bScale—The new scaling property.
Return Type: HRESULT
Return Values: See Direct3D Retained-Mode Return Values.
See Also: IDirect3DViewport::GetUniformScaling

Transform

Interface: IDirect3DRMViewport
Declaration: `HRESULT Transform(D3DRMVECTOR4D * lprvDst, D3DVECTOR * lprvSrc);`
Description: This method transforms a vector in world coordinates to homogeneous screen coordinates.
Notes: The result of the transformation is a four-element homogeneous vector. The point represented by the resulting vector is visible if the following equations are true:

$$w \times x_{min} <= x < w \times x_{max}$$

$$w \times y_{min} <= y < w \times y_{max}$$

$$0 <= z < w$$

where:

$$x_{min} = viewport_x - (viewport_{width} / 2)$$

$$x_{max} = viewport_x + (viewport_{width} / 2)$$

$$y_{min} = viewport_y - (viewport_{height} / 2)$$

$$y_{max} = viewport_y + (viewport_{height} / 2)$$

Arguments: D3DRMVECTOR4D * lprvDst—The address of a D3DRMVECTOR4D structure to be filled with the resultant vector in screen coordinates.

continues

continued

                D3DVECTOR * lprvSrc—The address of a D3DVECTOR structure containing the source vector.

Return Type: HRESULT

Return Values: See Direct3D Retained-Mode Return Values.

See Also: IDirect3DViewport::InverseTransform

IDirect3DRMwinDevice

The IDirect3DRMWinDevice interface implements two methods that enable a Direct3D Retained-Mode application to respond to the Windows WM_PAINT and WM_ACTIVATE messages.

IDirect3DRMWinDevice, as with all COM interfaces, is derived from IUnknown and inherits its methods. An IDirect3DRMWinDevice object can be obtained by calling IDirect3DRM::CreateWinDevice(). IDirect3DRMWinDevice implements the following methods:

HandleActivate

HandlePaint

HandleActivate

Interface:	IDirect3DRMWinDevice
Declaration:	`HRESULT HandleActivate(WORD wParam);`
Description:	This method informs Direct3D that the application has received a WM_ACTIVATE message.
Notes:	This ensures that the colors are correct in the active rendering window.
Arguments:	WORD wParam—The wParam parameter passed to the message-processing procedure with the WM_ACTIVATE message.
Return Type:	HRESULT
Return Values:	See Direct3D Retained-Mode Return Values.
See Also:	None

HandlePaint

Interface:	IDirect3DRMWinDevice
Declaration:	`HRESULT HandlePaint(HDC hDC);`
Description:	This method informs Direct3D that the application has received a WM_PAINT message.
Notes:	The hDC argument should be taken from the PAINTSTRUCT structure given to the Windows BeginPaint function. BeginPaint should be called to obtain the handle of the Windows device context to be used as the argument to HandlePaint. Each call to BeginPaint must have a matching call to EndPaint.
Arguments:	hDC—The handle of the Windows device context to repaint.
Return Type:	HRESULT
Return Values:	See Direct3D Retained-Mode Return Values.
See Also:	None

IDirect3DRMWrap

The IDirect3DRMWrap interface provides functionality for generating the texture coordinates of a set of vertices from a wrap object previous created with IDirect3DRM::CreateWrap().

IDirect3DRMWrap, as with all COM interfaces, is derived from IUnknown and inherits its methods. A Direct3DRMWrap object can be obtained by calling IDirect3DRM::CreateWrap(). IDirect3DRMWrap implements the following methods:

Apply

ApplyRelative

Init

Apply

Interface:	IDirect3DRMWrap
Declaration:	`HRESULT Apply(LPDIRECT3DRMOBJECT lpObject);`
Description:	This method applies a Direct3D Retained-Mode wrap to a Direct3D Retained-Mode object.
Notes:	The destination object is typically a face or a mesh.
Arguments:	LPDIRECT3DRMOBJECT lpObject—The address of the destination object.
Return Type:	HRESULT
Return Values:	See Direct3D Retained-Mode Return Values.
See Also:	IDirect3DRMWrap::ApplyRelative

ApplyRelative

Interface:	IDirect3DRMWrap
Declaration:	`HRESULT ApplyRelative(LPDIRECT3DRMFRAME frame, LPDIRECT3DRMOBJECT mesh);`
Description:	This method applies a Direct3D Retained-Mode wrap to the vertices of a Direct3D Retained-Mode object, first transforming each vertex by a Direct3D Retained-Mode frame's world transformation, and the inverse world transformation of the wrap's reference frame.
Notes:	None
Arguments:	LPDIRECT3DRMFRAME lpFrame—The Direct3D frame used for transforming vertices of the destination object before applying wrap.
	LPDIRECT3DRMOBJECT mesh—The address of the destination object.
Return Type:	HRESULT
Return Values:	See Direct3D Retained-Mode Return Values.
See Also:	IDirect3DRMWrap::Apply

Init

Interface:	IDirect3DRMWrap
Declaration:	`HRESULT Init(D3DRMWRAPTYPE d3drmwt, LPDIRECT3DRMFRAME lpd3drmfRef, D3DVALUE ox, D3DVALUE oy, D3DVALUE oz, D3DVALUE dx, D3DVALUE dy, D3DVALUE dz, D3DVALUE ux, D3DVALUE uy, D3DVALUE uz, D3DVALUE ou, D3DVALUE ov, D3DVALUE su, D3DVALUE sv);`
Description:	This method initializes a Direct3D Retained-Mode wrap object.
Notes:	This method is only used in conjunction with IDirect3DRM::CreateObject(). IDirect3DRM::CreateWrap() encapsulates the functionality of both IDirect3DRM::CreateObject() and IDirect3DRMWrap::Init().

Arguments:	D3DRMWRAPTYPE d3drmwt—One of the members of the D3DRMWRAPTYPE enumerated type (D3DRMWRAP_FLAT, D3DRMWRAP_CYLINDER, D3DRMWRAP_SPHERE, or D3DRMWRAP_CHROME).
	LPDIRECT3DRMFRAME lpd3drmfRef—The pointer to a Direct3D frame representing the reference frame for this wrap object.
	D3DVALUE ox—The x coordinate of the origin of the wrap.
	D3DVALUE oy—The y coordinate of the origin of the wrap.
	D3DVALUE oz—The z coordinate of the origin of the wrap.
	D3DVALUE dx—The x coordinate of the z-axis of the wrap.
	D3DVALUE dy—The y coordinate of the z-axis of the wrap.
	D3DVALUE dz—The z coordinate of the z-axis of the wrap.
	D3DVALUE ux—The x coordinate of the y-axis of the wrap.
	D3DVALUE uy—The y coordinate of the y-axis of the wrap.
	D3DVALUE uz—The z coordinate of the y-axis of the wrap.
	D3DVALUE ou—The u coordinate of the origin in the texture.
	D3DVALUE ov—The v coordinate of the origin in the texture.
	D3DVALUE su—The u coordinate scale factor in the texture.
	D3DVALUE sv—The v coordinate scale factor in the texture.
Return Type:	HRESULT
Return Values:	See Direct3D Retained-Mode Return Values.
See Also:	IDirect3DRM::CreateWrap

Retained-Mode Structures

D3DRMBOX

Definition:
```
typedef struct _D3DRMBOX
{
    D3DVECTOR min, max;
} D3DRMBOX;
typedef D3DRMBOX *LPD3DRMBOX;
```

Description: This structure defines the bounding box retrieved by the IDirect3DRMMesh::GetBox() and IDirect3DRMMeshBuilder::GetBox() functions. The two Direct3D vectors define the box.

Members: D3DVECTOR min—Vector to the minimum x-, y-, and z- coordinates of the box.

D3DVECTOR max—Vector to the maximum x-, y-, and z- coordinates of the box.

See Also: IDirect3DRMMesh::GetBox, IDirect3DRMMeshBuilder::GetBox

D3DRMIMAGE

Definition:
```
typedef struct _D3DRMIMAGE
{
    int width, height;
    int aspectx, aspecty;
    int depth;
    int rgb;
    int bytes_per_line;
    void* buffer1;
    void* buffer2;
    unsigned long red_mask;
    unsigned long green_mask;
    unsigned long blue_mask;
    unsigned long alpha_mask;
```

continues

continued

```
            int palette_size;
            D3DRMPALETTEENTRY* palette;
    } D3DRMIMAGE;
    typedef D3DRMIMAGE, *LPD3DRMIMAGE;
```

Description: This structure describes an image that is attached to a texture. This structure is provided for backward compatibility with Reality Lab. Under Direct3D, IDirectDrawSurface is the preferred means of representing the image attached to a texture.

Members: int width—Width of the image, in pixels.

int height—Height of the image, in pixels.

int aspectx—X-Aspect ratio for non-square pixels.

int aspecty—Y-Aspect ratio for non-square pixels.

int depth—Bits per pixel.

int rgb—If this member is FALSE, pixels are indices into a palette. Otherwise, pixels encode RGB values.

int bytes_per_line—Number of bytes of memory for a scanline. This value must be a multiple of four.

void* buffer1—Buffer in which to render (first buffer for double buffering).

void* buffer2—Second rendering buffer for double buffering. Set this member to NULL for single buffering.

unsigned long red_mask, green_mask, blue_mask, and alpha_mask—If rgb is TRUE, these members are masks for the red, green, and blue parts of a pixel. Otherwise, they are masks for the significant bits of the red, green, and blue elements in the palette. For example, most SVGA displays use 64 intensities of red, green, and blue, so the masks should all be set to 0xfc.

int palette_size—Number of entries in the palette.

D3DRMPALETTEENTRY* palette—If rgb is FALSE, this member is the address of a D3DRMPALETTEENTRY structure describing the palette entry.

See Also: IDirect3DRM::CreateTexture, IDirect3DRMTexture::GetImage, D3DRMPALETTEENTRY

D3DRMLOADMEMORY

Definition:
```
typedef struct _D3DRMLOADMEMORY
{
    LPVOID lpMemory;
    DWORD dSize;
} D3DRMLOADMEMORY, *LPD3DRMLOADMEMORY;
```

Description: This structure identifies the location and size of the block of memory to be loaded when an application calls one of the Load functions and specifies D3DRMLOAD_FROMMEMORY.

Members: LPVOID lpMemory—The address of a block of memory to be loaded.

DWORD dSize—The size, in bytes, of the block of memory to be loaded.

See Also: IDirect3DRM::Load, IDirect3DRMAnimationSet::Load, IDirect3DRMFrame::Load, IDirect3DRMMeshBuilder::Load, D3DRMLOADOPTIONS

D3DRMLOADRESOURCE

Definition:
```
typedef struct _D3DRMLOADRESOURCE
{
    HMODULE hModule;
    LPCTSTR lpName;
    LPCTSTR lpType;
} D3DRMLOADRESOURCE, *LPD3DRMLOADRESOURCE;
```

Description: This structure identifies the module, name, and type of resource to be loaded when an application calls one of the Retained-Mode Load functions and specifies D3DRMLOAD_FROMRESOURCE.

If the high-order word of the lpName or lpType member is zero, the low-order word specifies the integer identifier of the name or type of the given resource. Otherwise, those parameters are long pointers to NULL-terminated strings. If the first character of the string is a pound sign (#), the remaining characters represent a decimal number that specifies the integer identifier of the resource's name or type. For example, the string "#258" represents the integer identifier 258.

continues

continued	An application should reduce the amount of memory required for the resources by referring to them by integer identifier rather than by name.
	When an application calls a Load function and specifies D3DRMLOAD_FROMRESOURCE, it does not need to find or unlock any resources; the system handles this automatically.
Members:	HMODULE hModule—The handle of the module containing the resource to be loaded. If this member is NULL, the resource must be attached to the calling executable file.
	LPCTSTR lpName—The name of the resource to be loaded. If the resource is a mesh, for example, this member should specify the name of the mesh file.
	LPCTSTR lpType—The user-defined type identifying the resource.
See Also:	IDirect3DRM::Load, IDirect3DRMAnimationSet::Load, IDirect3DRMFrame::Load, IDirect3DRMMeshBuilder::Load, D3DRMLOADOPTIONS

D3DRMPALETTEENTRY

| **Definition:** | ```
typedef struct _D3DRMPALETTEENTRY
{
    unsigned char red;
    unsigned char green;
    unsigned char blue;
    unsigned char flags;
} D3DRMPALETTEENTRY;
``` |
	`typedef D3DRMPALETTEENTRY *LPD3DRMPALETTEENTRY;`
Description:	This structure describes an entry in the color palette used by a D3DRMIMAGE structure. These palette entries are used only if the rgb member of the D3DRMIMAGE structure is FALSE. If the rgb member is TRUE, red, green, and blue component values are used to describe colors, and no palette is needed.
	The flags member specifies whether the particular palette entry is unused (D3DRMPALETTE_FREE), whether the entry may have other
```

colors mapped to it by Direct3D (D3DRMPALETTE_READONLY), or may not be used at all by Direct3D (D3DRMPALETTE_RESERVED). D3DRMPALETTE_RESERVED is required if the particular palette entry is to be animated.

Members: unsigned red—Red color component of this palette entry. This value should be in the range of 0–255.

unsigned green—Green color component of this palette entry. This value should be in the range of 0–255.

unsigned blue—Blue color component of this palette entry. This value should be in the range of 0–255.

flags—The value defining how this palette entry may be used by the renderer. This value is one of the members of the D3DRMPALETTEFLAGS enumerated type:

D3DRMPALETTE_FREE

D3DRMPALETTE_READONLY

D3DRMPALETTE_RESERVED

See Also: IDirect3DRM::CreateTexture, IDirect3DRMTexture::GetImage, D3DRMIMAGE, D3DRMPALETTEFLAGS

D3DRMPICKDESC

Definition:
```
typedef struct _D3DRMPICKDESC
{
    ULONG ulFaceIdx;
    LONG lGroupIdx;
    D3DVECTOR vPosition;
} D3DRMPICKDESC, *LPD3DRMPICKDESC;
```

Description: This structure contains the pick position, face, and group identifiers of the Direct3D objects retrieved by IDirect3DRMPickedArray::GetPick().

Members: ULONG ulFaceIdx—The face index of the retrieved Direct3D object.

LONG lGroupIdx—The group index of the retrieved Direct3D object.

continues

continued

	D3DVECTOR vPosition—The value describing the position of the retrieved Direct3D object. This value is a D3DVECTOR structure.
See Also:	IDirect3DRMPickedArray::GetPick()

D3DRMQUATERNION

| **Definition:** | ```
typedef struct _D3DRMQUATERNION
{
    D3DVALUE s;
    D3DVECTOR v;
} D3DRMQUATERNION, *LPD3DRMQUATERNION;
``` |
Description:	This structure describes the rotation used by IDirect3DRMAnimation::AddRotateKey(). It is also used in several of Direct3D's quaternion functions.
	A *quaternion* consists of a D3DVECTOR that describes an axis around which rotation is to occur and a D3DVALUE that specifies the amount, in radians, to rotate around the axis.
	A quaternion is the most compact way to represent an arbitrary rotation in three dimensions. It is also a convenient representation in which to interpolate between orientations in an animation.
Members:	D3DVALUE s—Amount of rotation around the axis of rotation, in radians.
	D3DVECTOR v—Vector specifying the axis around which to rotate.
See Also:	D3DRMMatrixFromQuaternion, D3DRMQuaternionFromRotation, D3DRMQuaternionMultiply, D3DRMQuaternionSlerp, IDirect3DRMAnimation::AddRotateKey

D3DRMVECTOR4D

| **Definition:** | ```
typedef struct _D3DRMVECTOR4D
{
``` |

```
            D3DVALUE x;
            D3DVALUE y;
            D3DVALUE z;
            D3DVALUE w;
    } D3DRMVECTOR4D, *LPD3DRMVECTOR4D;
```

Description: This structure defines a four-dimensional vector suitable for holding the homogeneous coordinates produced by a call to IDirect3DRMViewport::Transform() or IDirect3DRMViewport::InverseTransform().

Members: D3DVALUE x—X-coordinate of the homogeneous vector.

D3DVALUE y—Y-coordinate of the homogeneous vector.

D3DVALUE z—Z-coordinate of the homogeneous vector.

D3DVALUE w—W-coordinate of the homogeneous vector.

See Also: IDirect3DRMViewport::InverseTransform, IDirect3DRMViewport::Transform

D3DRMVERTEX

Definition:
```
typedef struct _D3DRMVERTEX
{
    D3DVECTOR position;
    D3DVECTOR normal;
    D3DVALUE tu, tv;
    D3DCOLOR color;
} D3DRMVERTEX;
```

Description: This structure describes a vertex in a Direct3D mesh object.

Members: D3DVECTOR position—Position of the vertex in model coordinates.

D3DVECTOR normal—The normal vector for the vertex.

D3DVALUE tu—The horizontal texture coordinate for the vertex.

D3DVALUE tv—The vertical texture coordinate for the vertex.

D3DCOLOR color—The vertex color. If the alpha component is zero, the vertex may be completely transparent.

See Also: IDirect3DRMMesh::GetVertices, IDirect3DRMMesh::SetVertices

Retained-Mode Enumerated and Other Types

D3DRCOLORSOURCE

Definition:
```
typedef enum _D3DRMCOLORSOURCE
{
    D3DRMCOLOR_FROMFACE,
    D3DRMCOLOR_FROMVERTEX
} D3DRMCOLORSOURCE;
```

Description: This enumerated type describes the color source of a Direct3D mesh builder object. You can set the color source by using IDirect3DRMMeshBuilder::SetColorSource(). To retrieve it, use IDirect3DRMMeshBuilder::GetColorSource().

Members: D3DRMCOLOR_FROMFACE—The object's color source is a face.

D3DRMCOLOR_FROMVERTEX—The object's color source is a vertex.

See Also: IDirect3DRMMeshBuilder::GetColorSource, IDirect3DRMMeshBuilder::SetColorSource

D3DRMCOMBINETYPE

Definition:
```
typedef enum _D3DRMCOMBINETYPE
{
    D3DRMCOMBINE_REPLACE,
    D3DRMCOMBINE_BEFORE,
    D3DRMCOMBINE_AFTER
} D3DRMCOMBINETYPE;
```

continues

continued

Description:	This enumerated type specifies how to combine two transforms when setting a frame object's position, orientation, scale, ±r general transform. The order in which transforms are composed is important because composition is not commutative.
Members:	D3DRMCOMBINE_REPLACE—The supplied transform replaces the frame's current transform.
	D3DRMCOMBINE_BEFORE—The supplied transform is composed with the frame's current transform and precedes the current transform in the composition.
	D3DRMCOMBINE_AFTER—The supplied transform is composed with the frame's current transform and follows the current transform in the composition.
See Also:	IDirect3DRMFrame::AddRotation, IDirect3DRMFrame::AddScale, IDirect3DRMFrame::AddTransform, IDirect3DRMFrame::AddTranslation

D3DRMFILLMODE

| **Definition:** | ```
typedef enum _D3DRMFILLMODE
{
    D3DRMFILL_POINTS = 0 * D3DRMLIGHT_MAX,
    D3DRMFILL_WIREFRAME = 1 * D3DRMLIGHT_MAX,
    D3DRMFILL_SOLID = 2 * D3DRMLIGHT_MAX,
    D3DRMFILL_MASK = 7 * D3DRMLIGHT_MAX,
    D3DRMFILL_MAX = 8 * D3DRMLIGHT_MAX
} D3DRMFILLMODE;
``` |
Description:	This enumerated type is used to help define the D3DRMRENDERQUALITY enumerated type. These values can be used independently for setting or retrieving the rendering quality of a device.
Members:	D3DRMFILL_POINTS—Fills points only, minimum fill mode.
	D3DRMFILL_WIREFRAME—Fill wireframes.
	D3DRMFILL_SOLID—Fill solid objects.
```

	D3DRMFILL_MASK—Fill using a mask.
	D3DRMFILL_MAX—Maximum value for fill mode.
See Also:	IDirect3DRMDevice::GetQuality, IDirect3DRMDevice::SetQuality, IDirect3DRMMesh::GetGroupQuality, IDirect3DRMMesh::SetGroupQuality, IDirect3DRMMeshBuilder::GetQuality, IDirect3DRMMeshBuilder::SetQuality, D3DRMSHADEMODE, D3DRMLIGHTMODE, D3DRMRENDERQUALITY

D3DRMFOGMODE

Definition:
```
typedef enum _D3DRMFOGMODE
{
    D3DRMFOG_LINEAR,
    D3DRMFOG_EXPONENTIAL,
    D3DRMFOG_EXPONENTIALSQUARED
} D3DRMFOGMODE;
```

Description: This enumerated type contains the values that describe the method in which the fog effect intensifies with increasing distance from the camera. Note that fog can be considered a measure of visibility; the lower the fog value produced by one of the fog equations, the less visible an object is. You can specify the fog's density and start and end points by using IDirect3DRMFrame::SetSceneFogParams().

In the formulas for the exponential fog modes, e is the base of the natural logarithms; its value is approximately 2.71828. Direct3D only supports the linear fog model, however.

Members: D3DRMFOG_LINEAR—The fog effect intensifies linearly between the start and end points, according to the following formula:

$f = (end - z) / (end - start)$

where start and end are the fog start and end points (specified by IDirect3DRMFrame::SetSceneFogParams) and z is the depth of the frame. This is the only fog mode currently supported.

continues

continued

D3DRMFOG_EXPONENTIAL—The fog effect intensifies exponentially, according to the following formula:

$$f = e \wedge (-(\text{density} \times z))$$

where density is the fog density (specified by IDirect3DRMFrame::SetSceneFogParams) and z is the depth of the frame. This fog mode is not currently supported.

D3DRMFOG_EXPONENTIALSQUARED—The fog effect intensifies exponentially with the square of the distance, according to the following formula:

$$f = e \wedge (-((\text{density} \times z) \wedge 2))$$

where density is the fog density (specified by IDirect3DRMFrame::SetSceneFogParams) and z is the depth of the frame. This fog mode is not currently supported.

See Also: IDirect3DRMFrame::GetSceneFogMode,
IDirect3DRMFrame::SetSceneFogMode,
IDirect3DRMFrame::SetSceneFogParams

D3DRMFRAMECONSTRAINT

Definition:
```
typedef enum _D3DRMFRAMECONSTRAINT
{
        D3DRMCONSTRAIN_Z,
        D3DRMCONSTRAIN_Y,
        D3DRMCONSTRAIN_X
} D3DRMFRAMECONSTRAINT;
```

Description: This enumerated type describes the axes of rotation to constrain when changing the orientation of a Direct3DRMFrame object with IDirect3DRMFrame::LookAt().

Members: D3DRMCONSTRAIN_Z—Use only x and y rotations.

D3DRMCONSTRAIN_Y—Use only x and z rotations.

D3DRMCONSTRAIN_X—Use only y and z rotations.

See Also: IDirect3DRMFrame::LookAt

D3DRMLIGHTMODE

Definition:
```
typedef enum _D3DRMLIGHTMODE
{
        D3DRMLIGHT_OFF  = 0 * D3DRMSHADE_MAX,
        D3DRMLIGHT_ON   = 1 * D3DRMSHADE_MAX,
        D3DRMLIGHT_MASK = 7 * D3DRMSHADE_MAX,
        D3DRMLIGHT_MAX  = 8 * D3DRMSHADE_MAX
} D3DRMLIGHTMODE;
```

Description: This enumerated type is used to help define the D3DRMRENDERQUALITY enumerated type. These values can be used independently for setting or retrieving the rendering quality of a device.

Members: D3DRMLIGHT_OFF—Lighting is off.

D3DRMLIGHT_ON—Lighting is on.

D3DRMLIGHT_MASK—Lighting uses a mask.

D3DRMLIGHT_MAX—Maximum lighting value.

See Also: IDirect3DRMDevice::GetQuality, IDirect3DRMDevice::SetQuality, IDirect3DRMMesh::GetGroupQuality, IDirect3DRMMesh::SetGroupQuality, IDirect3DRMMeshBuilder::GetQuality, IDirect3DRMMeshBuilder::SetQuality, D3DRMSHADEMODE, D3DRMFILLMODE, D3DRMRENDERQUALITY

D3DRMLIGHTTYPE

Definition:
```
typedef enum _D3DRMLIGHTTYPE
{
        D3DRMLIGHT_AMBIENT,
        D3DRMLIGHT_POINT,
        D3DRMLIGHT_SPOT,
        D3DRMLIGHT_DIRECTIONAL,
        D3DRMLIGHT_PARALLELPOINT
} D3DRMLIGHTTYPE;
```

Description: This enumerated type defines the light types available in Direct3D.

continues

continued

Members: D3DRMLIGHT_AMBIENT—Light is an ambient source.

D3DRMLIGHT_POINT—Light is a point source. Sometimes called "omnidirectional."

D3DRMLIGHT_SPOT—Light is a spotlight source.

D3DRMLIGHT_DIRECTIONAL—Light is a directional source.

D3DRMLIGHT_PARALLELPOINT—Light is a parallel point source.

See Also: IDirect3DRM::CreateLight, IDirect3DRM::CreateLightRGB, IDirect3DRMLight::GetType, IDirect3DRMLight::SetType

D3DRMMATERIALMODE

Definition:
```
typedef enum _D3DRMMATERIALMODE
{
        D3DRMMATERIAL_FROMMESH,
        D3DRMMATERIAL_FROMPARENT,
        D3DRMMATERIAL_FROMFRAME
} D3DRMMATERIALMODE;
```

Description: This enumerated type describes from where material information about Direct3D objects is retrieved.

Members: D3DRMMATERIAL_FROMMESH—Material information is retrieved from the visual object (the mesh) itself. This is the default setting.

D3DRMMATERIAL_FROMPARENT—Material information, along with color or texture information, is inherited from the parent frame.

D3DRMMATERIAL_FROMFRAME—Material information is retrieved from the frame, overriding any previous material information that the visual object may have possessed.

See Also: IDirect3DRMFrame::GetMaterialMode, IDirect3DRMFrame::SetColor, IDirect3DRMFrame::SetColorRGB, IDirect3DRMFrame::SetMaterialMode, IDirect3DRMFrame::SetTexture

D3DRMPALETTEFLAGS

Definition:
```
typedef enum _D3DRMPALETTEFLAGS
{
    D3DRMPALETTE_FREE,
    D3DRMPALETTE_READONLY,
    D3DRMPALETTE_RESERVED
} D3DRMPALETTEFLAGS;
```

Description: This enumerated type tells the renderer what it can do with a specific palette entry.

Members: D3DRMPALETTE_FREE—The renderer may use this entry freely.

D3DRMPALETTE_READONLY—The render may not change this value, but it may map other colors to it.

D3DRMPALETTE_RESERVED—May not be used by the renderer.

See Also: IDirect3DRM::CreateTexture, IDirect3DRMTexture::GetImage, D3DRMPALETTEENTRY, D3DRMIMAGE

D3DRMPROJECTIONTYPE

Definition:
```
typedef enum _D3DRMPROJECTIONTYPE
{
    D3DRMPROJECT_PERSPECTIVE,
    D3DRMPROJECT_ORTHOGRAPHIC
} D3DRMPROJECTIONTYPE;
```

Description: Defines the type of projection used for viewing a scene with a Direct3D viewport object.

Members: D3DRMPROJECT_PERSPECTIVE—Use a perspective viewing projection.

D3DRMPROJECT_ORTHOGRAPHIC—Use an orthographic viewing projection.

See Also: IDirect3DRMViewport::GetProjection, IDirect3DRMViewport::SetProjection

D3DRMRENDERQUALITY

Definition: `typedef DWORD D3DRMRENDERQUALITY;`

```
#define D3DRMRENDER_WIREFRAME (D3DRMSHADE_FLAT + D3DRMLIGHT_OFF +
D3DRMFILL_WIREFRAME)
#define D3DRMRENDER_UNLITFLAT (D3DRMSHADE_FLAT + D3DRMLIGHT_OFF +
D3DRMFILL_SOLID)
#define D3DRMRENDER_FLAT (D3DRMSHADE_FLAT + D3DRMLIGHT_ON +
D3DRMFILL_SOLID)
#define D3DRMRENDER_GOURAUD (D3DRMSHADE_GOURAUD + D3DRMLIGHT_ON +
D3DRMFILL_SOLID)
#define D3DRMRENDER_PHONG (D3DRMSHADE_PHONG + D3DRMLIGHT_ON +
D3DRMFILL_SOLID)
```

Description: Not a true enumerated type, this set of definitions combines the values of the D3DRMFILLMODE, D3DRMLIGHTMODE, and D3DRMSHADEMODE enumerated types to specify the rendering quality for a Direct3D mesh object, a Direct3D mesh builder object, or a Direct3D device.

Members: D3DRMRENDER_WIREFRAME—Display only the edges of the geometry.

D3DRMRENDER_UNLITFLAT—Flat shaded without lighting.

D3DRMRENDER_FLAT—Flat shaded with lighting.

D3DRMRENDER_GOURAUD—Gouraud shaded.

D3DRMRENDER_PHONG—Phong shaded. Phong shading is not currently supported.

See Also: IDirect3DRMDevice::GetQuality, IDirect3DRMDevice::SetQuality, IDirect3DRMMesh::GetGroupQuality, IDirect3DRMMesh::SetGroupQuality, IDirect3DRMMeshBuilder::GetQuality, IDirect3DRMMeshBuilder::SetQuality, D3DRMSHADEMODE, D3DRMFILLMODE, D3DRMLIGHTMODE

D3DRMSHADEMODE

Definition:
```
typedef enum _D3DRMSHADEMODE
{
        D3DRMSHADE_FLAT = 0,
        D3DRMSHADE_GOURAUD = 1,
        D3DRMSHADE_PHONG = 2,
        D3DRMSHADE_MASK = 7,
        D3DRMSHADE_MAX = 8
} D3DRMSHADEMODE;
```

Description: This enumerated type is used to help define the D3DRMRENDER QUALITY enumerated type. These values, however, can be used independently for setting or retrieving the rendering quality of a device.

Members: D3DRMSHADE_FLAT—Flat shading is used for rendering.

D3DRMSHADE_GOURAUD—Gouraud shading is used for rendering.

D3DRMSHADE_PHONG—Phong shading is used. Phong shading is not currently supported.

D3DRMSHADE_MASK—Shading uses a mask.

D3DRMSHADE_MAX—Maximum shading value.

See Also: IDirect3DRMDevice::GetQuality, IDirect3DRMDevice::SetQuality, IDirect3DRMMesh::GetGroupQuality, IDirect3DRMMesh::SetGroupQuality, IDirect3DRMMeshBuilder::GetQuality, IDirect3DRMMeshBuilder::SetQuality, D3DRMFILLMODE, D3DRMLIGHTMODE, D3DRMRENDERQUALITY

D3DRMSORTMODE

Definition:
```
typedef enum _D3DRMSORTMODE
{
        D3DRMSORT_FROMPARENT,
        D3DRMSORT_NONE,
        D3DRMSORT_FRONTTOBACK,
        D3DRMSORT_BACKTOFRONT
} D3DRMSORTMODE;
```

Description: This enumerated type describes how child frames are sorted in a scene. If z-buffering is off, polygons typically should be sorted back to front to take advantage of the painter's algorithm. If z-buffering is on, sorting polygons from front to back minimizes overdraw.

Members: D3DRMSORT_FROMPARENT—Child frames inherit the sorting order of their parents. This is the default setting.

D3DRMSORT_NONE—Child frames are not sorted.

D3DRMSORT_FRONTTOBACK—Child frames are sorted front to back.

D3DRMSORT_BACKTOFRONT—Child frames are sorted back to front.

See Also: IDirect3DRMFrame::GetSortMode, IDirect3DRMFrame::SetSortMode

D3DRMTEXTUREQUALITY

Definition:
```
typedef enum _D3DRMTEXTUREQUALITY
{
        D3DRMTEXTURE_NEAREST,
        D3DRMTEXTURE_LINEAR,
        D3DRMTEXTURE_MIPNEAREST,
        D3DRMTEXTURE_MIPLINEAR,
        D3DRMTEXTURE_LINEARMIPNEAREST,
        D3DRMTEXTURE_LINEARMIPLINEAR
} D3DRMTEXTUREQUALITY;
```

Description: This enumerated type defines values for specifying the algorithm used to compute texel values when texture mapping a texture onto an arbitrarily-oriented face. Different values provide different levels of quality and require different amounts of processing for each texel. Specific devices may support none, some, or all of these values.

Members: D3DRMTEXTURE_NEAREST—Texels come from the nearest pixel in the texture.

D3DRMTEXTURE_LINEAR—Texels are computed by linearly interpolating the four nearest pixels.

D3DRMTEXTURE_MIPNEAREST—Similar to D3DRMTEXTURE_NEAREST, but uses the appropriate mipmap.

D3DRMTEXTURE_MIPLINEAR—Similar to D3DRMTEXTURE_LINEAR, but uses the appropriate mipmap and linearly interpolates the four nearest pixels in the mipmap.

D3DRMTEXTURE_LINEARMIPNEAREST—Similar to D3DRMTEXTURE_MIPNEAREST, but interpolates between the two nearest mipmaps.

D3DRMTEXTURE_LINEARMIPLINEAR—Similar to D3DRMTEXTURE_MIPLINEAR, but interpolates between the four nearest pixels in the two nearest mipmaps.

See Also: IDirect3DRMDevice::GetTextureQuality, IDirect3DRMDevice::SetTextureQuality

D3DRMUSERVISUALREASON

Definition:
```
typedef enum _D3DRMUSERVISUALREASON
{
        D3DRMUSERVISUAL_CANSEE,
        D3DRMUSERVISUAL_RENDER
} D3DRMUSERVISUALREASON;
```

Description: This enumerated type defines values for the reasons the system may call a user-visual callback function.

Members: D3DRMUSERVISUAL_CANSEE—The callback function should return TRUE if the user-visual object is visible in the viewport.

continues

continued

D3DRMUSERVISUAL_RENDER—The callback function should render the user-visual object.

See Also: D3DRMUSERVISUALCALLBACK

D3DRMWRAPTYPE

Definition:
```
typedef enum _D3DRMWRAPTYPE
{
    D3DRMWRAP_FLAT,
    D3DRMWRAP_CYLINDER,
    D3DRMWRAP_SPHERE,
    D3DRMWRAP_CHROME
} D3DRMWRAPTYPE;
```

Description: This enumerated type defines the method for assigning texture coordinates to faces and meshes.

Members: D3DRMWRAP_FLAT—The wrap is flat.

D3DRMWRAP_CYLINDER—The wrap is cylindrical.

D3DRMWRAP_SPHERE—The wrap is spherical.

D3DRMWRAP_CHROME—The wrap allocates texture coordinates so that the texture appears to be reflected onto the objects.

See Also: IDirect3DRM::CreateWrap, IDirect3DRMWrap::Init

D3DRMXOFFORMAT

Definition:
```
typedef enum _D3DRMXOFFORMAT
{
    D3DRMXOF_BINARY,
    D3DRMXOF_COMPRESSED,
    D3DRMXOF_TEXT
} D3DRMXOFFORMAT;
```

Description: Defines the file type used by IDirect3DRMMeshBuilder::Save(). The D3DRMXOF_BINARY and D3DRMXOF_TEXT settings are mutually exclusive.

Members: D3DRMXOF_BINARY—File is in binary format. This is the default setting.

D3DRMXOF_COMPRESSED—Not currently supported.

D3DRMXOF_TEXT—File is in text format.

See Also: IDirect3DRMMeshBuilder::Save

D3DRMZBUFFERMODE

Definition:
```
typedef enum _D3DRMZBUFFERMODE
{
    D3DRMZBUFFER_FROMPARENT,
    D3DRMZBUFFER_ENABLE,
    D3DRMZBUFFER_DISABLE
} D3DRMZBUFFERMODE;
```

Description: This enumerated type describes the z-buffering for a Direct3D frame.

Members: D3DRMZBUFFER_FROMPARENT—The frame inherits the z-buffer setting from its parent frame. This is the default setting.

D3DRMZBUFFER_ENABLE—Z-buffering is enabled.

D3DRMZBUFFER_DISABLE—Z-buffering is disabled.

See Also: IDirect3DRMFrame::GetZbufferMode,
IDirect3DRMFrame::SetZbufferMode

Retained-Mode Other Types

D3DRMANIMATIONOPTIONS

Definition: `typedef DWORD D3DRMANIMATIONOPTIONS;`

```
#define D3DRMANIMATION_CLOSED 0x02L
#define D3DRMANIMATION_LINEARPOSITION 0x04L
#define D3DRMANIMATION_OPEN 0x01L
#define D3DRMANIMATION_POSITION 0x00000020L
#define D3DRMANIMATION_SCALEANDROTATION 0x00000010L
#define D3DRMANIMATION_SPLINEPOSITION 0x08L
```

Description: This set of definitions defines how a Direct3D animation is played.

Members: D3DRMANIMATION_CLOSED—The animation plays continually, looping back to the beginning when it reaches the end. In a closed animation, the last key in the animation should be a repeat of the first. This repeated key is used to indicate the time difference between the last and first keys in the looping animation.

D3DRMANIMATION_LINEARPOSITION—The animation's position is set linearly.

D3DRMANIMATION_OPEN—The animation plays once and stops.

D3DRMANIMATION_POSITION—The animation's position matrix should overwrite any transformation matrices that could be set by other methods.

D3DRMANIMATION_SCALEANDROTATION—The animation's scale and rotation matrix should overwrite any transformation matrices that could be set by other methods.

D3DRMANIMATION_SPLINEPOSITION—The animation's position is interpolated by using splines.

See Also: IDirect3DRMAnimation::GetOptions, IDirect3DRMAnimation::SetOptions

D3DRMCOLORMODEL

Definition: `typedef D3DCOLORMODEL D3DRMCOLORMODEL;`

Description: This data type is a synonym for D3DCOLORMODEL, which is used in conjunction with IDirect3DRMDevice::GetColorModel().

Members: None

See Also: D3DCOLORMODEL

D3DRMLOADOPTIONS

Definition: `typedef DWORD D3DRMLOADOPTIONS;`

```
#define D3DRMLOAD_FROMFILE              0x00L
#define D3DRMLOAD_FROMRESOURCE          0x01L
#define D3DRMLOAD_FROMMEMORY            0x02L
#define D3DRMLOAD_FROMSTREAM            0x03L
#define D3DRMLOAD_BYNAME                0x10L
#define D3DRMLOAD_BYPOSITION            0x20L
#define D3DRMLOAD_BYGUID                0x30L
#define D3DRMLOAD_FIRST                 0x40L
#define D3DRMLOAD_INSTANCEBYREFERENCE   0x100L
#define D3DRMLOAD_INSTANCEBYCOPYING     0x200L
```

Description: This set of definitions describes how a Direct3D object is loaded.

Each of the Load functions uses the lpvObjSource parameter to specify the source of the object and the lpvObjID parameter to identify the object. The system interprets the contents of the lpvObjSource parameter based on the choice of source flags, and it interprets the contents of the lpvObjID parameter based on the choice of identifier flags.

The instance flags do not change the interpretation of any of the parameters. By using the D3DRMLOAD_INSTANCEBYREFERENCE flag, an application can load the same file twice without creating any new objects. If an object does not have a name, setting the D3DRMLOAD_INSTANCEBYREFERENCE flag has the same effect

continues

continued

as setting the D3DRMLOAD_INSTANCEBYCOPYING flag; the loader creates each unnamed object as a new one, even if some of the objects are identical. In DirectX 3, D3DRMLOAD_INSTANCEBYCOPYING is not supported.

Members: *Source flags*:

D3DRMLOAD_FROMFILE—Load from a file. This is the default setting.

D3DRMLOAD_FROMRESOURCE—Load from a resource. If this flag is specified, the lpvObjSource parameter of the calling Load function must point to a D3DRMLOADRESOURCE structure.

D3DRMLOAD_FROMMEMORY—Load from memory. If this flag is specified, the lpvObjSource parameter of the calling Load function must point to a D3DRMLOADMEMORY structure.

D3DRMLOAD_FROMSTREAM—Load from a stream. This flag is not currently supported.

Identifier flags:

D3DRMLOAD_BYNAME—Load any object by using a specified name.

D3DRMLOAD_BYPOSITION—Load a stand-alone object based on a given zero-based position (that is, the nth object in the file). Stand-alone objects can contain other objects, but are not contained by any other objects.

D3DRMLOAD_BYGUID—Load any object by using a specified globally unique identifier (GUID).

D3DRMLOAD_FIRST—This is the default setting. Load the first stand-alone object of the given type (for example, a mesh if the application calls IDirect3DRMMeshBuilder::Load()). Stand-alone objects can contain other objects, but are not contained by any other objects.

Instance flags:

> D3DRMLOAD_INSTANCEBYREFERENCE—Check whether an object already exists with the same name as specified and, if so, use an instance of that object instead of creating a new one. This flag is implied by default.
>
> D3DRMLOAD_INSTANCEBYCOPYING—Check whether an object already exists with the same name as specified and, if so, copy that object. This flag is not currently supported.

See Also: IDirect3DRM::Load, IDirect3DRMAnimationSet::Load, IDirect3DRMFrame::Load, IDirect3DRMMeshBuilder::Load

D3DRMMAPPING

Definition:
```
typedef DWORD D3DRMMAPPING, D3DRMMAPPINGFLAG;

static const D3DRMMAPPINGFLAG D3DRMMAP_WRAPU = 1;
static const D3DRMMAPPINGFLAG D3DRMMAP_WRAPV = 2;
static const D3DRMMAPPINGFLAG D3DRMMAP_PERSPCORRECT = 4;
```

Description: This set of definitions specifies how textures are mapped to a Direct3D mesh group.

The D3DRMMAP_WRAPU and D3DRMMAP_WRAPV flags determine how the rasterizer interprets texture coordinates. The rasterizer always interpolates the shortest distance between texture coordinates; that is, a line. The path taken by this line, and the valid values for the texture coordinates u and v, varies with the topology of the texture, which is specified by a combination of the D3DRMMAP_WRAPU and D3DRMMAP_WRAPV flags. If either the u flag or v flag is set, the line can wrap around the texture edge in the u or v direction, respectively, as if the texture had a cylindrical or toroidal topology. If both the u and v flags are set, the texture has a spherical topology.

Members: D3DRMMAPPINGFLAG—Type equivalent to D3DRMMAPPING.

D3DRMMAP_WRAPU—Texture wraps in the u direction.

continues

continued

D3DRMMAP_WRAPV—Texture wraps in the v direction.

D3DRMMAP_PERSPCORRECT—Texture mapping is perspective correct. This typically requires extra processing, and may only be necessary if the particular face spans a large z-range in the camera's coordinate system.

See Also: IDirect3DRMMesh::GetGroupMapping, IDirect3DRMMesh::SetGroupMapping

D3DRMMATRIX4D

Definition: `typedef D3DVALUE D3DRMMATRIX4D[4][4];`

Description: This definition expresses a 4×4 matrix as an array of D3DVALUEs (floats).

Members: None

See Also: D3DRMMatrixFromQuaternion, IDirect3DRMFrame::AddTransform, IDirect3DRMFrame::GetTransform

D3DRMSAVEOPTIONS

Definition: `typedef DWORD D3DRMSAVEOPTIONS;`

```
#define D3DRMXOFSAVE_NORMALS 1
#define D3DRMXOFSAVE_TEXTURECOORDINATES 2
#define D3DRMXOFSAVE_MATERIALS 4
#define D3DRMXOFSAVE_TEXTURENAMES 8
#define D3DRMXOFSAVE_ALL 15
#define D3DRMXOFSAVE_TEMPLATES 16
```

Description: This set of definitions defines options for IDirect3DRMMeshBuilder::Save().

Members: D3DRMXOFSAVE_NORMALS—Save normal vectors in addition to the basic geometry.

D3DRMXOFSAVE_TEXTURECOORDINATES—Save texture

coordinates in addition to the basic geometry.

D3DRMXOFSAVE_MATERIALS—Save materials in addition to the basic geometry.

D3DRMXOFSAVE_TEXTURENAMES—Save texture names in addition to the basic geometry.

D3DRMXOFSAVE_ALL—Save normal vectors, texture coordinates, materials, and texture names in addition to the basic geometry.

D3DRMXOFSAVE_TEMPLATES—Save templates with the file. By default, templates are not saved.

See Also: IDirect3DRMMeshBuilder::Save

Retained-Mode Data Types and Return Values

D3DRM_OK—No error

D3DRMERR_BADALLOC—Out of memory

D3DRMERR_BADDEVICE—Device is not compatible with renderer

D3DRMERR_BADFILE—Data file is corrupt

D3DRMERR_BADMAJORVERSION—Bad DLL major version

D3DRMERR_BADMINORVERSION—Bad DLL minor version

D3DRMERR_BADOBJECT—Pointer to object was bad

D3DRMERR_BADTYPE—Bad argument type passed

D3DRMERR_BADVALUE—Bad argument value passed

D3DRMERR_FACEUSED—Face already used in a mesh

D3DRMERR_FILENOTFOUND—File cannot be opened

D3DRMERR_NOTDONEYET—Unimplemented function

D3DRMERR_NOTFOUND—Object not found in specified place

D3DRMERR_UNABLETOEXECUTE—Unable to carry out procedure

Part III

Immediate-Mode Function Reference

Immediate-Mode Functions *307*

Immediate-Mode Functions

Immediate-Mode Macros

The Direct3D Immediate-Mode Macros provide basic functionality for division, multiplication, and color manipulation, as well as a macro for overriding Direct3D states in an execute buffer. The Immediate-Mode Macros include:

D3DDivide

D3DMultiply

D3DRGB

D3DRGBA

D3DSTATE_OVERRIDE

D3DVAL

D3DVALP

RGB_GETBLUE

RGB_GETGREEN

RGB_GETRED

RGB_MAKE

RGB_TORGBA

RGBA_GETALPHA

RGBA_GETBLUE

RGBA_GETGREEN

RGBA_GETRED

RGBA_MAKE

RGBA_SETALPHA

RGBA_TORGB

D3DDivide

Interface:	None
Description:	This macro divides two values.
Notes:	D3DDivide(a, b) is defined as (float)((double)(a)/(double)(b))
Arguments:	a—Dividend in the computation.
	b—Divisor in the computation.
Return Type:	float
Return Values:	Returns the computed quotient.
See Also:	D3DMultiply

D3DMultiply

Interface:	None
Description:	This macro multiplies two values.
Notes:	D3DMultiply (a, b) is defined as: $((a) \times (b))$
Arguments:	a—First multiplicand.
	b—Second multiplicand.
Return Type:	Depends on the types of the arguments.
Return Values:	Returns the product of the two arguments.
See Also:	D3DDivide

D3DRGB

Interface:	None
Description:	This macro creates a D3DCOLOR from the supplied red, green, and blue values.

Notes:	D3DRGB(r, g, b) is defined as: (0xff000000L	(((long)((r) × 255)) << 16)	(((long)((g) × 255)) << 8)	(long)((b) × 255)). The color component arguments should be in the range 0.0 to 1.0.
	D3DRGB creates D3DCOLOR values with the maximum alpha component (1.0 or 255, depending on the representation). This is different than RGB_MAKE, which creates D3DCOLOR values with 0 alpha component.
Arguments:	r—Red component of color.
	g—Green component of color.
	b—Blue component of color.
Return Type:	D3DCOLOR
Return Values:	The D3DCOLOR constructed to represent the specified component values.
See Also:	D3DCOLOR, D3DRGBA, RGB_GETBLUE, RGB_GETGREEN, RGB_GETRED, RGB_MAKE, RGB_TORGBA, RGBA_GETALPHA, RGBA_GETBLUE, RGBA_GETGREEN, RGBA_GETRED, RGBA_MAKE, RGBA_SETALPHA, RGBA_TORGB

D3DRGBA

Interface:	None
Description:	This macro creates a D3DCOLOR from the supplied red, green, blue, and alpha values.
Notes:	D3DRGBA(r, g, b, a) is defined as: ((((long)((a) × 255)) << 24)	(((long)((r) × 255)) << 16)	(((long)((g) × 255)) << 8)	(long)((b) × 255))
	The color and alpha component arguments must all be in the range 0.0 to 1.0.
Arguments:	r—Red component of color.
	g—Green component of color.

continues

continued	
	b—Blue component of color.
	a—Alpha component of color.
Return Type:	D3DCOLOR
Return Values:	Returns the D3DCOLOR constructed to represent the specified component values.
See Also:	D3DCOLOR, D3DRGB, RGB_GETBLUE, RGB_GETGREEN, RGB_GETRED, RGB_MAKE, RGB_TORGBA, RGBA_GETALPHA, RGBA_GETBLUE, RGBA_GETGREEN, RGBA_GETRED, RGBA_MAKE, RGBA_SETALPHA, RGBA_TORGB

D3DSTATE_OVERRIDE

Interface:	None
Description:	This macro is used to disable or enable subsequent state changes to the transform, lighting, or rasterization module states from within an execute buffer.
Notes:	D3DSTATE_OVERRIDE(type) is defined as: ((DWORD) (type) + D3DSTATE_OVERRIDE_BIAS)
	The D3DSTATE_OVERRIDE macro is used in constructing a D3DINSTRUCTION to enable or disable subsequent changes to specific states within the transform, lighting, or rasterization modules during execution of the execute buffer. State overrides can be used to implement various execute buffer reuse schemes.
Arguments:	type—State to override. This parameter should be one of the members of the D3DTRANSFORMSTATETYPE, D3DLIGHTSTATETYPE, or D3DRENDERSTATETYPE enumerated types.
Return Type:	None
Return Values:	None
See Also:	D3DINSTRUCTION, D3DSTATE

D3DVAL

Interface:	None
Description:	This macro casts a value to the same type as D3DVALUE.
Notes:	D3DVAL(val) is defined as: ((float)val)
	D3DVAL returns a 32-bit, IEEE floating point number that can represent values within the range of approximately 3.4E–38 to 3.4E+38, with 6 to 7 significant digits.
	This convenience macro is provided for use when assigning values of various types (such as double or int) to a D3DVALUE.
Arguments:	val—Value to be converted.
Return Type:	D3DVALUE (float)
Return Values:	Returns the converted value.
See Also:	D3DVALP

D3DVALP

Interface:	None
Description:	This macro casts a value to the same type as D3DVALUE.
Notes:	D3DVALP(val, prec) is defined as: ((float)val)
	Currently, the precision argument is ignored. This macro behaves identically to the D3DVAL.
Arguments:	val—Value to be converted.
	prec—This parameter is ignored.
Return Type:	D3DVALUE (float)
Return Values:	Returns the converted value.
See Also:	D3DVAL

RGB_GETBLUE

Interface:	None
Description:	This macro retrieves the blue component of a D3DCOLOR.
Notes:	RGB_GETBLUE(rgb) is defined as: ((rgb) & 0xff)
Arguments:	rgb—D3DCOLOR from which to extract the blue component.
Return Type:	DWORD
Return Values:	The blue component of the D3DCOLOR, a number between 0 and 255.
See Also:	D3DCOLOR, D3DRGB, D3DRGBA, RGB_GETGREEN, RGB_GETRED, RGB_MAKE, RGB_TORGBA, RGBA_GETALPHA, RGBA_GETBLUE, RGBA_GETGREEN, RGBA_GETRED, RGBA_MAKE, RGBA_SETALPHA, RGBA_TORGB

RGB_GETGREEN

Interface:	None
Description:	This macro retrieves the green component of a D3DCOLOR.
Notes:	RGB_GETGREEN(rgb) is defined as: (((rgb) >> 8) & 0xff)
Arguments:	rgb—D3DCOLOR from which to extract the green component.
Return Type:	DWORD
Return Values:	The green component of the D3DCOLOR, a number between 0 and 255.
See Also:	D3DCOLOR, D3DRGB, D3DRGBA, RGB_GETBLUE, RGB_GETRED, RGB_MAKE, RGB_TORGBA, RGBA_GETALPHA, RGBA_GETBLUE, RGBA_GETGREEN, RGBA_GETRED, RGBA_MAKE, RGBA_SETALPHA, RGBA_TORGB

RGB_GETRED

Interface:	None
Description:	This macro retrieves the red component of a D3DCOLOR.
Notes:	RGB_GETRED(rgb) is defined as: (((rgb) >> 16) & 0xff)
Arguments:	rgb—D3DCOLOR from which to extract the red component.
Return Type:	DWORD
Return Values:	The red component of D3DCOLOR, a number between 0 and 255.
See Also:	D3DCOLOR, D3DRGB, D3DRGBA, RGB_GETBLUE, RGB_GETGREEN, RGB_MAKE, RGB_TORGBA, RGBA_GETALPHA, RGBA_GETBLUE, RGBA_GETGREEN, RGBA_GETRED, RGBA_MAKE, RGBA_SETALPHA, RGBA_TORGB

RGB_MAKE

Interface:	None
Description:	This macro creates a D3DCOLOR from the supplied red, green, and blue values.
Notes:	RGB_MAKE(r, g, b) is defined as: ((D3DCOLOR) (((r) << 16)	((g) << 8)	(b)))
	The color component arguments must be integers in the range 0–255.
	Unlike the D3DRGB macro, RGB_MAKE makes a D3DCOLOR with an alpha component of 0. If RGB_MAKE is used to construct a D3DCOLOR in a situation that requires an alpha component, the resulting color may be invisible because an alpha component of 0 may mean the color is completely transparent.
Arguments:	r—Red component of color.
	g—Green component of color.
	b—Blue component of color.

continues

continued

Return Type:	D3DCOLOR (DWORD)
Return Values:	The D3DCOLOR created from the specified values.
See Also:	D3DCOLOR, D3DRGB, D3DRGBA, RGB_GETBLUE, RGB_GETGREEN, RGB_GETRED, RGB_TORGBA, RGBA_GETALPHA, RGBA_GETBLUE, RGBA_GETGREEN, RGBA_GETRED, RGBA_MAKE, RGBA_SETALPHA, RGBA_TORGB

RGB_TORGBA

Interface:	None
Description:	This macro creates a D3DCOLOR with the maximum alpha component value from the RGB components of the specified D3DCOLOR.
Notes:	RGB_TORGBA(rgb) is defined as: ((D3DCOLOR) ((rgb) | 0xff000000))
	This macro automatically sets the alpha value of the result D3DCOLOR to 255.
	This macro can be used to convert a D3DCOLOR created with RGB_MAKE to one suitable for use when an RGBA color is required.
Arguments:	rgb—D3DCOLOR to be converted.
Return Type:	D3DCOLOR (DWORD)
Return Values:	Returns the converted D3DCOLOR.
See Also:	D3DCOLOR, D3DRGB, D3DRGBA, RGB_GETBLUE, RGB_GETGREEN, RGB_GETRED, RGB_MAKE, RGBA_GETALPHA, RGBA_GETBLUE, RGBA_GETGREEN, RGBA_GETRED, RGBA_MAKE, RGBA_SETALPHA, RGBA_TORGB

RGBA_GETALPHA

Interface:	None
Description:	This macro retrieves the alpha component of a D3DCOLOR.
Notes:	RGBA_GETALPHA(rgb) is defined as: ((rgb) >> 24)
Arguments:	rgb—D3DCOLOR from which to extract the alpha component.
Return Type:	DWORD
Return Values:	The alpha component of the D3DCOLOR, a number between 0 and 255.
See Also:	D3DCOLOR, D3DRGB, D3DRGBA, RGB_GETBLUE, RGB_GETGREEN, RGB_GETRED, RGB_MAKE, RGB_TORGBA, RGBA_GETBLUE, RGBA_GETGREEN, RGBA_GETRED, RGBA_MAKE, RGBA_SETALPHA, RGBA_TORGB

RGBA_GETBLUE

Interface:	None
Description:	This macro retrieves the blue component of a D3DCOLOR.
Notes:	RGBA_GETBLUE(rgb) is defined as: ((rgb) & 0xff)
Arguments:	rgb—D3DCOLOR from which to extract the blue component.
Return Type:	DWORD
Return Values:	The blue component of the D3DCOLOR, a number between 0 and 255.
See Also:	D3DCOLOR, D3DRGB, D3DRGBA, RGB_GETBLUE, RGB_GETGREEN, RGB_GETRED, RGB_MAKE, RGB_TORGBA, RGBA_GETALPHA, RGBA_GETGREEN, RGBA_GETRED, RGBA_MAKE, RGBA_SETALPHA, RGBA_TORGB

RGBA_GETGREEN

Interface:	None
Description:	This macro retrieves the green component of a D3DCOLOR.
Notes:	RGBA_GETGREEN(rgb) is defined as: (((rgb) >> 8) & 0xff)
Arguments:	rgb—D3DCOLOR from which to extract the green component.
Return Type:	DWORD
Return Values:	The green component of the D3DCOLOR, a number between 0 and 255.
See Also:	D3DCOLOR, D3DRGB, D3DRGBA, RGB_GETBLUE, RGB_GETGREEN, RGB_GETRED, RGB_MAKE, RGB_TORGBA, RGBA_GETALPHA, RGBA_GETBLUE, RGBA_GETRED, RGBA_MAKE, RGBA_SETALPHA, RGBA_TORGB

RGBA_GETRED

Interface:	None
Description:	This macro retrieves the red component of a D3DCOLOR.
Notes:	RGBA_GETRED(rgb) is defined as: (((rgb) >> 16) & 0xff)
Arguments:	rgb—D3DCOLOR from which to extract the red component.
Return Type:	DWORD
Return Values:	The red component of the D3DCOLOR, a number between 0 and 255.
See Also:	D3DCOLOR, D3DRGB, D3DRGBA, RGB_GETBLUE, RGB_GETGREEN, RGB_GETRED, RGB_MAKE, RGB_TORGBA, RGBA_GETALPHA, RGBA_GETBLUE, RGBA_GETGREEN, RGBA_MAKE, RGBA_SETALPHA, RGBA_TORGB

RGBA_MAKE

Interface:	None
Description:	This macro creates a D3DCOLOR from the supplied red, green, blue, and alpha values.
Notes:	RGBA_MAKE(r, g, b, a) is defined as: ((D3DCOLOR) (((a) << 24)	((r) << 16)	((g) << 8)	(b)))
	The color and alpha component arguments should be integers in the range 0–255.
Arguments:	r—Red component of color.
	g—Green component of color.
	b—Blue component of color.
	a—Alpha component of color.
Return Type:	D3DCOLOR (DWORD)
Return Values:	The D3DCOLOR created from the specified values.
See Also:	D3DCOLOR, D3DRGB, D3DRGBA, RGB_GETBLUE, RGB_GETGREEN, RGB_GETRED, RGB_MAKE, RGB_TORGBA, RGBA_GETALPHA, RGBA_GETBLUE, RGBA_GETGREEN, RGBA_GETRED, RGBA_SETALPHA, RGBA_TORGB

RGBA_SETALPHA

Interface:	None
Description:	This macro sets the alpha component of a D3DCOLOR.
Notes:	RGBA_SETALPHA(rgba, x) is defined as: (((x) << 24)	((rgba) & 0x00ffffff))
	The new alpha component value should be between 0 and 255.
Arguments:	rgba—D3DCOLOR whose alpha color will be changed.
	x—New alpha component value.

continues

continued

Return Type:	D3DCOLOR (DWORD)
Return Values:	The new D3DCOLOR.
See Also:	D3DCOLOR, D3DRGB, D3DRGBA, RGB_GETBLUE, RGB_GETGREEN, RGB_GETRED, RGB_MAKE, RGB_TORGBA, RGBA_GETALPHA, RGBA_GETBLUE, RGBA_GETGREEN, RGBA_GETRED, RGBA_MAKE, RGBA_TORGB

RGBA_TORGB

Interface:	None
Description:	This macro creates a new D3DCOLOR value from just the red, green, and blue components of the argument, ignoring the alpha component.
Notes:	RGBA_TORGB(rgba) is defined as: ((D3DCOLOR) ((rgba) & 0xffffff))
	This macro automatically sets the alpha value of the result D3DCOLOR to be 0.
Arguments:	rgba—D3DCOLOR to be converted.
Return Type:	D3DCOLOR (DWORD)
Return Values:	The converted D3DCOLOR.
See Also:	D3DCOLOR, D3DRGB, D3DRGBA, RGB_GETBLUE, RGB_GETGREEN, RGB_GETRED, RGB_MAKE, RGB_TORGBA, RGBA_GETALPHA, RGBA_GETBLUE, RGBA_GETGREEN, RGBA_GETRED, RGBA_MAKE, RGBA_SETALPHA

Immediate-Mode Callbacks

There are currently only two implemented Immediate-Mode Callbacks. D3DENUMDEVICES is used to call a function for each available device driver and D3DENUMTEXTUREFORMATSCALLBACK is to call a function for each available texture format. The Immediate-Mode Callbacks are:

D3DENUMDEVICESCALLBACK

D3DENUMTEXTUREFORMATSCALLBACK

D3DVALIDATECALLBACK

D3DENUMDEVICESCALLBACK

Interface:	None

Declaration:	`HRESULT (FAR PASCAL * LPD3DENUMDEVICESCALLBACK)(`
	`    LPGUID lpGuid,`
	`    LPSTR lpDeviceDescription,`
	`    LPSTR lpDeviceName,`
	`    LPD3DDEVICEDESC,`
	`    LPD3DDEVICEDESC,`
	`    LPVOID);`

Description:	This function prototype defines the signature of the Direct3D device enumeration callback type.
Notes:	This callback is used in conjunction with IDirect3D::EnumDevices(). The callback function is called for each Direct3D device driver found by IDirect3D::EnumDevices().
	This function can be used during application initialization to enable the user to choose a specific device based on its capabilities. It can also be used to verify the capabilities of a specific device to choose the best device for the particular application.

continues

continued	
	Note that the software renderer devices do not have any hardware capabilities; thus the device descriptor pointed to by the lpD3HWDeviceDesc argument will be filled with 0s when the device is a software renderer.
	After a suitable device has been found, the callback can avoid enumerating any further devices by returning D3DENUMRET_CANCEL from the function.
Arguments:	LPGUID lpGuid—Address of a globally unique identifier (GUID) of a device driver.
	LPSTR lpDeviceDescription—Address of a textual description of the device.
	LPSTR lpDeviceName—Address of the device name.
	LPD3DDEVICEDESC lpD3DHWDeviceDesc—Address of a D3DDEVICEDESC structure that contains the hardware capabilities of the Direct3D device.
	LPD3DDEVICEDESC lpD3DHELDeviceDesc—Address of a D3DDEVICEDESC structure that contains the emulated capabilities of the Direct3D device.
	LPVOID lpUserArg—Address of application-defined data passed to this callback function.
Return Type:	HRESULT
Return Values:	D3DENUMRET_CANCEL—Cancel the enumeration.
	D3DENUMRET_OK—Continue the enumeration.
See Also:	IDirect3D::EnumDevices

D3DENUMTEXTUREFORMATSCALLBACK

Interface:	None
| **Declaration:** | ```
HRESULT (WINAPI* LPD3DENUMTEXTUREFORMATSCALLBACK)(
    LPDDSURFACEDESC lpDdsd,
    LPVOID lpContext);
``` |
```

Description:	This function prototype defines the signature of the Direct3D texture format enumeration callback type.
Notes:	The callback function will be called for each texture format found by IDirect3DDevice::EnumTextureFormats().
	This function can be used during application initialization to enable the user to choose a specific texture format based on available capabilities. It can also be used to verify the available texture formats to perform the most optimal texture code.
	After a suitable texture format has been found, the callback can avoid enumerating any further texture formats by returning D3DENUMRET_CANCEL from the function.
Arguments:	LPDDSURFACEDESC lpDdsd—Address of the DDSURFACEDESC structure containing the texture information.
	LPVOID lpUserArg—Address of application-defined data passed to this callback function.
Return Type:	HRESULT
Return Values:	This callback should return one of the following values:
	D3DENUMRET_CANCEL—Cancel the enumeration.
	D3DENUMRET_OK—Continue the enumeration.
See Also:	IDirect3DDevice::EnumTextureFormats

D3DVALIDATECALLBACK

Interface:	None
Declaration:	```HRESULT (WINAPI* LPD3DVALIDATECALLBACK)(
LPVOID lpUserArg,
DWORD dwOffset);```
Description:	This function prototype defines the signature of the Direct3D validate callback type.

continues

continued

Notes:	The IDirect3DExecuteBuffer::Validate() function allows for overriding its default error handler function, which has type D3DVALIDATECALLBACK. In DirectX 3, Validate is not implemented, so there is currently no use for this type.
	Future versions of Direct3D may support the IDirect3DExecuteBuffer::Validate function. In that event, a validate callback could be used to handle execute buffer errors.
Arguments:	LPVOID lpUserArg—Address of application-defined data passed to this callback function.
	DWORD dwOffset—Offset into the execute buffer at which the system found an error.
Return Type:	HRESULT
Return Values:	D3D_OK if the error was fixed, otherwise an error value.
See Also:	IDirect3DExecuteBuffer::Validate

IDirect3D

The IDirect3D interface is an interface to a DirectDraw object and provides the functionality to create Immediate-Mode lights, materials, and viewports. Additionally, applications can use the IDirect3D interface to enumerate the available devices and to find a device with certain capabilities.

IDirect3D, as with all COM interfaces, is derived from IUnknown and inherits its methods. A Direct3D object is initially obtained by calling QueryInterface() on a DirectDraw object. It can also be obtained by calling IDirect3DDevice::GetDirect3D(). IDirect3D implements the following methods:

- CreateLight
- CreateMaterial
- CreateViewport
- EnumDevices
- FindDevice
- Initialize

CreateLight

Interface:	IDirect3D

Declaration:	`HRESULT CreateLight(`
	`    LPDIRECT3DLIGHT* lplpDirect3DLight,`
	`    IUnknown* pUnkOuter);`

Description:	This function creates a new Direct3D light object.
Notes:	After the Direct3D light object has been created, it can be added to a viewport object with IDirect3DViewport::AddLight().
Arguments:	LPDIRECT3DLIGHT* lplpDirect3DLight—The address that will be filled with a pointer to a Direct3D light object if the call succeeds.

continues

continued

	IUnknown* pUnkOuter—This parameter must be NULL. It is provided for future compatibility with COM aggregation features.
Return Type:	HRESULT
Return Values:	Returns D3D_OK if successful, or an error otherwise, which may be one of the following values: 　　DDERR_INVALIDOBJECT 　　DDERR_INVALIDPARAMS
See Also:	IDirect3DViewport::AddLight(), IDirect3DViewport::DeleteLight(), IDirect3DViewport::LightElements(), IDirect3DViewport::NextLight()

CreateMaterial

Interface:	IDirect3D
Declaration:	```HRESULT CreateMaterial(
LPDIRECT3DMATERIAL* lplpDirect3DMaterial,
IUnknown* pUnkOuter);```
Description:	This function creates a new Direct3D material object.
Notes:	A material, once created, is typically used through its D3DMATERIALHANDLE, which can be embedded in execute buffers or set as the background of a viewport.
Arguments:	LPDIRECT3DMATERIAL* lplpDirect3DMaterial—Address that will be filled with a pointer to a Direct3D material object if the call succeeds.
	IUnknown* pUnkOuter—This parameter must be NULL. It is provided for future compatibility with COM aggregation features.
Return Type:	HRESULT
Return Values:	See Direct3D Immediate-Mode Return Values.
See Also:	IDirect3DViewport::SetBackground, IDirect3DMaterial::GetHandle

CreateViewport

Interface:	IDirect3D

Declaration:	`HRESULT CreateViewport(`
	`  LPDIRECT3DVIEWPORT* lplpD3DViewport,`
	`  IUnknown* pUnkOuter);`

Description:	This function creates a new Direct3D viewport object.
Notes:	After the viewport has been created, it can be associated with a Direct3D device with IDirect3DDevice::AddViewport().
Arguments:	LPDIRECT3DVIEWPORT* lplpD3DViewport—Address that will be filled with a pointer to an IDirect3D viewport object if the call succeeds.
	IUnknown* pUnkOuter—This parameter must be NULL. It is provided for future compatibility with COM aggregation features.
Return Type:	HRESULT
Return Values:	Returns D3D_OK if successful, or an error otherwise, which may be one of the following values:
	DDERR_INVALIDOBJECT
	DDERR_INVALIDPARAMS
See Also:	IDirect3DDevice::AddViewport

EnumDevices

Interface:	IDirect3D

Declaration:	`HRESULT EnumDevices(`
	`  LPD3DENUMDEVICESCALLBACK lpEnumDevicesCallback,`
	`  LPVOID lpUserArg);`

Description:	This function enumerates all Direct3D device drivers installed on the system.

continues

continued

Notes:	This function can be used in conjunction with the D3DENUMDEVICESCALLBACK to enable the user to choose a specific device based on its capabilities. It can also be used to verify the capabilities that a specific device has to perform the most optimal code for the device.
Arguments:	LPD3DENUMDEVICESCALLBACK lpEnumDevicesCallback—Address of the D3DENUMDEVICESCALLBACK callback function that the enumeration procedure will call every time a device is found.
	LPVOID lpUserArg—Address of application-defined data passed to the callback function.
Return Type:	HRESULT
Return Values:	Returns D3D_OK if successful, or an error otherwise, which may be one of the following values:
	DDERR_INVALIDOBJECT
	DDERR_INVALIDPARAMS
See Also:	IDirect3D::FindDevice, D3DENUMDEVICESCALLBACK

FindDevice

Interface:	IDirect3D
Declaration:	```HRESULT FindDevice(
LPD3DFINDDEVICESEARCH lpD3DFDS,
LPD3DFINDDEVICERESULT lpD3DFDR);```
Description:	This function finds a Direct3D device with the specified characteristics.
Notes:	FindDevice obviates the need to enumerate the available devices to find a particular device. Rather, a description of a suitable device is constructed by setting various capabilities bits in the D3DFINDDEVICESEARCH structure, which is passed to FindDevice. FindDevice attempts to locate a device that matches the requested capabilities.

	The contents of the D3DFINDDEVICESEARCH structure are preserved across calls to FindDevice. If a particular found device is not suitable, therefore, incremental changes to the D3DFINDDEVICESEARCH struct can be made and FindDevice can be called again.
Arguments:	LPD3DFINDDEVICESEARCH lpD3DFDS—Address of the D3DFINDDEVICESEARCH structure describing the device to be located.
	LPD3DFINDDEVICERESULT lpD3DFDR—Address of the D3DFINDDEVICERESULT structure describing the device if it is found.
Return Type:	HRESULT
Return Values:	See Direct3D Immediate-Mode Return Values.
See Also:	IDirect3D::EnumDevices

Initialize

Interface:	IDirect3D
Declaration:	`HRESULT Initialize(REFIID lpREFIID);`
Description:	This function should never be called. It is provided for compliance with the COM protocol.
Notes:	Because the IDirect3D object is created via a call to IDirectDraw2::QueryInterface, the IDirectDraw2 object takes care of properly initializing the IDirect3D object.
Arguments:	REFIID lpREFIID—Address of a globally unique identifier (GUID).
Return Type:	HRESULT
Return Values:	Returns DDERR_ALREADYINITIALIZED.
See Also:	None

IDirect3DDevice

The IDirect3DDevice interface provides an abstraction for a 3D accelerator device. Through this interface an application can create execute buffers and matrices, associate viewports with the device, render a scene by processing execute buffers, and retrieve information about the device.

IDirect3DDevice, as with all COM interfaces, is derived from IUnknown and inherits its methods. A Direct3DDevice object can be obtained by calling QueryInterface() on a DirectDraw surface object that was created as a 3D-capable surface. The GUID passed to QueryInterface is usually obtained either through a call to FindDevice or by examining the available devices through a call to IDirect3D::EnumDevices(). IDirect3DDevice implements the following methods:

AddViewport	GetDirect3D
BeginScene	GetMatrix
CreateExecuteBuffer	GetPickRecords
CreateMatrix	GetStats
DeleteMatrix	Initialize
DeleteViewport	NextViewport
EndScene	Pick
EnumTextureFormats	SetMatrix
Execute	SwapTextureHandles
GetCaps	

AddViewport

Interface: IDirect3DDevice

Declaration:
```
HRESULT AddViewport(
    LPDIRECT3DVIEWPORT lpDirect3DViewport);
```

Description:	This function adds a viewport to the list of a device's viewport objects.
Notes:	Viewports must be added explicitly to a particular device. This enables viewports to survive independently of any particular device, for instance, between full-screen and windowed mode.
	AddViewport calls the viewport object's AddRef function to increase its reference count.
Arguments:	LPDIRECT3DVIEWPORT lpDirect3DViewport—Address of the Direct3D viewport object that should be associated with this Direct3D device object.
Return Type:	HRESULT

Return Values:	Returns D3D_OK if successful, or an error otherwise, which may be one of the following values:
	    DDERR_INVALIDOBJECT
	    DDERR_INVALIDPARAMS

See Also:	IDirect3D::DeleteViewport, IDirect3D::NextViewport

BeginScene

Interface:	IDirect3DDevice
Declaration:	`HRESULT BeginScene();`
Description:	This function prepares the device to execute one or more execute buffers.
Notes:	Applications must call IDirect3DDevice::BeginScene() before executing any execute buffers, after which they must call IDirect3DDevice::EndScene().
Arguments:	None
Return Type:	HRESULT
Return Values:	See Direct3D Immediate-Mode Return Values.
See Also:	IDirect3DDevice::EndScene

CreateExecuteBuffer

Interface:	IDirect3DDevice
Declaration:	HRESULT CreateExecuteBuffer(LPDIRECT3DEXECUTEBUFFERDESC lpDesc, LPDIRECT3DEXECUTEBUFFER* lplpDirect3DExecuteBuffer, IUnknown* pUnkOuter);
Description:	This function creates a new Direct3D execute buffer object.
Notes:	This function is passed through an execute buffer descriptor that specifies the size of the execute buffer, and optionally, whether the execute buffer should be created in VRAM or system memory.
	The D3DEXECUTEBUFFERDESC structure describes the execute buffer to be created. At a minimum, the application must specify the size required. If the application specifies DEBCAPS_VIDEO_MEMORY in the capabilities member, Direct3D will attempt to keep the execute buffer in video memory. Currently, however, no cards can execute buffers natively, so execute buffers are always created in system memory. Future hardware accelerators may support execute buffers in VRAM.
	The application can use the IDirect3DExecuteBuffer::Lock method to request that the memory be moved into system memory so it can be modified by the application.
Arguments:	LPDIRECT3DEXECUTEBUFFERDESC lpDesc—The address of a D3DEXECUTEBUFFERDESC structure that describes the Direct3D execute buffer object to be created. The call will fail if a buffer of at least the specified size cannot be created.
	LPDIRECT3DEXECUTEBUFFER* lplpDirect3DExecuteBuffer—The address of a pointer that will be filled with the address of the new Direct3D execute buffer object.
	IUnknown* pUnkOuter—This parameter must be NULL. It is provided for future compatibility with COM aggregation features.
Return Type:	HRESULT

Return Values:	Returns D3D_OK if successful, or an error otherwise, which may be one of the following values: DDERR_INVALIDOBJECT .....DDERR_INVALIDPARAMS
See Also:	IDirect3DExecuteBuffer::Lock, IDirect3DExecuteBuffer::Unlock

CreateMatrix

Interface:	IDirect3DDevice
Declaration:	`HRESULT CreateMatrix(LPD3DMATRIXHANDLE lpD3DMatHandle);`
Description:	This function allocates a Direct3D matrix and returns a handle to it.
Notes:	Matrices are referred to by handle, in execute buffers. Various calculations can be performed directly in an execute buffer by referring to matrix handles. The contents of a matrix may be set by using SetMatrix.
Arguments:	LPD3DMATRIXHANDLE lpD3DMatHandle—The address of a variable that will contain a handle to the matrix that is created. The call will fail if a buffer of at least the size of the matrix cannot be created.
Return Type:	HRESULT
Return Values:	See Direct3D Immediate-Mode Return Values.
See Also:	IDirect3DDevice::DeleteMatrix, IDirect3DDevice::GetMatrix, IDirect3DDevice::SetMatrix

DeleteMatrix

Interface:	IDirect3DDevice
Declaration:	`HRESULT DeleteMatrix(D3DMATRIXHANDLE d3dMatHandle);`
Description:	This function deletes a matrix specified by its handle.

continues

continued

Notes:	The matrix handle to be deleted must have been created with IDirect3DDevice::CreateMatrix(), and it must not have been deleted already.
Arguments:	D3DMATRIXHANDLE d3dMatHandle—Matrix handle to be deleted.
Return Type:	HRESULT
Return Values:	See Direct3D Immediate-Mode Return Values.
See Also:	IDirect3DDevice::CreateMatrix, IDirect3DDevice::GetMatrix, IDirect3DDevice::SetMatrix

DeleteViewport

Interface:	IDirect3DDevice
Declaration:	`HRESULT DeleteViewport(` `    LPDIRECT3DVIEWPORT lpDirect3DViewport);`
Description:	This function removes the specified viewport from the device's list of viewport objects.
Notes:	Viewports are only loosely associated with devices, so that viewports can survive a change of device, for instance, going between full-screen and windowed mode.
	DeleteViewport calls the viewport's Release method to balance the fact that IDirect3DDevice::AddViewport calls its AddRef method.
Arguments:	LPDIRECT3DVIEWPORT lpDirect3DViewport—The address of the Direct3D viewport object that should be disassociated with this Direct3D device object.
Return Type:	HRESULT
Return Values:	Returns D3D_OK if successful, or an error otherwise, which may be one of the following values: 　　DDERR_INVALIDOBJECT 　　DDERR_INVALIDPARAMS
See Also:	IDirect3D::AddViewport, IDirect3D::NextViewport

EndScene

Interface:	IDirect3DDevice
Declaration:	`HRESULT EndScene();`
Description:	This function is called after a series of execute buffers are executed to signal the end of the scene.
Notes:	The call to EndScene() must match a corresponding call to IDirect3DDevice::BeginScene().
Arguments:	Applications must call IDirect3DDevice::BeginScene before any buffers are executed, and IDirect3DDevice::EndScene afterwards.
Return Type:	HRESULT
Return Values:	See Direct3D Immediate-Mode Return Values.
See Also:	IIDirect3DDevice::BeginScene

EnumTextureFormats

Interface:	IDirect3DDevice

Declaration:	`HRESULT EnumTextureFormats(`
	`LPD3DENUMTEXTUREFORMATSCALLBACK lpd3dEnumTextureProc,`
	`LPVOID lpArg);`

Description:	This function enumerates the available texture formats for a device.
Notes:	This function can be used in conjunction with the D3DENUMTEXTUREFORMATSCALLBACK to enable the user to choose a specific texture format based on available capabilities. It can be used also to verify the available texture formats to perform the most optimal texture code. After a suitable texture format has been found, the callback can avoid enumerating any further formats by returning D3DENUMRET_CANCEL from the callback function.

continues

continued

Arguments:	LPD3DENUMTEXTUREFORMATSCALLBACK lpd3dEnumTextureProc—The address of the D3DENUMTEXTUREFORMATSCALLBACK callback function that the enumeration procedure will call for each texture format.
	LPVOID lpArg—The address of application-defined data passed to the callback function.
Return Type:	HRESULT
Return Values:	Returns D3D_OK if successful, or an error otherwise, which may be one of the following values:
	DDERR_INVALIDOBJECT
	DDERR_INVALIDPARAMS
See Also:	D3DENUMTEXTUREFORMATSCALLBACK

Execute

Interface:	IDirect3DDevice
Declaration:	```HRESULT Execute(
LPDIRECT3DEXECUTEBUFFER lpDirect3DExecuteBuffer,
LPDIRECT3DVIEWPORT lpDirect3DViewport,
DWORD dwFlags);```
Description:	This function executes a Direct3D execute buffer.
Notes:	All calls to Execute must occur between matching calls to IDirect3DDevice::BeginScene and IDirect3DDevice::EndScene.
	Execute buffers can contain rendering primitives, as well as commands to change the state of the transformation, lighting, or rasterization modules.
	If only state is being changed, or the vertices in the execute buffer are known to lie within the view frustum, passing D3DEXECUTE_UNCLIPPED for the dwFlags argument may result in faster execution.
Arguments:	LPDIRECT3DEXECUTEBUFFER lpDirect3DExecuteBuffer—The address of the Direct3D execute buffer to be executed.

LPDIRECT3DVIEWPORT lpDirect3DViewport—The address of the Direct3D viewport object into which any rendering is to take place.

DWORD dwFlags—The flags specifying whether or not objects in the buffer should be clipped. This parameter must be one of the following values:

D3DEXECUTE_CLIPPED—Clip any primitives in the buffer that are outside or partially outside the viewport.

D3DEXECUTE_UNCLIPPED—All primitives in the buffer are contained within the viewport.

Return Type: HRESULT

Return Values: Returns D3D_OK if successful, or an error otherwise, which may be one of the following values:

DDERR_INVALIDOBJECT

DDERR_INVALIDPARAMS

See Also: IDirect3DDevice::CreateExecuteBuffer

GetCaps

Interface: IDirect3DDevice

Declaration:
```
HRESULT GetCaps(
LPD3DDEVICEDESC lpD3DHWDevDesc,
LPD3DDEVICEDESC lpD3DHELDevDesc);
```

Description: This function retrieves the capabilities of the Direct3D device object.

Notes: This method does not retrieve the capabilities of the display device. To retrieve this information, use the IDirectDraw2::GetCaps method.

See D3DDEVICEDESC for a detailed list of the allowed capabilities.

Arguments: LPD3DDEVICEDESC lpD3DHWDevDesc—The address of the D3DDEVICEDESC structure that will contain the hardware features of the device.

LPD3DDEVICEDESC lpD3DHELDevDesc—The address of the D3DDEVICEDESC structure that will contain the software emulation being provided.

continues

continued

Return Type:	HRESULT

Return Values:	Returns D3D_OK if successful, or an error otherwise, which may be one of the following values:
	    DDERR_INVALIDOBJECT
	    DDERR_INVALIDPARAMS

See Also:	IDirect3D::FindDevice, D3DDEVICEDESC

GetDirect3D

Interface:	IDirect3DDevice
Declaration:	`HRESULT GetDirect3D(LPDIRECT3D* lpD3D);`
Description:	This function retrieves the current Direct3D object.
Notes:	This function is provided as a convenience and for situations in which keeping a global variable holding the IDirect3D object is not convenient.
Arguments:	LPDIRECT3D* lpD3D—The address that will contain the Direct3D object when the function returns.
Return Type:	HRESULT
Return Values:	See Direct3D Immediate-Mode Return Values.
See Also:	IDirect3D

GetMatrix

Interface:	IDirect3DDevice

Declaration:	`HRESULT GetMatrix(`
	    `D3DMATRIXHANDLE lpD3DMatHandle,`
	    `LPD3DMATRIX lpD3DMatrix);`

Description:	This function retrieves the contents of a matrix from its matrix handle.
Notes:	The matrix handle must have been created by using IDirect3DDevice::CreateMatrix and not yet been deleted by IDirect3DDevice::DeleteMatrix.

Arguments: D3DMATRIXHANDLE D3DMatHandle—The matrix handle.

LPD3DMATRIX lpD3DMatrix—The address of a D3DMATRIX structure that will contain the matrix when the function returns.

Return Type: HRESULT

Return Values: See Direct3D Immediate-Mode Return Values.

See Also: IDirect3DDevice::CreateMatrix, IDirect3DDevice::DeleteMatrix, IDirect3DDevice::SetMatrix

GetPickRecords

Interface: IDirect3DDevice

Declaration:
```
HRESULT GetPickRecords(
LPDWORD lpCount,
LPD3DPICKRECORD lpD3DPickRec);
```

Description: This function retrieves the pick records for a Direct3D device. This function can also report the number of pick records.

Notes: If the pick record pointer argument is NULL, this function will return the number of pick records the Direct3D device has. After the application knows how many records exists, it can allocate the required amount of memory and call IDirect3DDevice::GetPickRecords() with the pick record pointer argument pointing to the newly allocated memory, into which to retrieve the actual records.

Arguments: LPDWORD lpCount—If lpD3DPickRec is NULL, the variable pointed to by lpCount will contain the total number of pick records for the device object when the function returns. Otherwise, lopCount should be the address of a variable that contains the number of D3DPICKRECORD structures to retrieve.

LPD3DPICKRECORD lpD3DPickRec—If this argument is NULL, the variable pointed to by lpCount will contain the total number of pick records for the device object. Otherwise lpD3DPickRec should be the address of an array of D3DPICKRECORD structures which will hold the pick records when the method returns.

continues

continued

Return Type:	HRESULT
Return Values:	See Direct3D Immediate-Mode Return Values.
See Also:	IDirect3DDevice::Pick

GetStats

Interface:	IDirect3DDevice
Declaration:	`HRESULT GetStats(LPD3DSTATS lpD3DStats);`
Description:	This function retrieves geometry and rendering statistics about a device.
Notes:	The D3DSTATS structure reports the number of triangles, lines, points, and spans drawn since the device was created as well as the number of vertices processed since the device was created.
Arguments:	LPD3DSTATS lpD3DStats—The address of a D3DSTATS structure that will be filled with the statistics.
Return Type:	HRESULT

Return Values:	Returns D3D_OK if successful, or an error otherwise, which may be one of the following values:
	    DDERR_INVALIDOBJECT
	    DDERR_INVALIDPARAMS

See Also:	D3DSTATS

Initialize

Interface:	IDirect3DDevice

Declaration:	`HRESULT Initialize(`
	    `LPDIRECT3D lpd3d,`
	    `LPGUID lpGUID,`
	    `LPD3DDEVICEDESC lpd3ddvdesc);`

Description:	This function should never be called. It is provided for compliance with the COM protocol.
Notes:	Because the IDirect3DDevice object is created via a call to IDirectDrawSurface::QueryInterface, the IDirectDrawSurface object takes care of properly initializing the IDirect3D object.
Arguments:	LPDIRECT3D lpd3d—The address of the Direct3D object to use as an initializer.
	LPGUID lpGUID—The address of the globally unique identifier (GUID) used as the interface identifier.
	LPD3DDEVICEDESC lpd3ddvdesc—The address of a D3DDEVICEDESC structure describing the Direct3DDevice object to be initialized.
Return Type:	HRESULT
Return Values:	Returns DDERR_ALREADYINITIALIZED.
See Also:	None

NextViewport

Interface:	IDirect3DDevice
Declaration:	```HRESULT NextViewport(
LPDIRECT3DVIEWPORT lpDirect3DViewport,
LPDIRECT3DVIEWPORT* lplpDirect3DViewport,
DWORD dwFlags);```
Description:	This function enumerates a Direct3D device's viewport objects.
Notes:	NextViewport can be used to retrieve the first, last, or next viewport in the device's list of viewports.
Arguments:	LPDIRECT3DVIEWPORT lpDirect3DViewport—The address of a viewport in the list of viewports associated with this device.
	LPDIRECT3DVIEWPORT* lplpDirect3DViewport—The address of the next viewport in the list of viewports associated with this device.
	DWORD dwFlags—The flags specifying which viewport to retrieve from the list of viewports. The default setting is D3DNEXT_NEXT.

continues

continued

	D3DNEXT_HEAD—Retrieves the item at the beginning of the list.
	D3DNEXT_NEXT—Retrieves the next item in the list.
	D3DNEXT_TAIL—Retrieves the item at the end of the list.
Return Type:	HRESULT
Return Values:	D3D_OK if successful, or an error otherwise, which may be one of the following values:
	DDERR_INVALIDOBJECT
	DDERR_INVALIDPARAMS
See Also:	IDirect3DDevice::AddViewport, IDirect3DDevice::DeleteViewport

Pick

Interface:	IDirect3DDevice
| **Declaration:** | ```
HRESULT Pick(
LPDIRECT3DEXECUTEBUFFER lpDirect3DExecuteBuffer,
LPDIRECT3DVIEWPORT lpDirect3DViewport,
DWORD dwFlags,
LPD3DRECT lpRect);
``` |
Description:	This function is used to map screen coordinates to objects in a 3D scene.
Notes:	Pick executes the supplied execute buffer and generates a z-ordered list of the D3DOPCODEs that rendered into the rectangle pointed to by the lpRect parameter. The generated list is accessed via IDirect3DDevice::GetPickRecords().
	If the rectangle's top-left point is the same as its bottom right, Pick selects only those primitives that modify the single pixel at that point.
	Using Pick in a complex scene can be complicated because typically several execute buffers are used to generate the scene. Pick must be called for each execute buffer, and IDirect3DDevice::GetPickRecords must be called between each call to Pick or else the results of the previous Pick operation will be lost.
	This call fails if the Direct3D execute buffer object is locked.
```

Arguments:	LPDIRECT3DEXECUTEBUFFER lpDirect3DExecuteBuffer—The address of the execute buffer.
	LPDIRECT3DVIEWPORT lpDirect3DViewport—The address of the viewport that the execute buffer is executed into for display.
	DWORD dwFlags—Must be 0. No flags are currently defined for this method.
	LPD3DRECT lpRect—The address of a D3DRECT structure specifying the range of device coordinates to be picked.
Return Type:	HRESULT
Return Values:	Returns D3D_OK if successful, or an error otherwise, which may be one of the following values:
	DDERR_EXECUTE_LOCKED
	DDERR_INVALIDOBJECT
	DDERR_INVALIDPARAMS
See Also:	IDirect3DDevice::Execute, IDirect3DDevice::GetPickRecords

SetMatrix

Interface:	IDirect3DDevice
Declaration:	```HRESULT SetMatrix(D3DMATRIXHANDLE d3dMatHandle, LPD3DMATRIX lpD3DMatrix);```
Description:	This function sets the value of a matrix.
Notes:	Matrix handles are typically embedded in execute buffers. SetMatrix enables the application to change the value of a matrix from outside an execute buffer.
Arguments:	D3DMATRIXHANDLE d3dMatHandle—The handle of the matrix to be set.
	LPD3DMATRIX lpD3DMatrix—The address of a D3DMATRIX structure that contains the new value for the matrix.
Return Type:	HRESULT

continues

continued

Return Values: See Direct3D Immediate-Mode Return Values.

See Also: IDirect3DDevice::CreateMatrix, IDirect3DDevice::DeleteMatrix, IDirect3DDevice::GetMatrix

SwapTextureHandles

Interface: IDirect3DDevice

Declaration:
```
HRESULT SwapTextureHandles(
LPDIRECT3DTEXTURE lpD3DTex1,
LPDIRECT3DTEXTURE lpD3DTex2);
```

Description: This function swaps two texture handles.

Notes: SwapTextureHandles can be used to change the texture referred to by a particular texture handle. This is faster, typically, than locking an execute buffer, changing the texture handle values in it, and then unlocking it. This allows changing the appearance of an object, without changing its meshes.

SwapTextureHandles can also be used as part of a scheme to share execute buffers among different, similar objects in a scene. By changing the texture referred to by a particular handle value, the same execute buffer can render a mesh in different places with different textures, without modifying the contents of the execute buffer.

Arguments: LPDIRECT3DTEXTURE lpD3DTex1—The address of the first texture whose handle will be swapped.

LPDIRECT3DTEXTURE lpD3DTex2—The address of the second texture whose handle will be swapped.

Return Type: HRESULT

Return Values: See Direct3D Immediate-Mode Return Values.

See Also: IDirect3DTexture::GetHandle

IDirect3DExecuteBuffer

The IDirect3DExecuteBuffer interface enables an application to create execute buffers that describe the 3D scene. Through this interface, applications can obtain and release exclusive access to the execute buffer contents, as well as set and retrieve the execute buffer data and state.

IDirect3DExecuteBuffer, as with all COM interfaces, is derived from IUnknown and inherits its methods. A Direct3DExecuteBuffer object can be obtained by calling IDirect3DDevice::CreateExecuteBuffer(). IDirect3DExecuteBuffer implements the following methods:

- GetExecuteData
- Initialize
- Lock
- Optimize
- SetExecuteData
- Unlock
- Validate

GetExecuteData

Interface:	IDirect3DExecuteBuffer
Declaration:	`HRESULT GetExecuteData(LPD3DEXECUTEDATA lpData);`
Description:	This function retrieves the execute data state from a Direct3D execute buffer object.
Notes:	The execute data is used to describe the contents of a Direct3D execute buffer object. In particular, the dsStatus field of the D3DEXECUTEDATA struct contains the damage extent rectangle,

continues

continued

which is the bounding rectangle of all pixels that were changed by the most recent call to IDirect3DExecuteBuffer::Execute. The dsStatus field also contains the clipping flags, which indicate if any clipping occurred and in which direction.

Arguments: LPD3DEXECUTEDATA lpData—The address of a D3DEXECUTEDATA structure that will be filled with the current execute data state of the Direct3D execute buffer object.

Return Type: HRESULT

Return Values: Returns D3D_OK if successful, or an error otherwise, which may be one of the following values:

    DDERR_EXECUTE_LOCKED

    DDERR_INVALIDOBJECT

    DDERR_INVALIDPARAMS

See Also: IDirect3DExecuteBuffer::SetExecuteData, D3DEXECUTEDATA, D3DSTATUS

Initialize

Interface: IDirect3DExecuteBuffer

Declaration:
```
HRESULT Initialize(
LPDIRECT3DDEVICE lpDirect3DDevice,
LPD3DEXECUTEBUFFERDESC lpDesc);
```

Description: This function should never be called. It is provided for compliance with the COM protocol.

Notes: Because an IDirect3DExecuteBuffer object is created via a call to IDirect3DDevice::CreateExecuteBuffer, the IDirect3DDevice object takes care of properly initializing the execute buffer object.

Arguments: LPDIRECT3DDEVICE lpDirect3DDevice—The address of the device that created the execute buffer.

LPD3DEXECUTEBUFFERDESC lpDesc—The address of a D3DEXECUTEBUFFERDESC structure that describes the

Direct3DExecuteBuffer object to be created. The call fails if a buffer of at least the specified size cannot be created.

Return Type: HRESULT

Return Values: Returns DDERR_ALREADYINITIALIZED because the Direct3D execute buffer object is initialized when it is created.

See Also: IDirect3D::Initialize, IDirect3DLight::Initialize, IDirect3DMaterial::Initialize, IDirect3DViewport::Initialize

Lock

Interface: IDirect3DExecuteBuffer

Declaration: `HRESULT Lock(LPD3DEXECUTEBUFFERDESC lpDesc);`

Description: This function locks an execute buffer so an application can modify its contents.

Notes: The execute buffer may reside in system or video memory as specified by the dwCaps member. The application may use Lock to request that Direct3D move the data into system memory so that it may be altered by the application.

This call fails if the Direct3DExecuteBuffer object is already locked or if a call to IDirect3DDevice::Execute() on this buffer has not yet completed.

After Lock executes, the execute buffer descriptor pointed to by the lpDesc argument will contain whether the execute buffer lives in video or system memory, its size, and a pointer to its data.

Arguments: lpDesc—The address of a D3DEXECUTEBUFFERDESC structure. When this function returns, the lpData member will point to the buffer contents to which the application has been granted access.

Return Type: HRESULT

Return Values: Returns D3D_OK if successful, or an error otherwise, which may be one of the following values:

DDERR_EXECUTE_LOCKED

DDERR_INVALIDOBJECT

continues

continued	DDERR_INVALIDPARAMS
	DDERR_WASSTILLDRAWING
See Also:	IDirect3DExecuteBuffer::Unlock, D3DEXECUTEBUFFERDESC

Optimize

Interface:	IDirect3DExecuteBuffer
Declaration:	`HRESULT Optimize(DWORD);`
Description:	This function is not currently implemented.
Notes:	Future versions of Direct3D may implement this function to optimize an execute buffer in-place based on various heuristics chosen with respect to the particular driver.
Arguments:	DWORD—This parameter is not documented by Microsoft.
Return Type:	HRESULT
Return Values:	DDERR_UNSUPPORTED

SetExecuteData

Interface:	IDirect3DExecuteBuffer
Declaration:	`HRESULT SetExecuteData(LPD3DEXECUTEDATA lpData);`
Description:	This function sets the execute data state of the Direct3DExecuteBuffer object.
Notes:	After unlocking an execute buffer that has been modified, an application must use SetExecuteData to provide the execute buffer with the offset of the first vertex in the execute buffer, the number of vertices in the execute buffer, the offset of the first instruction, and the number of instructions.
	SetExecuteData can also be used to reset the status word and to reset the damage extent rectangle, though this is usually done by instructions in an execute buffer.

	This call fails if the Direct3DExecuteBuffer object is locked.
Arguments:	LPD3DEXECUTEDATA lpData—Address of a D3DEXECUTEDATA structure that describes the execute buffer layout.
Return Type:	HRESULT
Return Values:	Returns D3D_OK if successful, or an error otherwise, which may be one of the following values:
	DDERR_EXECUTE_LOCKED
	DDERR_INVALIDOBJECT
	DDERR_INVALIDPARAMS
See Also:	IDirect3DExecuteBuffer::GetExecuteData

Unlock

Interface:	IDirect3DExecuteBuffer
Declaration:	`HRESULT Unlock();`
Description:	This function unlocks an execute buffer that was previously locked with IDirect3DExecuteBuffer::Lock.
Notes:	After the contents of an execute buffer have changed, the execute buffer must be unlocked. After being unlocked, its contents are no longer available to be examined or modified until it is locked again. Depending on the particular driver, accelerator card, and descriptor used to create the execute buffer, unlocking an execute buffer may cause it to be copied into VRAM for faster processing.
	Currently, no accelerator cards can execute buffers in VRAM.
	IDirect3DExecuteBuffer::Unlock() must be called prior to calling IDirect3DDevice::SetExecuteData() and IDirect3DDevice::Execute().
Arguments:	None
Return Type:	HRESULT

continues

continued

Return Values: Returns D3D_OK if successful, or an error otherwise, which may be one of the following values:

    DDERR_EXECUTE_NOT_LOCKED

    DDERR_INVALIDOBJECT

See Also: IDirect3DExecuteBuffer::Lock

Validate

Interface: IDirect3DExecuteBuffer

Declaration:
```
HRESULT Validate(
LPDWORD lpdwOffset,
LPD3DVALIDATECALLBACK lpFunc,
LPVOID lpUserArg,
DWORD dwReserved);
```

Description: This function is not currently implemented.

Notes: Future versions of Direct3D may check execute buffers for consistency and proper syntax.

Arguments: LPDWORD lpdwOffset—The pointer to a DWORD holding the offset into the execute buffer at which to start validating. After the call, the DWORD will hold the offset into the execute buffer of the first error found by Validate.

LPD3DVALIDATECALLBACK lpFunc—The address of user-supplied callback function, or NULL.

LPVOID lpUserArg—User-supplied argument to user-supplied callback function.

DWORD dwReserved—Must be 0.

Return Type: HRESULT

Return Values: DDERR_UNSUPPORTED

See Also: D3DVALIDATECALLBACK

IDirect3DLight

The IDirect3DLight interface enables an application to set and retrieve the attributes of Immediate-Mode light objects. Through this interface, applications can adjust the characteristics of the various light types supported in Direct3D.

IDirect3DLight, as with all COM interfaces, is derived from IUnknown and inherits its methods. A Direct3DLight object can be obtained by calling IDirect3D::CreateLight(). IDirect3DLight implements the following methods:

GetLight

Initialize

SetLight

GetLight

Interface:	IDirect3DLight
Declaration:	`HRESULT GetLight(LPD3DLIGHT lpLight);`
Description:	This function retrieves the light information for a Direct3D light object.
Notes:	The D3DLIGHT structure reports light type, color, position, direction, range, falloff, attenuation values, and penumbra angle (for spotlights).
Arguments:	LPD3DLIGHT lpLight—The address of a D3DLIGHT structure that will be filled with the current light data.
Return Type:	HRESULT

Return Values:	Returns D3D_OK if successful, or an error otherwise, which may be one of the following values:
	    DDERR_INVALIDOBJECT
	    DDERR_INVALIDPARAMS

See Also:	IDirect3DLight::SetLight

Initialize

Interface:	IDirect3DLight
Declaration:	`HRESULT Initialize(LPDIRECT3D lpDirect3D);`
Description:	This function should never be called. It is provided for compliance with the COM protocol.
Notes:	Because an IDirect3DLight object is created via a call to IDirect3D::CreateLight, the IDirect3D object takes care of properly initializing the light object.
Arguments:	LPDIRECT3D lpDirect3D—The address of the Direct3D structure representing the Direct3D object.
Return Type:	HRESULT
Return Values:	DDERR_ALREADYINITIALIZED.
See Also:	None

SetLight

Interface:	IDirect3DLight
Declaration:	`HRESULT SetLight(LPD3DLIGHT lpLight);`
Description:	This function sets the light information for a Direct3D light object.
Notes:	The D3DLIGHT structure reports light type, color, position, direction, range, falloff, attenuation values, and umbra and penumbra angle (for spotlights).
Arguments:	LPD3DLIGHT lpLight—The address of a D3DLIGHT structure that will be used to set the current light data.
Return Type:	HRESULT

Return Values:	Returns D3D_OK if successful, or an error otherwise, which may be one of the following values:
	    DDERR_INVALIDOBJECT
	    DDERR_INVALIDPARAMS

See Also:	IDirect3DLight::GetLight

IDirect3DMaterial

The IDirect3DMaterial interface enables an application to set and retrieve the attributes of Immediate-Mode material objects. Through this interface, applications can adjust the characteristics of a material such as its diffuse, ambient, specular, and emissive colors, its specular exponent, and its ramp size.

IDirect3DMaterial, as with all COM interfaces, is derived from IUnknown and inherits its methods. A Direct3DMaterial object can be obtained by calling IDirect3D::Create Material(). IDirect3D implements the following methods:

- GetHandle
- GetMaterial
- Initialize
- Reserve
- SetMaterial
- Unreserve

GetHandle

Interface:	IDirect3DMaterial

Declaration:	`HRESULT GetHandle(`
	`LPDIRECT3DDEVICE lpDirect3DDevice,`
	`LPD3DMATERIALHANDLE lpHandle);`

Description:	This function retrieves the material handle for a Direct3D material object.
Notes:	Material handles are typically embedded in execute buffers to set the material for a face or collection of faces.
Arguments:	LPDIRECT3DDEVICE lpDirect3DDevice—The address of the Direct3D device object in which the material is being used.

continues

continued

	LPD3DMATERIALHANDLE lpHandle—The address of a handle that will be filled with the material's handle.
Return Type:	HRESULT
Return Values:	Returns D3D_OK if successful, or DDERR_INVALIDOBJECT otherwise.
See Also:	IDirect3DMaterial, IDirect3DDevice::CreateMaterial, D3DLIGHTSTATE_MATERIAL

GetMaterial

Interface:	IDirect3DMaterial
Declaration:	`HRESULT GetMaterial(LPD3DMATERIAL lpMat);`
Description:	This function retrieves the material data for a Direct3D material object.
Notes:	The D3DMATERIAL structure reports the diffuse, ambient, specular, and emissive colors of a material as well as the specular exponent, the color ramp size, and the handle of the texture map, if any. If the material is not associated with a texture, the texture handle will be 0.
Arguments:	LPD3DMATERIAL lpMat—The address of a D3DMATERIAL structure that will be filled with the current material properties.
Return Type:	HRESULT
Return Values:	Returns D3D_OK if successful, or an error otherwise, which may be one of the following values:
	DDERR_INVALIDOBJECT
	DDERR_INVALIDPARAMS
See Also:	IDirect3DMaterial::SetMaterial

Initialize

Interface:	IDirect3DMaterial
Declaration:	`HRESULT Initialize(LPDIRECT3D lpDirect3D);`
Description:	This function should never be called. It is provided for compliance with the COM protocol.
Notes:	Because an IDirect3DMaterial object is created via a call to IDirect3D::CreateMaterial, the IDirect3D object takes care of properly initializing the material object.
Arguments:	LPDIRECT3D lpDirect3D—The address of the Direct3D object that created the material.
Return Type:	HRESULT
Return Values:	Returns DDERR_ALREADYINITIALIZED because the Direct3D material object is initialized when it is created.
See Also:	None

Reserve

Interface:	IDirect3DMaterial
Declaration:	`HRESULT Reserve();`
Description:	This function is not currently implemented.
Notes:	Reserve and IDirect3DMaterial::Unreserve may be used in future versions of Direct3D to enable the application a finer level of control over which materials are active, on-card, and using entries in the palette.
Arguments:	None
Return Type:	HRESULT
Return Values:	DDERR_UNSUPPORTED
See Also:	IDirect3DMaterial::Unreserve

SetMaterial

Interface:	IDirect3DMaterial
Declaration:	`HRESULT SetMaterial(LPD3DMATERIAL lpMat);`
Description:	This function sets the material data for the Direct3DMaterial object.
Notes:	The D3DMATERIAL structure contains the new diffuse, ambient, specular, and emissive colors for the material. It also contains the specular exponent, the color ramp size, and the handle of the texture map, which may be 0 if no texture is associated with the material.
Arguments:	lpMat—The address of a D3DMATERIAL structure that contains the material properties.
Return Type:	HRESULT

Return Values:	Returns D3D_OK if successful, or an error otherwise, which may be one of the following values:
	    DDERR_INVALIDOBJECT
	    DDERR_INVALIDPARAMS

See Also:	IDirect3DMaterial::GetMaterial

Unreserve

Interface:	IDirect3DMaterial
Declaration:	`HRESULT Unreserve();`
Description:	This function is not currently implemented.
Notes:	IDirect3DMaterial::Reserve and Unreserve may be used in future versions of Direct3D to allow the application a finer level of control over which materials are active, on-card, and using entries in the palette.
Arguments:	None
Return Type:	HRESULT
Return Values:	DDERR_UNSUPPORTED
See Also:	IDirect3DMaterial::Reserve

IDirect3DTexture

The IDirect3DTexture interface enables an application to set and retrieve the attributes of Immediate-Mode texture objects. Through this interface, an application can obtain a texture handle, inform the system that the palette for a texture has changed, and load or unload a texture to or from display memory.

Some hardware drivers limit texture dimensions to 64×64, 128×128, and 256×256 pixels.

IDirect3DTexture, as with all COM interfaces, is derived from IUnknown and inherits its methods. A Direct3DTexture object can be obtained through the appropriate call to QueryInterface() on a DirectDraw surface object that was created as a texture map. IDirect3DTexture implements the following methods:

GetHandle

Initialize

Load

PaletteChanged

Unload

GetHandle

Interface:	IDirect3DTexture

Declaration:	`HRESULT GetHandle(`
	`    LPDIRECT3DDEVICE lpDirect3DDevice,`
	`    LPD3DTEXTUREHANDLE lpHandle);`

Description:	This function retrieves the texture handle from a Direct3D texture object.
Notes:	This handle is typically embedded in execute buffers to specify a texture for a face or collection of faces.

continues

continued

Arguments:	LPDIRECT3DDEVICE lpDirect3DDevice—The address of a Direct3D device object into which the texture is to be loaded.
	LPD3DTEXTUREHANDLE lpHandle—The address of a handle that will contain the handle corresponding to the Direct3D texture object.
Return Type:	HRESULT
Return Values:	Returns D3D_OK if successful, or an error otherwise, which may be one of the following values:
	DDERR_BADOBJECT
	DDERR_INVALIDPARAMS
See Also:	D3DRENDERSTATE_TEXTUREHANDLE

Initialize

Interface:	IDirect3DTexture
Declaration:	```HRESULT Initialize(
LPDIRECT3DDEVICE lpD3DDevice,
LPDIRECTDRAWSURFACE lpDDSurface);```
Description:	This function should never be called. It is provided for compliance with the COM protocol.
Notes:	Because an IDirect3DMaterial object is created via a call to IDirectDrawSurface::QueryInterface, the IDirectDrawSurface object takes care of properly initializing the texture object.
Arguments:	LPDIRECT3D lpDirect3D—The address of IDirect3D object.
Return Type:	HRESULT
Return Values:	Returns DDERR_ALREADYINITIALIZED because the Direct3D viewport object is initialized when it is created.
See Also:	None

Load

Interface:	IDirect3DTexture
Declaration:	`HRESULT Load(LPDIRECT3DTEXTURE lpD3DTexture);`
Description:	This function loads a texture on-card that was created with the DDSCAPS_ALLOCONLOAD flag.
Notes:	A texture created with the DDSCAPS_ALLOCONLOAD flag from a surface in system memory should be loaded on-card, if supported, for best performance.
	Load may radically alter the format of the texture, compressing if necessary. To dynamically change the contents of an on-card texture, an application must call IDirect3DTexture::Unload before changing the texture contents and then Load again to move it back on-card.
Arguments:	LPDIRECT3DTEXTURE lpD3DTexture—The address of the texture to load.
Return Type:	HRESULT
Return Values:	See Direct3D Immediate-Mode Return Values.
See Also:	IDirect3DTexture::Unload

PaletteChanged

Interface:	IDirect3DTexture
Declaration:	`HRESULT PaletteChanged(DWORD dwStart, DWORD dwCount);`
Description:	This function informs the driver that the palette has changed on a surface.
Notes:	This method is particularly useful for applications that play video clips into a texture surface or modify texture contents directly, which requires changing the palette periodically.

continues

continued

Arguments:	DWORD dwStart—The index of first palette entry that has changed.
	DWORD dwCount—The number of palette entries that have changed.
Return Type:	HRESULT
Return Values:	See Direct3D Immediate-Mode Return Values.
See Also:	None

Unload

Interface:	IDirect3DTexture
Declaration:	`HRESULT Unload();`
Description:	This function unloads a texture from on-card to system memory.
Notes:	A texture that is on-card may have an undocumented format. Thus, to change the contents of a texture surface, if it was loaded on-card with IDirect3DTexture::Load, the texture should be unloaded from the card before being modified.
Arguments:	None
Return Type:	HRESULT
Return Values:	See Direct3D Immediate-Mode Return Values.
See Also:	IDirect3DTexture::Load

IDirect3DViewport

The IDirect3DViewport interface provides the functionality to control an Immediate-Mode viewport object. Through this interface, an application can adjust the viewport attributes, set the viewport background material, manipulate lights, and transform vertices.

IDirect3DViewport, as with all COM interfaces, is derived from IUnknown and inherits its methods. A Direct3DViewport object can be obtained by calling IDirect3D::CreateViewport(). IDirect3DViewport implements the following methods:

AddLight

Clear

DeleteLight

GetBackground

GetBackgroundDepth

GetViewport

Initialize

LightElements

NextLight

SetBackground

SetBackgroundDepth

SetViewport

TransformVertices

AddLight

Interface:	IDirect3DViewport
Declaration:	`HRESULT AddLight(LPDIRECT3DLIGHT lpDirect3DLight);`
Description:	This function adds the specified light to the list of a Direct3D viewport's lights.
Notes:	A light only illuminates objects after it has been added to the viewport of the scene to be illuminated.
	AddLight calls the light's AddRef member function.
Arguments:	LPDIRECT3DLIGHT lpDirect3DLight—The address of the Direct3D light object to associate with the Direct3D viewport object.
Return Type:	HRESULT
Return Values:	Returns D3D_OK if successful, or an error otherwise, which may be one of the following values:
	DDERR_INVALIDOBJECT
	DDERR_INVALIDPARAMS
See Also:	IDirect3DViewport::DeleteLight, IDirect3DViewport::LightElements, IDirect3DViewport::NextLight

Clear

Interface:	IDirect3DViewport

Declaration:	`HRESULT Clear(`
	`  DWORD dwCount,`
	`  LPD3DRECT lpRects,`
	`  DWORD dwFlags);`

Description:	This function clears one or more rectangular regions of a Direct3D viewport to the current background material and depth.
Notes:	Clear can be used to clear the back buffer and/or z-buffer associated with the viewport.

	A viewport may have a background material and/or a background z-buffer, the contents of which Clear will use to initialize the back buffer and z-buffer. Otherwise, the back buffer is filled with black and the z-buffer is filled with z-values corresponding to the maximum distance from the camera.

Several rectangles may be passed to this function so that the driver can clear them all faster than it would if several calls to Clear were required.

Arguments: DWORD dwCount—The number of rectangles pointed to by lpRects.

LPD3DRECT lpRects—The address of an array of D3DRECT structures.

DWORD dwFlags—The flags indicating what to clear: the rendering target, the z-buffer, or both.

D3DCLEAR_TARGET—Clear the rendering target to the background material (if set).

D3DCLEAR_ZBUFFER—Clear the z-buffer or set it to the current background depth field (if set).

Return Type: HRESULT

Return Values: Returns D3D_OK if successful, or an error otherwise, which may be one of the following values:

DDERR_INVALIDOBJECT

DDERR_INVALIDPARAMS

See Also: IDirect3DViewport::GetBackground,
IDirect3DViewport::GetBackgroundDepth,
IDirect3DViewport::SetBackground,
IDirect3DViewport::SetBackgroundDepth

DeleteLight

Interface: IDirect3DViewport

Declaration: `HRESULT DeleteLight(LPDIRECT3DLIGHT lpDirect3DLight);`

continues

continued

Description:	This function removes the specified light from the list of a Direct3D viewport's lights.
Notes:	The light must have been previously added to the viewport via IDirect3DViewport::AddLight.
	A light that is removed from a viewport no longer lights objects in that viewport's scene.
	This function calls the light's Release method to match the call to AddRef when the light was added via IDirect3DViewport::AddLight.
Arguments:	LPDIRECT3DLIGHT lpDirect3DLight—The address of the Direct3D light object that should be disassociated with the Direct3D viewport object.
Return Type:	HRESULT
Return Values:	Returns D3D_OK if successful, or an error otherwise, which may be one of the following values:
	DDERR_INVALIDOBJECT
	DDERR_INVALIDPARAMS
See Also:	IDirect3DViewport::AddLight, IDirect3DViewport::LightElements, IDirect3DViewport::NextLight

GetBackground

Interface:	IDirect3DViewport

Declaration:	`HRESULT GetBackground(`
	`LPD3DMATERIALHANDLE lphMat,`
	`LPBOOL lpValid );`

Description:	This function retrieves the handle of a material that is the Direct3D viewport's current background material.
Notes:	The background material controls the color and, optionally, a texture for the background of the viewport.
	The software renderer can support textures of arbitrary sizes, but some hardware accelerators limit textures to 64×64, 128×128, and 256×256 pixels.

Arguments:	LPD3DMATERIALHANDLE lphMat—The address that will contain the handle of the material being used as the background. LPBOOL lpValid—The address of a variable that will be filled to indicate whether a background is associated with the viewport. If this parameter returns FALSE, no background is associated with the viewport.
Return Type:	HRESULT
Return Values:	Returns D3D_OK if successful, or an error otherwise, which may be one of the following values: 　　DDERR_INVALIDOBJECT 　　DDERR_INVALIDPARAMS
See Also:	IDirect3DViewport::Clear, IDirect3DViewport::GetBackgroundDepth, IDirect3DViewport::SetBackground, IDirect3DViewport::SetBackgroundDepth

GetBackgroundDepth

Interface:	IDirect3DViewport
Declaration:	```HRESULT GetBackgroundDepth(` `LPDIRECTDRAWSURFACE* lplpDDSurface,` `LPBOOL lpValid);```
Description:	This function retrieves the DirectDraw surface, if any, that is the Direct3D viewport's current background-depth field.
Notes:	Applications may provide a second z-buffer, the contents of which is used by IDirect3DViewport::Clear() to initialize the z-buffer actually used for rendering. If the viewport does not have a background depth associated with it, the BOOL pointed to by lpValid is set to FALSE; otherwise it is set to TRUE.
Arguments:	LPDIRECTDRAWSURFACE* lplpDDSurface—The address that will be initialized to point to the DirectDrawSurface object representing the background depth.

continues

continued

	LPBOOL lpValid—The address of a variable that is set to FALSE if no background depth is associated with the viewport.
Return Type:	HRESULT
Return Values:	Returns D3D_OK if successful, or an error otherwise, which may be one of the following values: 　　DDERR_INVALIDOBJECT 　　DDERR_INVALIDPARAMS
See Also:	IDirect3DViewport::Clear, IDirect3DViewport::GetBackground, IDirect3DViewport::SetBackground, IDirect3DViewport::SetBackgroundDepth

GetViewport

Interface:	IDirect3DViewport
Declaration:	`HRESULT GetViewport(LPD3DVIEWPORT lpData);`
Description:	This function retrieves the viewport state data of a Direct3D viewport object.
Notes:	The D3DVIEWPORT structure reports the coordinates of a viewport's top-left corner, the width and height of a viewport in pixels, the canonical view volume-to-device scale values, and the maximum and minimum homogeneous coordinates.
Arguments:	LPD3DVIEWPORT lpData—The address of a D3DVIEWPORT structure representing the viewport.
Return Type:	HRESULT
Return Values:	Returns D3D_OK if successful, or an error otherwise, which may be one of the following values: 　　DDERR_INVALIDOBJECT 　　DDERR_INVALIDPARAMS
See Also:	IDirect3DViewport::SetViewport, D3DVIEWPORT

Initialize

Interface:	IDirect3DViewport
Declaration:	`HRESULT Initialize(LPDIRECT3D lpDirect3D);`
Description:	This function should never be called. It is provided for compliance with the COM protocol.
Notes:	Because an IDirect3DViewport object is created via a call to IDirect3D::CreateViewport, the IDirect3D object takes care of properly initializing the viewport object.
Arguments:	LPDIRECT3D lpDirect3D—The address of the Direct3D structure representing the Direct3D object.
Return Type:	HRESULT
Return Values:	Returns DDERR_ALREADYINITIALIZED because the Direct3D material object is initialized when it is created.
See Also:	None

LightElements

Interface:	IDirect3DViewport

Declaration:	`HRESULT LightElements(`
	`DWORD dwElementCount,`
	`LPD3DLIGHTDATA lpData);`

Description:	This function is not currently implemented.
Notes:	Future versions of Direct3D may support this function by using the current lighting module to light a collection of vertices, skipping the transformation and rasterization modules.
Arguments:	DWORD dwElementCount—The number of D3DLIGHTDATA structs pointed to by lpData. LPD3DLIGHTDATA lpData—The pointer to the first D3DLIGHTDATA struct.
Return Type:	HRESULT

continues

continued

Return Values:	None
See Also:	IDirect3DViewport::TransformVertices, D3DLIGHTDATA

NextLight

Interface:	IDirect3DViewport

Declaration:	`HRESULT NextLight(`
	`LPDIRECT3DLIGHT lpDirect3DLight,`
	`LPDIRECT3DLIGHT* lplpDirect3DLight,`
	`DWORD dwFlags);`

Description:	This function enumerates a Direct3D viewport's light objects.
Notes:	NextLight can be used to retrieve the first, last, or next light in the viewport's list of light objects.

Arguments:	LPDIRECT3DLIGHT lpDirect3DLight—The address of a light in the list of lights associated with this Direct3D viewport object.
	
	LPDIRECT3DLIGHT* lplpDirect3DLight—The address of a pointer that will contain the requested light in the list of lights associated with this Direct3D viewport object. The requested light is specified in the dwFlags parameter.
	
	DWORD dwFlags—The flags specifying which light to retrieve from the list of lights. The default setting is D3DNEXT_NEXT. The settings are as follows:
	
	    D3DNEXT_HEAD—Retrieves the item at the beginning of the list.
	
	    D3DNEXT_NEXT—Retrieves the next item in the list.
	
	    D3DNEXT_TAIL—Retrieves the item at the end of the list.

Return Type:	HRESULT

Return Values:	Returns D3D_OK if successful, or an error otherwise, which may be one of the following values:
	
	    DDERR_INVALIDOBJECT
	
	    DDERR_INVALIDPARAMS

See Also:	IDirect3DViewport::AddLight, IDirect3DViewport::DeleteLight, IDirect3DViewport::LightElements

SetBackground

Interface:	IDirect3DViewport
Declaration:	`HRESULT SetBackground(D3DMATERIALHANDLE hMat);`
Description:	This function sets the background material for a Direct3D viewport.
Notes:	The background material controls the color and, optionally, a texture for the background of the viewport.
	The software renderer can support textures of arbitrary sizes, but some hardware accelerators limit textures to 64×64, 128×128, and 256×256 pixels.
Arguments:	D3DMATERIALHANDLE hMat—The material handle that will be used as the background.
Return Type:	HRESULT
Return Values:	Returns D3D_OK if successful, or an error otherwise, which may be one of the following values:
	DDERR_INVALIDOBJECT
	DDERR_INVALIDPARAMS
See Also:	IDirect3DViewport::Clear, IDirect3DViewport::GetBackground, IDirect3DViewport::GetBackgroundDepth, IDirect3DViewport::SetBackgroundDepth

SetBackgroundDepth

Interface:	IDirect3DViewport
Declaration:	`HRESULT SetBackgroundDepth(` `    LPDIRECTDRAWSURFACE lpDDSurface);`

continues

continued

Description:	This function associates a background depth, or z-buffer, with a Direct3D viewport.
Notes:	If a background depth is attached to a viewport with SetBackgroundDepth, the z-buffer used for rendering is filled with the contents of the specified depth field when IDirect3DViewport::Clear() is called and the D3DCLEAR_ZBUFFER flag is specified.
	The format for the z-buffer is undocumented and may vary between devices. It is always safe, however, to supply SetBackgroundDepth with a z-buffer that was generated by the current device.
Arguments:	LPDIRECTDRAWSURFACE lpDDSurface—The address of the DirectDrawSurface object representing the background depth.
Return Type:	HRESULT

Return Values:	Returns D3D_OK if successful, or an error otherwise, which may be one of the following values:
	    DDERR_INVALIDOBJECT
	    DDERR_INVALIDPARAMS

See Also:	IDirect3DViewport::Clear, IDirect3DViewport::GetBackground, IDirect3DViewport::GetBackgroundDepth, IDirect3DViewport::SetBackground

SetViewport

Interface:	IDirect3DViewport
Declaration:	`HRESULT SetBackgroundDepth(` `    LPDIRECTDRAWSURFACE lpDDSurface);`
Description:	This function sets the viewport state data of a Direct3D viewport object.
Notes:	The D3DVIEWPORT structure reports the coordinates of a viewport's top-left corner, the width and height of a viewport, the canonical view volume-to-device scale values, and the maximum and minimum homogeneous coordinates.

Arguments:	LPD3DVIEWPORT lpData—The address of a D3DVIEWPORT structure that contains the new viewport.
Return Type:	HRESULT

Return Values:	Returns D3D_OK if successful, or an error otherwise, which may be one of the following values:
	    DDERR_INVALIDOBJECT
	    DDERR_INVALIDPARAMS

See Also:	IDirect3DViewport::GetViewport

TransformVertices

Interface:	IDirect3DViewport
| **Declaration:** | ```
HRESULT TransformVertices(
    DWORD dwVertexCount,
    LPD3DTRANSFORMDATA lpData,
    DWORD dwFlags,
    LPDWORD lpOffscreen);
``` |
Description:	This function transforms a set of vertices from their model coordinates into the canonical view volume.
Notes:	The current transformation is the composition of the world, view, and projection matrices. The world matrix should be set to take vertices from model coordinates to world coordinates. The view matrix should be set to take world coordinates into camera coordinates. The projection matrix should be set to take camera coordinates into canonical view volume coordinates.
	If the dwFlags parameter is set to D3DTRANSFORM_CLIPPED, this function uses the current transformation matrix to transform a set of vertices, checking the resulting vertices to see if they are within the viewing frustum. The homogeneous part of the D3DLVERTEX structure within lpData will be set if the vertex is clipped; otherwise, only the screen coordinates will be set. The clip intersection of all the vertices transformed is returned in lpOffscreen. That is, if lpOffscreen is nonzero, all the vertices were off-screen and not straddling the

continues
```

continued

viewport. The drExtent member of the D3DTRANSFORMDATA structure also will be set to the 2D bounding rectangle of the resulting vertices.

If the dwFlags parameter is set to D3DTRANSFORM_UNCLIPPED, this method uses the current transformation matrix to transform a set of vertices. In this case, the system assumes that all the resulting coordinates will be within the viewing frustum. The drExtent member of the D3DTRANSFORMDATA structure will be set to the bounding rectangle of the resulting vertices.

The dwClip member of D3DTRANSFORMDATA can help the transformation module determine whether the geometry will need clipping against the viewing volume. Before transforming a geometry, high-level software often can test whether bounding boxes or convex hulls are wholly within the viewing volume (enabling clipping tests to be skipped), or wholly outside the viewing volume (enabling the geometry to be skipped entirely).

Arguments: DWORD dwVertexCount—The number of vertices in the lpData parameter to be transformed.

LPD3DTRANSFORMDATA lpData—The address of a D3DTRANSFORMDATA structure that contains the vertices to be transformed.

DWORD dwFlags—One of the following flags:

D3DTRANSFORM_CLIPPED

D3DTRANSFORM_UNCLIPPED

LPDWORD lpOffscreen—The address of a variable that is set to a nonzero value if the resulting vertices are all off-screen.

Return Type: HRESULT

Return Values: Returns D3D_OK if successful or an error otherwise, which may be one of the following values:

DDERR_INVALIDOBJECT

DDERR_INVALIDPARAMS

See Also: IDirect3DViewport::LightElements

Immediate-Mode Function Reference

Immediate-Mode Structures

D3DBRANCH

Definition:
```
typedef struct _D3DBRANCH
{
    DWORD dwMask;
    DWORD dwValue;
    BOOL  bNegate;
    DWORD dwOffset;
} D3DBRANCH, *LPD3DBRANCH;
```

Description: Performs a conditional branch operation inside an execute buffer based on the result of a bitwise AND operation on the driver status mask.

The Transformation Module sets the bits of the driver's status register as it clips vertices during transformation. The result of the clip tests can be used to determine a conditional branch.

Members: dwMask—The bit mask for the branch. This mask is combined with the driver-status mask by using the bitwise AND operator. For a list of the available driver-status masks, see the dwStatus member of the D3DSTATUS structure.

dwValue—The value to compare with the result of the operation described for the dwMask member. Execution branches if dwValue is equal to the combined mask and bNegate is FALSE or if dwValue is not equal to the combined mask and bNegate is TRUE.

bNegate—If TRUE, the branch occurs if the result of the AND is equal to dwValue. If FALSE, the branch occurs if the result of the AND is not equal to dwValue.

continues

continued

dwOffset—How far to branch forward, or zero to exit. This value is the number of bytes from the first byte of the D3DINSTRUCTION containing the D3DBRANCH data to the first byte of the D3DINSTRUCTION to execute after branching.

See Also: IDirect3DDevice::Execute, IDirect3DExecuteBuffer::GetExecuteData, IDirect3DExecuteBuffer::SetExecuteData, D3DOPCODE

D3DCOLORVALUE

Definition:
```
typedef struct _D3DCOLORVALUE
{
        union
        {
                D3DVALUE r;
                D3DVALUE dvR;
        };
        union
        {
                D3DVALUE g;
                D3DVALUE dvG;
        };
        union
        {
                D3DVALUE b;
                D3DVALUE dvB;
        };
        union
        {
                D3DVALUE a;
                D3DVALUE dvA;
        };
} D3DCOLORVALUE;
```

Description: This structure describes a color value for use with the D3DLIGHT and D3DMATERIAL structures.

The red, green, and blue components of D3DCOLORVALUE are usually between 0.0 and 1.0. Material colors must always be in this range. Lights may have values outside this range, with different results on different drivers. Alpha values are ignored for lights.

Members: r, dvR—The red component of color.

g, dvG—The green component of color.

b, dvB—The blue component of color.

a, dvA—The alpha component of color.

See Also: IDirect3DLight::SetLight, IDirect3DLight::GetLight, D3DLIGHT, IDirect3DMaterial::GetMaterial, IDirect3DMaterial::SetMaterial, D3DMATERIAL

D3DDEVICEDESC

Definition:
```
typedef struct _D3DDeviceDesc
{
        DWORD dwSize;
        DWORD dwFlags;
        D3DCOLORMODEL dcmColorModel;
        DWORD dwDevCaps;
        D3DTRANSFORMCAPS dtcTransformCaps;
        BOOL bClipping;
        D3DLIGHTINGCAPS dlcLightingCaps;
        D3DPRIMCAPS dpcLineCaps;
        D3DPRIMCAPS dpcTriCaps;
        DWORD dwDeviceRenderBitDepth;
        DWORD dwDeviceZBufferBitDepth;
        DWORD dwMaxBufferSize;
        DWORD dwMaxVertexCount;
} D3DDEVICEDESC, *LPD3DDEVICEDESC;
```

Description: This structure contains a description of the current Direct3D device.

Members: dwSize—The size, in bytes, of this structure.

dwFlags—The flags identifying which data is valid. Each value below defines a bitmask, which may be combined together by using a bitwise OR.

The following flags are defined:

D3DDD_BCLIPPING—The bClipping member is valid.

D3DDD_COLORMODEL—The dcmColorModel member is valid.

D3DDD_DEVCAPS—The dwDevCaps member is valid.

continues

continued

> D3DDD_LIGHTINGCAPS—The dlcLightingCaps member is valid.
>
> D3DDD_LINECAPS—The dpcLineCaps member is valid.
>
> D3DDD_MAXBUFFERSIZE—The dwMaxBufferSize member is valid.
>
> D3DDD_MAXVERTEXCOUNT—The dwMaxVertexCount member is valid.
>
> D3DDD_TRANSFORMCAPS—The dtcTransformCaps member is valid.
>
> D3DDD_TRICAPS—The dpcTriCaps member is valid.

dcmColorModel—Color models the device supports. This may be one or the other or both of D3DCOLOR_MONO or D3DCOLOR_RGB.

dwDevCaps—Flags identifying the capabilities of the device. This member can contain one or more of the following values:

> D3DDEVCAPS_EXECUTESYSTEMMEMORY—This device can process execute buffers in system memory.
>
> D3DDEVCAPS_EXECUTEVIDEOMEMORY—This device can process execute buffers in video memory.
>
> D3DDEVCAPS_FLOATTLVERTEX—This device accepts floating point for post-transform vertex data.
>
> D3DDEVCAPS_SORTDECREASINGZ—This device requires faces sorted back-to-front.
>
> D3DDEVCAPS_SORTEXACT—This device requires faces sorted with respect to depth. This flag is always coupled with D3DDEVCAPS_SORTINCREASINGZ or D3DDEVCAPS_SORTDECREASINGZ.
>
> D3DDEVCAPS_SORTINCREASINGZ—This device requires faces sorted front-to-back.
>
> D3DDEVCAPS_TEXTURESYSTEMMEMORY—This device can access textures in system memory.

D3DDEVCAPS_TEXTUREVIDEOMEMORY—This device can access textures in video memory.

D3DDEVCAPS_TLVERTEXSYSTEMMEMORY—This device can process execute buffers in system memory built from transformed and lit vertices.

D3DDEVCAPS_TLVERTEXVIDEOMEMORY—This device can process execute buffers in video memory built from transformed and lit vertices.

dtcTransformCaps—An instance of the D3DTRANSFORMCAPS structure, which specifies the transformation capabilities of the device.

bClipping—TRUE if the device can perform 3D clipping.

dlcLightingCaps—An instance of the D3DLIGHTINGCAPS structure, which specifies the lighting capabilities of the device.

dpcLineCaps and dpcTriCaps—Instances of the D3DPRIMCAPS structure, which describe the device's support for line-drawing and triangle primitives.

dwDeviceRenderBitDepth—Bit depths this device can support. This may be one or more of the following DirectDraw bit-depth constants, combined by bitwise OR: DDBD_8, DDBD_16, DDBD_24, or DDBD_32.

dwDeviceZBufferBitDepth—Z-buffer bit depths this device can support. This may be one (or, someday, more) of the following DirectDraw bit-depth constants: DDBD_8, DDBD_16, DDBD_24, or DDBD_32.

dwMaxBufferSize—The maximum execute buffer size, in bytes, this device can support. If this member is 0, the device supports any size up to a maximum of 64 K.

dwMaxVertexCount—The maximum number of vertices allowed per execute buffer.

See Also: D3DENUMDEVICESCALLBACK, IDirect3D::FindDevice, D3DFINDDEVICERESULT, D3DFINDDEVICESEARCH, IDirect3DDevice::GetCaps, IDirect3DDevice::Initialize, D3DLIGHTINGCAPS, D3DPRIMCAPS, D3DRENDERSTATETYPE, D3DTRANSFORMCAPS

D3DEXECUTEBUFFERDESC

Definition:
```
typedef struct _D3DExecuteBufferDesc
{
        DWORD dwSize;
        DWORD dwFlags;
        DWORD dwCaps;
        DWORD dwBufferSize;
        LPVOID lpData;
} D3DEXECUTEBUFFERDESC, *LPD3DEXECUTEBUFFERDESC;
```

Description: This structure describes the memory status, size, and location of an execute buffer. It is used as an argument to IDirect3DDevice::CreateExecuteBuffer to provide the size and preferred memory location (system or video) of the execute buffer data. It is also used as an argument to IDirect3DExecuteBuffer::Lock, which returns a pointer to the execute buffer contents in the lpData member.

Members: dwSize—The size of this structure, in bytes.

dwFlags—The flags identifying which data is valid.

Each of the following values defines a bitmask, which may be combined together by using a bitwise OR. The following flags are defined:

D3DDEB_BUFSIZE—The dwBufferSize member is valid.

D3DDEB_CAPS—The dwCaps member is valid.

D3DDEB_LPDATA—The lpData member is valid.

dwCaps—The location in memory of the execute buffer. This member can contain one of the following:

D3DDEBCAPS_MEM—A logical OR of D3DDEBCAPS_SYSTEMMEMORY and D3DDEBCAPS_VIDEOMEMORY. This flag is used when creating an execute buffer to specify that execute buffer data may reside in video or system memory. The device must support video memory execute buffers to use this flag.

D3DDEBCAPS_SYSTEMMEMORY—The execute buffer contents should reside in system memory.

D3DDEBCAPS_VIDEOMEMORY—The execute buffer contents should reside in device memory.

dwBufferSize—The size of the execute buffer contents, in bytes.

lpData—The address of the buffer contents. Filled in by IDirect3DExecuteBuffer::Lock.

See Also: IDirect3DExecuteBuffer::GetExecuteData, IDirect3DExecuteBuffer::SetExecuteData, IDirect3DExecuteBuffer::Lock, IDirect3DExecuteBuffer::Unlock, IDirect3DExecuteBuffer::Initialize, IDirect3DExecuteBuffer::Optimize, IDirect3DExecuteBuffer::Validate, IDirect3DDevice::CreateExecuteBuffer

D3DEXECUTEDATA

Definition:
```
typedef struct _D3DEXECUTEDATA
{
    DWORD dwSize;
    DWORD dwVertexOffset;
    DWORD dwVertexCount;
    DWORD dwInstructionOffset;
    DWORD dwInstructionLength;
    DWORD dwHVertexOffset;
    D3DSTATUS dsStatus;
} D3DEXECUTEDATA, *LPD3DEXECUTEDATA;
```

Description: This structure describes the layout of an execute buffer, the value of the driver status register, and the accumulated damage extent in device coordinates.

Members: dwSize—Size of this structure, in bytes.

dwVertexOffset—Offset from the start of the buffer, in bytes, of the first vertex.

dwVertexCount—Number of vertices in the execute buffer.

dwInstructionOffset—Offset from the start of the buffer, in bytes, of the first instruction to execute.

continues

continued

dwInstructionLength—Length of the entire block of instructions, in bytes.

dwHVertexOffset—Offset from the start of the buffer, in bytes, of the first homogeneous vertex used when the application is supplying screen coordinates that need clipping.

dsStatus—An instance of the D3DSTATUS structure, storing the damage extent of the rendered geometry and the value of the device's status register. This is filled in by IDirect3DExecuteBuffer::GetExecuteData.

See Also: IDirect3DDevice::Execute, IDirect3DExecuteBuffer::GetExecuteData, IDirect3DExecuteBuffer::SetExecuteData, D3DSTATUS

D3DFINDDEVICERESULT

Definition:
```
typedef struct _D3DFINDDEVICERESULT
{
        DWORD dwSize;
        GUID guid;
        D3DDEVICEDESC ddHwDesc;
        D3DDEVICEDESC ddSwDesc;
} D3DFINDDEVICERESULT, *LPD3DFINDDEVICERESULT;
```

Description: This structure identifies a Direct3D device found with IDirect3D::FindDevice().

Members: dwSize—The size, in bytes, of this structure.

guid—Globally unique identifier (GUID) of the device found.

ddHwDesc—D3DDEVICEDESC structure describing the hardware capabilities of the device.

ddSwDesc—D3DDEVICEDESC structure describing the software capabilities of the device.

See Also: IDirect3D::FindDevice, D3DFINDDEVICESEARCH

D3DFINDDEVICESEARCH

Definition:
```
typedef struct _D3DFINDDEVICESEARCH
{
        DWORD dwSize;
        DWORD dwFlags;
        BOOL bHardware;
        D3DCOLORMODEL dcmColorModel;
        GUID guid;
        DWORD dwCaps;
        D3DPRIMCAPS dpcPrimCaps;
} D3DFINDDEVICESEARCH, *LPD3DFINDDEVICESEARCH;
```

Description: This structure is used with IDirect3D::FindDevice() to specify characteristics of a desired Direct3D device.

Members: dwSize—The size, in bytes, of this structure.

dwFlags—The flags that define which properties a device must possess to be found by IDirect3D::FindDevice().

Each of the following values defines a bitmask; these values may be combined with a bitwise OR to specify several device properties for which to search:

D3DFDS_ALPHACMPCAPS—Compare the dwAlphaCmpCaps member of the D3DPRIMCAPS structures.

D3DFDS_COLORMODEL—Compare the color model of the device, specified in dcmColorModel.

D3DFDS_DSTBLENDCAPS—Compare the dwDestBlendCaps member of the D3DPRIMCAPS structures.

D3DFDS_GUID—Compare the globally unique identifier (GUID) specified in the guid member of this structure with the device's GUID.

D3DFDS_HARDWARE—Match only hardware or software devices, based on the value of the bHardware member. If bHardware is TRUE, only hardware devices will be sought. If bHardware is FALSE, only software-only devices will be sought.

continues

continued

D3DFDS_LINES—Specifies that the members of the dpcPrimCaps member of this structure should be compared with the members of the dpcLineCaps member of a candidate device's D3DDEVICEDESC structure. This flag is used to indicate that the search is for a device with the specified line-rendering capabilities.

D3DFDS_RASTERCAPS—Compare the dwRasterCaps member of the dpcPrimCaps member of this structure with the dwRasterCaps member of the candidate device descriptor's dpcLineCaps or dpcTriCaps members (or both), depending on whether the D3DFDS_LINES and D3DFDS_TRIANGLES flags are set in the dwFlags member of this structure.

D3DFDS_SHADECAPS—Compare the dwShadeCaps member of the dpcPrimCaps member of this structure with the dwShadeCaps member of the candidate device descriptor's dpcLineCaps or dpcTriCaps members (or both), depending on whether the D3DFDS_LINES and D3DFDS_TRIANGLES flags are set in the dwFlags member of this structure.

D3DFDS_SRCBLENDCAPS—Compare the dwSrcBlendCaps member of the dpcPrimCaps member of this structure with the dwSrcBlendCaps member of the candidate device descriptor's dpcLineCaps or dpcTriCaps members (or both), depending on whether the D3DFDS_LINES and D3DFDS_TRIANGLES flags are set in the dwFlags member of this structure.

D3DFDS_TEXTUREBLENDCAPS—Compare the dwTextureBlendCaps member of the dpcPrimCaps member of this structure with the dwTextureBlendCaps member of the candidate device descriptor's dpcLineCaps or dpcTriCaps members (or both), depending on whether the D3DFDS_LINES and D3DFDS_TRIANGLES flags are set in the dwFlags member of this structure.

D3DFDS_TEXTURECAPS—Compare the dwTextureCaps member of the dpcPrimCaps member of this structure with the dwTextureCaps member of the candidate device descriptor's dpcLineCaps or dpcTriCaps members (or both), depending on whether the D3DFDS_LINES and D3DFDS_TRIANGLES flags are set in the dwFlags member of this structure.

D3DFDS_TEXTUREFILTERCAPS—Compare the dwTextureFilterCaps member of the dpcPrimCaps member of this structure with the dwTextureFilterCaps member of the candidate device descriptor's dpcLineCaps or dpcTriCaps members (or both), depending on whether the D3DFDS_LINES and D3DFDS_TRIANGLES flags are set in the dwFlags member of this structure.

D3DFDS_TRIANGLES—Specifies that the dpcPrimCaps member of this structure should be compared with the dpcTriCaps member of a candidate device's D3DDEVICEDESC structure. This flag is used to indicate that the search is for a device with the specified triangle rendering capabilities.

D3DFDS_ZCMPCAPS—Compare the dwZCmpCaps member of the dpcPrimCaps member of this structure with the dwZCmpCaps member of the candidate device descriptor's dpcLineCaps or dpcTriCaps members (or both), depending on whether the D3DFDS_LINES and D3DFDS_TRIANGLES flags are set in the dwFlags member of this structure.

bHardware—The flag specifying whether the device to find must be implemented as hardware or software. This member is ignored unless the D3DFDS_HARDWARE flag is set in the dwFlags member.

dcmColorModel—The flag specifying which color model a found device should support, either D3DCOLOR_MONO, D3DCOLOR_RGB, or both. This member is ignored unless the D3DFDS_COLORMODEL flag is set in the dwFlags member.

guid—Globally unique identifier (GUID) of the device to find. This member is ignored unless the D3DFDS_GUID flag is set in the dwFlags member. Note that a GUID completely specifies a particular device.

continues

continued

dwCaps—Capability flags. This field is not currently used and should be 0.

dpcPrimCaps—Specifies a D3DPRIMCAPS structure defining the device's capabilities for each primitive type. Each member of dpcPrimCaps has a corresponding flag that may be set in the dwFlags field to force IDirect3D::FindDevice() to compare the particular member with the corresponding member of the candidate device's relevant D3DPRIMCAPS. The particular D3DPRIMCAPS used is specified by either the D3DFDS_LINES or D3DFDS_TRIANGLES flag.

See Also: IDirect3D::FindDevice(),

D3DHVERTEX

Definition:

```
typedef struct _D3DHVERTEX
{
        DWORD       dwFlags;
        union
    {
                D3DVALUE hx;
                D3DVALUE dvHX;
        };
        union
    {
                D3DVALUE hy;
                D3DVALUE dvHY;
        };
        union
    {
                D3DVALUE hz;
                D3DVALUE dvHZ;
        };
} D3DHVERTEX, *LPD3DHVERTEX;
```

Description: This structure defines a homogeneous vertex used when the application is supplying screen coordinate data that needs clipping. This structure is part of the D3DTRANSFORMDATA structure.

Members: dwFlags—The flags defining the clip status of the homogeneous vertex. This member must be one or more of the flags described in the dwClip member of the D3DTRANSFORMDATA structure.

hx, dvHX—The value of the transformed homogeneous x coordinate of the vertex.

hy, dvHY—The value of the transformed homogeneous y coordinate of the vertex.

hz, dvHZ—The value of the transformed homogeneous z coordinate of the vertex.

See Also: IDirect3DViewport::TransformVertices, D3DTRANSFORMDATA

D3DINSTRUCTION

Definition:
```
typedef struct _D3DINSTRUCTION
{
        BYTE bOpcode;
        BYTE bSize;
        WORD wCount;
} D3DINSTRUCTION, *LPD3DINSTRUCTION;
```

Description: This structure defines an instruction in an execute buffer.

Execute buffers are comprised of a list of vertices followed by a list of variable-length instructions. Each instruction begins with a common instruction header and is followed by zero or more data blocks. Each data block for a given instruction is the same size. This architecture facilitates efficient processing of large batches of similar instructions, such as the faces of a polygon mesh.

Members: bOpcode—This value specifies the specific instruction. Its value must be a member of the D3DOPCODE enumerated type.

bSize—The size of each instruction data unit.

wCount—The number of instruction data units for this instruction.

See Also: IDirect3DDevice::Execute, IDirect3DExecuteBuffer::GetExecuteData, IDirect3DExecuteBuffer::SetExecuteData, D3DOPCODE

D3DLIGHT

Definition:
```
typedef struct _D3DLIGHT
{
        DWORD dwSize;
        D3DLIGHTTYPE dltType;
        D3DCOLORVALUE dcvColor;
        D3DVECTOR dvPosition;
        D3DVECTOR  dvDirection;
        D3DVALUE dvRange;
        D3DVALUE dvFalloff;
        D3DVALUE dvAttenuation0;
        D3DVALUE dvAttenuation1;
        D3DVALUE dvAttenuation2;
        D3DVALUE dvTheta;
        D3DVALUE dvPhi;
} D3DLIGHT, *LPD3DLIGHT;
```

Description: Defines the Direct3D light type.

Notes: The total attenuation of the light at a particular vertex is computed from the light's constant, linear, and quadratic attenuation values by using the following formula:

$$\text{attenuation}_{Total} = \text{attenuation}_{Constant} + r \times \text{attenuation}_{Linear} + r^2 \times \text{attenuation}_{Quadratic}$$

where r is the distance from the light to the vertex being lit.

The total attenuation affects the intensity of the light at a particular vertex as an inverse proportion, that is:

$$I_{Vertex} = I_{Light} / \text{attenuation}_{Total}$$

Members: dwSize—The size, in bytes, of this structure.

dltType—The type of the light source. This value may be one of the members of the D3DLIGHTTYPE enumerated type, D3DLIGHT_POINT, D3DLIGHT_SPOT, D3DLIGHT_DIRECTIONAL, D3DLIGHT_PARALLELPOINT, or D3DLIGHT_GLSPOT.

dcvColor—The light's color. In ramp mode, the alpha value sets the intensity of the light. In RGB mode, alpha is ignored, and the red, green, and blue components define the color of the light.

dvPosition—The position vector of the light in world coordinates.

dvDirection—The direction vector of the light in world coordinates.

dvRange—The maximum distance light may travel from the light in world coordinates.

dvFalloff—The decrease in illumination between the center of the umbra and the outer edge of the penumbra. The intensity of the light at any point in the penumbra is described by the following equation:

$$I \cdot \cos^{dvFalloff}((p/2) \cdot ((2 \cdot r - dvTheta)/(dvPhi - dvTheta)))$$

where I is the intensity of the light, and ρ is the angle between the direction vector of the spotlight and the point (in radians).

dvAttenuation0—The constant attenuation of the light. Specifies an attenuation that is independent of the distance from the light of the point being lit, within the cutoff distance specified by the dvRange member.

dvAttenuation1—The linear attenuation of the light. A non-zero value specifies attenuation proportional to the distance from the light (r), or intensity that decreases like $1/r$.

dvAttenuation2—The quadratic attenuation of the light. A non-zero value specifies attenuation proportional to the square of the distance from the light (r^2), or intensity that descreases like $1/r^2$.

dvTheta—The angle, in radians, of the spotlight's umbra—that is, the fully illuminated inner cone.

dvPhi—The angle, in radians, defining the outer edge of the spotlight's penumbra. Points outside this cone are not lit by the spotlight.

See Also: IDirect3DLight::GetLight, IDirect3DLight::SetLight

D3DLIGHTDATA

Definition:
```
typedef struct _D3DLIGHTDATA
{
        DWORD dwSize;
        LPD3DLIGHTINGELEMENT lpIn;
        DWORD dwInSize;
        LPD3DTLVERTEX lpOut;
        DWORD dwOutSize;
} D3DLIGHTDATA, *LPD3DLIGHTDATA;
```

continues

continued

Description: This structure describes the points to be lit and their resulting colors in calls to IDirect3DViewport::LightElements, which is not currently implemented.

Members: dwSize—The size, in bytes, of this structure.

lpIn—The address of an array of D3DLIGHTINGELEMENT structures specifying the position and normal vectors to be lit.

dwInSize—The number of bytes between each D3DLIGHTINGELEMENT in the array pointed to by lpIn. This enables the application to store extra data inline between each D3DLIGHTINGELEMENT structure.

lpOut—The address of an array of D3DTLVERTEX structures specifying the output colors.

dwOutSize—The number of bytes between each D3DTLVERTEX in the array pointed to by lpOut. This enables the application to store extra data inline between D3DTLVERTEX each structure.

See Also: IDirect3DViewport::LightElements, D3DLIGHTINGELEMENT, D3DTLVERTEX

D3DLIGHTINGCAPS

Definition:
```
typedef struct _D3DLIGHTINGCAPS
{
        DWORD dwSize;
        DWORD dwCaps;
        DWORD dwLightingModel;
        DWORD dwNumLights;
} D3DLIGHTINGCAPS, *LPD3DLIGHTINGCAPS;
```

Description: This structure describes the lighting capabilities of a device. An instance of this structure is a member of the D3DDEVICEDESC structure.

Members: dwSize—The size, in bytes, of this structure.

dwCaps—The flags describing the capabilities of the lighting module.

The following flags are defined:

> D3DLIGHTCAPS_DIRECTIONAL—Supports directional lights.
>
> D3DLIGHTCAPS_GLSPOT—Supports OpenGL-style spot lights.
>
> D3DLIGHTCAPS_PARALLELPOINT—Supports parallel point lights.
>
> D3DLIGHTCAPS_POINT—Supports point (omni-directional) lights.
>
> D3DLIGHTCAPS_SPOT—Supports spotlights.

dwLightingModel—The flags defining whether the device supports the RGB or monochrome lighting models, or both.

The following flags are defined:

> D3DLIGHTINGMODEL_MONO—Monochromatic (ramp) lighting model.
>
> D3DLIGHTINGMODEL_RGB—RGB lighting model.

dwNumLights—The maximum number of lights allowed in a scene.

See Also: IDirect3DDevice::GetCaps, D3DDEVICEDESC

D3DLIGHTINGELEMENT

Definition:
```
typedef struct _D3DLIGHTINGELEMENT
{
        D3DVECTOR dvPosition;
        D3DVECTOR dvNormal;
} D3DLIGHTINGELEMENT, *LPD3DLIGHTINGELEMENT;
```

Description: This structure describes the points in model space to be lit. The D3DLIGHTDATA structure contains a pointer to an array of D3DLIGHTINGELEMENT structures, which is used as input to IDirect3DViewport::LightElements. IDirect3DViewport::LightElements is currently not implemented.

Members: dvPosition—The value specifying the point in model coordinates to light. This value is a D3DVECTOR structure.

continues

continued

dvNormal—The normalized unit vector normal to the vertex. This value is a D3DVECTOR structure.

See Also: IDirect3DViewport::LightElements, D3DLIGHTDATA

D3DLINE

Definition:
```
typedef struct _D3DLINE
{
        union
        {
                WORD v1;
                WORD wV1;
        };
        union
        {
                WORD v2;
                WORD wV2;
        };
} D3DLINE, *LPD3DLINE;
```

Description: This structure, one or more of which is used as instruction data for a D3DINSTRUCTION with the D3DOP_LINE opcode, defines a line segment between two vertices.

The vertices are specified as indices into the array of vertices in the execute buffer.

Members: v1, wV1—The vertex index of first line endpoint.

v2, wV2—The vertex index of second line endpoint.

See Also: IDirect3DDevice::Execute, IDirect3DExecuteBuffer::GetExecuteData, IDirect3DExecuteBuffer::SetExecuteData, D3DOPCODE

D3DLINEPATTERN

Definition:
```
typedef struct _D3DLINEPATTERN
{
        WORD wRepeatFactor;
        WORD wLinePattern;
} D3DLINEPATTERN;
```

Description: This structure describes a line pattern. It is used as instruction data for a D3DINSTRUCTION with the D3DOP_STATERENDER opcode.

Members: wRepeatFactor—The number of bits in wLinePattern to use in generating a pattern.

wLinePattern—Bit mask to use as a pixel mask for generating a line pattern.

See Also: IDirect3DDevice::GetCaps, D3DPRIMCAPS

D3DLVERTEX

Definition:
```
typedef struct _D3DLVERTEX
{
    union
    {
        D3DVALUE x;
        D3DVALUE dvX;
    };
    union
    {
        D3DVALUE y;
        D3DVALUE dvY;
    };
    union
    {
        D3DVALUE z;
        D3DVALUE dvZ;
    };
    DWORD    dwReserved;
    union
    {
        D3DCOLOR color;
        D3DCOLOR dcColor;
    };
    union
    {
        D3DCOLOR specular;
        D3DCOLOR dcSpecular;
    };
    union
    {
        D3DVALUE tu;
        D3DVALUE dvTU;
    };
```

continues

continued

```
        union
        {
                D3DVALUE tv;
                D3DVALUE dvTV;
        };
} D3DLVERTEX, *LPD3DLVERTEX;
```

Description: This structure defines an untransformed and lit vertex in model coordinates. An application which does its own vertex lighting can disable the lighting module and use this structure to represent vertices in an execute buffer.

Members: x, dvX—The value of the x coordinate of the vertex.

y, dvY—The value of the y coordinate of the vertex.

z, dvZ—The value of the z coordinate of the vertex.

dwReserved—Reserved; must be zero.

color, dcColor—The value of the color component of the vertex.

specular, dcSpecular—The value of the specular component of the vertex.

tu, dvTU—The value of the texture u coordinate of the vertex.

tv, dvTV—The value of the texture v coordinate of the vertex.

See Also: IDirect3DViewport::TransformVertices, D3DTRANSFORMDATA

D3DMATERIAL

Definition:
```
typedef struct _D3DMATERIAL
{
        DWORD dwSize;
        union
        {
                D3DCOLORVALUE diffuse;
                D3DCOLORVALUE dcvDiffuse;
        };
        union
        {
                D3DCOLORVALUE ambient;
                D3DCOLORVALUE dcvAmbient;
        };
        union
```

```
        {
                D3DCOLORVALUE specular;
                D3DCOLORVALUE dcvSpecular;
        };
        union
        {
                D3DCOLORVALUE emissive;
                D3DCOLORVALUE dcvEmissive;
        };
        union
        {
                D3DVALUE power;
                D3DVALUE dvPower;
        };
        D3DTEXTUREHANDLE hTexture;
        DWORD dwRampSize;
} D3DMATERIAL, *LPD3DMATERIAL;
```

Description: This structure specifies properties of a Direct3D material.

The diffuse color is specified as RGBA, while the ambient, specular, and emissive colors are specified as RGB.

The material parameters are used to light vertices by using the Phong reflection model.

Members: dwSize—The size, in bytes, of this structure.

diffuse, dcvDiffuse—The value specifying the diffuse color of the material.

ambient, dcvAmbient—The value specifying the ambient color of the material.

specular, dcvSpecular—The value specifying the specular color of the material.

emissive, dcvEmissive—The value specifying the emissive color of the material.

dvPower—The value determining the sharpness of the specular highlights. A value of 5 gives a metallic look, and higher values look more like smooth plastic. A perfect mirror would have an infinite power value.

hTexture—The handle for a texture, or NULL if there is no texture. The texture must be loaded into the device using IDirect3DTexture::Load().

continues

dwRampSize—The number of colors in the shade ramp for this material. For background materials (see IDirect3DViewport::SetBackground), this value should be less than or equal to 1.

See Also: IDirect3DMaterial::GetMaterial, IDirect3DMaterial::SetMaterial, D3DCOLORVALUE

D3DMATRIX

Definition:
```
typedef struct _D3DMATRIX
{
        D3DVALUE _11, _12, _13, _14;
        D3DVALUE _21, _22, _23, _24;
        D3DVALUE _31, _32, _33, _34;
        D3DVALUE _41, _42, _43, _44;
} D3DMATRIX, *LPD3DMATRIX;
```

Description: This structure describes a 4×4 matrix.

The _44 member may not be negative.

Members: _RC—Row R, Column C matrix element.

See Also: IDirect3DDevice::GetMatrix, IDirect3DDevice::SetMatrix, D3DMATRIXLOAD, D3DMATRIXMULTIPLY

D3DMATRIXLOAD

Definition:
```
typedef struct _D3DMATRIXLOAD
{
        D3DMATRIXHANDLE hDestMatrix;
        D3DMATRIXHANDLE hSrcMatrix;
} D3DMATRIXLOAD, *LPD3DMATRIXLOAD;
```

Description: This structure describes the instruction data for a D3DINSTRUCTION with the D3DOP_MATRIXLOAD opcode.

A D3DMATRIXLOAD specifies that the contents of the matrix whose handle is hDestMatrix be replaced with the contents of the matrix whose handle is hSrcMatrix.

Members: hDestMatrix—The handle of the destination matrix.

hSrcMatrix—The handle of the source matrix.

See Also: IDirect3DDevice::Execute, D3DMATRIX, D3DOPCODE, D3DINSTRUCTION

D3DMATRIXMULTIPLY

Definition:
```
typedef struct _D3DMATRIXMULTIPLY
{
        D3DMATRIXHANDLE hDestMatrix;
        D3DMATRIXHANDLE hSrcMatrix1;
        D3DMATRIXHANDLE hSrcMatrix2;
} D3DMATRIXMULTIPLY, *LPD3DMATRIXMULTIPLY;
```

Description: This structure describes the instruction data for a D3DINSTRUCTION with the D3DOP_MATRIXMULTIPLY opcode.

A D3DMATRIXMULTIPLY specifies the handle of a matrix, hDestMatrix, which will hold the result of multiplying the two matrices whose handles are hSrcMatrix1 and hSrcMatrix2. The matrices are multiplied with hSrcMatrix1 on the left.

Members: hDestMatrix—The handle of the destination matrix.

hSrcMatrix1—The handle of the first matrix multiplicand.

hSrcMatrix2—The handle of the second matrix multiplicand.

See Also: IDirect3DDevice::Execute, IDirect3DExecuteBuffer::GetExecuteData, IDirect3DExecuteBuffer::SetExecuteData, D3DMATRIX, D3DOPCODE

D3DPICKRECORD

Definition:
```
typedef struct _D3DPICKRECORD
{
        BYTE bOpcode;
        BYTE bPad;
        DWORD dwOffset;
        D3DVALUE dvZ;
} D3DPICKRECORD, *LPD3DPICKRECORD;
```

Description: A D3DPICKRECORD structure specifies a primitive within an execute buffer that, upon rendering, is mapped to at least one pixel within a certain rectangle.

A primitive that modifies a pixel with the specified rectangle is considered "picked." IDirect3DDevice::GetPickRecords() is used to retrieve an array of D3DPICKRECORDs, which is generated by a call to IDirect3DDevice::Pick().

Members: bOpcode—Picked primitive's opcode.

bPad—Pad byte.

dwOffset—Offset into the execute buffer, in bytes, at which the picked primitive was found.

dvZ—The distance along the z-axis of the primitive from the camera, in canonical-view volume coordinates.

See Also: IDirect3DDevice::GetPickRecords, IDirect3DDevice::Pick

D3DPOINT

Definition:
```
typedef struct _D3DPOINT
{
        WORD wCount;
        WORD wFirst;
} D3DPOINT, *LPD3DPOINT;
```

Description: This structure describes instruction data for a D3DINSTRUCTION with the D3DOP_POINT opcode.

Members: wCount—Number of points.

wFirst—Index of the first vertex.

See Also: IDirect3DDevice::Execute, IDirect3DExecuteBuffer::GetExecuteData, IDirect3DExecuteBuffer::SetExecuteData, D3DOPCODE

D3DPRIMCAPS

Definition:
```
typedef struct _D3DPrimCaps
{
        DWORD dwSize;
        DWORD dwMiscCaps;
        DWORD dwRasterCaps;
        DWORD dwZCmpCaps;
        DWORD dwSrcBlendCaps;
        DWORD dwDestBlendCaps;
        DWORD dwAlphaCmpCaps;
        DWORD dwShadeCaps;
        DWORD dwTextureCaps;
        DWORD dwTextureFilterCaps;
        DWORD dwTextureBlendCaps;
        DWORD dwTextureAddressCaps;
        DWORD dwStippleWidth;
        DWORD dwStippleHeight;
} D3DPRIMCAPS, *LPD3DPRIMCAPS;
```

Ddescription: This structure defines the device capabilities for each primitive type (triangles and lines). This structure is used when creating a device and when querying the capabilities of a device. The D3DDEVICEDESC structure contains two members of this type, dpcLineCaps and dpcTriCaps.

Members: dwSize—The size, in bytes, of this structure.

dwMiscCaps—Miscellaneous capabilities of the device when rendering the particular primitive. This member may contain one or more of the following values, combined with a bitwise OR:

D3DPMISCCAPS_CONFORMANT—The device conforms to the OpenGL standard.

D3DPMISCCAPS_CULLCCW—The device supports counter clockwise culling of triangles. This flag only applies to triangle primitives.

continues

continued

> D3DPMISCCAPS_CULLCW—The device supports clockwise culling of triangles. This flag only applies to triangle primitives.
>
> D3DPMISCCAPS_CULLNONE—The device does not cull triangles. This flag only applies to triangle primitives.
>
> D3DPMISCCAPS_LINEPATTERNREP—The device supports repeating patterns. This means the wRepeatFactor member of the D3DLINEPATTERN structure may have values greater than 1. This flag only applies to line drawing primitives.
>
> D3DPMISCCAPS_MASKPLANES—The device can perform a bitmask of color planes.
>
> D3DPMISCCAPS_MASKZ—The device can dynamically enable and disable z-buffer writes when rendering.

dwRasterCaps—The raster-drawing capabilities of the device. This member may contain one or more of the following values, combined with a bitwise OR:

> D3DPRASTERCAPS_DITHER—The device supports dithering.
>
> D3DPRASTERCAPS_FOGTABLE—The device supports a lookup table for fog values, indexed by z-distance from the camera.
>
> D3DPRASTERCAPS_FOGVERTEX—The device computes fog values in the lighting module, storing the values in the alpha component of the D3DCOLOR value of the specular member of D3DTLVERTEX structures. In this case, fog values are interpolated during rasterization.
>
> D3DPRASTERCAPS_PAT—The device can perform patterned drawing. This flag applies to line drawing or triangle filling and the D3DRENDERSTATE_LINEPATTERN and D3DRENDERSTATE_STIPPLEPATTERN render states.
>
> D3DPRASTERCAPS_ROP2—The device supports raster operations other than the default R2_COPYPEN. The raster operations supported when this flag is set are reported in the dwRops member of the DDCAPS structure of the current DirectDraw device.

D3DPRASTERCAPS_STIPPLE—The device can stipple polygons to simulate translucency during rasterization.

D3DPRASTERCAPS_SUBPIXEL—The device can perform sub-pixel placement of z, color, and texture data. This helps avoid z-buffer artifacts due to z value quantization, as well as color jitter when rendering pixels. Sub-pixel rendering cannot be enabled or disabled, but is a static property of the device.

D3DPRASTERCAPS_SUBPIXELX—The device can perform sub-pixel placement of z, color, and texture data the x-direction only. Placement is clamped to integer values in the y-direction. See D3DPRASTERCAPS_SUBPIXEL previously shown.

D3DPRASTERCAPS_XOR—The device supports exclusive-ORoperations. If this flag is not set but the D3DPRIM_RASTER_ROP2 flag is, the XOR operation may still be supported if so indicated by the dwRops member of the DDCAPS structure of the current DirectDraw device.

D3DPRASTERCAPS_ZTEST—The device supports z-test operations.

dwZCmpCaps—The z-buffer comparison functions the device supports. This member may contain one or more of the following values, combined with a bitwise OR:

D3DPCMPCAPS_ALWAYS—Always pass the z test.

D3DPCMPCAPS_EQUAL—Pass the z test if the new z equals the current z.

D3DPCMPCAPS_GREATER—Pass the z test if the new z is greater than the current z.

D3DPCMPCAPS_GREATEREQUAL—Pass the z test if the new z is greater than or equal to the current z.

D3DPCMPCAPS_LESS—Pass the z test if the new z is less than the current z.

D3DPCMPCAPS_LESSEQUAL—Pass the z test if the new z is less than or equal to the current z.

continues

continued

D3DPCMPCAPS_NEVER—Always fail the z test.

D3DPCMPCAPS_NOTEQUAL—Pass the z test if the new z does not equal the current z.

dwSrcBlendCaps—The source surface blending capabilities of the device. See D3DBLEND for an explanation of the meaning of the different blending types and factors. This member may contain one or more of the following values, combined with a bitwise OR (the RGBA values of the source and destination surfaces are indicated with the subscripts s and d):

D3DPBLENDCAPS_BOTHINVSRCALPHA—The source blend factor is $(1-A_s, 1-A_s, 1-A_s, 1-A_s)$, and the destination blend factor is (A_s, A_s, A_s, A_s). The destination blend selection is overridden.

D3DPBLENDCAPS_BOTHSRCALPHA—The source blend factor is (A_s, A_s, A_s, A_s), and the destination blend factor is $(1-A_s, 1-A_s, 1-A_s, 1-A_s)$. The destination blend selection is overridden.

D3DPBLENDCAPS_DESTALPHA—The blend factor is (A_d, A_d, A_d, A_d).

D3DPBLENDCAPS_DESTCOLOR—The blend factor is (R_d, G_d, B_d, A_d).

D3DPBLENDCAPS_INVDESTALPHA—The blend factor is $(1-A_d, 1-A_d, 1-A_d, 1-A_d)$.

D3DPBLENDCAPS_INVDESTCOLOR—The blend factor is $(1-R_d, 1-G_d, 1-B_d, 1-A_d)$.

D3DPBLENDCAPS_INVSRCALPHA—The blend factor is $(1-A_s, 1-A_s, 1-A_s, 1-A_s)$.

D3DPBLENDCAPS_INVSRCCOLOR—The blend factor is $(1-R_d, 1-G_d, 1-B_d, 1-A_d)$.

D3DPBLENDCAPS_ONE—The blend factor is $(1, 1, 1, 1)$.

D3DPBLENDCAPS_SRCALPHA—The blend factor is (A_s, A_s, A_s, A_s).

D3DPBLENDCAPS_SRCALPHASAT—The blend factor is
$(f, f, f, 1); f = \min(A_s, 1-A_d)$.

D3DPBLENDCAPS_SRCCOLOR—The blend factor is (R_s, G_s, B_s, A_s).

D3DPBLENDCAPS_ZERO—The blend factor is $(0, 0, 0, 0)$.

dwDestBlendCaps—The destination surface blending capabilities of the device. This member may have the same values as the flags defined for the dwSrcBlendCaps member previously described.

dwAlphaCmpCaps—The alpha-test comparison functions the device supports. This member may have the same values as the dwZCmpCaps member.

dwShadeCaps—The shading operations the device supports. Flat shading mode is assumed, and need not be tested. On devices that do not support alpha blending, or when alpha blending is disabled, all RGB values are implicitly converted to RGBA values with the maximum alpha value. When alpha blending is supported, the alpha value for a face is taken to be the alpha value of the face's first vertex. This member may contain one or more of the following values, combined with a bitwise OR:

D3DPSHADECAPS_ALPHAFLATBLEND—The device supports alpha blending in the flat shading model.

D3DPSHADECAPS_ALPHAFLATSTIPPLED—The device supports alpha stippling in the flat shading model.

D3DPSHADECAPS_ALPHAGOURAUDBLEND—The device supports alpha blending in the Gouraud shading model.

D3DPSHADECAPS_ALPHAGOURAUDSTIPPLED—The device supports alpha stippling in the Gouraud shading model.

D3DPSHADECAPS_ALPHAPHONGBLEND—The device supports alpha blending in the Phong shading model. Phong shading currently is not supported.

D3DPSHADECAPS_ALPHAPHONGSTIPPLED—The device supports alpha stippling in the Phong shading model. Phong shading currently is not supported.

continues

continued

D3DPSHADECAPS_COLORFLATMONO—The device supports flat shading in ramp color model.

D3DPSHADECAPS_COLORFLATRGB—The device supports flat shading in the RGB color model.

D3DPSHADECAPS_COLORGOURAUDMONO—The device supports Gouraud shading in the ramp color model.

D3DPSHADECAPS_COLORGOURAUDRGB—The device supports Gouraud shading in the RGB color model.

D3DPSHADECAPS_COLORPHONGMONO—The device supports Phong shading in the ramp color model. Phong shading currently is not supported.

D3DPSHADECAPS_COLORPHONGRGB—The device supports Phong shading in the RGB color model. Phong shading currently is not supported.

D3DPSHADECAPS_FOGFLAT—The device supports fog in the flat shading model.

D3DPSHADECAPS_FOGGOURAUD—The device supports fog in the Gouraud shading model.

D3DPSHADECAPS_FOGPHONG—The device supports fog in the Phong shading model. Phong shading currently is not supported.

D3DPSHADECAPS_SPECULARFLATMONO—The device supports specular highlights in the flat shading model and ramp color model.

D3DPSHADECAPS_SPECULARFLATRGB—The device supports specular highlights in the flat shading model and RGB color model.

D3DPSHADECAPS_SPECULARGOURAUDMONO—The device supports specular highlights in the Gouraud shading model and ramp color model.

D3DPSHADECAPS_SPECULARGOURAUDRGB—The device supports specular highlights in the Gouraud shading model and ramp color model.

D3DPSHADECAPS_SPECULARPHONGMONO—The device supports specular highlights in the Phong shading model and ramp color model. Phong shading currently is not supported.

D3DPSHADECAPS_SPECULARPHONGRGB—The device supports specular highlights in the Phong shading model and RGB color model. Phong shading currently is not supported.

dwTextureCaps—The miscellaneous texture-mapping capabilities of the device. This member may contain one or more of the following values, combined with a bitwise OR:

D3DPTEXTURECAPS_ALPHA—The device supports RGBA textures in the D3DTEX_DECAL and D3DTEX_MODULATE texture filtering modes. If this capability is not present, only RGB textures are supported in the D3DTEX_DECAL and D3DTEX_MODULATE modes. Regardless of the setting of this flag, alpha must always be supported in D3DTBLEND_DECALMASK, D3DTBLEND_DECALALPHA, or D3DTBLEND_MODULATEALPHA texture-blending modes if those modes are reported as supported in the dwTextureBlendCaps field.

D3DPTEXTURECAPS_BORDER—The device supports texture mapping along borders.

D3DPTEXTURECAPS_PERSPECTIVE—The device supports perspective-correct texture mapping.

D3DPTEXTURECAPS_POW2—The device requires that all textures, not just mipmapped textures, must have widths and heights that are exact powers of two.

D3DPTEXTURECAPS_SQUAREONLY—The device only supports square textures.

D3DPTEXTURECAPS_TRANSPARENCY—The device supports texture transparency through color keying.

dwTextureFilterCaps—The texture filtering capabilities of the device. This member may contain one or more of the following values, combined with a bitwise OR:

continues

continued

D3DPTFILTERCAPS_NEAREST—The device supports nearest-texel filtering. In this mode, pixel colors are chosen to be the color of the nearest texel.

D3DPTFILTERCAPS_LINEAR—The device supports linear filtering. In this mode, pixel colors are computed as the average of the four nearest texel colors.

D3DPTFILTERCAPS_MIPNEAREST—The device supports nearest-texel filtering with mipmapping. In this mode, pixel colors are computed from the color of the nearest texel in the nearest mipmap in the mipmapping chain.

D3DPTFILTERCAPS_MIPLINEAR—The device supports linear filtering with mipmapping. In this mode, pixel colors are computed as the average of the four nearest texel colors in the nearest mipmap in the mipmapping chain.

D3DPTFILTERCAPS_LINEARMIPNEAREST—The device supports nearest-texel filtering with interpolative mipmapping. In this mode, pixel colors are computed by linearly interpolating between the nearest texel color in the two nearest mipmaps.

D3DPTFILTERCAPS_LINEARMIPLINEAR—The device supports linear filtering with interpolative mipmapping. In this mode, pixel colors are computed by linearly interpolating between the average of the four nearest texel colors in the two nearest mipmaps.

dwTextureBlendCaps—The texture-blending capabilities of the device. See the D3DTEXTUREBLEND enumerated type for discussions of the various texture-blending modes. This member may contain one or more of the following values, combined with a bitwise OR:

D3DPTBLENDCAPS_COPY—The device supports copy mode texture-blending.

D3DPTBLENDCAPS_DECAL—The device supports decal mode texture-blending.

D3DPTBLENDCAPS_DECALALPHA—The device supports decal-alpha mode texture-blending.

D3DPTBLENDCAPS_DECALMASK—The device supports decal-mask mode texture-blending.

D3DPTBLENDCAPS_MODULATE—The device supports modulate mode texture-blending.

D3DPTBLENDCAPS_MODULATEALPHA—The device supports modulate-alpha mode texture-blending.

D3DPTBLENDCAPS_MODULATEMASK—The device supports modulate-mask mode texture-blending.

dwTextureAddressCaps—The texture-addressing capabilities of the device. This member may contain one or more of the following values, combined with a bitwise OR:

D3DPTADDRESSCAPS_CLAMP—The device can clamp textures coordinates to within 0 and 1.

D3DPTADDRESSCAPS_MIRROR—The device can tile textures by using the mirror tiling, in which each tile is surrounded by mirror images of itself (though at different rotations).

D3DPTADDRESSCAPS_WRAP—The device can wrap texture coordinates by using a flat, cylindrical, or spherical topology.

dwStippleWidth—The maximum width of a stipple pattern. The maximum allowed is 32.

dwStippleHeight—The maximum height of a stipple pattern. The maximum allowed is 32.

See Also: IDirect3DDevice::GetCaps, IDirect3DRM::CreateDeviceFromClipper, D3DDEVICEDESC, D3DFINDDEVICESEARCH

D3DPROCESSVERTICES

Definition:
```
typedef struct _D3DPROCESSVERTICES
{
        DWORD   dwFlags;
        WORD    wStart;
        WORD    wDest;
        DWORD   dwCount;
        DWORD   dwReserved;
} D3DPROCESSVERTICES, *LPD3DPROCESSVERTICES
```

Description: This structure describes the instruction data for a D3DINSTRUCTION with the D3DOP_PROCESSVERTICES opcode. It specifies a range of vertices to be processed by the renderer, according to its current state and the contents of the dwFlags parameter.

Members: dwFlags—One or more of the following flags indicating how the driver should process the vertices:

D3DPROCESSVERTICES_COPY—Vertices should be copied to the driver as-is because they have already been transformed, clipped, and lit. This flag implies all vertices in the execute buffer are specified in D3DTLVERTEX structures.

D3DPROCESSVERTICES_NOCOLOR—Vertices should not be colored.

D3DPROCESSVERTICES_OPMASK—Bitmask of the other flags that imply a particular vertex structure, and defined whether the transformation and lighting modules should be used. Currently, these flags are D3DPROCESSVERTICES_TRANSFORMLIGHT, D3DPROCESSVERTICES_TRANSFORM, and D3DPROCESSVERTICES_COPY.

D3DPROCESSVERTICES_TRANSFORM—Vertices should be transformed but not lit. Implies vertices are stored in D3DLVERTEX structures.

D3DPROCESSVERTICES_TRANSFORMLIGHT—Vertices should be transformed and lit. Implies vertices are stored in D3DVERTEX structures.

D3DPROCESSVERTICES_UPDATEEXTENTS—The damage extent rectangle (in device coordinates) should be updated to enclose all the processed vertices. This information is returned in the drExtent member of the D3DSTATUS structure.

wStart—The index of the first vertex to be transformed, transformed and lit, or copied.

wDest—The index of the first destination vertex. This feature is not currently supported, and wDest should be the same as wStart.

dwCount—The number of vertices to be processed.

dwReserved—Reserved; must be zero.

See Also: IDirect3DDevice::Execute, IDirect3DExecuteBuffer::GetExecuteData, IDirect3DExecuteBuffer::SetExecuteData, D3DOPCODE, D3DSTATUS

D3DRECT

Definition:

```
typedef struct _D3DRECT
{
        union
        {
                LONG x1;
                LONG lX1;
        };
        union
        {
                LONG y1;
                LONG lY1;
        };
        union
        {
                LONG x2;
                LONG lX2;
        };
        union
        {
                LONG y2;
                LONG lY2;
        };
} D3DRECT, *LPD3DRECT;
```

continues

continued

Description:	This structure defines a two-dimensional rectangle with integer coordinates.
Members:	x1, lX1—X coordinate of the upper-left corner of the rectangle.
	y1, lY1—Y coordinate of the upper-left corner of the rectangle.
	x2, lX2—X coordinate of the lower-right corner of the rectangle.
	y2, lY2—Y coordinate of the lower-right corner of the rectangle.
See Also:	D3DRMUPDATECALLBACK, IDirect3DDevice::Pick, IDirect3DViewport::Clear, D3DSTATUS, D3DTRANSFORMDATA

D3DSPAN

Definition:
```
typedef struct _D3DSPAN
{
        WORD wCount;
        WORD wFirst;
} D3DSPAN, *LPD3DSPAN;
```

Description: This structure describes the instruction data for a D3DINSTRUCTION with the D3DOP_SPAN opcode. A span is a group of vertices with the same y coordinate in screen space, which are thus on the same scanline.

Members: wCount—The number of vertices to span. WCount is the number of spans, not the number of vertices.

wFirst—Index of the first vertex.

See Also: IDirect3DDevice::Execute, IDirect3DExecuteBuffer::GetExecuteData, IDirect3DExecuteBuffer::SetExecuteData, D3DOPCODE

D3DSTATE

Definition:
```
typedef struct _D3DSTATE
{
        union
        {
```

```
                        D3DTRANSFORMSTATETYPE dtstTransformStateType;
                        D3DLIGHTSTATETYPE dlstLightStateType;
                        D3DRENDERSTATETYPE drstRenderStateType;
            };
                union
                {
                        DWORD dwArg[1];
                        D3DVALUE dvArg[1];
                };
        } D3DSTATE, *LPD3DSTATE;
```

Description: This structure describes the instruction data for a D3DINSTRUCTION with the D3DOP_STATETRANSFORM, D3DOP_STATELIGHT, or D3DOP_STATERENDER opcode.

Members: dtstTransformStateType, dlstLightStateType, drstRenderStateType— One of the members of the D3DTRANSFORMSTATETYPE, D3DLIGHTSTATETYPE, or D3DRENDERSTATETYPE enumerated type, depending on the D3DINSTRUCTION's opcode.

dvArg—This value holds the new state value. Its meaning depends on the state type specified in the first member.

See Also: IDirect3DDevice::Execute, IDirect3DExecuteBuffer::GetExecuteData, IDirect3DExecuteBuffer::SetExecuteData, D3DLIGHTSTATETYPE, D3DRENDERSTATETYPE, D3DTRANSFORMSTATETYPE, D3DOPCODE

D3DSTATS

Definition:
```
typedef struct _D3DSTATS
{
        DWORD dwSize;
        DWORD dwTrianglesDrawn;
        DWORD dwLinesDrawn;
        DWORD dwPointsDrawn;
        DWORD dwSpansDrawn;
        DWORD dwVerticesProcessed;
} D3DSTATS, *LPD3DSTATS;
```

Description: This structure is used to hold statistics retrieved from IDirect3DDevice::GetStats().

continues

continued

Members: dwSize—The size, in bytes, of this structure.

dwTrianglesDrawn—The number of triangles drawn since the device was created.

dwLinesDrawn—The number of lines drawn since the device was created.

dwPointsDrawn—The number of points drawn since the device was created.

dwSpansDrawn—The number of spans drawn since the device was created.

dwVerticesProcessed—The number of vertices processed since the device was created.

See Also: IDirect3DDevice::GetStats

D3DSTATUS

Definition:
```
typedef struct _D3DSTATUS
{
        DWORD    dwFlags;
        DWORD    dwStatus;
        D3DRECT  drExtent;
} D3DSTATUS, *LPD3DSTATUS;
```

Description: This structure describes the current status of the execute buffer. The D3DEXECUTEDATA structure has a member of this type, and it is also used as instruction data for a D3DINSTRUCTION with the D3DOP_SETSTATUS opcode.

Members: dwFlags—The flags indicating whether the driver's status register, the current damage extent rectangle, or both should be set. Its value may be one or more of the following, combined with a bitwise OR:

D3DSETSTATUS_STATUS—Set the status register.

D3DSETSTATUS_EXTENTS—Set the damage extent rectangle to that specified in the drExtent member.

D3DSETSTATUS_ALL—Set both the status register and the extent rectangle.

dwStatus—The current clipping flags. Its value may be one or more of the following, combined with a bitwise OR:

Combination and General Flags

D3DSTATUS_CLIPINTERSECTION—Combination of all CLIPINTERSECTION flags.

D3DSTATUS_CLIPUNIONALL—Combination of all CLIPUNION flags.

D3DSTATUS_DEFAULT—Combination of D3DSTATUS_CLIPINTERSECTION and D3DSTATUS_ZNOTVISIBLE flags. This value is typically used to initialize the status register before any clipping takes place.

D3DSTATUS_ZNOTVISIBLE—If the D3DRENDERSTATE_ZVISIBLE state is supported on the device and enabled, this flag indicates whether z-checking has culled.

Clip Intersection Flags

D3DSTATUS_CLIPINTERSECTIONBACK—This flag is set in the status register if all vertices were clipped by the back clipping plane.

D3DSTATUS_CLIPINTERSECTIONBOTTOM—This flag is set in the status register if all vertices were clipped by the bottom of the view frustum.

D3DSTATUS_CLIPINTERSECTIONFRONT—This flag is set in the status register if all vertices were clipped by the front clipping plane.

D3DSTATUS_CLIPINTERSECTIONGEN0 through D3DSTATUS_CLIPINTERSECTIONGEN5—These flags are reserved.

D3DSTATUS_CLIPINTERSECTIONLEFT—This flag is set in the status register if all vertices were clipped by the left side of the view frustum.

continues

continued

D3DSTATUS_CLIPINTERSECTIONRIGHT—This flag is set in the status register if all vertices were clipped by the right side of the view frustum.

D3DSTATUS_CLIPINTERSECTIONTOP—This flag is set in the status register if all vertices were clipped by the top of the view frustum.

Clip Union Flags

D3DSTATUS_CLIPUNIONBACK—This flag is set if any vertex was clipped by the back clipping plane.

D3DSTATUS_CLIPUNIONBOTTOM—This flag is set if any vertex was clipped by the bottom of the view frustum.

D3DSTATUS_CLIPUNIONFRONT—This flag is set if any vertex was clipped by the front of the view frustum.

D3DSTATUS_CLIPUNIONGEN0 through D3DSTATUS_CLIPUNIONGEN5—These values are reserved.

D3DSTATUS_CLIPUNIONLEFT—This flag is set if any vertex was clipped by the left side of the view frustum.

D3DSTATUS_CLIPUNIONRIGHT—This flag is set if any vertex was clipped by the right side of the view frustum.

D3DSTATUS_CLIPUNIONTOP—This flag is set if any vertex was clipped by the top of the view frustum.

Basic Clipping Flags

D3DCLIP_BACK—Used to specify clipping against the back clipping plane. Same as D3DSTATUS_CLIPUNIONBACK.

D3DCLIP_BOTTOM—Used to specify clipping against the bottom of the view frustum. Same as D3DSTATUS_CLIPUNIONBOTTOM.

D3DCLIP_FRONT—Used to specify clipping against the front clipping plane. Same as D3DSTATUS_CLIPUNIONFRONT.

D3DCLIP_LEFT—Used to specify clipping against the left of the view frustum. Same as D3DSTATUS_CLIPUNIONLEFT.

D3DCLIP_RIGHT—Used to specify clipping against the right of the view frustum. Same as D3DSTATUS_CLIPUNIONRIGHT.

D3DCLIP_TOP—Used to specify clipping against the top of the view frustum. Same as D3DSTATUS_CLIPUNIONTOP.

D3DCLIP_GEN0 through D3DCLIP_GEN5—Reserved. Same as D3DSTATUS_CLIPUNIONGEN0 through D3DSTATUS_CLIPUNIONGEN5.

drExtent—A D3DRECT structure that defines an extent box in device coordinates that encloses all modified bits in the device since it was last reset for all the relevant vertices. The structure, for example, might define the area containing the output of the D3DOP_PROCESSVERTICES opcode, assuming the D3DPROCESSVERTICES_UPDATEEXTENTS flag is set in the D3DPROCESSVERTICES structure.

See Also: D3DBRANCH, D3DEXECUTEDATA, D3DOPCODE, D3DPROCESSVERTICES, IDirect3DDevice::Execute, IDirect3DExecuteBuffer::GetExecuteData, IDirect3DExecuteBuffer::SetExecuteData

D3DTEXTURELOAD

Definition:
```
typedef struct _D3DTEXTURELOAD
{
        D3DTEXTUREHANDLE hDestTexture;
        D3DTEXTUREHANDLE hSrcTexture;
} D3DTEXTURELOAD, *LPD3DTEXTURELOAD;
```

Description: This structure describes instruction data for a D3DINSTRUCTION with the D3DOP_TEXTURELOAD opcode. The textures referred to by the hDestTexture and hSrcTexture members must have the same dimensions.

Members: hDestTexture—The destination texture handle.

hSrcTexture—The source texture handle.

See Also: IDirect3DDevice::Execute, IDirect3DExecuteBuffer::GetExecuteData, IDirect3DExecuteBuffer::SetExecuteData, D3DOPCODE

D3DTLVERTEX

Definition:
```
typedef struct _D3DTLVERTEX
{
        union
        {
                D3DVALUE sx;
                D3DVALUE dvSX;
        };
        union
        {
                D3DVALUE sy;
                D3DVALUE dvSY;
        };
        union
        {
                D3DVALUE sz;
                D3DVALUE dvSZ;
        };
        union
        {
                D3DVALUE rhw;
                D3DVALUE dvRHW;
        };
        union
        {
                D3DCOLOR color;
                D3DCOLOR dcColor;
        };
        union
        {
                D3DCOLOR specular;
                D3DCOLOR dcSpecular;
        };
        union
        {
                D3DVALUE tu;
                D3DVALUE dvTU;
        };
        union
        {
                D3DVALUE tv;
                D3DVALUE dvTV;
        };
} D3DTLVERTEX, *LPD3DTLVERTEX;
```

Description: This structure defines a transformed and lit vertex.

Members: sx, dvSX—The screen x coordinate of the vertex.

sy, dvSY—The screen y coordinate of the vertex.

sz, dvSZ—The screen z coordinate of the vertex.

rhw, dvRHW—The value of the reciprocal of the homogeneous w coordinate. It is proportional to 1 divided by the distance along the z-axis from camera to the object.

color, dcColor—The value of the color component of the vertex.

specular, dcSpecular—The value of the specular component of the vertex.

tu, dvTU—The value of the texture u coordinate of the vertex.

tv, dvTV—The value of the texture v coordinate of the vertex.

See Also: IDirect3DViewport::TransformVertices, D3DLIGHTDATA, D3DPRIMCAPS

D3DTRANSFORMCAPS

Definition:
```
typedef struct _D3DTransformCaps
{
        DWORD dwSize;
        DWORD dwCaps;
} D3DTRANSFORMCAPS, *LPD3DTRANSFORMCAPS;
```

Description: This structure describes the transformation capabilities of a device. This structure is part of the D3DDEVICEDESC structure.

Members: dwSize—The size, in bytes, of this structure.

dwCaps—The flag specifying whether the system clips while transforming. This member can be zero or the following flag:

D3DTRANSFORMCAPS_CLIP—The system clips while transforming.

See Also: IDirect3DDevice::GetCaps, D3DDEVICEDESC

D3DTRANSFORMDATA

Definition:
```
typedef struct _D3DTRANSFORMDATA
{
        DWORD dwSize;
        LPVOID lpIn;
        DWORD dwInSize;
        LPVOID lpOut;
        DWORD dwOutSize;
        LPD3DHVERTEX lpHOut;
        DWORD dwClip;
        DWORD dwClipIntersection;
        DWORD dwClipUnion;
        D3DRECT drExtent;
} D3DTRANSFORMDATA, *LPD3DTRANSFORMDATA;
```

Description: This structure encapsulates various data for transforming vertices with IDirect3DViewport::TransformVertices().

Members: dwSize—The size of the structure, in bytes.

lpIn—The address of the first element of an array of D3DLVERTEX structures, to be transformed.

dwInSize—The number of bytes between D3DLVERTEXs in the array pointed to by lpIn. This enables the application to store extra data inline with the vertex.

lpOut—The address of the first element of an array of D3DTLVERTEX vertices used to store the transformed vertices.

dwOutSize—The number of bytes between D3DTLVERTEX's in the array pointed to by lpOut. This enables the application to store extra data inline with the vertex.

lpHOut—The address of the first element of an array of D3DHVERTEX structures, used to store the clipped vertices.

dwClip—The flags indicating against which side of the view frustum vertices should be clipped. This member may contain zero or more of the following values, combined with bitwise OR:

D3DCLIP_BACK—Clip against the back clipping plane.

D3DCLIP_BOTTOM—Clip against the bottom of the view frustum.

D3DCLIP_FRONT—Clip against the front clipping plane.

D3DCLIP_GEN0 through D3DCLIP_GEN5—These values are reserved.

D3DCLIP_LEFT—Clip against the left side of the view frustum.

D3DCLIP_RIGHT—Clip against the right side of the view frustum.

D3DCLIP_TOP—Clip against the top of the view frustum.

dwClipIntersection—The flags denoting the intersection of the clip flags. Before processing the vertices, this flag is initialized to D3DSTATUS_CLIPINTERSECTIONALL. Then whenever a vertex is *not* clipped on a side, the corresponding flag is cleared. After processing the vertices, if any flag is set, then all vertices were clipped on that side, and no vertex is visible. This member can be one or more of the following values, combined with bitwise OR:

D3DSTATUS_CLIPINTERSECTIONBACK—This flag is set in the status register if all vertices were clipped by the back clipping plane.

D3DSTATUS_CLIPINTERSECTIONBOTTOM—This flag is set in the status register if all vertices were clipped by the bottom of the view frustum.

D3DSTATUS_CLIPINTERSECTIONFRONT—This flag is set in the status register if all vertices were clipped by the front clipping plane.

D3DSTATUS_CLIPINTERSECTIONGEN0 through D3DSTATUS_CLIPINTERSECTIONGEN5—These flags are reserved.

D3DSTATUS_CLIPINTERSECTIONLEFT—This flag is set in the status register if all vertices were clipped by the left side of the view frustum.

D3DSTATUS_CLIPINTERSECTIONRIGHT—This flag is set in the status register if all vertices were clipped by the right side of the view frustum.

continues

continued

D3DSTATUS_CLIPINTERSECTIONTOP—This flag is set in the status register if all vertices were clipped by the top of the view frustum.

dwClipUnion—Flags indicating whether any vertices were clipped, and if so, the side of the view frustum against which clipping occurred. This member may contain zero or more of the following values, combined with bitwise OR:

D3DSTATUS_CLIPUNIONBACK—At least one vertex was clipped by the back-clipping plane.

D3DSTATUS_CLIPUNIONBOTTOM—At least one vertex was clipped by the bottom of the view frustum.

D3DSTATUS_CLIPUNIONFRONT—At least one vertex was clipped by the front-clipping plane.

D3DSTATUS_CLIPUNIONGEN0 through D3DSTATUS_CLIPUNIONGEN5—These values are reserved.

D3DSTATUS_CLIPUNIONLEFT—At least one vertex was clipped by the left side of the view frustum.

D3DSTATUS_CLIPUNIONRIGHT—At least one vertex was clipped by the right side of the view frustum.

D3DSTATUS_CLIPUNIONTOP—At least one vertex was clipped by the top of the view frustum.

drExtent—The smallest rectangle in device coordinates that contains all the vertices that were not clipped.

See Also: IDirect3DViewport::TransformVertices, D3DHVERTEX, D3DLVERTEX, D3DRECT

D3DTRIANGLE

Definition:
```
typedef struct _D3DTRIANGLE
{
        union
        {
```

```
                    WORD    v1;
                    WORD    wV1;
            };
            union
            {
                    WORD    v2;
                    WORD    wV2;
            };
            union
            {
                    WORD    v3;
                    WORD    wV3;
            };
            WORD        wFlags;
    } D3DTRIANGLE, *LPD3DTRIANGLE;
```

Description: This structure describes instruction data for a D3DINSTRUCTION with the D3DOP_TRIANGLE opcode.

Notes: If flat shading is enabled, the color of the first vertex is used to shade the triangle.

Enabled edges are visible in wireframe mode and may be anti-aliased if the driver supports them. If z-buffering is not enabled, only one edge of two flush edges need be enabled.

To minimize the amount of data that has to cross the bus onto an accelerator card and to facilitate various optimized triangle-rendering algorithms, strips and fans may be constructed that exploit symmetries in the face structure to reduce the amount of data required to represent a face. Fans are particularly useful for triangulating polygons.

The D3DTRIFLAG_ODD and D3DTRIFLAG_EVEN flags are used when constructing a strip. The D3DTRIFLAG_EVEN flag is used when constructing a fan. The most compact representation of a strip requires triangles with both clockwise and counterclockwise vertex ordering. The D3DTRIFLAG_ODD flag is used to signal a triangle in a strip that has the opposite ordering required for it to be visible. The D3DTRIFLAG_EVEN flag is used to signal a triangle in a strip that has the correct vertex ordering. If, for example, a triangle strip had five triangles, the following flags would be set in subsequent triangles in a strip of five triangles:

continues

continued

> D3DTRIFLAG_START
>
> D3DTRIFLAG_ODD
>
> D3DTRIFLAG_EVEN
>
> D3DTRIFLAG_ODD
>
> D3DTRIFLAG_EVEN
>
> The following flags would be set in subsequent triangles in a triangle fan with five triangles:
>
> D3DTRIFLAG_START
>
> D3DTRIFLAG_EVEN
>
> D3DTRIFLAG_EVEN
>
> D3DTRIFLAG_EVEN
>
> D3DTRIFLAG_EVEN
>
> If all the triangles in the fan are coplanar, the whole fan can be culled based on the result of culling one of the triangles. The following flags would be set in subsequent triangles in a flat triangle fan with five triangles:
>
> D3DTRIFLAG_STARTFLAT(4)
>
> D3DTRIFLAG_EVEN
>
> D3DTRIFLAG_EVEN
>
> D3DTRIFLAG_EVEN
>
> D3DTRIFLAG_EVEN

Members: v1, wV1—The first vertex of the triangle.

v2, wV2—The second vertex of the triangle.

v3, wV3—The third vertex of the triangle.

wFlags—The flags describing which edges of the triangle to edge-enable, and various strip and fan flags. In wireframe mode, only edge-enabled edges are drawn, and only one of two adjacent edges need be edge-enabled to be rendered in wireframe mode if z-buffer is disabled. Hardware anti-aliasing algorithms typically operate only on edge-enabled edges. This value may be a combination of the following flags, combined with a bitwise OR:

Edge Flags

D3DTRIFLAG_EDGEENABLE1—The edge defined by vertices 1 and 2 is edge-enabled.

D3DTRIFLAG_EDGEENABLE2—The edge defined by vertices 2 and 3 is edge-enabled.

D3DTRIFLAG_EDGEENABLE3—The edge defined by vertices 3 and 1 is edge-enabled.

D3DTRIFLAG_EDGEENABLETRIANGLE—All the edges are edge-enabled.

Strip and Fan Flags

D3DTRIFLAG_EVEN—The edge formed by vertices 1 and 2 of the current triangle is adjacent to the edge formed by vertices 3 and 1 of the previous triangle. This implies that vertex 1 is shared between the two triangles, and the current triangle's vertex 2 is the previous triangle's vertex 3.

D3DTRIFLAG_ODD—Indicates the winding order of this triangle is opposite what it should be to be visible. This flag is used in creating strips, when the edge formed by vertices 1 and 2 of the current triangle is adjacent to the edge formed by vertices 2 and 3 of the previous triangle. This implies that the winding order has changed between the two triangles, and unless provisions are made by the renderer, the current triangle will be culled. This flag is only used when constructing a strip.

D3DTRIFLAG_START—Indicates this triangle is the first triangle in a strip or fan.

D3DTRIFLAG_STARTFLAT(len)—Indicates this triangle is the first triangle of a strip or fan of len coplanar triangles.

See Also: IDirect3DDevice::Execute, IDirect3DExecuteBuffer::GetExecuteData, IDirect3DExecuteBuffer::SetExecuteData, D3DOPCODE

D3DVECTOR

Definition:
```
typedef struct _D3DVECTOR
{
        union
        {
                D3DVALUE x;
                D3DVALUE dvX;
        };
        union
        {
                D3DVALUE y;
                D3DVALUE dvY;
        };
        union
        {
                D3DVALUE z;
                D3DVALUE dvZ;
        };
} D3DVECTOR, *LPD3DVECTOR;
```

Description: This structure defines a vector in three-dimensional space.

Members: x, dvX—X value of the vector.

y, dvY—Y value of the vector.

z, dvZ—Z value of the vector.

See Also: D3DRMVectorAdd, D3DRMVectorCrossProduct, D3DRMVectorDotProduct, D3DRMVectorNormalize, D3DRMVectorRandom, D3DRMVectorReflect, D3DRMVectorRotate, D3DRMVectorScale, D3DRMVectorSubtract

D3DVERTEX

Definition:
```
typedef struct _D3DVERTEX
{
        union
        {
                D3DVALUE x;
                D3DVALUE dvX;
        };
        union
        {
                D3DVALUE y;
```

```
                        D3DVALUE dvY;
        };
        union
        {
                D3DVALUE z;
                D3DVALUE dvZ;
        };
        union
        {
                D3DVALUE nx;
                D3DVALUE dvNX;
        };
        union
        {
                D3DVALUE ny;
                D3DVALUE dvNY;
        };
        union
        {
                D3DVALUE nz;
                D3DVALUE dvNZ;
        };
        union
        {
                D3DVALUE tu;
                D3DVALUE dvTU;
        };
        union
        {
                D3DVALUE tv;
                D3DVALUE dvTV;
        };
} D3DVERTEX, *LPD3DVERTEX;
```

Description: This structure defines an untransformed and unlit vertex. It has a position, normal vector, and texture coordinates.

The normal vector is typically the normalized sum of the normal vector for each face that shares this vertex. The correct lighting of a mesh may require several vertices with the same position vector but different normal vectors.

Members: x, dvX—The value of the x coordinate of the vertex.

y, dvY—The value of the y coordinate of the vertex.

z, dvZ—The value of the z coordinate of the vertex.

x, dvNX—The value of the x coordinate of the vertex normal.

y, dvNY—The value of the y coordinate of the vertex normal.

continues

continued

z, dvNZ—The value of the z coordinate of the vertex normal.

tu, dvTU—The value of the vertex's texture u coordinate.

tv, dvTV—The value of the vertex's texture v coordinate.

See Also: D3DPROCESSVERTICES

D3DVIEWPORT

Definition:
```
typedef struct _D3DVIEWPORT
{
        DWORD dwSize;
        DWORD dwX;
        DWORD dwY;
        DWORD dwWidth;
        DWORD dwHeight;
        D3DVALUE dvScaleX;
        D3DVALUE dvScaleY;
        D3DVALUE dvMaxX;
        D3DVALUE dvMaxY;
        D3DVALUE dvMinZ;
        D3DVALUE dvMaxZ;
} D3DVIEWPORT, *LPD3DVIEWPORT;
```

Description: Describes the visible 3D volume and the 2D screen area onto which a 3D volume projects. Currently, Direct3D only uses the dwX, dwY, dwWidth, dwHeight, dwScaleX and dwScaleY parameters. Projection matrix management is up to the application.

Members: dwSize—The size of this structure, in bytes.

dwX—X coordinate of the top-left corner of the viewport in device coordinates.

dwY—Y coordinate of the top-left corner of the viewport in device coordinates.

dwWidth—The width of the viewport in pixels.

dwHeight—The height of the viewport in pixels.

dvScaleX—The value of the x-scaling quantity homogeneous to the screen. Typically $1/2$ the width of the screen in pixels.

dvScaleY—The value of the y-scaling quantity homogeneous to the screen. Typically $1/2$ the width of the screen in pixels.

dvMaxX—The value of the maximum visible x coordinate in camera coordinates.

dvMaxY—The value of the maximum visible y coordinate in camera coordinates.

dvMinZ—The distance of the front clipping plane from the camera, in world coordinates.

dvMaxZ—The distance of the back clipping plane from the camera, in world coordinates.

See Also: IDirect3DViewport::GetViewport, IDirect3DViewport::SetViewport

Immediate-Mode Enumerated Types

D3DBLEND

Definition:

```
typedef enum _D3DBLEND
{
        D3DBLEND_ZERO = 1,
        D3DBLEND_ONE = 2,
        D3DBLEND_SRCCOLOR = 3,
        D3DBLEND_INVSRCCOLOR = 4,
        D3DBLEND_SRCALPHA = 5,
        D3DBLEND_INVSRCALPHA = 6,
        D3DBLEND_DESTALPHA = 7,
        D3DBLEND_INVDESTALPHA = 8,
        D3DBLEND_DESTCOLOR = 9,
        D3DBLEND_INVDESTCOLOR = 10,
        D3DBLEND_SRCALPHASAT = 11,
        D3DBLEND_BOTHSRCALPHA = 12,
        D3DBLEND_BOTHINVSRCALPHA = 13
} D3DBLEND;
```

Description: This enumerated type defines values for the different source and destination blending modes that may be invoked in an execute buffer by a D3DOP_STATERENDER instruction with state type D3DRENDERSTATE_SRCBLEND or D3DRENDERSTATE_DESTBLEND. The dwArg member of the D3DSTATE for the render state should hold one of the values defined by D3DBLEND.

A blending mode specifies how source and destination pixel values are combined to create a new destination pixel value by the blitter.

New pixel values are computed using the following e

$$\text{New Pixel} = (\text{Source Pixel} \times \phi_S) + (\text{Dest. Pixel} \times \phi_D)$$

where ϕ_S and ϕ_D are the source and destination blend factors, described later.

continues

continued

Take care when choosing a source and destination blend factor so that for all possible pixel values, the resulting R, G, B, and A values are between 0 and 1.

To use blending, the device must support it. Blending must be enabled by executing a D3DOP_STATERENDER instruction of type D3DRENDERSTATE_BLENDENABLE with the state value set to TRUE.

In the following descriptions, the R, G, B, and A values of the source and destination pixels are indicated with the subscripts s and d.

Members: D3DBLEND_ZERO—The blend factor is (0, 0, 0, 0).

D3DBLEND_ONE—The blend factor is (1, 1, 1, 1).

D3DBLEND_SRCCOLOR—The blend factor is (R_s, G_s, B_s, A_s). Setting this factor on the destination surface serves to modulate the colors.

D3DBLEND_INVSRCCOLOR—The blend factor is (A_s, A_s, A_s, A_s, $1 - A_s$).

D3DBLEND_SRCALPHA—The blend factor is (A_s, A_s, A_s, A_s).

D3DBLEND_INVSRCALPHA—The blend factor is ($1 - A_s$, $1 - A_s$, $1 - A_s$).

D3DBLEND_DESTALPHA—The blend factor is (A_d, A_d, A_d, A_d).

D3DBLEND_INVDESTALPHA—The blend factor is ($1 - A_d$, $1 - A_d$, $1 - A_d$, $1 - A_d$).

D3DBLEND_DESTCOLOR—The blend factor is (R_d, G_d, B_d, A_d).

D3DBLEND_INVDESTCOLOR—The blend factor is ($1 - R_d$, $1 - G_d$, $1 - B_d$, $1 - A_d$).

D3DBLEND_SRCALPHASAT—The blend factor is (ϕ, ϕ, ϕ, 1), where ϕ is the minimum of A_d and $1 - A_d$.

D3DBLEND_BOTHSRCALPHA—The source blend factor is (A_s, A_s, A_s, A_s), and the destination blend factor is ($1 - A_s$, $1 - A_s$, $1 - A_s$, $1 - A_s$). This is a common blending function for achieving basic transparency. This mode should be set for the source, and it overrides any previous mode set for the destination.

D3DBLEND_BOTHINVSRCALPHA—The source blend factor is $(1 - A_s, 1 - A_s, 1 - A_s, 1 - A_s)$, and the destination blend factor is (A_s, A_s, A_s, A_s). This mode should be set for the source, and it overrides any previous mode set for the destination.

See Also: D3DPRIMCAPS

D3DCMPFUNC

Definition:
```
typedef enum _D3DCMPFUNC
{
        D3DCMP_NEVER = 1,
        D3DCMP_LESS = 2,
        D3DCMP_EQUAL = 3,
        D3DCMP_LESSEQUAL = 4,
        D3DCMP_GREATER = 5,
        D3DCMP_NOTEQUAL = 6,
        D3DCMP_GREATEREQUAL = 7,
        D3DCMP_ALWAYS = 8
} D3DCMPFUNC;
```

Description: This enumerated type defines values for the supported compare functions to be used by the z-buffer and alpha-blending algorithms.

A particular algorithm is specified in an execute buffer by a D3DOP_STATERENDER instruction with state type D3DRENDERSTATE_ZFUNC or D3DRENDERSTATE_ALPHAFUNC. The dwArg member of the D3DSTATE for the render state should hold one of the values defined by D3DCMPFUNC.

The default z-buffer algorithm is D3DCMP_LESSEQUAL, which means a new pixel is only written if its distance from the camera is less than or equal to the last pixel written at that location's distance from the camera.

The default algorithm for alpha blending is D3DCMP_ALWAYS, which means a new pixel is always written. The actual pixel value written depends on the current blending modes of the source and destination surfaces.

continues

continued

Members: D3DCMP_NEVER—Do not write any pixels.

D3DCMP_LESS—Write a pixel if the new pixel value is less than the old pixel value.

D3DCMP_EQUAL—Write a pixel if the new pixel value is the same value as the old pixel value.

D3DCMP_LESSEQUAL—Write a pixel if the new pixel value is less than or equal to the old pixel value.

D3DCMP_GREATER—Write a pixel if the new pixel value is greater than the old pixel value.

D3DCMP_NOTEQUAL—Write a pixel if the new pixel value is not equal to the old pixel value.

D3DCMP_GREATEREQUAL—Write a pixel if the new pixel value is greater than or equal to the old pixel value.

D3DCMP_ALWAYS—Write all pixels.

See Also: D3DPRIMCAPS

D3DCOLORMODEL

Definition:
```
typedef enum _D3DCOLORMODEL
{
        D3DCOLOR_MONO = 1,
        D3DCOLOR_RGB = 2,
} D3DCOLORMODEL;
```

Description: This enumerated type defines values for the allowable device color models.

A particular color model is specified in an execute buffer by a D3DOP_STATELIGHT instruction with state type D3DLIGHTSTATE_COLORMODEL. The dwArg member of the D3DSTATE should hold one of the values defined by D3DCOLORMODEL.

Not all devices support changing the color model dynamically. The dcmColorModel member of the D3DDEVICEDESC for the device indicates whether the particular device supports one or both color models.

Members: D3DCOLOR_MONO—Specifies the monochromatic, or ramp, color model.

D3DCOLOR_RGB—Specifies the RGB model.

See Also: IDirect3DRMDevice::GetColorModel, IDirect3DDevice::GetCaps

D3DCULL

Definition:
```
typedef enum _D3DCULL
{
        D3DCULL_NONE = 1,
        D3DCULL_CW = 2,
        D3DCULL_CCW = 3,
} D3DCULL;
```

Description: This enumerated type defines values for the possible cull modes.

Not all drivers support all cull modes. Check the dwMiscCaps member of the D3DPRIMCAPS struct for each device.

Members: D3DCULL_NONE—Draw all faces.

D3DCULL_CW—Do not draw faces whose vertices are listed in clockwise order with respect to the camera.

D3DCULL_CCW—Do not draw faces whose vertices are listed in counterclockwise order with respect to the camera.

See Also: IDirect3DDevice::GetCaps, D3DPRIMCAPS.

D3DFILLMODE

Definition:
```
typedef enum _D3DFILLMODE
{
        D3DFILL_POINT = 1,
        D3DFILL_WIREFRAME = 2,
        D3DFILL_SOLID = 3
} D3DFILLMODE;
```

continues

continued

Description: This enumerated type defines values for the different fill modes. A particular fill mode is specified in an execute buffer by a D3DOP_STATERENDER instruction with state type D3DRENDERSTATE_FILLMODE. The dwArg member of the D3DSTATE for the render state should hold one of the values defined by D3DFILLMODE.

Members: D3DFILL_POINT—Render only a pixel for each vertex.

D3DFILL_WIREFRAME—Render only a line for each edge-enabled triangle edge.

D3DFILLSOLID—Render solid faces.

See Also: D3DRENDERSTATE, D3DINSTRUCTION, D3DPRIMCAPS

D3DFOGMODE

Definition:
```
typedef enum _D3DFOGMODE
{
        D3DFOG_NONE = 0,
        D3DFOG_EXP = 1,
        D3DFOG_EXP2 = 2,
        D3DFOG_LINEAR = 3
} D3DFOGMODE;
```

Description: This enumerated type defines values for the different fog modes. A particular fog mode is specified in an execute buffer by a D3DOP_STATERENDER instruction with state type D3DRENDERSTATE_FOGTABLEMODE. The dwArg member of the D3DSTATE for the render state should hold one of the values defined by D3DFOGMODE.

Fog values describe the transparency of the fog, not its thickness. This means that the smaller the fog value, the thicker the fog.

Currently, only the linear fog model is supported.

In the monochromatic (ramp) color model, only fog values of 0 and 1 are supported; that is, fog is either all the way on (0) or all the way off (1) at a particular location.

Members: D3DFOG_NONE—No fog effect.

D3DFOG_EXP—The fog thickens exponentially with z-distance from the camera:

$$\text{fog value} = e \char`^ (-(d \times z))$$

where d is the fog density (part of the lighting module state, see D3DLIGHTSTATETYPE that follows) and z is the distance from the camera along the z-axis. This fog mode is not currently supported.

D3DFOG_EXP2—The fog thickens exponentially with the square of the z-distance from the camera:

$$\text{fog value} = e \char`^ (-((d \times z) \char`^ 2))$$

where d is the fog density (part of the lighting module state, see D3DLIGHTSTATETYPE that follows) and z is the distance from the camera along the z-axis. This fog mode is not currently supported.

D3DFOG_LINEAR—The fog thickens linearly between the start and end points:

$$\text{fog value} = (\text{end} - z) / (\text{end} - \text{start})$$

where start and end are the fog start and end points (part of the lighting module state, see D3DLIGHTSTATETYPE that follows) and z is the distance from the camera along the z-axis. This is the only fog mode currently supported.

See Also: D3DPRIMCAPS, D3DLIGHTSTATETYPE

D3DLIGHTSTATETYPE

Definition:
```
typedef enum _D3DLIGHTSTATETYPE
{
        D3DLIGHTSTATE_MATERIAL = 1,
        D3DLIGHTSTATE_AMBIENT = 2,
        D3DLIGHTSTATE_COLORMODEL = 3,
        D3DLIGHTSTATE_FOGMODE = 4,
        D3DLIGHTSTATE_FOGSTART = 5,
        D3DLIGHTSTATE_FOGEND = 6,
        D3DLIGHTSTATE_FOGDENSITY = 7
} D3DLIGHTSTATETYPE;
```

continues

continued

Description: This enumerated type defines values for the different lighting module states that may be set in an execute buffer by D3DOP_STATELIGHT instruction.

Each D3DOP_STATELIGHT has one or more D3DSTATE structures as its instruction data, and each of the D3DSTATE structures must have its dlstLightStateType member set to one of these values.

For each of these state types, the meaning of the dwArg or dvArg value or values—and whether dwArg or dvArg applies—depends on the state type.

Members: D3DLIGHTSTATE_MATERIAL—Defines the current material used when rendering surfaces. dwArg is the D3DMATERIALHANDLE of the material.

D3DLIGHTSTATE_AMBIENT—Sets the color and intensity of the current ambient light. The dwArg member of the D3DSTATE structure should be the D3DCOLOR representing the desired ambient light color. In the monochromatic (ramp) color model, which does not support colored lights, only the alpha value of the D3DCOLOR is used to set the intensity of the ambient light. In the RGB model, the alpha value is ignored.

D3DLIGHTSTATE_COLORMODEL—Sets the current color model. The dwArg member of the D3DSTATE structure should be one of the members of the D3DCOLORMODEL enumerated type. If the device supports the RGB color model, then the default value is D3DCOLOR_RGB; otherwise, the default value is D3DCOLOR_MONO.

D3DLIGHTSTATE_FOGMODE—Sets the current fog mode. The dwArg member of the D3DSTATE structure should be one of the members of the D3DFOGMODE enumerated type. The default value is D3DFOG_NONE.

D3DLIGHTSTATE_FOGSTART—Sets the z-distance from the camera at which fog should begin. The dvArg member of the D3DSTATE holds the start distance. The default value is 1.0.

D3DLIGHTSTATE_FOGEND—Sets the z-distance from the camera at which fog should reach maximum intensity. The dvArg member of the D3DSTATE holds the end distance. The default value is 100. This only applies to the linear fog model.

D3DLIGHTSTATE_FOGDENSITY—Sets the fog density parameter. The dvArg member of the D3DSTATE structure should hold the density, a value between 0 and 1. The default value is 1.0. This state only applies to the exponential fog models, which are not supported.

See Also: D3DSTATE, D3DFOGMODE, D3DLIGHT, D3DLIGHTTYPE

D3DLIGHTTYPE

Definition:
```
typedef enum _D3DLIGHTTYPE
{
        D3DLIGHT_POINT = 1,
        D3DLIGHT_SPOT = 2,
        D3DLIGHT_DIRECTIONAL = 3,
        D3DLIGHT_PARALLELPOINT = 4,
        D3DLIGHT_GLSPOT = 5
} D3DLIGHTTYPE;
```

Description: This enumerated type defines values for each of the supported light types. The D3DLIGHT structure has a member of this type identifying the type of light.

Members: D3DLIGHT_POINT—Specifies a point source light.

D3DLIGHT_SPOT—Specifies a spotlight.

D3DLIGHT_DIRECTIONAL—Specifies a directional light.

D3DLIGHT_PARALLELPOINT—Specifies a parallel point source light.

D3DLIGHT_GLSPOT—Specifies an OpenGL-style spotlight.

See Also: IDirect3DLight::GetLight, IDirect3DLight::SetLight, D3DLIGHT

D3DOPCODE

Definition:
```
typedef enum D3DOPCODE
{
        D3DOP_POINT = 1,
        D3DOP_LINE = 2,
        D3DOP_TRIANGLE = 3,
        D3DOP_MATRIXLOAD = 4,
        D3DOP_MATRIXMULTIPLY = 5,
        D3DOP_STATETRANSFORM = 6,
        D3DOP_STATELIGHT = 7,
        D3DOP_STATERENDER = 8,
        D3DOP_PROCESSVERTICES = 9,
        D3DOP_TEXTURELOAD = 10,
        D3DOP_EXIT = 11,
        D3DOP_BRANCHFORWARD = 12,
        D3DOP_SPAN = 13,
        D3DOP_SETSTATUS = 14,
} D3DOPCODE;
```

Description: This enumerated type defines the opcodes for all the instructions permitted in execute buffers.

Each instruction may include a variable number of instruction data blocks. For a given opcode, each block must be the same size and correspond to a particular structure. The particular structure corresponding to each opcode is listed in the following Members section.

Members: D3DOP_POINT—Instructs the renderer to render one or more points, as described by the subsequent D3DPOINT structure(s).

D3DOP_LINE—Instructs the renderer to render one or more lines, as described by the subsequent D3DLINE structures(s).

D3DOP_TRIANGLE—Instructs the renderer to render one or more triangles, as described by the subsequent D3DTRIANGLE structure(s).

D3DOP_MATRIXLOAD—Executes one or more matrix load instructions, each of which loads the contents of one matrix into another. The source and destination matrices are specified by the subsequent D3DMATRIXLOAD structure(s).

D3DOP_MATRIXMULTIPLY—Executes one or more matrix multiply instructions, each of which multiplies two matrices together and places the results in a third. The multiplicands and destination matrix handles are specified in the subsequent D3DMATRIXMULTIPLY structure(s).

D3DOP_STATETRANSFORM—Sets the value(s) of one or more state variable in the transformation module. Each state and its new value are specified in a D3DSTATE structure following the D3DINSTRUCTION as instruction data. The D3DSTATE structure must have its dlstTransformStateType member set to one of the members of the D3DTRANSFORMSTATETYPE enumerated type, and its dvArg or dwArg must hold the new state value, depending on which state is being changed.

D3DOP_STATELIGHT—Sets the value(s) of one or more state variable in the lighting module. Each state and its new value are specified in a D3DSTATE structure following the D3DINSTRUCTION as instruction data. The D3DSTATE structure must have its dlstLightStateType member set to one of the members of the D3DLIGHTSTATETYPE enumerated type, and its dvArg or dwArg must hold the new state value, depending on which state is being changed.

D3DOP_STATERENDER—Sets the value(s) of one or more state variables in the render module. Each state and its new value are specified in a D3DSTATE structure following the D3DINSTRUCTION as instruction data. The D3DSTATE structure must have its drstRenderStateType member set to one of the members of the D3DRENDERSTATETYPE enumerated type, and its dvArg or dwArg must hold the new state value, depending on which state is being changed.

D3DOP_PROCESSVERTICES—Instructs the renderer to process one or more collections of vertices as specified by the subsequent D3DPROCESSVERTICES structure.

D3DOP_TEXTURELOAD—Instructs the renderer to load one or more textures specified (by handle) in the subsequent D3DTEXTURELOAD structures.

D3DOP_EXIT—Instructs the renderer to stop executing this execute buffer. There is no instruction data for this instruction.

continues

continued

D3DOP_BRANCHFORWARD—Instructs the renderer to branch forward based on the contents of the subsequent D3DBRANCH structure and the contents of the driver's status register.

D3DOP_SPAN—Instructs the renderer to render faces from the vertex spans defined by the subsequent D3DSPAN structure(s).

D3DOP_SETSTATUS—Sets the driver's status register and accumulated damage extent rectangle based on the contents of the subsequent D3DSTATUS structure.

See Also: D3DINSTRUCTION, D3DPOINT, D3DLINE, D3DTRIANGLE, D3DMATRIXLOAD, D3DMATRIXMULTIPLY, D3DSTATE, D3DPROCESSVERTICES, D3DTEXTURELOAD, D3DBRANCH, D3DSPAN, D3DSTATUS

D3DRENDERSTATETYPE

Definition:

```
typedef enum _D3DRENDERSTATETYPE
{
        D3DRENDERSTATE_TEXTUREHANDLE = 1,
        D3DRENDERSTATE_ANTIALIAS = 2,
        D3DRENDERSTATE_TEXTUREADDRESS = 3,
        D3DRENDERSTATE_TEXTUREPERSPECTIVE = 4,
        D3DRENDERSTATE_WRAPU = 5,
        D3DRENDERSTATE_WRAPV = 6,
        D3DRENDERSTATE_ZENABLE = 7,
        D3DRENDERSTATE_FILLMODE = 8,
        D3DRENDERSTATE_SHADEMODE = 9,
        D3DRENDERSTATE_LINEPATTERN = 10,
        D3DRENDERSTATE_MONOENABLE = 11,
        D3DRENDERSTATE_ROP2 = 12,
        D3DRENDERSTATE_PLANEMASK = 13,
        D3DRENDERSTATE_ZWRITEENABLE = 14,
        D3DRENDERSTATE_ALPHATESTENABLE = 15,
        D3DRENDERSTATE_LASTPIXEL = 16,
        D3DRENDERSTATE_TEXTUREMAG = 17,
        D3DRENDERSTATE_TEXTUREMIN = 18,
        D3DRENDERSTATE_SRCBLEND = 19,
        D3DRENDERSTATE_DESTBLEND = 20,
        D3DRENDERSTATE_TEXTUREMAPBLEND = 21,
        D3DRENDERSTATE_CULLMODE = 22,
        D3DRENDERSTATE_ZFUNC = 23,
        D3DRENDERSTATE_ALPHAREF = 24,
        D3DRENDERSTATE_ALPHAFUNC = 25,
```

```
                        D3DRENDERSTATE_DITHERENABLE = 26,
                        D3DRENDERSTATE_BLENDENABLE = 27,
                        D3DRENDERSTATE_FOGENABLE = 28,
                        D3DRENDERSTATE_SPECULARENABLE = 29,
                        D3DRENDERSTATE_ZVISIBLE = 30,
                        D3DRENDERSTATE_SUB-PIXEL = 31,
                        D3DRENDERSTATE_SUB-PIXELX = 32,
                        D3DRENDERSTATE_STIPPLEDALPHA = 33,
                        D3DRENDERSTATE_FOGCOLOR = 34,
                        D3DRENDERSTATE_FOGTABLEMODE = 35,
                        D3DRENDERSTATE_FOGTABLESTART = 36,
                        D3DRENDERSTATE_FOGTABLEEND = 37,
                        D3DRENDERSTATE_FOGTABLEDENSITY = 38,
                        D3DRENDERSTATE_STIPPLEENABLE = 39,
                        D3DRENDERSTATE_STIPPLEPATTERN00 = 64,
                        // Stipple patterns 01 through 30 omitted here.
                        D3DRENDERSTATE_STIPPLEPATTERN31 = 95
                    } D3DRENDERSTATETYPE;
```

Description: This enumerated type defines values for the different render module states that may be set in an execute buffer by D3DOP_STATERENDER instruction.

Each D3DOP_STATERENDER has one or more D3DSTATE structures as its instruction data, and each of the D3DSTATE structures must have its dlstRenderStateType member set to one of these values.

For each of these state types, the meaning of the dwArg or dvArg value or values—and whether dwArg or dvArg applies—depends on the state type.

Note that many of these states may or may not exist in a particular driver, as specified by the driver's cap bits.

Members: D3DRENDERSTATE_TEXTUREHANDLE—Sets the current texture to the D3DTEXTUREHANDLE specified in dwArg.

D3DRENDERSTATE_ANTIALIAS—Enables anti-aliasing of triangle edges which are edge-enabled if dwArg is TRUE or disables anti-alias if dwArg is FALSE. The default value is FALSE.

D3DRENDERSTATE_TEXTUREADDRESS—Sets the texture address mode. The dwArg value should be set to one of D3DTADDRESS_WRAP, D3DTADDRESS_MIRROR, or D3DTADDRESS_CLAMP. The default value is D3DTADDRESS_WRAP.

continues

continued

D3DRENDERSTATE_TEXTUREPERSPECTIVE—Enables perspective texture mapping if dwArg is TRUE or disables it if dwArg is FALSE. The default value is FALSE.

D3DRENDERSTATE_WRAPU—Sets the horizontal texture wrapping topology. If dwArg is TRUE, texture addresses wrap in the horizontal direction (cylindrical topology). If dwArg is FALSE, texture addresses do not wrap. If both horizontal and vertical texture wrapping topologies are set to wrap, then the total texture wrapping topology is spherical. The default value is FALSE.

D3DRENDERSTATE_WRAPV—Sets the vertical texture wrapping topology. If dwArg is TRUE, texture addresses wrap in the vertical direction (cylindrical topology). If dwArg is FALSE, texture addresses do not wrap. If both horizontal and vertical texture wrapping topologies are set to wrap, then the total texture wrapping topology is spherical. The default value is FALSE.

D3DRENDERSTATE_ZENABLE—Used to enable or disable the z-buffer algorithm for hidden surface removal. If dwArg is TRUE, the z-buffer is enabled. If dwArg is FALSE, the z-buffer is disabled. The default value is FALSE.

D3DRENDERSTATE_FILLMODE—Sets the current fill mode for the renderer. The dwArg value must be one of the values defined by the D3DFILLMODE enumerated type. The default value is D3DFILL_SOLID.

D3DRENDERSTATE_SHADEMODE—Sets the current shade mode for the renderer. The dwArg value must be one of the values defined by the D3DSHADEMODE enumerated type. The default value is D3DSHADE_GOURAUD.

D3DRENDERSTATE_LINEPATTERN—Sets the current line pattern for the renderer. The dwArg value must contain an instance of the D3DLINEPATTERN structure. The default values are 0 for wRepeatPattern and 0 for wLinePattern.

D3DRENDERSTATE_MONOENABLE—If dwArg is TRUE, it sets the renderer to use the monochromatic rendering model, if supported.

If dwArg is FALSE, the renderer uses the RGB rendering model, if supported. The default value is FALSE.

D3DRENDERSTATE_ROP2—Sets the current ROP2 rasterization model, which specifies how pixels on the source surface are combined with pixels on the destination surface. The dwArg value should contain one of the GDI raster operations. The allowable values are: R2_BLACK, R2_NOTMERGEPEN, R2_MASKNOTPEN, R2_NOTCOPYPEN, R2_MASKPENNOT, R2_NOT, R2_XORPEN, R2_NOTMASKPEN, R2_MASKPEN, R2_NOTXORPEN, R2_NOP, R2_MERGENOTPEN, R2_COPYPEN, R2_MERGEPENNOT, R2_MERGEPEN, or R2_WHITE. The default value is R2_COPYPEN. The D3DPRASTERCAPS_ROP2 flag in the dwRasterCaps member of the D3DPRIMCAPS structure specifies which raster operations the driver supports.

D3DRENDERSTATE_PLANEMASK—Sets the physical plane mask for the renderer. The dwArg value should contain the new, 32-bit mask. The default value is 0xFFFFFFFF.

D3DRENDERSTATE_ZWRITEENABLE—If dwArg is TRUE, it instructs the renderer to write new values into the z-buffer when rendering according to the current z-buffer algorithm. If dwArg is FALSE, it instructs the renderer not to write values into the z-buffer when rendering. The default value is TRUE.

D3DRENDERSTATE_ALPHATESTENABLE—If dwArg is TRUE, it instructs the renderer to use the current alpha blending algorithm when rendering pixels. If dwArg is FALSE, it instructs the renderer not to use the current alpha blending algorithm. The default value is FALSE.

D3DRENDERSTATE_LASTPIXEL—If dwArg is TRUE, it instructs the renderer to not draw the last pixel in a line. If dwArg is FALSE, it instructs the renderer to draw the last pixel in a line. The default value is TRUE.

D3DRENDERSTATE_TEXTUREMAG—Sets the texture filter model to use when magnifying a texture. The dwArg value should be one of the values of the D3DTEXTUREFILTER enumerated type. The default value is D3DFILTER_NEAREST.

continues

continued

D3DRENDERSTATE_TEXTUREMIN—Sets the texture filter model to use when shrinking a texture. The dwArg value should be one of the values of the D3DTEXTUREFILTER enumerated type. The default value is D3DFILTER_NEAREST.

D3DRENDERSTATE_SRCBLEND—Sets the blending mode for the source pixels. The dwArg value should be one of the values of the D3DBLEND enumerated type. The default value is D3DBLEND_ONE.

D3DRENDERSTATE_DESTBLEND—Sets the blending mode for the destination pixels. The dwArg value should be one of the values of the D3DBLEND enumerated type. The default value is D3DBLEND_ZERO.

D3DRENDERSTATE_TEXTUREMAPBLEND—Sets the texture blending mode. The dwArg value should be one of the values of the D3DTEXTUREBLEND enumerated type. The default value is D3DTBLEND_MODULATE.

D3DRENDERSTATE_CULLMODE—Sets the renderer's cull mode. The dwArg value should contain one of the values of the D3DCULL enumerated type. The default value is D3DCULL_CCW.

D3DRENDERSTATE_ZFUNC—Sets the renderer's z-buffer algorithm. The dwArg value must be one of the values of the D3DCMPFUNC enumerated type. The default value is D3DCMP_LESSEQUAL.

D3DRENDERSTATE_ALPHAREF—Sets the reference alpha value against which pixels are tested when alpha-blending is enabled. The dwArg value should hold a D3DFIXED type, specifying the alpha value. The default value is 0.

D3DRENDERSTATE_ALPHAFUNC—Sets the renderer's alpha blending algorithm. The dwArg value must be one of the values of the D3DCMPFUNC enumerated type. The default value is D3DCMP_ALWAYS.

D3DRENDERSTATE_DITHERENABLE—Enables or disables dithering. If dwArg is TRUE, dithering is enabled. If dwArg is FALSE, dithering is disabled. The default value is FALSE.

D3DRENDERSTATE_BLENDENABLE—Enables or disables alpha blending. If dwArg is TRUE, alpha blending is enabled. If dwArg is FALSE, alpha blending is disabled. The default value is FALSE.

D3DRENDERSTATE_FOGENABLE—Enables or disables fog. If dwArg is TRUE, fog is enabled. If dwArg is FALSE, fog is disabled. The default value is FALSE.

D3DRENDERSTATE_SPECULARENABLE—Enables or disables specular highlights. If dwArg is TRUE, specular highlights are enabled. If dwArg is FALSE, specular highlights are disabled.

D3DRENDERSTATE_ZVISIBLE—Enables or disables polygon-level, z-visibility testing. If dwArg is TRUE, entire polygons are tested for z-visibility. If dwArg is FALSE, visibility testing is disabled. The default value is FALSE.

D3DRENDERSTATE_SUBPIXEL—Enables or disables sub-pixel correction. If dwArg is TRUE, sub-pixel correction is enabled. If dwArg is FALSE, sub-pixel correction is disabled. The default value is FALSE.

D3DRENDERSTATE_SUBPIXELX—Enables or disables sub-pixel correction in the x-direction only. If dwArg is TRUE, sub-pixel correction is enabled. If dwArg is FALSE, sub-pixel correction is disabled. The default value is FALSE.

D3DRENDERSTATE_STIPPLEDALPHA—Enables or disables alpha stippling. If dwArg is TRUE, alpha stippling is enabled. If dwArg is FALSE, alpha stippling is disabled. The default value is FALSE.

D3DRENDERSTATE_FOGCOLOR—Sets the fog color. The dwArg value should be a D3DCOLOR representing the fog color.

D3DRENDERSTATE_FOGTABLEMODE—Sets the current fog mode. The dwArg value must be one of the values of the D3DFOGMODE enumerated type. The default value is D3DFOG_NONE.

continues

continued

D3DRENDERSTATE_FOGTABLESTART—Sets the z-distance away from the camera at which fog should start. The dvArg value should hold the z-distance from the camera to start fog. The default value is 1. This state only applies to the linear fog mode.

D3DRENDERSTATE_FOGTABLEEND—Sets the z-distance away from the camera at which fog should become maximally thick. The dvArg value should hold the z-distance from the camera at which the fog should reach its maximum value. The default value is 100. This state only applies to the linear fog model.

D3DRENDERSTATE_FOGTABLEDENSITY—Sets the density parameter for the exponential fog modes. The dvArg value should contain the density, between 0 and 1.

D3DRENDERSTATE_STIPPLEENABLE—Enables or disables stippling. If the dwArg value is TRUE, stippling is enabled. If dwArg is FALSE, stippling is disabled. If alpha stippling is also enabled, its stippling algorithm overrides the stipple pattern.

D3DRENDERSTATE_STIPPLEPATTERN00 through D3DRENDERSTATE_STIPPLEPATTERN31—Specify each of the 32 lines of a stipple pattern. The dwArg value holds the 32-bit pattern for the particular line of the pattern.

See Also: D3DLIGHTSTATETYPE, D3DTRANSFORMSTATETYPE, D3DINSTRUCTION, D3DOPCODE, D3DSTATE

D3DSHADEMODE

Definition:
```
typedef enum _D3DSHADEMODE
{
        D3DSHADE_FLAT = 1,
        D3DSHADE_GOURAUD = 2,
        D3DSHADE_PHONG = 3
} D3DSHADEMODE;
```

Description: This enumerated type defines values for each of the possible shade modes. A particular shade mode is specified in an execute buffer by a D3DOP_STATERENDER instruction with state type D3DRENDERSTATE_SHADEMODE. The dwArg member of the D3DSTATE for the render state should hold one of the values defined by D3DSHADEMODE.

Members: D3DSHADE_FLAT—Specifies the flat shade mode.

D3DSHADE_GOURAUD—Specifies the Gouraud shade mode.

D3DSHADE_PHONG—Phong shade mode. Phong shading is not currently supported.

See Also: D3DRENDERSTATETYPE, D3DINSTRUCTION, D3DOPCODE, D3DSTATE

D3DTEXTUREADDRESS

Definition:
```
typedef enum _D3DTEXTUREADDRESS
{
        D3DTADDRESS_WRAP = 1,
        D3DTADDRESS_MIRROR = 2,
        D3DTADDRESS_CLAMP = 3
} D3DTEXTUREADDRESS;
```

Description: This enumerated type defines values for each of the possible texture address modes.

A particular address mode is specified in an execute buffer by a D3DOP_STATERENDER instruction with state type D3DRENDERSTATE_TEXTUREADDRESS. The dwArg member of the D3DSTATE for the render state should hold one of the values defined by D3DTEXTUREADDRESS.

Members: D3DTADDRESS_WRAP—Specifies wrapping in both the horizontal and vertical directions.

D3DTADDRESS_MIRROR—Specifies no wrapping, but the texture is flipped as it is tiled.

continues

continued

D3DTADDRESS_CLAMP—Specifies that texture coordinates greater than 1.0 are clamped to 1.0, and values less than 0.0 are clamped to 0.0.

See Also: D3DRENDERSTATETYPE, D3DINSTRUCTION, D3DOPCODE, D3DSTATE

D3DTEXTUREBLEND

Definition:
```
typedef enum _D3DTEXTUREBLEND
{
        D3DTBLEND_DECAL = 1,
        D3DTBLEND_MODULATE = 2,
        D3DTBLEND_DECALALPHA = 3,
        D3DTBLEND_MODULATEALPHA = 4,
        D3DTBLEND_DECALMASK = 5,
        D3DTBLEND_MODULATEMASK = 6,
        D3DTBLEND_COPY = 7,
} D3DTEXTUREBLEND;
```

Description: This enumerated type defines values for the possible texture-blending modes.

A particular address mode is specified in an execute buffer by a D3DOP_STATERENDER instruction with state type D3DRENDERSTATE_TEXTUREMAPBLEND. The dwArg member of the D3DSTATE for the render state should hold one of the values defined by D3DTEXTUREBLEND.

Modulation typically decreases the brightness of the colors being blended unless one of them is pure white.

Members: D3DTBLEND_DECAL—Sets the texture-blending mode to decal. In decal mode, RGB and alpha values in the texture replace the colors on the surface to which they are mapped.

D3DTBLEND_MODULATE—Sets the texture-blending mode to modulate. In modulate mode, RGB values from the texture are multiplied with RGB values from the face being mapped. The texture's alpha values replace the alpha values of the face being mapped.

D3DTBLEND_DECALALPHA—Sets the texture-blending mode to decal-alpha texture-blending mode. In decal-alpha mode, RGB and alpha values from the texture are blended with the face's colors using the formula:

$$\text{Pixel color} = ((1 - A_t) \times C_f) + (A_t \times C_t)$$

where C_f is the face's color, and A_t is the texture pixel's alpha value. In this mode, the texture's alpha value replaces the face's alpha value.

D3DTBLEND_MODULATEALPHA—Sets the texture-blending mode to modulate-alpha texture-blending mode. In this mode, a pixel's RGB value is computed by multiplying the RGB value from the texture with the RGB value from the face. The alpha value is computed by multiplying the texture's alpha value and the face's alpha value.

D3DTBLEND_DECALMASK—Sets the texture-blending mode to decal-mask texture-blending mode.

D3DTBLEND_MODULATEMASK—Sets the texture-blending mode to modulate-mask texture-blending mode.

D3DTBLEND_COPY—Sets the texture-blending mode to copy texture-blending mode.

See Also: D3DRENDERSTATETYPE, D3DINSTRUCTION, D3DOPCODE, D3DSTATE

D3DTEXTUREFILTER

Definition:
```
typedef enum _D3DTEXTUREFILTER
{
        D3DFILTER_NEAREST = 1,
        D3DFILTER_LINEAR = 2,
        D3DFILTER_MIPNEAREST = 3,
        D3DFILTER_MIPLINEAR = 4,
        D3DFILTER_LINEARMIPNEAREST = 5,
        D3DFILTER_LINEARMIPLINEAR = 6
} D3DTEXTUREFILTER;
```

Description: This enumerated type defines values for the possible texture filter modes.

continues

continued

A particular texture filter mode is specified in an execute buffer by a D3DOP_STATERENDER instruction with state type D3DRENDERSTATE_TEXTUREMAG or D3DRENDERSTATE_TEXTUREMIN. The dwArg member of the D3DSTATE for the render state should hold one of the values defined by D3DTEXTUREFILTER.

Members: D3DFILTER_NEAREST—Sets the texture filter mode to use the nearest texel.

D3DFILTER_LINEAR—Sets the texture filter mode to use a weighted average of a 2×2 area of texels surrounding the target texel.

D3DFILTER_MIPNEAREST—Sets the texture filter mode to use the D3DFILTER_NEAREST algorithm with the nearest mipmap.

D3DFILTER_MIPLINEAR—Sets the texture filter mode to use the D3DTILER_LINEAR algorithm with mipmaps.

D3DFILTER_LINEARMIPNEAREST—Sets the texture filter mode to use the D3DFILTER_MIPNEAREST algorithm, but includes interpolation between the two nearest mipmaps.

D3DFILTER_LINEARMIPLINEAR—Sets the texture filter mode to use the D3DFILTER_MIPLINEAR algorithm, but includes interpolation between the two nearest mipmaps.

See Also: D3DRENDERSTATETYPE, D3DINSTRUCTION, D3DOPCODE, D3DSTATE

D3DTRANSFORMSTATETYPE

Definition:
```
typedef enum _D3DTRANSFORMSTATETYPE
{
        D3DTRANSFORMSTATE_WORLD = 1,
        D3DTRANSFORMSTATE_VIEW = 2,
        D3DTRANSFORMSTATE_PROJECTION = 3,
} D3DTRANSFORMSTATETYPE;
```

Description:	This enumerated type defines values for the three standard transforms: world, view, and projection.
	A particular transform is specified in an execute buffer by a D3DOP_STATERENDER instruction with a state type of one of the values of D3DTRANSFORMSTATETYPE. The dwArg member of the D3DSTATE should hold the matrix handle of the matrix whose value is to be used to generate the world, view, or projection transform.
	The default value for each of these matrices is the identity matrix.
Members:	D3DTRANSFORMSTATE_WORLD—Specifies that dwArg holds a matrix handle to the matrix whose value is to define the world matrix.
	D3DTRANSFORMSTATE_VIEW—Specifies that dwArg holds a matrix handle to the matrix whose value is to define the view matrix.
	D3DTRANSFORMSTATE_PROJECTION—Specifies that dwArg holds a matrix handle to the matrix whose value is to define the projection matrix.
See Also:	D3DINSTRUCTION, D3DOPCODE, D3DSTATE

Immediate-Mode Other Values

D3DCOLOR

Definition: `typedef DWORD D3DCOLOR, D3DCOLOR, *LPD3DCOLOR;`

Description: A D3DCOLOR species the red, green, blue, and alpha components of a color.

The color components of a D3DCOLOR are specified as values between 0 and 255. An alpha value of zero may mean the color is completely transparent; that is, not visible on the screen. Typically, lights ignore the alpha component, but materials typically do not, depending on the current driver and its state.

D3DVALUE

Definition: `typedef float D3DVALUE, *LPD3DVALUE;`

Description: A D3DVALUE is the typdef used to encapsulate the underlying floating point type, which is a 32-bit, IEEE format floating point number.

Immediate-Mode Data Types and Return Values

D3D_OK—Indicates no error.

D3DERR_BADMAJORVERSION—Indicates an incompatible DLL.

D3DERR_BADMINORVERSION—Indicates an incompatible DLL.

D3DERR_EXECUTE_CLIPPED_FAILED—Indicates an execute buffer failure while clipping.

D3DERR_EXECUTE_CREATE_FAILED—Indicates that the requested execute buffer could not be created.

D3DERR_EXECUTE_DESTROY_FAILED—Indicates an execute buffer could not be destroyed.

D3DERR_EXECUTE_FAILED—Indicates a generic error executing an execute buffer.

D3DERR_EXECUTE_LOCK_FAILED—Indicates an execute buffer could not be locked.

D3DERR_EXECUTE_LOCKED—Indicates an execute buffer could not be locked because it is already locked.

D3DERR_EXECUTE_NOT_LOCKED—Indicates an execute buffer could not be unlocked because it is already unlocked.

D3DERR_EXECUTE_UNLOCK_FAILED—Indicates an execute buffer could not be unlocked for reasons unknown.

D3DERR_LIGHT_SET_FAILED—Indicates the light could not be placed.

D3DERR_MATERIAL_CREATE_FAILED—Indicates the requested material could not be created.

D3DERR_MATERIAL_DESTROY_FAILED—Indicates a material could not be destroyed.

D3DERR_MATERIAL_GETDATA_FAILED—Indicates a call to IDirect3DMaterial::GetMaterial() could not succeed.

D3DERR_MATERIAL_SETDATA_FAILED—Indicates a call to IDirect3DMaterial::SetMaterial() could not succeed.

D3DERR_MATRIX_CREATE_FAILED—Indicates the requested matrix could not be created.

D3DERR_MATRIX_DESTROY_FAILED—Indicates a matrix could not be deleted.

D3DERR_MATRIX_GETDATA_FAILED—Indicates the contents of a matrix could not be accessed via a call to IDirect3DDevice::GetMatrix().

D3DERR_MATRIX_SETDATA_FAILED—Indicates the contents of a matrix could not be set via a call to IDirect3DDevice::SetMatrix().

D3DERR_SCENE_BEGIN_FAILED—Indicates scene setup failed.

D3DERR_SCENE_END_FAILED—Indicates scene clean-up failed.

D3DERR_SCENE_IN_SCENE—Indicates IDirect3DDevice::BeginScene() was called again before a corresponding call to IDirect3DDevice::EndScene().

D3DERR_SCENE_NOT_IN_SCENE—Indicates a call to IDirect3DDevice::EndScene() was made without a corresponding earlier call to IDirect3DDevice::BeginScene().

D3DERR_SETVIEWPORTDATA_FAILED—Indicates the viewport data could not be set.

D3DERR_TEXTURE_CREATE_FAILED—Indicates the requested texture could not be created.

D3DERR_TEXTURE_DESTROY_FAILED—Indicates a texture could not be deleted.

D3DERR_TEXTURE_GETSURF_FAILED—Indicates access to the texture's surface was denied.

D3DERR_TEXTURE_LOAD_FAILED—Indicates a texture could not be loaded.

D3DERR_TEXTURE_LOCK_FAILED—Indicates a texture surface could not be locked.

D3DERR_TEXTURE_LOCKED—Indicates a texture surface could not be locked because it is already locked.

D3DERR_TEXTURE_NO_SUPPORT—Indicates the texture interface does not support the request.

D3DERR_TEXTURE_NOT_LOCKED—Indicates a texture surface could not be unlocked because it was not locked.

D3DERR_TEXTURE_SWAP_FAILED—Indicates the texture handles could not be swapped.

D3DERR_TEXTURE_UNLOCK_FAILED—Indicates the texture could not be unlocked.

Part IV

Appendix

DirectX File Format *455*

APPENDIX A

DirectX File Format

This appendix specifies the DirectX file format, version 1.13. Currently, this file format is only used by Direct3D Retained-Mode for storing geometry and animation; however, the file format has been designed with more general goals in mind. The DirectX file format is application- and context-independent and can be used with applications or APIs other than DirectX. Currently, the DirectX file format is used only with Direct3D's Retained-Mode, but it is likely that Microsoft will provide new templates as the DirectX file format grows to encompass all of DirectX.

The DirectX file format provides a basic set of data types upon which more complex data structures, or templates, are built. A mechanism for the definition of user-defined data structures provides extensibility to fit a developer's application needs. The DirectX file format was introduced with DirectX 2 with only a text data representation implemented. DirectX 3 brought the implementation of the binary data representation, allowing for more compact representation and quicker load times.

In its current form, the DirectX file format provides support for the following:

- Storage of meshes
- Mesh attributes
- Object hierarchy
- Textures
- Animation
- User-definable objects

Objects can also utilize references to other data objects, eliminating the need for multiple instances of the same data object in a file. This appendix details the general concepts of the file format as well as the current features for use in Direct3D Retained-Mode.

File Format Syntax

The DirectX file format uses the extension .x for DirectX files. The DirectX file format consists of four parts:

- Header—Contains information regarding the file and format version number.
- Comments—Allow information in the form of text to be embedded inside the file.
- Templates—Describe the data structures that are contained in each file.
- Data Objects—Objects describe the actual information contained in the file.

Reserved Words

The following words are reserved and must not be used:

ARRAY	BYTE
CHAR	CSTRING
DOUBLE	DWORD
FLOAT	STRING
TEMPLATE	UCHAR
UNICODE	WORD

Header

All DirectX files must begin with a header. The header contains the file type, the file version number, the data format type, and the size of floating-point numbers. If the file is compressed as specified in the data format type, then the header contains the compression type. Table A.1 describes the elements of the header.

Table A.1 Header Elements

Field	Size (in bytes)	Contents	Description
Magic Number	4	"xof "	file type
Version Number-Major Number	2	03	major version 3
Version Number-Major Number	2	02	minor version 2
Format Type	4	"txt "	text file
		"bin "	binary file
		"com "	compressed file
Compression Type	4	"lzw "	
		"zip "	
Float Size	4	0064	64-bit floats
		0032	32-bit floats

All the preceding fields are required except for compression type, which is only required if the Format Type field is "com ".

Comments

Comments enable an application to embed information inside a DirectX file. Comments can only be used with DirectX text files and can occur anywhere within file. A comment line begins with either the pound sign character ("#") or a double forward-slash ("//") and continues until the next new line character.

For example:

```
# This is a comment.
// This is another comment.
```

Templates

Templates define the data structures that describe how the data in the file should be parsed. A template has the following form:

```
template <template-name>
{
    <GUID>
    <member 1>;
    ...
    <member n>;
    [restriction-type]
}
```

The template name identifies the template for data instancing and for referencing by other templates. The template name can contain alphanumeric characters and underscore characters ("_"). The name cannot begin with a digit.

The GUID represents a globally unique identifier, preceded with a left angle bracket character ("<") and followed by a right angle bracket character (">"). The GUID is 16 bytes long and must be formatted to the OSF DCE standard.

The members of a template describe the elements, order, and types of the data. Each member of a template consists of a data type followed by the member name or member array name. Basic data types are included in table A.2.

Table A.2 Basic Data Types

Type	Size
WORD	16 bits
DWORD	32 bits
FLOAT	IEEE float
DOUBLE	64 bits
CHAR	8 bits
UCHAR	8 bits
BYTE	8 bits
STRING	NULL-terminated string

Type	Size
CSTRING	Formatted C-string (unsupported)
UNICODE	UNICODE string (unsupported)

Data types can also be previously defined templates. No forward references to template definitions are allowed.

In the following example, the ColorRGBA template is used as a data type in the IndexedColor template. However, the IndexedColor template could not be used as a data type in the ColorRGBA template because the IndexedColor template follows it:

```
template ColorRGBA
{
    <35FF44E0-6C7C-11cf-8F52-0040333594A3>
    FLOAT red;
    FLOAT green;
    FLOAT blue;
    FLOAT alpha;
}
template IndexedColor
{
    <1630B820-7842-11cf-8F52-0040333594A3>
    DWORD index;
    ColorRGBA indexColor;
}
```

Data types can also be arrays of basic data types or templates. The basic syntax for an array is:

```
array <data-type> <member-name>[<dimension-size>];
```

where <dimension-size> can either be an integer or a named reference to another template member whose value is then substituted. Multi-dimensional arrays are permitted through the use of multiple paired brackets, one for each dimension of the array.

For example:

```
array FLOAT matrix[16];
array IndexedColor vertexColors[nVertexColors];
array ColorRGBA pixelMap[32][32];
```

Each template has an associated restriction type that applies to the instances of a template in the object hierarchy. The restriction type defines the object data types that can be children of the template instances. The three restriction types are:

- Open
- Closed
- Restricted

An instance of an open template can have child objects with any data type. Open templates are specified with [...] at the end of the template. A restricted template defines a list of data types that can exist as children of the template instance. Restricted templates are specified with a comma-separated list of named templates, optionally followed by the template GUIDs, as follows:

    [<data-type0> [GUID], <data-type1> [GUID], ..., <data-typen> [GUID]]

Instances of closed templates cannot have child objects of any type.

An example of an open template:

```
template Mesh
{
    <3D82AB44-62DA-11cf-AB39-0020AF71E433>
    DWORD nVertices;
    array Vector vertices[nVertices];
    DWORD nFaces;
    array MeshFace faces[nFaces];
    [...]
}
```

An example of a restricted template:

```
template MeshMaterialList
{
    <F6F23F42-7686-11cf-8F52-0040333594A3>
    DWORD nMaterials;
    DWORD nFaceIndexes;
    array DWORD faceIndexes[nFaceIndexes];
    [Material]
}
```

An example of a closed template:

```
template MeshVertexColors
{
    <1630B821-7842-11cf-8F52-0040333594A3>
    DWORD nVertexColors;
    array IndexedColor vertexColors[nVertexColors];
}
```

In addition to the set of templates, applications may define a special Header template to define application-specific information. Applications defining this Header must include the template member flags of data type DWORD. The first bit (bit 0) of the flags member will be used to determine if the data in the Header template is text (bit 0 = 1) or binary (bit 0 = 0). Multiple Header instances can be used to switch between binary and text throughout a DirectX file.

For example:

```
template Header
{
    <3D82AB43-62DA-11cf-AB39-0020AF71E433>
    WORD major;
    WORD minor;
    DWORD flags;
}
```

Instances

Instances of templates contain the actual data or reference to the actual data. Each element of a template instance is an instance of a template member. The type of the template member dictates the type of the instanced element. A semicolon terminates each data item in a template instance. Commas separate array elements within a data item. Instances have the following form:

```
<Identifier> [name]
{
    <member 1>;
    ...
    <member n>;
}
```

The Identifier is required and must match a previously defined data type or template. The name is optional, but necessary if a reference to this instance is needed. Instanced elements can be integer lists, float lists, string lists, data references, or instances of templates. Integer, float, and string lists are semicolon-separated lists of one or more integers, floats, or strings, respectively. Data references are references to previously defined and named data objects. Additionally, instances can be nested inside other instances, subject to the restrictions specified by the corresponding template's restriction type.

For example:

```
// This instance of the Material template defines a material with red
// face color.
Material RedMaterial
{
        1.000000;0.000000;0.000000;1.000000;;
        0.000000;
        0.000000;0.000000;0.000000;;
        0.000000;0.000000;0.000000;;
}

// This instance of the Material template defines a material with green
// face color.
Material GreenMaterial
{
        0.000000;1.000000;0.000000;1.000000;;
        0.000000;
        0.000000;0.000000;0.000000;;
        0.000000;0.000000;0.000000;;
}

// This instance defines a sample mesh with 8 vertices and 12 faces.
// This instance uses an optional template member in the mesh to
// specify materials.
Mesh SampleMesh
{
        8;                                      // 8 vertices
        1.000000;1.000000;-1.000000;,           // vertex 0
        -1.000000;1.000000;-1.000000;,          // vertex 1
        -1.000000;1.000000;1.000000;,
        1.000000;1.000000;1.000000;,
        1.000000;-1.000000;-1.000000;,
        -1.000000;-1.000000;-1.000000;,
        -1.000000;-1.000000;1.000000;,
        1.000000;-1.000000;1.000000;;

        12;                                     // 12 faces
        3;0,1,2;,                               // face 0 (3 vertices)
        3;0,2,3;,
        3;0,4,5;,
        3;0,5,1;,
        3;1,5,6;,
        3;1,6,2;,
        3;2,6,7;,
        3;2,7,3;,
        3;3,7,4;,
        3;3,4,0;,
        3;4,7,6;,
        3;4,6,5;;

        // This is the optional instance that defines the material
        // for each face.
        MeshMaterialList
        {
```

```
                2;                      // Number of materials used
                12;                     // A material for each face
                0,                      // face 0 uses the first material
                0,
                0,
                0,
                0,
                0,
                0,
                0,
                1,                      // face 8 uses the second material
                1,
                1,
                1;;
                {RedMaterial}           // References to the defini-
                {GreenMaterial}         // tions of material 0 and 1
        }
}
```

Template Reference

This template reference describes the currently defined DirectX templates. Each template has a GUID, a description, a table of members, member types, array sizes, a list of templates that can be used to create child instances, and a template definition.

Header

GUID: <3D82AB43-62DA-11cf-AB39-0020AF71E433>

Description: This template defines the application-specific header for the Direct3D Retained-Mode usage of the DirectX file format. The Retained-Mode uses the major and minor flags to specify the current major and minor versions for the Retained-Mode file format.

Table A.3 Members

Member Name	Type	Array Size
Major	WORD	
Minor	WORD	
Flags	DWORD	

Child Templates: None

Definition:
```
template Header
{
    <3D82AB43-62DA-11cf-AB39-0020AF71E433>
    WORD major;
    WORD minor;
    DWORD flags;
}
```

Vector

GUID: <3D82AB5E-62DA-11cf-AB39-0020AF71E433>

Description: This template defines a vector.

Table A.4 Members

Member Name	Type	Array Size
X	FLOAT	
Y	FLOAT	
Z	FLOAT	

Child Templates: None

Definition:
```
template Vector
{
    <3D82AB5E-62DA-11cf-AB39-0020AF71E433>
    FLOAT x;
    FLOAT y;
    FLOAT z;
}
```

Coords2d

GUID: <F6F23F44-7686-11cf-8F52-0040333594A3>

Description: A two-dimensional vector used to define a mesh's texture coordinates.

Table A.5 Members

Member Name	Type	Array Size
U	FLOAT	
V	FLOAT	

Child Templates: None

Definition:
```
template Coords2D
{
    <F6F23F44-7686-11cf-8F52-0040333594A3>
    FLOAT u;
    FLOAT v;
}
```

Quaternion

GUID: <10DD46A3-775B-11cf-8F52-0040333594A3>

Description: A quaternion used to represent rotation around an axis. Currently is unused.

Table A.6 Members

Member Name	Type	Array Size
S	FLOAT	
V	Vector	

Child Templates: None

Definition:
```
template Quaternion
{
    <10DD46A3-775B-11cf-8F52-0040333594A3>
    FLOAT s;
    Vector v;
}
```

Matrix4x4

GUID: <F6F23F45-7686-11cf-8F52-0040333594A3>

Description: This template defines a 4×4 matrix. This template is used in the FrameTransformMatrix template.

Table A.7 Members

Member Name	Type	Array Size
Matrix	array FLOAT	16

Child Templates: None

Definition:
```
template Matrix4x4
{
    <F6F23F45-7686-11cf-8F52-0040333594A3>
    array FLOAT matrix[16];
}
```

ColorRGBA

GUID: <35FF44E0-6C7C-11cf-8F52-0040333594A3>

Description: This template defines a color object with an alpha component. This is used for the face color in the material template definition.

Table A.8 Members

Member Name	Type	Array Size
Red	FLOAT	
Green	FLOAT	
Blue	FLOAT	
Alpha	FLOAT	

Child Templates: None

Definition:
```
template ColorRGBA
{
    <35FF44E0-6C7C-11cf-8F52-0040333594A3>
    FLOAT red;
    FLOAT green;
    FLOAT blue;
    FLOAT alpha;
}
```

ColorRGB

GUID: `   <D3E16E81-7835-11cf-8F52-0040333594A3>

Description: This template defines the basic RGB color object.

Table A.9   Members

Member Name	Type	Array Size
Red	FLOAT	
Green	FLOAT	
Blue	FLOAT	

Child Templates: None

Definition:
```
template ColorRGB
{
    <D3E16E81-7835-11cf-8F52-0040333594A3>
    FLOAT red;
    FLOAT green;
    FLOAT blue;
}
```

IndexedColor

GUID: <1630B820-7842-11cf-8F52-0040333594A3>

Description: This template consists of an index parameter and a RGBA color and is used in defining mesh vertex colors. The index defines the vertex to which the color is applied.

Table A.10 Members

Member Name	Type	Array Size
Index	DWORD	
indexColor	ColorRGBA	

Child Templates: None

Definition:
```
template IndexedColor
{
    <1630B820-7842-11cf-8F52-0040333594A3>
    DWORD index;
    ColorRGBA indexColor;
}
```

Boolean

GUID: <4885AE61-78E8-11cf-8F52-0040333594A3>

Description: Defines a simple boolean type. Should be set to 0 or 1.

Table A.11 Members

Member Name	Type	Array Size
truefalse	WORD	

Child Templates: None

Definition:
```
template Boolean
{
    <4885AE61-78E8-11cf-8F52-0040333594A3>
    WORD truefalse;
}
```

Boolean2d

GUID: <4885AE63-78E8-11cf-8F52-0040333594A3>

Description: This defines a set of two boolean values used in the MeshFaceWraps template in order to define the texture topology of an individual face.

Table A.12 Members

Member Name	Type	Array Size
U	Boolean	
V	Boolean	

Child Templates: None

Definition:
```
template Boolean2d
{
    <4885AE63-78E8-11cf-8F52-0040333594A3>
    Boolean u;
    Boolean v;
}
```

Material

GUID: <3D82AB4D-62DA-11cf-AB39-0020AF71E433>

Description: This template defines a basic material color, which can be applied to either a complete mesh or a mesh's individual faces. The power member is the specular exponent of the material.

Note that this template is open, however, currently only the TextureFileName template is used as a child instance. If a TextureFileName is not specified, this material is untextured.

Table A.13 Members

Member Name	Type	Array Size
FaceColor	ColorRGBA	
Power	FLOAT	
SpecularColor	ColorRGB	
EmissiveColor	ColorRGB	

Child Templates: Any

Definition:
```
template Material
{
    <3D82AB4D-62DA-11cf-AB39-0020AF71E433>
    ColorRGBA faceColor;
    FLOAT power;
    ColorRGB specularColor;
    ColorRGB emissiveColor;
    [...]
}
```

TextureFilename

GUID: <A42790E1-7810-11cf-8F52-0040333594A3>

Description: This template enables you to specify the file name of a texture to apply to a mesh or a face. This should appear within a material object.

Table A.14 Members

Member Name	Type	Array Size
Filename	STRING	

Child Templates: None

Definition:
```
template TextureFilename
{
    <A42790E1-7810-11cf-8F52-0040333594A3>
    STRING filename;
}
```

MeshFace

GUID: <3D82AB5F-62DA-11cf-AB39-0020AF71E433>

Description: This template is used by the Mesh template to define a mesh's faces. Each element of the nFaceVertexIndices array indexes a vertex in the associated Mesh instance's list of vertices.

Table A.15 Members

Member Name	Type	Array Size
NFaceVertexIndices	DWORD	
FaceVertexIndices	array DWORD	nFaceVertexIndices

Child Templates: None

Definition:
```
template MeshFace
{
    <3D82AB5F-62DA-11cf-AB39-0020AF71E433>
    DWORD nFaceVertexIndices;
    array DWORD faceVertexIndices[nFaceVertexIndices];
}
```

MeshFaceWraps

GUID: <4885AE62-78E8-11cf-8F52-0040333594A3>

Description: This template is used to define the texture topology of each face in a wrap. nFaceWrapValues should be equal to the number of faces in a mesh.

Table A.16 Members

Member Name	Type	Array Size
nFaceWrapValues	DWORD	
faceWrapValues	Boolean2d	

Child Templates: None

Definition:
```
template MeshFaceWraps
{
    <4885AE62-78E8-11cf-8F52-0040333594A3>
    DWORD nFaceWrapValues;
    Boolean2d faceWrapValues;
}
```

MeshTextureCoords

GUID: <F6F23F40-7686-11cf-8F52-0040333594A3>

Description: This template defines a mesh's texture coordinates.

Table A.17 Members

Member Name	Type	Array Size
nTextureCoords	DWORD	
TextureCoords	array Coords2d	nTextureCoords

Child Templates: None

Definition:
```
template MeshTextureCoords
{
    <F6F23F40-7686-11cf-8F52-0040333594A3>
    DWORD nTextureCoords;
    array Coords2d textureCoords[nTextureCoords];
}
```

MeshNormals

GUID: <F6F23F43-7686-11cf-8F52-0040333594A3>

Description: This template defines normals for a mesh. The first array of vectors are the normal vectors themselves, and the second array is an array of indexes specifying which normals should be applied to a given face. nFaceNormals should be equal to the number of faces in a mesh.

Table A.18 Members

Member Name	Type	Array Size
nNormals	DWORD	
normals	array Vector	nNormals
nFaceNormals	DWORD	
faceNormals	array MeshFace	nFaceNormals

Child Templates: None

Definition:
```
template MeshNormals
{
    <F6F23F43-7686-11cf-8F52-0040333594A3>
    DWORD nNormals;
    array Vector normals[nNormals];
    DWORD nFaceNormals;
    array MeshFace faceNormals[nFaceNormals];
}
```

MeshVertexColors

GUID: <1630B821-7842-11cf-8F52-0040333594A3>

Description: This template specifies vertex colors for a mesh, as opposed to applying a material per face or per mesh.

Table A.19 Members

Member Name	Type	Array Size
nVertexColors	DWORD	
VertexColors	array IndexedColor	nVertexColors

Child Templates: None

Definition:
```
template MeshVertexColors
{
    <1630B821-7842-11cf-8F52-0040333594A3>
    DWORD nVertexColors;
    array IndexedColor vertexColors[nVertexColors];
}
```

MeshMaterialList

GUID: <F6F23F42-7686-11cf-8F52-0040333594A3>

Description: This template is used in a mesh object to specify which material applies to which faces. nMaterials specifies how many materials are present, and materials specify which material to apply.

If the Material instance is not present, the default material is applied to all faces.

Table A.20 Members

Member Name	Type	Array Size
nMaterials	DWORD	
nFaceIndexes	DWORD	
faceIndexes	array DWORD	nFaceIndexes

Child Templates: Material

Definition:
```
template MeshMaterialList
{
    <F6F23F42-7686-11cf-8F52-0040333594A3>
    DWORD nMaterials;
    DWORD nFaceIndexes;
    array DWORD faceIndexes[nFaceIndexes];
    [Material]
}
```

Mesh

GUID: <3D82AB44-62DA-11cf-AB39-0020AF71E433>

Description: This template defines a simple mesh. The first array is a list of vertices and the second array defines the faces of the mesh by indexing into the vertex array.

If the MeshFaceWraps instance is not present, wrapping for both u and v defaults is set to false. If the MeshTextureCoords instance is not present, there are no texture coordinates. If the MeshNormals instance is not present, normals are generated by using IDirect3DRMMesh Builder::GenerateNormals(). If the MeshVertexColors instance is not present, the colors default to white. If the MeshMaterialList instance is not present, the material defaults to white.

Table A.21 Members

Member Name	Type	Array Size
nVertices	DWORD	
vertices	array Vector	nVertices
nFaces	DWORD	
faces	array MeshFace	nFaces

Child Templates: Any

Definition:
```
template Mesh
{
    <3D82AB44-62DA-11cf-AB39-0020AF71E433>
    DWORD nVertices;
    array Vector vertices[nVertices];
    DWORD nFaces;
    array MeshFace faces[nFaces];
    [...]
}
```

FrameTransformMatrix

GUID: <F6F23F41-7686-11cf-8F52-0040333594A3>

Description: This template defines a local transformation for a frame (and all its child objects). The data in the matrix represents a frame's position, translation, rotation, and scale.

Table A.21

Members

Member Name	Type	Array Size
FrameMatrix	Matrix4×4	

Child Templates: None

Definition:
```
template FrameTransformMatrix
{
    <F6F23F41-7686-11cf-8F52-0040333594A3>
    Matrix4x4 frameMatrix;
}
```

Frame

GUID: <3D82AB46-62DA-11cf-AB39-0020AF71E433>

Description: This template defines a frame. Currently, the frame can contain objects of the type Mesh and a FrameTransformMatrix. If a FrameTransformMatrix instance is not present, no local transform is applied to the frame. Mesh instances that are children of the frame can be specified in-line or by reference.

Table A.22 Members

Member Name	Type	Array Size
none		

Child Templates: Any

Definition:
```
template Frame
{
    <3D82AB46-62DA-11cf-AB39-0020AF71E433>
    [...]
}
```

FloatKeys

GUID: <10DD46A9-775B-11cf-8F52-0040333594A3>

Description: This template defines an array of floats and the number of floats in that array. This is used for defining sets of animation keys.

Table A.23 Members

Member Name	Type	Array Size
NValues	DWORD	
Values	array FLOAT	nValues

Child Templates: None

Definition:
```
template FloatKeys
{
    <10DD46A9-775B-11cf-8F52-0040333594A3>
    DWORD nValues;
    array FLOAT values[nValues];
}
```

TimedFloatKeys

GUID: <F406B180-7B3B-11cf-8F52-0040333594A3>

Description: This template defines a set of floats and a positive time used in the animation templates.

Table A.24 Members

Member Name	Type	Array Size
time	DWORD	
tfkeys	FloatKeys	

Child Templates: None

Definition:
```
template TimedFloatKeys
{
    <F406B180-7B3B-11cf-8F52-0040333594A3>
    DWORD time;
    FloatKeys tfkeys;
}
```

AnimationKey

GUID: <10DD46A8-775B-11cf-8F52-0040333594A3>

Description: This template defines a set of animation keys. The keyType parameter specifies whether the keys are rotation, scale, or position keys (using the integers 0, 1, or 2, respectively).

Table A.25 Members

Member Name	Type	Array Size
KeyType	DWORD	
nKeys	DWORD	
Keys	array	
TimedFloatKeys		nKeys

Child Templates: None

Definition:
```
template AnimationKey
{
    <10DD46A8-775B-11cf-8F52-0040333594A3>
    DWORD keyType;
    DWORD nKeys;
    array TimedFloatKeys keys[nKeys];
}
```

AnimationOptions

GUID: <E2BF56C0-840F-11cf-8F52-0040333594A3>

Description: This template enables you to set the D3DRM Animation options. The Openclosed parameter can be either 0 for a closed or 1 for an open animation. The Positionquality parameter is used to set the position quality for any position keys specified and can either be 0 for spline positions or 1 for linear positions. By default, an animation is open and uses linear position keys.

Table A.26 Members

Member Name	Type	Array Size
Openclosed	DWORD	
Positionquality	DWORD	

Child Templates: None

Definition:
```
template AnimationOptions
{
    <E2BF56C0-840F-11cf-8F52-0040333594A3>
    DWORD openclosed;
    DWORD positionquality;
}
```

Animation

GUID: <3D82AB4F-62DA-11cf-AB39-0020AF71E433>

Description: This template contains the data that defines an animation. It should contain at least one AnimationKeys. It can also contain an AnimationOptions instance. If the AnimationOptions instance is not present, an Animation is open and uses linear position keys.

Table A.27 Members

Member Name	Type	Array Size
none		

Child Templates: Any

Definition:
```
template Animation
{
    <3D82AB4F-62DA-11cf-AB39-0020AF71E433>
    [...]
}
```

AnimationSet

GUID: <3D82AB50-62DA-11cf-AB39-0020AF71E433>

Description: An AnimationSet can contain one or more Animation instances. This allows a set of animations to be controlled by the same time value.

Table A.28 Members

Member Name	Type	Array Size
none		

Child Templates: Animation

Definition:
```
template AnimationSet
{
    <3D82AB50-62DA-11cf-AB39-0020AF71E433>
    [Animation]
}
```

Binary Format Specification

The binary format of the DirectX file format is a tokenized representation of the text format and was introduced with DirectX 3. There are two types of tokens: stand-alone and record-bearing. Stand-alone tokens provide structure to the file format and record-bearing tokens provide the actual data of the file format. As with the text format, a valid DirectX file must contain a header and zero or more templates and data objects. No comments are permitted in the binary file format. All data in the binary format is in little-endian format (low bytes in lower memory).

Header

The following C-style definitions describe the data of the binary format header:

```
#define XOFFILE_FORMAT_MAGIC \
    ((long)'x' + ((long)'o' << 8) + ((long)'f' << 16) + ((long)' ' << 24))

#define XOFFILE_FORMAT_VERSION \
    ((long)'0' + ((long)'3' << 8) + ((long)'0' << 16) + ((long)'2' << 24))
```

```
#define XOFFILE_FORMAT_BINARY \
    ((long)'b' + ((long)'i' << 8) + ((long)'n' << 16) + ((long)' ' << 24))

#define XOFFILE_FORMAT_TEXT    \
    ((long)'t' + ((long)'x' << 8) + ((long)'t' << 16) + ((long)' ' << 24))

#define XOFFILE_FORMAT_COMPRESSED \
    ((long)'c' + ((long)'m' << 8) + ((long)'p' << 16) + ((long)' ' << 24))

#define XOFFILE_FORMAT_FLOAT_BITS_32 \
    ((long)'0' + ((long)'0' << 8) + ((long)'3' << 16) + ((long)'2' << 24))

#define XOFFILE_FORMAT_FLOAT_BITS_64 \
    ((long)'0' + ((long)'0' << 8) + ((long)'6' << 16) + ((long)'4' << 24))
```

Templates

The template grammar is as follows:

```
Template   : TOKEN_TEMPLATE name TOKEN_OBRACE
                     class_id
                     template_parts
                     TOKEN_CBRACE

template_parts            : template_members_part TOKEN_OBRACKET
             template_option_info
             TOKEN_CBRACKET
        ¦ template_members_list

template_members_part    : /* Empty */
        ¦ template_members_list

template_option_info     : ellipsis
        ¦ template_option_list

template_members_list    : template_members
        ¦ template_members_list template_members

template_Members         : primitive
        ¦ array
        ¦ template_reference

primitive                : primitive_type optional_name TOKEN_SEMICOLON

array                    : TOKEN_ARRAY array_data_type name dimension_list
        TOKEN_SEMICOLON

template_reference       : name optional_name YT_SEMICOLON
```

```
primitive_type          : TOKEN_WORD
            | TOKEN_DWORD
            | TOKEN_FLOAT
            | TOKEN_DOUBLE
            | TOKEN_CHAR
            | TOKEN_UCHAR
            | TOKEN_SWORD
            | TOKEN_SDWORD
            | TOKEN_LPSTR
            | TOKEN_UNICODE
            | TOKEN_CSTRING

array_data_type         : primitive_type
            | name

dimension_list          : dimension
            | dimension_list dimension

dimension               : TOKEN_OBRACKET dimension_size TOKEN_CBRACKET

dimension_size          : TOKEN_INTEGER
            | name

template_option_list    : template_option_part
            | template_option_list template_option_part

template_option_part    : name optional_class_id

name                    : TOKEN_NAME

optional_name           : /* Empty */
            | name

class_id                : TOKEN_GUID

optional_class_id       : /* Empty */
            | class_id

ellipsis                : TOKEN_DOT TOKEN_DOT TOKEN_DOT
```

Data

The data grammar is as follows:

```
Object          : identifier optional_name    TOKEN_OBRACE
                  optional_class_id
                  data_parts_list
                  TOKEN_CBRACE

data_parts_list       : data_part
            | data_parts_list data_part
```

```
data_part         : data_reference
                  ¦ object
                  ¦ number_list
                  ¦ float_list
                  ¦ string_list

number_list       : TOKEN_INTEGER_LIST

float_list        : TOKEN_FLOAT_LIST

string_list       : string_list_1 list_separator

string_list_1     : string
                  ¦ string_list_1 list_separator string

list_separator    : comma
                  ¦ semicolon

string            : TOKEN_STRING

identifier        : name
                  ¦ primitive_type

data_reference    : TOKEN_OBRACE name optional_class_id TOKEN_CBRACE
```

Tokens

Tokens are stored as little-endian DWORD values. The list of record-bearing tokens is as follows:

```
#define TOKEN_NAME 1
#define TOKEN_STRING 2
#define TOKEN_INTEGER 3
#define TOKEN_GUID 5
#define TOKEN_INTEGER_LIST 6
#define TOKEN_REALNUM_LIST 7
```

The list of stand-alone tokens is as follows:

```
#define TOKEN_OBRACE 10
#define TOKEN_CBRACE 11
#define TOKEN_OPAREN 12
#define TOKEN_CPAREN 13
#define TOKEN_OBRACKET 14
#define TOKEN_CBRACKET 15
#define TOKEN_OANGLE 16
#define TOKEN_CANGLE 17
#define TOKEN_DOT 18
#define TOKEN_COMMA 19
#define TOKEN_SEMICOLON 20
#define TOKEN_TEMPLATE 31
```

```
#define TOKEN_WORD     40
#define TOKEN_DWORD    41
#define TOKEN_FLOAT    42
#define TOKEN_DOUBLE   43
#define TOKEN_CHAR     44
#define TOKEN_UCHAR    45
#define TOKEN_SWORD    46
#define TOKEN_SDWORD   47
#define TOKEN_VOID     48
#define TOKEN_LPSTR    49
#define TOKEN_UNICODE  50
#define TOKEN_CSTRING  51
#define TOKEN_ARRAY    52
```

Record-Bearing Token Reference

TOKEN_NAME

Description: TOKEN_NAME is a variable length record. The token is followed by a count value, which specifies the number of bytes that follow in the name field. An ASCII name of length count completes the record.

Table A.29 Members

Fields	FieldType	Size (in bytes)	Contents
Token	DWORD	4	TOKEN_NAME
Count	DWORD	4	Length of name field in bytes
Name	BYTE array	count	ASCII name

TOKEN_STRING

Description: TOKEN_STRING is a variable length record. The token is followed by a count value that specifies the number of bytes that follow in the string field. An ASCII string of length count continues the record that is completed by a terminating token. The choice of terminator is based on the instance data as described in the File Format Syntax Instance section.

Table A.30 Members

Fields	FieldType	Size (in bytes)	Contents
Token	DWORD	4	Length of string field in bytes
String	BYTE array	count	ASCII string
Terminator	DWORD	4	TOKEN_SEMICOLON or TOKEN_COMMA

TOKEN_INTEGER

Description: TOKEN_INTEGER is a fixed length record. The token is followed by the integer value required.

Table A.31 Members

Fields	FieldType	Size (in bytes)	Contents
Token	DWORD	4	TOKEN_INTEGER
Value	DWORD	4	Single integer

TOKEN_GUID

Description: TOKEN_GUID is a fixed length record. The token is followed by the four data fields—as defined by the OSF's DCE standard. More information on that standard can be found at http://www.opengroup.org/tech/dce.

Table A.32 Members

Fields	FieldType	Size (in bytes)	Contents
data1	DWORD	4	uuid data field1
data2	WORD	2	uuid data field2
data3	WORD	2	uuid data field3
data4	BYTEarray	8	uuid data field4

TOKEN_INTEGER_LIST

Description: TOKEN_INTEGER_LIST is a variable length record. The token is followed by a count value, which specifies the number of integers that follow in the list field. For efficiency, consecutive integer lists should be compounded into a single list.

Table A.33 Members

Fields	FieldType	Size (in bytes)	Contents
Token	DWORD	4	TOKEN_INTEGER_LIST
Count	DWORD	4	Number of integers in list field
List	DWORD	4 × count	Integer list array

TOKEN_REALNUM_LIST

Description: TOKEN_REALNUM_LIST is a variable length record. The token is followed by a count value that specifies the number of floats or doubles that follow in the list field. The size of the floating point value (float or double) is determined by the value of float size specified in the file header discussed elsewhere. For efficiency, consecutive realnum lists should be compounded into a single list.

Table A.34 Members

Fields	FieldType	Size (in bytes)	Contents
Token	DWORD	4	TOKEN_REALNUM_LIST
Count	DWORD	4	Number of floats or doubles in list field
List	float/	4 or 8 × count	Float or double list double array

INDEX

Symbols

3D objects
   coordinate systems, 4
      origin, 6
   geometry, 5-9
      faces (polygons), 7
      lines, 7
      meshes, 9
      normal vectors (normals), 8
      vectors, 8
      vertices, 6
   visual characteristics, 10-13
      lights, 10-12
      materials, 10

3D scenes, 14-17
   converting to 2D representations, 16-17
   frames of reference, 14
   geometric transformations, 14-15
   rasterization, 17-19
   viewing volume, 15

A

AddAnimation method (IDirect3DRMAnimationSet interface), 102
AddChild method (IDirect3DRMFrame interface), 136-137
AddDestroyCallback method (IDirect3DRMObject interface), 231-232
AddFace method (IDirect3DRMMeshBuilder interface), 205
AddFaces method (IDirect3DRMMeshBuilder interface), 205-207
AddFrame method (IDirect3DRMMeshBuilder interface), 207
AddGroup method (IDirect3DRMMesh interface), 191
AddLight method, 360
   IDirect3DRMFrame interface, 137
   IDirect3DViewport interface, 360
AddMesh method (IDirect3DRMMeshBuilder interface), 207-208
AddMeshBuilder method (IDirect3DRMMeshBuilder interface), 208
AddMoveCallback method (IDirect3DRMFrame interface), 137-138
AddNormal method (IDirect3DRMMeshBuilder interface), 208-209
AddPositionKey method (IDirect3DRMAnimation interface), 95-98
AddRef method (IUnknown interface), 37-38
AddRotateKey method (IDirect3DRMAnimation interface), 97
AddRotation method (IDirect3DRMFrame interface), 138-139
AddScale method (IDirect3DRMFrame interface), 139-140
AddScaleKey method (IDirect3DRMAnimation interface), 97-98

AddSearchPath method (IDirect3DRM interface), 68
AddTransform method (IDirect3DRMFrame interface), 140
AddTranslation method (IDirect3DRMFrame interface), 140-141
AddUpdateCallback method (IDirect3DRMDevice interface), 107
AddVertex method
　IDirect3DRMFace interface, 123
　IDirect3DRMMeshBuilder interface, 209
AddVertexAndNormalIndexed method (IDirect3DRMFace interface), 123-124
AddViewport method (IDirect3DDevice interface), 328-329
AddVisual method (IDirect3DRMFrame interface), 141-142
alpha-blending algorithms, 427-428
ambient color, 10
ambient light, 11
animation
　defined, 3
　defining play, 296
Animation options, enabling/disabling, 100-101
animation sets
　Animation objects
　　adding, 102
　　deleting, 103
　loading from files, 103-105
　time, setting, 105-106
Animation template reference guide, 479
AnimationKey template reference guide, 478
AnimationOptions template reference guide, 478-479
AnimationSet template reference guide, 480
APIs
　Immediate-Mode, 29-32
　Retained-Mode, 29-32

Apply method (IDirect3DRMWrap interface), 271
ApplyRelative method (IDirect3DRMWrap interface), 272
Array interfaces (Retained-Mode), 63-67
　GetElement method, 64-65
　GetPick method, 65-67
　GetSize method, 64
Arrays, 459
attenuation (lights), 12

B

back clipping plane (viewing volume), 15
backface culling, 19
basic data types, 458-459
BeginScene method (IDirect3DDevice interface), 329
binary format (DirectX file format), 480-484
　data grammar, 482-483
　headers, 480-481
　record-bearing tokens, 483
　　TOKEN_GUID, 485
　　TOKEN_INTEGER, 485
　　TOKEN_INTEGER_LIST, 486
　　TOKEN_NAME, 484
　　TOKEN_REALNUM_LIST, 486
　　TOKEN_STRING, 484-485
　stand-alone tokens, 483-484
　template grammar, 481-482
bitmaps (textures), 12-14
　mipmapping, 13
　texture coordinates, 13
　texture mapping, 13
blending modes, 425-427
Boolean template reference guide, 468
Boolean2d template reference guide, 468-469
BYTE data type, 458

C

C, accessing COM objects, 25
C++, 25
callback functions
   Immediate-Mode
      D3DENUMDEVICESCALLBACK, 319-320
      D3DENUMTEXTUREFORMATSCALLBACK, 320-321
      D3DVALIDATECALLBACK, 321-323
   Retained-Mode, 56
      D3DRMDEVICEPALETTECALLBACK, 56-57
      D3DRMFRAMEMOVECALLBACK, 57
      D3DRMLOADCALLBACK, 58
      D3DRMLOADTEXTURECALLBACK, 58-59
      D3DRMOBJECTCALLBACK, 59-60
      D3DRMUPDATECALLBACK, 60
      D3DRMUSERVISUALCALLBACK, 61-62
      D3DRMWRAPCALLBACK, 62-63
Changed method (IDirect3DRMTexture interface), 239-240
CHAR data type, 458
child frames, sorting, 292
chrome wrap (texture mapping), 13
Clear method
   IDirect3DRMViewport interface, 252
   IDirect3DViewport interface, 360-361
Clone method (IDirect3DRMObject interface), 232-233
closed templates, 460
CoCreateInstance method (IUnknown interface), 39-40
CoInitialize method (IUnknown interface), 40-41
color models (devices), 428-429
color palette (D3DRMIMAGE), 278-279

ColorRGB template reference guide, 467
ColorRGBA template reference guide, 466-467
colors
   creating from supplied color components, 45
   returning components, 44-45
   textures, setting usable colors, 91
comments (DirectX file format), 457
Component Object Model (COM), 24-25
   C++, 25
   library
      initializing, 40-41
      uninitializing, 41-42
   methods, 37-42
      AddRef, 37-38
      CoCreateInstance, 39-40
      CoInitialize, 40-41
      CoUninitialize, 41-42
      QueryInterface, 38
      Release, 38-39
   objects, 24-25
      accessing with C, 25
Compression Type field (header elements), 457
computer graphics, coordinate systems, 4
Configure method (IDirect3DRMViewport interface), 252
coordinate systems, 4
   origins, 6
Coords2d template reference guide, 464-465
CoUninitialize method (IUnknown interface), 41-42
CreateAnimation method (IDirect3DRM interface), 68-69
CreateAnimationSet method (IDirect3DRM interface), 69
CreateDevice method (IDirect3DRM interface), 69

CreateDeviceFromClipper method
  (IDirect3DRM interface), 70-71
CreateDeviceFromD3D method
  (IDirect3DRM interface), 71-72
CreateDeviceFromSurface method
  (IDirect3DRM interface), 73-74
CreateExecuteBuffer method
  (IDirect3DDevice), 330-331
CreateFace method
  IDirect3DRM interface, 74
  IDirect3DRMMeshBuilder interface, 210
CreateFrame method (IDirect3DRM
  interface), 75
CreateLight method
  IDirect3D interface, 323-324
  IDirect3DRM interface, 75-76
CreateLightRGB method (IDirect3DRM
  interface), 76-77
CreateMaterial method
  IDirect3D interface, 324
  IDirect3DRM interface, 77
CreateMatrix method (IDirect3DDevice
  interface), 331
CreateMesh method
  IDirect3DRM interface, 78
  IDirect3DRMMeshBuilder interface,
    210-211
CreateMeshBuilder method (IDirect3DRM
  interface), 78
CreateObject method (IDirect3DRM
  interface), 79
CreateShadow method (IDirect3DRM
  interface), 80-81
CreateTexture method (IDirect3DRM
  interface), 81
CreateUserVisual method (IDirect3DRM
  interface), 82-83
CreateViewport method
  IDirect3D interface, 325

  IDirect3DRM interface, 83
CreateWrap method (IDirect3DRM
  interface), 84-85
CSTRING data type, 459
cull modes, 429
cylindrical wrap (texture mapping), 13

D

D3DBLEND enumerated type, 425-427
D3DBRANCH structure (Immediate-
  Mode), 371-372
D3DCMPFUNC enumerated type, 427-428
D3DCOLORMODEL enumerated type,
  428-429
D3DCOLORVALUE structure (Immediate-
  Mode), 372-373
D3DCULL enumerated type, 429
D3DDEVICEDESC structure (Immediate-
  Mode), 373-375
D3DDivide macro (Immediate-Mode), 308
D3DENUMDEVICESCALLBACK
  arguments, 319-320
  callbacks (Immediate-Mode), 319-320
D3DENUMTEXTUREFORMATSCALLBACK
  arguments, 320-321
  callbacks (Immediate-Mode), 320-321
D3DEXECUTEBUFFERDESC structure
  (Immediate-Mode), 376-377
D3DEXECUTEDATA structure
  (Immediate-Mode), 377-378
D3DFILLMODE enumerated type, 429-430
D3DFINDDEVICERESULT structure
  (Immediate-Mode), 378
D3DFINDDEVICESEARCH structure
  (Immediate-Mode), 379-382
D3DFOGMODE enumerated type, 430-431
D3DHVERTEX structure (Immediate-
  Mode), 382-383

D3DINSTRUCTION structure (Immediate-Mode), 383
D3DLIGHT structure (Immediate-Mode), 384-385
D3DLIGHTDATA structure (Immediate-Mode), 385-386
D3DLIGHTINGCAPS structure (Immediate-Mode), 386-387
D3DLIGHTINGELEMENT structure (Immediate-Mode), 387-388
D3DLIGHTSTATETYPE enumerated type, 431-433
D3DLIGHTTYPE enumerated type, 433
D3DLINE structure (Immediate-Mode), 388
D3DLINEPATTERN structure (Immediate-Mode), 388-389
D3DLVERTEX structure (Immediate-Mode), 389-390
D3DMATERIAL structure (Immediate-Mode), 390-392
D3DMATRIX structure (Immediate-Mode), 392
D3DMATRIXLOAD structure (Immediate-Mode), 392-393
D3DMATRIXMULTIPLY structure (Immediate-Mode), 393
D3DMultiply macro (Immediate-Mode), 308
D3DOPCODE enumerated type, 434-436
D3DPICKRECORD structure (Immediate-Mode), 394
D3DPOINT structure (Immediate-Mode), 394-395
D3DPRIMCAPS structure (Immediate-Mode), 395-403
D3DPROCESSVERTICES structure (Immediate-Mode), 404-405
D3DRCOLORSOURCE enumerated type, 283

D3DRECT structure (Immediate-Mode), 405-406
D3DRENDERSTATETYPE enumerated type, 436-442
D3DRGB macro (Immediate-Mode), 308-309
D3DRGBA macro (Immediate-Mode), 309-310
D3DRMANIMATIONOPTIONS type definitions, 296
D3DRMBOX structure (Retained-Mode), 275
D3DRMColorGetAlpha function, 44-45
D3DRMColorGetBlue function, 44-45
D3DRMColorGetGreen function, 44-45
D3DRMColorGetRed function, 44-45
D3DRMCOLORMODEL type definitions, 297
D3DRMCOMBINETYPE enumerated type, 283-284
D3DRMCreateColorRGB function, 45
D3DRMCreateColorRGBA function, 45
D3DRMDEVICEPALETTECALLBACK function, 56-57
D3DRMFILLMODE enumerated type, 284-285
D3DRMFOGMODE enumerated type, 285-286
D3DRMFRAMECONTSRAINT enumerated type, 286
D3DRMFRAMEMOVECALLBACK function, 57
D3DRMIMAGE structure (Retained-Mode), 275-276
D3DRMLIGHTMODE enumerated type, 287
D3DRMLIGHTTYPE enumerated type, 287-288
D3DRMLOADCALLBACK function, 58

D3DRMLOADMEMORY structure
 (Retained-Mode), 277
D3DRMLOADOPTIONS type definitions,
 297-299
    source flags, 298-299
D3DRMLOADRESOURCE structure
 (Retained-Mode), 277-278
D3DRMLOADTEXTURECALLBACK
 function, 58-59
D3DRMMAPPING type definitions,
 299-300
D3DRMMATERIALMODE enumerated
 type, 288
D3DRMMATRIX4D type definitions, 300
D3DRMMatrixFromQuaternion function,
 46
D3DRMOBJECTCALLBACK function,
 59-60
D3DRMPALETTEENTRY structure
 (Retained-Mode), 278-279
D3DRMPALETTEFLAGS enumerated
 type, 289
D3DRMPICKDESC structure (Retained-
 Mode), 279-280
D3DRMPROJECTIONTYPE enumerated
 type, 289
D3DRMQUATERNION structure
 (Retained-Mode), 280
D3DRMQuaternionFromRotation function,
 46-47
D3DRMQuaternionMultiply function, 47
D3DRMQuaternionSlerp function, 48
D3DRMRENDERQUALITY enumerated
 type, 290
D3DRMSHADEMODE enumerated type,
 291
D3DRMSORTMODE enumerated type, 292
D3DRMTEXTUREQUALITY enumerated
 type, 292-293
D3DRMUPDATECALLBACK function, 60

D3DRMUSERVISUALCALLBACK
 function, 61-62
D3DRMUSERVISUALREASON
 enumerated type, 293-294
D3DRMVECTOR4D structure (Retained-
 Mode), 280-281
D3DRMVectorAdd function, 49
D3DRMVectorCrossProduct function,
 49-50
D3DRMVectorDotProduct function, 50
D3DRMVectorModulus function, 51
D3DRMVectorNormalize function, 51
D3DRMVectorRandom function, 52
D3DRMVectorReflect function, 52-53
D3DRMVectorRotate function, 53
D3DRMVectorScale function, 54
D3DRMVectorSubtract function, 55-56
D3DRMVERTEX structure (Retained-
 Mode), 281
D3DRMWRAPCALLBACK function,
 62-63
D3DRMWRAPTYPE enumerated type, 294
D3DRMXOFFORMAT enumerated type,
 294-295
D3DRMZBUFFERMODE enumerated
 type, 295-296
D3DSHADEMODE enumerated type,
 442-443
D3DSPAN structure (Immediate-Mode),
 406
D3DSTATE structure (Immediate-Mode),
 406-407
D3DSTATE_OVERRIDE macro
 (Immediate-Mode), 310
D3DSTATS structure (Immediate-Mode),
 407-408
D3DSTATUS structure (Immediate-Mode),
 408-411
D3DTEXTUREADDRESS enumerated
 type, 443-444
D3DTEXTUREBLEND enumerated type,
 444-445

D3DTEXTUREFILTER enumerated type, 445-446
D3DTEXTURELOAD structure (Immediate-Mode), 411
D3DTLVERTEX structure (Immediate-Mode), 412-413
D3DTRANSFORMCAPS structure (Immediate-Mode), 413
D3DTRANSFORMDATA structure (Immediate-Mode), 414-416
D3DTRANSFORMSTATETYPE enumerated type, 446-448
D3DTRIANGLE structure (Immediate-Mode), 416-422
D3DVAL macro (Immediate-Mode), 311
D3DVALIDATECALLBACK
 arguments, 321-323
 callbacks (Immediate-Mode), 321-323
D3DVALP macro (Immediate-Mode), 311
D3DVALUE value, 448
D3DVECTOR structure (Immediate-Mode), 420
D3DVERTEX structure (Immediate-Mode), 420-422
D3DVIEWPORT structure (Immediate-Mode), 422-423
data, binary format, 482-483
data types
 Immediate-Mode return values, 449-451
 Retained-Mode return values, 303
 templates, 458-459
DCE standard, 485
DeleteAnimation method (IDirect3DRMAnimationSet interface), 103
DeleteChild method (IDirect3DRMFrame interface), 142
DeleteDestroyCallback method (IDirect3DRMObject interface), 233
DeleteKey method (IDirect3DRMAnimation interface), 98-99

DeleteLight method
 IDirect3DRMFrame interface, 142-143
 IDirect3DViewport interface, 361-362
DeleteMatrix method (IDirect3DDevice interface), 331-332
DeleteMoveCallback method (IDirect3DRMFrame interface), 143
DeleteUpdateCallback method (IDirect3DRMDevice interface), 107-108
DeleteViewport method (IDirect3DDevice interface), 332
DeleteVisual method (IDirect3DRMFrame interface), 143-144
devices
 color models, 428-429
   returning, 108-109
 copying images rendered in viewports, 120-122
 dithering, 110
   enabling/disabling, 117
 height (in pixels), returning, 110
 pointers, retrieving, 109
 rendering quality
   returning, 111-112
   specifying, 290
 shades
   returning number in color ramps, 112
   setting number per color ramp, 119
 texture quality
   retrieving, 112-113
   setting, 119-120
 triangles, returning number drawn, 110-111
 updates
   returning number of buffers, 108
   setting number of buffers, 117
 viewports, 113-114
 width (in pixels), returning, 114
 wireframe options, returning, 114-115
diffuse color, 10

Direct3D, 23
   architecture, 28-32
      Hardware Abstraction Layer (HAL), 30-32
      Hardware Emulation Layer (HEL), 30-32
      Immediate-Mode API, 29-32
      rendering engine, 30-32
      Retained-Mode API, 29-32
   coordinate systems, 4
   history, 27-28
Direct3DRMCreate function, 44
DirectDraw, 23, 32
DirectInput, 24
directional light, 11
directories, adding to search paths, 68
DirectPlay, 23
DirectSetup, 24
DirectSound, 23
DirectX file format, 455-463
   binary format, 480-484
      data grammar, 482-483
      headers, 480-481
      record-bearing tokens, 483-486
      stand-alone tokens, 483-484
      template grammar, 481-482
   comments, 457
   headers, 456-457
   instances, 461-463
   reserved words, 456
   templates, 458-461
      Animation, 479
      AnimationKey, 478
      AnimationOptions, 478-479
      AnimationSet, 480
      arrays, 459
      Boolean, 468
      Boolean2d, 468-469
      ColorRGB, 467
      ColorRGBA, 466-467
      Coords2d, 464-465
      data types, 458-459
      FloatKeys, 476-477
      Frame, 476
      FrameTransformMatrix, 475-476
      Header, 461, 463-464
      IndexedColor, 467-468
      Material, 469-470
      Matrix4x4, 466
      Mesh, 474-475
      MeshFace, 470-471
      MeshFaceWraps, 471
      MeshMaterialList, 473-474
      MeshNormals, 472-473
      MeshTextureCoords, 472
      MeshVertexColors, 473
      Quaternion, 465
      restriction types, 459-460
      TextureFilename, 470
      TimedFloatKeys, 477
      Vector, 464
DirectX SDK (software development kit), 22-23
   Component Object Model (COM), 24-25
      C, 25
      C++, 25
   components, 23-24
DOUBLE data type, 458
DWORD data type, 458

E

emissive color, 10
EndScene method (IDirect3DDevice interface), 333
EnumDevices method (IDirect3D interface), 325-326
enumerated types
   D3DBLEND (Immediate-Mode), 425-427
   D3DCMPFUNC (Immediate-Mode), 427-428
   D3DCOLORMODEL (Immediate-Mode), 428-429

Index—**fields** 495

D3DCULL (Immediate-Mode), 429
D3DFILLMODE (Immediate-Mode), 429-430
D3DFOGMODE (Immediate-Mode), 430-431
D3DLIGHTSTATETYPE (Immediate-Mode), 431-433
D3DLIGHTTYPE (Immediate-Mode), 433
D3DOPCODE (Immediate-Mode), 434-436
D3DRCOLORSOURCE (Retained-Mode), 283
D3DRENDERSTATETYPE (Immediate-Mode), 436-442
D3DRMCOMBINETYPE (Retained-Mode), 283-284
D3DRMFILLMODE (Retained-Mode), 284-285
D3DRMFOGMODE (Retained-Mode), 285-286
D3DRMFRAMECONTSRAINT (Retained-Mode), 286
D3DRMLIGHTMODE (Retained-Mode), 287
D3DRMLIGHTTYPE (Retained-Mode), 287-288
D3DRMMATERIALMODE (Retained-Mode), 288
D3DRMPALETTEFLAGS (Retained-Mode), 289
D3DRMPROJECTIONTYPE (Retained-Mode), 289
D3DRMRENDERQUALITY (Retained-Mode), 290
D3DRMSHADEMODE (Retained-Mode), 291
D3DRMSORTMODE (Retained-Mode), 292
D3DRMTEXTUREQUALITY (Retained-Mode), 292-293
D3DRMUSERVISUALREASON (Retained-Mode), 293-294
D3DRMWRAPTYPE (Retained-Mode), 294
D3DRMXOFFORMAT (Retained-Mode), 294-295
D3DRMZBUFFERMODE (Retained-Mode), 295-296
D3DSHADEMODE (Immediate-Mode), 442-443
D3DTEXTUREADDRESS (Immediate-Mode), 443-444
D3DTEXTUREBLEND (Immediate-Mode), 444-445
D3DTEXTUREFILTER (Immediate-Mode), 445-446
D3DTRANSFORMSTATETYPE (Immediate-Mode), 446-448
EnumerateObjects method (IDirect3DRM interface), 85
enumerating, Retained-Mode objects, 85
EnumTextureFormats method (IDirect3DDevice interface), 333-334
execute buffers, 32
    opcodes, 434-436
Execute method (IDirect3DDevice interface), 334-335

F

face normals, 8
faces (polygons), 7
field of view (viewing volume), 15
fields
    Compression Type (header elements), 457
    Float Size (header elements), 457
    Format Type (header elements), 457
    Magic Number (header elements), 457
    Version Number-Major Number (header elements), 457
    Version Number-Minor Number (header elements), 457

file formats
  DirectX, 455-463
    Animation template, 479
    AnimationKey template, 478
    AnimationOptions template, 478-479
    AnimationSet template, 480
    binary format, 480-484
    Boolean template, 468
    Boolean2d template, 468-469
    ColorRGB template, 467
    ColorRGBA template, 466-467
    comments, 457
    Coords2d template, 464-465
    FloatKeys template, 476-477
    Frame template, 476
    FrameTransformMatrix template, 475-476
    Header template, 463-464
    headers, 456-457
    IndexedColor template, 467-468
    instances, 461-463
    Material template, 469-470
    Matrix4x4 template, 466
    Mesh template, 474-475
    MeshFace template, 470-471
    MeshFaceWraps template, 471
    MeshMaterialList template, 473-474
    MeshNormals template, 472-473
    MeshTextureCoords template, 472
    MeshVertexColors template, 473
    Quaternion template, 465
    reserved words, 456
    templates, 458-461
    TextureFilename template, 470
    TimedFloatKeys template, 477
    Vector template, 464
fill modes, 429-430
FindDevice method (IDirect3D interface), 326-327
flat shading, 18
flat wrap (texture mapping), 13

FLOAT data type, 458
Float Size field (header elements), 457
FloatKeys template reference guide, 476-477
fog effect, 285-286
fog modes, defining values, 430-431
ForceUpdate method (IDirect3DRMViewport interface), 253
Format Type field (header elements), 457
Frame template reference guide, 476
frames, z-buffering, 295-296
FrameTransformMatrix template reference guide, 475-476
front clipping plane (viewing volume), 15
frustum (viewing volume), 15
functions (Retained-Mode), 43, 56
  D3DRMColorGetAlpha, 44-45
  D3DRMColorGetBlue, 44-45
  D3DRMColorGetGreen, 44-45
  D3DRMColorGetRed, 44-45
  D3DRMCreateColorRGB, 45
  D3DRMCreateColorRGBA, 45
  D3DRMDEVICEPALETTECALLBACK, 56-57
  D3DRMFRAMEMOVECALLBACK, 57
  D3DRMLOADCALLBACK, 58
  D3DRMLOADTEXTURECALLBACK, 58-59
  D3DRMMatrixFromQuaternion, 46
  D3DRMOBJECTCALLBACK, 59-60
  D3DRMQuaternionFromRotation, 46-47
  D3DRMQuaternionMultiply, 47
  D3DRMQuaternionSlerp, 48
  D3DRMUPDATECALLBACK, 60
  D3DRMUSERVISUALCALLBACK, 61-62
  D3DRMVectorAdd, 49
  D3DRMVectorCrossProduct, 49-50
  D3DRMVectorDotProduct, 50
  D3DRMVectorModulus, 51
  D3DRMVectorNormalize, 51

D3DRMVectorRandom, 52
D3DRMVectorReflect, 52-53
D3DRMVectorRotate, 53
D3DRMVectorScale, 54
D3DRMVectorSubtract, 55-56
D3DRMWRAPCALLBACK, 62-63
Direct3DRMCreate, 44

G

GenerateNormals method
 (IDirect3DRMMeshBuilder interface), 211
GetAppData method (IDirect3DRMObject
 interface), 233-234
GetBack method (IDirect3DRMViewport
 interface), 253-254
GetBackground method
 (IDirect3DViewport interface), 362-363
GetBackgroundDepth method
 (IDirect3DViewport interface), 363-364
GetBox method
 IDirect3DRMMesh interface, 192
 IDirect3DRMMeshBuilder interface,
  211-212
GetBufferCount method
 (IDirect3DRMDevice interface), 108
GetCamera method
 (IDirect3DRMViewport interface), 254
GetCaps method (IDirect3DDevice
 interface), 335-336
GetChildren method (IDirect3DRMFrame
 interface), 144
GetClassName method
 (IDirect3DRMObject interface), 234
GetColor method
 IDirect3DRMFace interface, 124
 IDirect3DRMFrame interface, 145
 IDirect3DRMLight interface, 174-175
GetColorModel method
 (IDirect3DRMDevice interface), 108-109
GetColors method (IDirect3DRMTexture
 interface), 240

GetColorSource method
 (IDirect3DRMMeshBuilder interface), 212
GetConstantAttenuation method
 (IDirect3DRMLight interface), 175
GetDecalOrigin method
 (IDirect3DRMTexture interface), 241
GetDecalScale method
 (IDirect3DRMTexture interface), 241
GetDecalSize method
 (IDirect3DRMTexture interface), 242
GetDecalTransparency method
 (IDirect3DRMTexture interface), 242
GetDecalTransparentColor method
 (IDirect3DRMTexture interface), 243
GetDevice method (IDirect3DRMViewport
 interface), 254-255
GetDevices method (IDirect3DRM
 interface), 85-86
GetDirect3D method (IDirect3DDevice
 interface), 336
GetDirect3DDevice method
 (IDirect3DRMDevice interface), 109
GetDirect3DViewport method
 (IDirect3DRMViewport interface), 255
GetDither method (IDirect3DRMDevice
 interface), 110
GetElement method (array interfaces),
 64-65
GetEmissive method
 (IDirect3DRMMaterial interface), 186-187
GetEnableFrame method
 (IDirect3DRMLight interface), 176
GetExecuteBuffer method
 (IDirect3DExecuteBuffer interface),
 343-344
GetFaceCount method
 (IDirect3DRMMeshBuilder interface),
 212-213
GetFaces method
 (IDirect3DRMMeshBuilder interface), 213

GetField method (IDirect3DRMViewport interface), 255-256
GetFront method (IDirect3DRMViewport interface), 256
GetGroup method (IDirect3DRMMesh interface), 192-193
GetGroupColor method (IDirect3DRMMesh interface), 193
GetGroupCount method (IDirect3DRMMesh interface), 194
GetGroupMapping method (IDirect3DRMMesh interface), 194-195
GetGroupMaterial method (IDirect3DRMMesh interface), 195
GetGroupQuality method (IDirect3DRMMesh interface), 196
GetGroupTexture method (IDirect3DRMMesh interface), 196
GetHandle method
 IDirect3DMaterial interface, 351-352
 IDirect3DTexture interface, 355-356
GetHeight method
 IDirect3DRMDevice interface, 110
 IDirect3DRMViewport interface, 256-257
GetImage method (IDirect3DRMTexture interface), 243
GetLight method (IDirect3DLight interface), 349
GetLights method (IDirect3DRMFrame interface), 145
GetLinearAttenuation method (IDirect3DRMLight interface), 176-177
GetMaterial method
 IDirect3DMaterial interface, 352
 IDirect3DRMFace interface, 124-125
GetMaterialMode method (IDirect3DRMFrame interface), 146
GetMatrix method (IDirect3DDevice interface), 336-337
GetName method (IDirect3DRMObject interface), 235

GetNamedObject method (IDirect3DRM interface), 86
GetNormal method (IDirect3DRMFace interface), 125
GetOptions method (IDirect3DRMAnimation interface), 99
GetOrientation method (IDirect3DRMFrame interface), 146-147
GetParent method (IDirect3DRMFrame interface), 147
GetPenumbra method (IDirect3DRMLight interface), 177
GetPerspective method (IDirect3DRMMeshBuilder interface), 214
GetPick method (array interfaces), 65-67
GetPickRecords method (IDirect3DDevice interface), 337-338
GetPlane method (IDirect3DRMViewport interface), 257
GetPosition method (IDirect3DRMFrame interface), 148
GetPower method (IDirect3DRMMaterial interface), 187
GetProjection method (IDirect3DRMViewport interface), 258
GetQuadraticAttenuation method (IDirect3DRMLight interface), 177-178
GetQuality method
 IDirect3DRMDevice interface, 111-112
 IDirect3DRMMeshBuilder interface, 214-215
GetRange method (IDirect3DRMLight interface), 178
GetRotation method (IDirect3DRMFrame interface), 148-149
GetScene method (IDirect3DRMFrame interface), 149
GetSceneBackground method (IDirect3DRMFrame interface), 149-150
GetSceneBackgroundDepth method (IDirect3DRMFrame interface), 150

GetSceneFogColor method
(IDirect3DRMFrame interface), 150-151
GetSceneFogEnable method
(IDirect3DRMFrame interface), 151
GetSceneFogMode method
(IDirect3DRMFrame interface), 151-152
GetSceneFogParams method
(IDirect3DRMFrame interface), 152
GetSearchPath method (IDirect3DRM
interface), 86-87
GetShades method
  IDirect3DRMDevice interface, 112
  IDirect3DRMTexture interface, 244
GetSize method (Array interfaces), 64
GetSortMode method (IDirect3DRMFrame
interface), 153
GetSpecular method
(IDirect3DRMMaterial interface), 187-188
GetStats method (IDirect3DDevice
interface), 338
GetTexture method
  IDirect3DRMFace interface, 125
  IDirect3DRMFrame interface, 153-154
GetTextureCoordinateIndex method
(IDirect3DRMFace interface), 126
GetTextureCoordinates method
  IDirect3DRMFace interface, 126-127
  IDirect3DRMMeshBuilder interface,
  215-216
GetTextureQuality method
(IDirect3DRMDevice interface), 112-113
GetTextureTopology method
  IDirect3DRMFace interface, 127
  IDirect3DRMFrame interface, 154
GetTransform method
(IDirect3DRMFrame interface), 155
GetTrianglesDrawn method
(IDirect3DRMDevice interface), 110-111
GetType method (IDirect3DRMLight
interface), 179

GetUmbra method (IDirect3DRMLight
interface), 179-180
GetUniformScaling method
(IDirect3DRMViewport interface),
258-259
GetVelocity method (IDirect3DRMFrame
interface), 155-156
GetVertex method (IDirect3DRMFace
interface), 127-128
GetVertexColor method
(IDirect3DRMMeshBuilder interface), 216
GetVertexCount method
  IDirect3DRMFace interface, 128
  IDirect3DRMMeshBuilder interface,
  216-217
GetVertexIndex method
(IDirect3DRMFace interface), 128-129
GetVertices method
  IDirect3DRMFace interface, 129-130
  IDirect3DRMMesh interface, 197
  IDirect3DRMMeshBuilder interface,
  217-218
GetViewport method (IDirect3DViewport
interface), 364
GetViewports method (IDirect3DRMDevice
interface), 113-114
GetVisuals method (IDirect3DRMFrame
interface), 156
GetWidth method
  IDirect3DRMDevice interface, 114
  IDirect3DRMViewport interface, 259
GetWireframeOptions method
(IDirect3DRMDevice interface), 114-115
GetX method (IDirect3DRMViewport
interface), 259-260
GetY method (IDirect3DRMViewport
interface), 260
GetZbufferMode method
(IDirect3DRMFrame interface), 156-157
Gouraud shading, 18

H

HAL (Hardware Abstraction Layer), 22, 30-32
HandleActivate method (IDirect3DRMwinDevice interface), 269
HandlePaint method (IDirect3DRMwinDevice interface), 270-271
Hardware Abstraction Layer (HAL), 22, 30-32
Hardware Emulation Layer (HEL), 22, 30-32
Header templates, 461
    reference guide, 463-464
headers
    binary format, 480-481
    DirectX file format, 456-457
HEL (Hardware Emulation Layer), 22, 30-32

I-J

IDirect3D interface methods, 323
    CreateLight, 323
    CreateMaterial, 324
    CreateViewport, 325
    EnumDevices, 325-326
    FindDevice, 326-327
    Initialize, 327-328
IDirect3DDevice interface methods, 328
    AddViewport, 328-329
    BeginScene, 329
    CreateExecuteBuffer, 330-331
    CreateMatrix, 331
    DeleteMatrix, 331-332
    DeleteViewport, 332
    EndScene, 333
    EnumTextureFormats, 333-334
    Execute, 334-335
    GetCaps, 335-336
    GetDirect3D, 336
    GetMatrix, 336-337
    GetPickRecords, 337-338
    GetStats, 338
    Initialize, 338-339
    NextViewport, 339-340
    Pick, 340-341
    SetMatrix, 341-342
    SwapTextureHandles, 342-343
IDirect3DExecuteBuffer interface methods, 343
    GetExecuteBuffer, 343-344
    Initialize, 344-345
    Lock, 345-346
    Optimize, 346
    SetExecuteData, 346-347
    Unlock, 347-348
    Validate, 348-349
IDirect3DLight interface methods, 349
    GetLight, 349
    Initialize, 350
    SetLight, 350-351
IDirect3DMaterial interface methods, 351
    GetHandle, 351-352
    GetMaterial, 352
    Initialize, 353
    Reserve, 353
    SetMaterial, 354
    Unreserve, 354-355
IDirect3DRM interface methods, 67-68
    AddSearchPath, 68
    CreateAnimation, 68-69
    CreateAnimationSet, 69
    CreateDevice, 69
    CreateDeviceFromClipper, 70-71
    CreateDeviceFromD3D, 71-72
    CreateDeviceFromSurface, 73-74
    CreateFace, 74
    CreateFrame, 75
    CreateLight, 75-76

CreateLightRGB, 76-77
CreateMaterial, 77
CreateMesh, 78
CreateMeshBuilder, 78
CreateObject, 79
CreateShadow, 80-81
CreateTexture, 81
CreateUserVisual, 82-83
CreateViewport, 83
CreateWrap, 84-85
EnumerateObjects, 85
GetDevices, 85-86
GetNamedObject, 86
GetSearchPath, 86-87
Load, 87-89
LoadTexture, 90
LoadTextureFromResource, 90-91
SetDefaultTextureColors, 91
SetDefaultTextureShades, 92
SetSearchPath, 93
Tick, 93-95

IDirect3DRMAnimation interface methods, 95
AddPositionKey, 95-96
AddRotateKey, 97
AddScaleKey, 97-98
DeleteKey, 98-99
GetOptions, 99
SetFrame, 99-100
SetOptions, 100-101
SetTime, 101-102

IDirect3DRMAnimationSet interface methods, 102
AddAnimation, 102
DeleteAnimation, 103
Load, 103-105
SetTime, 105-106

IDirect3DRMDevice interface methods, 106
AddUpdateCallback, 107
DeleteUpdateCallback, 107-108
GetBufferCount, 108

GetColorModel, 108-109
GetDirect3DDevice, 109
GetDither, 110
GetHeight, 110
GetQuality, 111-112
GetShades, 112
GetTextureQuality, 112-113
GetTrianglesDrawn, 110-111
GetViewports, 113-114
GetWidth, 114
GetWireframeOptions, 114-115
Init, 115
InitFromClipper, 115-116
InitFromD3D, 116-117
SetBufferCount, 117
SetDither, 117
SetShades, 119
SetTextureQuality, 119-120
Update, 120-122

IDirect3DRMFace interface methods, 122-123
AddVertex, 123
AddVertexAndNormalIndexed, 123-124
GetColor, 124
GetMaterial, 124-125
GetNormal, 125
GetTexture, 125
GetTextureCoordinateIndex, 126
GetTextureCoordinates, 126-127
GetTextureTopology, 127
GetVertex, 127-128
GetVertexCount, 128
GetVertexIndex, 128-129
GetVertices, 129-130
SetColor, 130
SetColorRGB, 131
SetMaterial, 131
SetTexture, 132
SetTextureCoordinates, 132-133
SetTextureTopology, 133

IDirect3DRMFrame interface methods, 135-136
   AddChild, 136-137
   AddLight, 137
   AddMoveCallback, 137-138
   AddRotation, 138-139
   AddScale, 139-140
   AddTransform, 140
   AddTranslation, 140-141
   AddVisual, 141-142
   DeleteChild, 142
   DeleteLight, 142-143
   DeleteMoveCallback, 143
   DeleteVisual, 143-144
   GetChildren, 144
   GetColor, 145
   GetLights, 145
   GetMaterialMode, 146
   GetOrientation, 146-147
   GetParent, 147
   GetPosition, 148
   GetRotation, 148-149
   GetScene, 149
   GetSceneBackground, 149-150
   GetSceneBackgroundDepth, 150
   GetSceneFogColor, 150-151
   GetSceneFogEnable, 151
   GetSceneFogMode, 151-152
   GetSceneFogParams, 152
   GetSortMode, 153
   GetTexture, 153-154
   GetTextureTopology, 154
   GetTransform, 155
   GetVelocity, 155-156
   GetVisuals, 156
   GetZbufferMode, 156-157
   InverseTransform, 157
   Load, 158-159
   LookAt, 159-160
   Move, 160-161
   SetColor, 161
   SetColorRGB, 161-162
   SetMaterialMode, 162-163
   SetOrientation, 163
   SetPosition, 164
   SetRotation, 164-165
   SetSceneBackground, 165
   SetSceneBackgroundDepth, 165-166
   SetSceneBackgroundImage, 166-167
   SetSceneBackgroundRGB, 167
   SetSceneFogColor, 168
   SetSceneFogEnable, 168
   SetSceneFogMode, 169
   SetSceneFogParams, 169-170
   SetSortMode, 170
   SetTexture, 170-171
   SetTextureTopology, 171
   SetVelocity, 172
   SetZbufferMode, 172-173
   Transform, 173-174

IDirect3DRMLight interface methods, 174
   GetColor, 174-175
   GetConstantAttenuation, 175
   GetEnableFrame, 176
   GetLinearAttenuation, 176-177
   GetPenumbra, 177
   GetQuadraticAttenuation, 177-178
   GetRange, 178
   GetType, 179
   GetUmbra, 179-180
   SetColor, 180
   SetColorRGB, 180-181
   SetConstantAttenuation, 181
   SetEnableFrame, 182
   SetLinearAttenuation, 182-183
   SetPenumbra, 183
   SetQuadraticAttenuation, 183-184
   SetRange, 184
   SetUmbra, 185-186

IDirect3DRMMaterial interface methods, 186
   GetEmissive, 186-187
   GetPower, 187
   GetSpecular, 187-188
   SetEmissive, 188
   SetPower, 189
   SetSpecular, 189-190

IDirect3DRMMesh interface methods, 190
   AddGroup, 191
   GetBox, 192
   GetGroup, 192-193
   GetGroupColor, 193
   GetGroupCount, 194
   GetGroupMapping, 194-195
   GetGroupMaterial, 195
   GetGroupQuality, 196
   GetGroupTexture, 196
   GetVertices, 197
   Scale, 198
   SetGroupColor, 198-199
   SetGroupColorRGB, 199
   SetGroupMapping, 199-200
   SetGroupMaterial, 200-201
   SetGroupQuality, 201
   SetGroupTexture, 201-202
   SetVertices, 202
   Translate, 203-204

IDirect3DRMMeshBuilder interface methods, 204-205
   AddFace, 205
   AddFaces, 205-207
   AddFrame, 207
   AddMesh, 207-208
   AddMeshBuilder, 208
   AddNormal, 208-209
   AddVertex, 209
   CreateFace, 210
   CreateMesh, 210-211
   GenerateNormals, 211
   GetBox, 211-212
   GetColorSource, 212
   GetFaceCount, 212-213
   GetFaces, 213
   GetPerspective, 214
   GetQuality, 214-215
   GetTextureCoordinates, 215-216
   GetVertexColor, 216
   GetVertexCount, 216-217
   GetVertices, 217-218
   Load, 218-220
   ReserveSpace, 220
   Save, 221
   Scale, 221
   SetColor, 222
   SetColorRGB, 222-223
   SetColorSource, 223
   SetMaterial, 224
   SetNormal, 224
   SetPerspective, 225
   SetQuality, 225-226
   SetTexture, 226
   SetTextureCoordinates, 227
   SetTextureTopology, 227-228
   SetVertex, 228
   SetVertexColor, 229
   SetVertexColorRGB, 229-230
   Translate, 230-231

IDirect3DRMObject interface methods, 231
   AddDestroyCallback, 231-232
   Clone, 232-233
   DeleteDestroyCallback, 233
   GetAppData, 233-234
   GetClassName, 234
   GetName, 235
   SetAppData, 235-236
   SetName, 236-237

IDirect3DRMShadow interface, Init method, 237-239

IDirect3DRMTexture interface methods, 239
- Changed, 239-240
- GetColors, 240
- GetDecalOrigin, 241
- GetDecalScale, 241
- GetDecalSize, 242
- GetDecalTransparency, 242
- GetDecalTransparentColor, 243
- GetImage, 243
- GetShades, 244
- InitFromFile, 244-245
- InitFromResource, 245
- InitFromSurface, 245-246
- SetColors, 246
- SetDecalOrigin, 247
- SetDecalScale, 247
- SetDecalSize, 248
- SetDecalTransparency, 248
- SetDecalTransparentColor, 249
- SetShades, 249-250

IDirect3DRMUserVisual interface, Init method, 250-251

IDirect3DRMViewport interface methods, 251
- Clear, 252
- Configure, 252
- ForceUpdate, 253
- GetBack, 253-254
- GetCamera, 254
- GetDevice, 254-255
- GetDirect3DViewport, 255
- GetField, 255-256
- GetFront, 256
- GetHeight, 256-257
- GetPlane, 257
- GetProjection, 258
- GetUniformScaling, 258-259
- GetWidth, 259
- GetX, 259-260
- GetY, 260
- Init, 260-261
- InverseTransform, 261
- Pick, 262
- Render, 262-263
- SetBack, 263
- SetCamera, 263
- SetField, 264
- SetFront, 264-265
- SetPlane, 265
- SetProjection, 266
- SetUniformScaling, 266-267
- Transform, 267-269

IDirect3DRMwinDevice interface methods, 269
- HandleActivate, 269
- HandlePaint, 270-271

IDirect3DRMWrap interface methods, 271
- Apply, 271
- ApplyRelative, 272
- Init, 272-273

IDirect3DTexture interface methods, 355
- GetHandle, 355-356
- Initialize, 356
- Load, 357
- PaletteChanged, 357-358
- Unload, 358-359

IDirect3DViewport interface methods, 359-360
- AddLight, 360
- Clear, 360-361
- DeleteLight, 361-362
- GetBackground, 362-363
- GetBackgroundDepth, 363-364
- GetViewport, 364
- Initialize, 365
- LightElements, 365-366
- NextLight, 366-367

SetBackground, 367
SetBackgroundDepth, 367-368
SetViewport, 368-369
TransformVertices, 369-370
image bitmaps, coordinate systems, 4
Immediate-Mode
  API, 29-32
  callbacks
    D3DENUMDEVICESCALLBACK, 319-320
    D3DENUMTEXTUREFORMATSCALLBACK, 320-321
    D3DVALIDATECALLBACK, 321-323
  data types, return values, 449-451
  enumerated types
    D3DBLEND, 425-427
    D3DCMPFUNC, 427-428
    D3DCOLORMODEL, 428-429
    D3DCULL, 429
    D3DFILLMODE, 429-430
    D3DFOGMODE, 430-431
    D3DLIGHTSTATETYPE, 431-433
    D3DLIGHTTYPE, 433
    D3DOPCODE, 434-436
    D3DRENDERSTATETYPE, 436-442
    D3DSHADEMODE, 442-443
    D3DTEXTUREADDRESS, 443-444
    D3DTEXTUREBLEND, 444-445
    D3DTEXTUREFILTER, 445-446
    D3DTRANSFORMSTATETYPE, 446-448
  macros
    D3DDivide, 308
    D3DMultiply, 308
    D3DRGB, 308-309
    D3DRGBA, 309-310
    D3DSTATE_OVERRIDE, 310
    D3DVAL, 311
    D3DVALP, 311
    RGB_GETBLUE, 312
    RGB_GETGREEN, 312
    RGB_GETRED, 313
    RGB_MAKE, 313-314
    RGB_TORGBA, 314
    RGBA_GETALPHA, 315
    RGBA_GETBLUE, 315
    RGBA_GETGREEN, 316
    RGBA_GETRED, 316
    RGBA_MAKE, 317
    RGBA_SETALPHA, 317-318
    RGBA_TORGB, 318-319
  structures
    D3DBRANCH, 371-372
    D3DCOLORVALUE, 372-373
    D3DDEVICEDESC, 373-375
    D3DEXECUTEBUFFERDESC, 376-377
    D3DEXECUTEDATA, 377-378
    D3DFINDDEVICERESULT, 378
    D3DFINDDEVICESEARCH, 379-382
    D3DHVERTEX, 382-383
    D3DINSTRUCTION, 383
    D3DLIGHT, 384-385
    D3DLIGHTDATA, 385-386
    D3DLIGHTINGCAPS, 386-387
    D3DLIGHTINGELEMENT, 387-388
    D3DLINE, 388
    D3DLINEPATTERN, 388-389
    D3DLVERTEX, 389-390
    D3DMATERIAL, 390-392
    D3DMATRIX, 392
    D3DMATRIXLOAD, 392-393
    D3DMATRIXMULTIPLY, 393
    D3DPICKRECORD, 394
    D3DPOINT, 394-395
    D3DPRIMCAPS, 395-403
    D3DPROCESSVERTICES, 404-405
    D3DRECT, 405-406
    D3DSPAN, 406
    D3DSTATE, 406-407
    D3DSTATS, 407-408

D3DSTATUS, 408-411
D3DTEXTURELOAD, 411
D3DTLVERTEX, 412-413
D3DTRANSFORMCAPS, 413
D3DTRANSFORMDATA, 414-416
D3DTRIANGLE, 416-419
D3DVECTOR, 420
D3DVERTEX, 420-422
D3DVIEWPORT, 422-423
values, D3DVALUE, 448
IndexedColor template reference guide, 467-468
Init method
  IDirect3DRMDevice interface, 115
  IDirect3DRMShadow interface, 237-239
  IDirect3DRMUserVisual interface, 250-251
  IDirect3DRMViewport interface, 260-261
  IDirect3DRMWrap interface, 272-273
InitFromClipper method (IDirect3DRMDevice interface), 115-116
InitFromD3D method (IDirect3DRMDevice interface), 116-117
InitFromFile method (IDirect3DRMTexture interface), 244-245
InitFromResource method (IDirect3DRMTexture interface), 245
InitFromSurface method (IDirect3DRMTexture interface), 245-246
Initialize method
  IDirect3D interface, 327-328
  IDirect3DDevice interface, 338-339
  IDirect3DExecuteBuffer interface, 344-345
  IDirect3DLight interface, 350
  IDirect3DMaterial interface, 353
  IDirect3DTexture interface, 356
  IDirect3DViewport interface, 365
instances (DirectX file format), 461-463

interfaces
  Array, 63-67
    GetElement method, 64-65
    GetPick method, 65-67
    GetSize method, 64
  Hardware Abstraction Layer (HAL), 22, 30-32
  Hardware Emulation Layer (HEL), 22, 30-32
  IDirect3D
    CreateLight method, 323
    CreateMaterial method, 324
    CreateViewport method, 325
    EnumDevices method, 325-326
    FindDevice method, 326-327
    Initialize method, 327-328
  IDirect3DDevice
    AddViewport method, 328-329
    BeginScene method, 329
    CreateExecuteBuffer method, 330-331
    CreateMatrix method, 331
    DeleteMatrix method, 331-332
    DeleteViewport method, 332
    EndScene method, 333
    EnumTextureFormats method, 333-334
    Execute method, 334-335
    GetCaps method, 335-336
    GetDirect3D method, 336
    GetMatrix method, 336-337
    GetPickRecords method, 337-338
    GetStats method, 338
    Initialize method, 338-339
    NextViewport method, 339-340
    Pick method, 340-341
    SetMatrix method, 341-342
    SwapTextureHandles method, 342-343
  IDirect3DExecuteBuffer
    GetExecuteBuffer method, 343-344
    Initialize method, 344-345
    Lock method, 345-346
    Optimize method, 346

SetExecuteData method, 346-347
Unlock method, 347-348
Validate method, 348-349
IDirect3DLight
   GetLight method, 349
   Initialize method, 350
   SetLight method, 350-351
IDirect3DMaterial
   GetHandle method, 351-352
   GetMaterial method, 352
   Initialize method, 353
   Reserve method, 353
   SetMaterial method, 354
   Unreserve method, 354-355
IDirect3DRM, 67-95
   AddSearchPath method, 68
   CreateAnimation method, 68-69
   CreateAnimationSet method, 69
   CreateDevice method, 69
   CreateDeviceFromClipper method, 70-71
   CreateDeviceFromD3D method, 71-72
   CreateDeviceFromSurface method, 73-74
   CreateFace method, 74
   CreateFrame method, 75
   CreateLight method, 75-76
   CreateLightRGB method, 76-77
   CreateMaterial method, 77
   CreateMesh method, 78
   CreateMeshBuilder method, 78
   CreateObject method, 79
   CreateShadow method, 80-81
   CreateTexture method, 81
   CreateUserVisual method, 82-83
   CreateViewport method, 83
   CreateWrap method, 84-85
   EnumerateObjects method, 85
   GetDevices method, 85-86
   GetNamedObject method, 86
   GetSearchPath method, 86-87
   Load method, 87-89
   LoadTexture method, 90
   LoadTextureFromResource method, 90-91
   SetDefaultTextureColors method, 91
   SetDefaultTextureShades method, 92
   SetSearchPath method, 93
   Tick method, 93-95
IDirect3DRMAnimation, 95-102
   AddPositionKey method, 95-96, 98
   AddRotateKey method, 97
   AddScaleKey method, 97-98
   DeleteKey method, 98-99
   GetOptions method, 99
   SetFrame method, 99-100
   SetOptions method, 100-101
   SetTime method, 101-102
IDirect3DRMAnimationSet, 102
   AddAnimation method, 102
   DeleteAnimation method, 103
   Load method, 103-105
   SetTime method, 105-106
IDirect3DRMDevice, 106
   AddUpdateCallback method, 107
   DeleteUpdateCallback method, 107-108
   GetBufferCount method, 108
   GetColorModel method, 108-109
   GetDirect3DDevice method, 109
   GetDither method, 110
   GetHeight method, 110
   GetQuality method, 111-112
   GetShades method, 112
   GetTextureQuality method, 112-113
   GetTrianglesDrawn method, 110-111
   GetViewports method, 113-114
   GetWidth method, 114
   GetWireframeOptions method, 114-115
   Init method, 115
   InitFromClipper method, 115-116
   InitFromD3D method, 116-117

SetBufferCount method, 117
SetDither method, 117
SetShades method, 119
SetTextureQuality method, 119-120
Update method, 120-122
IDirect3DRMFace, 122-123
   AddVertex method, 123
   AddVertexAndNormalIndexed method, 123-124
   GetColor method, 124
   GetMaterial method, 124-125
   GetNormal method, 125
   GetTexture method, 125
   GetTextureCoordinateIndex method, 126
   GetTextureCoordinates method, 126-127
   GetTextureTopology method, 127
   GetVertex method, 127-128
   GetVertexCount method, 128
   GetVertexIndex method, 128-129
   GetVertices method, 129-130
   SetColor method, 130
   SetColorRGB method, 131
   SetMaterial method, 131
   SetTexture method, 132
   SetTextureCoordinates method, 132-133
   SetTextureTopology method, 133
IDirect3DRMFrame, 135-136
   AddChild method, 136-137
   AddLight method, 137
   AddMoveCallback method, 137-138
   AddRotation method, 138-139
   AddScale method, 139-140
   AddTransform method, 140
   AddTranslation method, 140-141
   AddVisual method, 141-142
   DeleteChild method, 142
   DeleteLight method, 142-143
   DeleteMoveCallback method, 143
   DeleteVisual method, 143-144
   GetChildren method, 144
   GetColor method, 145
   GetLights method, 145
   GetMaterialMode method, 146
   GetOrientation method, 146-147
   GetPosition method, 148
   GetRotation method, 148-149
   GetScene method, 149
   GetSceneBackground method, 149-150
   GetSceneBackgroundDepth method, 150
   GetSceneFogColor method, 150-151
   GetSceneFogEnable method, 151
   GetSceneFogMode method, 151-152
   GetSceneFogParams method, 152
   GetSortMode method, 153
   GetTexture method, 153-154
   GetTextureTopology method, 154
   GetTransform method, 155
   GetVelocity method, 155-156
   GetVisuals method, 156
   GetZbufferMode method, 156-157
   InverseTransform method, 157
   Load method, 158-159
   LookAt method, 159-160
   Move method, 160-161
   SetColor method, 161
   SetColorRGB method, 161-162
   SetMaterialMode method, 162-163
   SetOrientation method, 163
   SetPosition method, 164
   SetRotation method, 164-165
   SetSceneBackground method, 165
   SetSceneBackgroundDepth method, 165-166
   SetSceneBackgroundImage method, 166-167
   SetSceneBackgroundRGB method, 167
   SetSceneFogColor method, 168
   SetSceneFogEnable method, 168
   SetSceneFogMode method, 169
   SetSceneFogParams method, 169-170

SetSortMode method, 170
SetTexture method, 170-171
SetTextureTopology method, 171
SetVelocity method, 172
SetZbufferMode method, 172-173
Transform method, 173-174
IDirect3DRMLight, 174
  GetColor method, 174-175
  GetConstantAttenuation method, 175
  GetEnableFrame method, 176
  GetLinearAttenuation method, 176-177
  GetPenumbra method, 177
  GetQuadraticAttenuation method, 177-178
  GetRange method, 178
  GetType method, 179
  GetUmbra method, 179-180
  SetColor method, 180
  SetColorRGB method, 180-181
  SetConstantAttenuation method, 181
  SetEnableFrame method, 182
  SetLinearAttenuation method, 182-183
  SetPenumbra method, 183
  SetQuadraticAttenuation method, 183-184
  SetRange method, 184
  SetUmbra method, 185-186
IDirect3DRMMaterial, 186
  GetEmissive method, 186-187
  GetPower method, 187
  GetSpecular method, 187-188
  SetEmissive method, 188
  SetPower method, 189
  SetSpecular method, 189-190
IDirect3DRMMesh, 190
  AddGroup method, 191
  GetBox method, 192
  GetGroup method, 192-193
  GetGroupColor method, 193
  GetGroupCount method, 194

GetGroupMapping method, 194-195
GetGroupMaterial method, 195
GetGroupQuality method, 196
GetGroupTexture method, 196
GetVertices method, 197
Scale method, 198
SetGroupColor method, 198-199
SetGroupColorRGB method, 199
SetGroupMapping method, 199-200
SetGroupMaterial method, 200-201
SetGroupQuality method, 201
SetGroupTexture method, 201-202
SetVertices method, 202
Translate method, 203-204
IDirect3DRMMeshBuilder, 204-205
  AddFace method, 205
  AddFaces method, 205-207
  AddFrame method, 207
  AddMesh method, 207-208
  AddMeshBuilder method, 208
  AddNormal method, 208-209
  AddVertex method, 209
  CreateFace method, 210
  CreateMesh method, 210-211
  GenerateNormals method, 211
  GetBox method, 211-212
  GetColorSource method, 212
  GetFaceCount method, 212-213
  GetFaces method, 213
  GetPerspective method, 214
  GetQuality method, 214-215
  GetTextureCoordinates method, 215-216
  GetVertexColor method, 216
  GetVertexCount method, 216-217
  GetVertices method, 217-218
  Load method, 218-220
  ReserveSpace method, 220
  Save method, 221
  Scale method, 221
  SetColor method, 222

SetColorRGB method, 222-223
SetColorSource method, 223
SetMaterial method, 224
SetNormal method, 224
SetPerspective method, 225
SetQuality method, 225-226
SetTexture method, 226
SetTextureCoordinates method, 227
SetTextureTopology method, 227-228
SetVertex method, 228
SetVertexColor method, 229
SetVertexColorRGB method, 229-230
Translate method, 230-231
IDirect3DRMObject, 231
   AddDestroyCallback method, 231-232
   Clone method, 232-233
   DeleteDestroyCallback method, 233
   GetAppData method, 233-234
   GetClassName method, 234
   GetName method, 235
   SetAppData method, 235-236
   SetName method, 236-237
IDirect3DRMShadow, 237
   Init method, 237-239
IDirect3DRMTexture, 239
   Changed method, 239-240
   GetColors method, 240
   GetDecalOrigin method, 241
   GetDecalScale method, 241
   GetDecalSize method, 242
   GetDecalTransparency method, 242
   GetDecalTransparentColor method, 243
   GetImage method, 243
   GetShades method, 244
   InitFromFile method, 244-245
   InitFromResource method, 245
   InitFromSurface method, 245-246
   SetColors method, 246
   SetDecalOrigin method, 247

   SetDecalScale method, 247
   SetDecalSize method, 248
   SetDecalTransparency method, 248
   SetDecalTransparentColor method, 249
   SetShades method, 249-250
IDirect3DRMUserVisual, 250
   Init method, 250-251
IDirect3DRMViewport, 251
   Clear method, 252
   Configure method, 252
   ForceUpdate method, 253
   GetBack method, 253-254
   GetCamera method, 254
   GetDevice method, 254-255
   GetDirect3DViewport method, 255
   GetField method, 255-256
   GetFront method, 256
   GetHeight method, 256-257
   GetPlane method, 257
   GetProjection method, 258
   GetUniformScaling method, 258-259
   GetWidth method, 259
   GetX method, 259-260
   GetY method, 260
   Init method, 260-261
   InverseTransform method, 261
   Pick method, 262
   Render method, 262-263
   SetBack method, 263
   SetCamera method, 263
   SetField method, 264
   SetFront method, 264-265
   SetPlane method, 265
   SetProjection method, 266
   SetUniformScaling method, 266-267
   Transform method, 267-269
IDirect3DRMwinDevice, 269
   HandleActivate method, 269
   HandlePaint method, 270-271

IDirect3DRMWrap, 271
   Apply method, 271
   ApplyRelative method, 272
   Init method, 272-273
IDirect3DTexture
   GetHandle method, 355-356
   Initialize method, 356
   Load method, 357
   PaletteChanged method, 357-358
   Unload method, 358-359
IDirect3DViewport
   AddLight method, 360
   Clear method, 360-361
   DeleteLight method, 361-362
   GetBackground method, 362-363
   GetBackgroundDepth method, 363-364
   GetViewport method, 364
   Initialize method, 365
   LightElements method, 365-366
   NextLight method, 366-367
   SetBackground method, 367
   SetBackgroundDepth method, 367-368
   SetViewport method, 368-369
   TransformVertices method, 369-370
Immediate-Mode API, 29-32
IUnknown, 37
   AddRef method, 37-38
   CoCreateInstance method, 39-40
   CoInitialize method, 40-41
   CoUninitialize method, 41-42
   QueryInterface method, 38
   Release method, 38-39
Retained-Mode API, 29-32
Intermediate-Mode objects
IDirect3D, 323-328
IDirect3DDevice, 328-343
IDirect3DExecuteBuffer, 343-349
IDirect3DLight, 349-351
IDirect3DMaterial, 351-355

IDirect3DTexture, 355-359
IDirect3DViewport, 359-370
InverseTransform method
IDirect3DRMFrame interface, 157
IDirect3DRMViewport interface, 261
IUnknown interface methods, 37
AddRef, 37-38
CoCreateInstance, 39-40
CoInitialize, 40-41
CoUninitialize, 41-42
QueryInterface, 38
Release, 38-39

K-L

key-frame animation, 19

left-handed coordinate systems, 4
light types
   defining, 287-288
   values, defining, 433
LightElements method (IDirect3DViewport interface), 365-366
Lighting Module (rendering engine), 31-32
lighting module states, defining values, 431-433
lights, 10-12
   ambient light, 11
   attenuation, 12
   directional light, 11
   parallel point light, 11-12
   point light, 11
   range, 12
   spot light, 12
lines, 7
Load method
   IDirect3DRM interface, 87-89
   IDirect3DRMAnimationSet interface, 103-105
   IDirect3DRMFrame interface, 158-159

IDirect3DRMMeshBuilder interface, 218-220
IDirect3DTexture interface, 357
loading
   IDirect3DRMObject objects, 87-89
   objects, 297-299
   textures, 90
      from resources, 90-91
LoadTexture method (IDirect3DRM interface), 90
LoadTextureFromResource method (IDirect3DRM interface), 90-91
Lock method (IDirect3DExecuteBuffer interface), 345-346
LookAt method (IDirect3DRMFrame interface), 159-160

M

macros (Immediate-Mode)
   D3DDivide, 308
   D3DMultiply, 308
   D3DRGB, 308-309
   D3DRGBA, 309-310
   D3DSTATE_OVERRIDE, 310
   D3DVAL, 311
   D3DVALP, 311
   RGB_GETBLUE, 312
   RGB_GETGREEN, 312
   RGB_GETRED, 313
   RGB_MAKE, 313-314
   RGB_TORGBA, 314
   RGBA_GETALPHA, 315
   RGBA_GETBLUE, 315
   RGBA_GETGREEN, 316
   RGBA_GETRED, 316
   RGBA_MAKE, 317
   RGBA_SETALPHA, 317-318
   RGBA_TORGB, 318-319

Magic Number field (header elements), 457
magnitude (vectors), 8
Material template reference guide, 469-470
materials (reflected light), 10
Matrix4×4 template reference guide, 466
mesh groups, texture mapping, 299-300
Mesh template reference guide, 474-475
meshes, 6, 9
MeshFace template reference guide, 470-471
MeshFaceWraps template reference guide, 471
MeshMaterialList template reference guide, 473-474
MeshNormals template reference guide, 472-473
MeshTextureCoords template reference guide, 472
MeshVertexColors template reference guide, 473
methods
   AddAnimation (IDirect3DRMAnimationSet interface), 102
   AddChild (IDirect3DRMFrame interface), 136-137
   AddDestroyCallback (IDirect3DRMObject interface), 231-232
   AddFace (IDirect3DRMMeshBuilder interface), 205
   AddFaces (IDirect3DRMMeshBuilder interface), 205-207
   AddFrame (IDirect3DRMMeshBuilder interface), 207
   AddGroup (IDirect3DRMMesh interface), 191
   AddLight
      IDirect3DRMFrame interface, 137
      IDirect3DViewport interface, 360

Index—**methods** 513

AddMesh (IDirect3DRMMeshBuilder interface), 207-208
AddMeshBuilder (IDirect3DRMMeshBuilder interface), 208
AddMoveCallback (IDirect3DRMFrame interface), 137-138
AddNormal (IDirect3DRMMeshBuilder interface), 208-209
AddPositionKey (IDirect3DRMAnimation interface), 95-96, 98
AddRotateKey (IDirect3DRMAnimation interface), 97
AddRotation (IDirect3DRMFrame interface), 138-139
AddScale (IDirect3DRMFrame interface), 139-140
AddScaleKey (IDirect3DRMAnimation interface), 97-98
AddSearchPath (IDirect3DRM interface), 68
AddTransform (IDirect3DRMFrame interface), 140
AddTranslation (IDirect3DRMFrame interface), 140-141
AddUpdateCallback (IDirect3DRMDevice interface), 107
AddVertex
　IDirect3DRMFace interface, 123
　IDirect3DRMMeshBuilder interface, 209
AddVertexAndNormalIndexed (IDirect3DRMFace interface), 123-124
AddViewport (IDirect3DDevice interface), 328-329
AddVisual (IDirect3DRMFrame interface), 141-142
Apply (IDirect3DRMWrap interface), 271
ApplyRelative (IDirect3DRMWrap interface), 272

BeginScene (IDirect3DDevice interface), 329
Changed (IDirect3DRMTexture interface), 239-240
Clear
　IDirect3DRMViewport interface, 252
　IDirect3DViewport, 360-361
Clone (IDirect3DRMObject interface), 232-233
Component Object Model (COM), 37-42
　AddRef, 37-38
　CoCreateInstance, 39-40
　CoInitialize, 40-41
　CoUninitialize, 41-42
　QueryInterface, 38
　Release, 38-39
Configure (IDirect3DRMViewport interface), 252
CreateAnimation (IDirect3DRM interface), 68-69
CreateAnimationSet (IDirect3DRM interface), 69
CreateDevice (IDirect3DRM interface), 69
CreateDeviceFromClipper (IDirect3DRM interface), 70-71
CreateDeviceFromD3D (IDirect3DRM interface), 71-72
CreateDeviceFromSurface (IDirect3DRM interface), 73-74
CreateExecuteBuffer (IDirect3DDevice), 330-331
CreateFace
　IDirect3DRM interface, 74
　IDirect3DRMMeshBuilder interface, 210
CreateFrame (IDirect3DRM interface), 75
CreateLight
　IDirect3D interface, 323
　IDirect3DRM interface, 75-76

CreateLightRGB (IDirect3DRM interface), 76-77
CreateMaterial
  IDirect3D interface, 324
  IDirect3DRM interface, 77
CreateMatrix (IDirect3DDevice interface), 331
CreateMesh
  IDirect3DRM interface, 78
  IDirect3DRMMeshBuilder interface, 210-211
CreateMeshBuilder (IDirect3DRM interface), 78
CreateObject (IDirect3DRM interface), 79
CreateShadow (IDirect3DRM interface), 80-81
CreateTexture (IDirect3DRM interface), 81
CreateUserVisual (IDirect3DRM interface), 82-83
CreateViewport
  IDirect3D interface, 325
  IDirect3DRM interface, 83
CreateWrap (IDirect3DRM interface), 84-85
DeleteAnimation (IDirect3DRMAnimationSet interface), 103
DeleteChild (IDirect3DRMFrame interface), 142
DeleteDestroyCallback (IDirect3DRMObject interface), 233
DeleteKey (IDirect3DRMAnimation interface), 98-99
DeleteLight
  IDirect3DRMFrame interface, 142-143
  IDirect3DViewport interface, 361-362
DeleteMatrix (IDirect3DDevice interface), 331-332
DeleteMoveCallback (IDirect3DRMFrame interface), 143

DeleteUpdateCallback (IDirect3DRMDevice interface), 107-108
DeleteViewport (IDirect3DDevice interface), 332
DeleteVisual (IDirect3DRMFrame interface), 143-144
EndScene (IDirect3DDevice interface), 333
EnumDevices (IDirect3D interface), 325-326
EnumerateObjects (IDirect3DRM interface), 85
EnumTextureFormats (IDirect3DDevice interface), 333-334
Execute (IDirect3DDevice interface), 334-335
FindDevice (IDirect3D interface), 326-327
ForceUpdate (IDirect3DRMViewport interface), 253
GenerateNormals (IDirect3DRMMeshBuilder interface), 211
GetAppData (IDirect3DRMObject interface), 233-234
GetBack (IDirect3DRMViewport interface), 253-254
GetBackground (IDirect3DViewport interface), 362-363
GetBackgroundDepth (IDirect3DViewport interface), 363-364
GetBox
  IDirect3DRMMesh interface, 192
  IDirect3DRMMeshBuilder interface, 211-212
GetBufferCount (IDirect3DRMDevice interface), 108
GetCamera (IDirect3DRMViewport interface), 254
GetCaps (IDirect3DDevice interface), 335-336
GetChildren (IDirect3DRMFrame interface), 144

GetClassName (IDirect3DRMObject interface), 234
GetColor
  IDirect3DRMFace interface, 124
  IDirect3DRMFrame interface, 145
  IDirect3DRMLight interface, 174-175
GetColorModel (IDirect3DRMDevice interface), 108-109
GetColors (IDirect3DRMTexture interface), 240
GetColorSource (IDirect3DRMMeshBuilder interface), 212
GetConstantAttenuation (IDirect3DRMLight interface), 175
GetDecalOrigin (IDirect3DRMTexture interface), 241
GetDecalScale (IDirect3DRMTexture interface), 241
GetDecalSize (IDirect3DRMTexture interface), 242
GetDecalTransparency (IDirect3DRMTexture interface), 242
GetDecalTransparentColor (IDirect3DRMTexture interface), 243
GetDevice (IDirect3DRMViewport interface), 254-255
GetDevices (IDirect3DRM interface), 85-86
GetDirect3D (IDirect3DDevice interface), 336
GetDirect3DDevice (IDirect3DRMDevice interface), 109
GetDirect3DViewport (IDirect3DRMViewport interface), 255
GetDither (IDirect3DRMDevice interface), 110
GetElement (Array interfaces), 64-65
GetEmissive (IDirect3DRMMaterial interface), 186-187

GetEnableFrame (IDirect3DRMLight interface), 176
GetExecuteBuffer (IDirect3DExecuteBuffer interface), 343-344
GetFaceCount (IDirect3DRMMeshBuilder interface), 212-213
GetFaces (IDirect3DRMMeshBuilder interface), 213
GetField (IDirect3DRMViewport interface), 255-256
GetFront (IDirect3DRMViewport interface), 256
GetGroup (IDirect3DRMMesh interface), 192-193
GetGroupColor (IDirect3DRMMesh interface), 193
GetGroupCount (IDirect3DRMMesh interface), 194
GetGroupMapping (IDirect3DRMMesh interface), 194-195
GetGroupMaterial (IDirect3DRMMesh interface), 195
GetGroupQuality (IDirect3DRMMesh interface), 196
GetGroupTexture (IDirect3DRMMesh interface), 196
GetHandle
  IDirect3DMaterial interface, 351-352
  IDirect3DTexture interface, 355-356
GetHeight
  IDirect3DRMDevice interface, 110
  IDirect3DRMViewport interface, 256-257
GetImage (IDirect3DRMTexture interface), 243
GetLight (IDirect3DLight interface), 349
GetLights (IDirect3DRMFrame interface), 145

GetLinearAttenuation (IDirect3DRMLight interface), 176-177
GetMaterial
IDirect3DMaterial interface, 352
IDirect3DRMFace interface, 124-125
GetMaterialMode (IDirect3DRMFrame interface), 146
GetMatrix (IDirect3DDevice interface), 336-337
GetName (IDirect3DRMObject interface), 235
GetNamedObject (IDirect3DRM interface), 86
GetNormal (IDirect3DRMFace interface), 125
GetOptions (IDirect3DRMAnimation interface), 99
GetOrientation (IDirect3DRMFrame interface), 146-147
GetParent (IDirect3DRMFrame interface), 147
GetPenumbra (IDirect3DRMLight interface), 177
GetPerspective (IDirect3DRMMeshBuilder interface), 214
GetPick (Array interfaces), 65-67
GetPickRecords (IDirect3DDevice), 337-338
GetPlane (IDirect3DRMViewport interface), 257
GetPosition (IDirect3DRMFrame interface), 148
GetPower (IDirect3DRMMaterial interface), 187
GetProjection (IDirect3DRMViewport interface), 258
GetQuadraticAttenuation (IDirect3DRMLight interface), 177-178
GetQuality
IDirect3DRMDevice interface, 111-112
IDirect3DRMMeshBuilder interface, 214-215
GetRange (IDirect3DRMLight interface), 178
GetRotation (IDirect3DRMFrame interface), 148-149
GetScene (IDirect3DRMFrame interface), 149
GetSceneBackground (IDirect3DRMFrame interface), 149-150
GetSceneBackgroundDepth (IDirect3DRMFrame interface), 150
GetSceneFogColor (IDirect3DRMFrame interface), 150-151
GetSceneFogEnable (IDirect3DRMFrame interface), 151
GetSceneFogMode (IDirect3DRMFrame interface), 151-152
GetSceneFogParams (IDirect3DRMFrame interface), 152
GetSearchPath (IDirect3DRM interface), 86-87
GetShades
IDirect3DRMDevice interface, 112
IDirect3DRMTexture interface, 244
GetSize (Array interfaces), 64
GetSortMode (IDirect3DRMFrame interface), 153
GetSpecular (IDirect3DRMMaterial interface), 187-188
GetStats (IDirect3DDevice interface), 338
GetTexture
IDirect3DRMFace interface, 125
IDirect3DRMFrame interface, 153-154
GetTextureCoordinateIndex (IDirect3DRMFace interface), 126

GetTextureCoordinates
  IDirect3DRMFace interface, 126-127
  IDirect3DRMMeshBuilder interface, 215-216
GetTextureQuality (IDirect3DRMDevice interface), 112-113
GetTextureTopology
  IDirect3DRMFace interface, 127
  IDirect3DRMFrame interface, 154
GetTransform (IDirect3DRMFrame interface), 155
GetTrianglesDrawn (IDirect3DRMDevice interface), 110-111
GetType (IDirect3DRMLight interface), 179
GetUmbra (IDirect3DRMLight interface), 179-180
GetUniformScaling (IDirect3DRMViewport interface), 258-259
GetVelocity (IDirect3DRMFrame interface), 155-156
GetVertex (IDirect3DRMFace interface), 127-128
GetVertexColor (IDirect3DRMMeshBuilder interface), 216
GetVertexCount
  IDirect3DRMFace interface, 128
  IDirect3DRMMeshBuilder interface, 216-217
GetVertexIndex (IDirect3DRMFace interface), 128-129
GetVertices
  IDirect3DRMFace interface, 129-130
  IDirect3DRMMesh interface, 197
  IDirect3DRMMeshBuilder interface, 217-218
GetViewport (IDirect3DViewport interface), 364
GetViewports (IDirect3DRMDevice interface), 113-114
GetVisuals (IDirect3DRMFrame interface), 156
GetWidth
  IDirect3DRMDevice interface, 114
  IDirect3DRMViewport interface, 259
GetWireframeOptions (IDirect3DRMDevice interface), 114-115
GetX (IDirect3DRMViewport interface), 259-260
GetY (IDirect3DRMViewport interface), 260
GetZbufferMode (IDirect3DRMFrame interface), 156-157
HandleActivate (IDirect3DRMwinDevice interface), 269
HandlePaint (IDirect3DRMwinDevice interface), 270-271
Init
  IDirect3DRMDevice interface, 115
  IDirect3DRMShadow interface, 237-239
  IDirect3DRMUserVisual interface, 250-251
  IDirect3DRMViewport interface, 260-261
  IDirect3DRMWrap interface, 272-273
InitFromClipper (IDirect3DRMDevice interface), 115-116
InitFromD3D (IDirect3DRMDevice interface), 116-117
InitFromFile (IDirect3DRMTexture interface), 244-245
InitFromResource (IDirect3DRMTexture interface), 245
InitFromSurface (IDirect3DRMTexture interface), 245-246

Initialize
  IDirect3D interface, 327-328
  IDirect3DDevice interface, 338-339
  IDirect3DExecuteBuffer interface, 344-345
  IDirect3DLight interface, 350
  IDirect3DMaterial interface, 353
  IDirect3DTexture interface, 356
  IDirect3DViewport interface, 365
InverseTransform
  IDirect3DRMFrame interface, 157
  IDirect3DRMViewport interface, 261
LightElements (IDirect3DViewport interface), 365-366
Load
  IDirect3DRM interface, 87-89
  IDirect3DRMAnimationSet interface, 103-105
  IDirect3DRMFrame interface, 158-159
  IDirect3DRMMeshBuilder interface, 218-220
  IDirect3DTexture interface, 357
LoadTexture (IDirect3DRM interface), 90
LoadTextureFromResource (IDirect3DRM interface), 90-91
Lock (IDirect3DExecuteBuffer interface), 345-346
LookAt (IDirect3DRMFrame interface), 159-160
Move (IDirect3DRMFrame interface), 160-161
NextLight (IDirect3DViewport interface), 366-367
NextViewport (IDirect3DDevice interface), 339-340
Optimize (IDirect3DExecuteBuffer interface), 346
PaletteChanged (IDirect3DTexture interface), 357-358

Pick
  IDirect3DDevice interface, 340-341
  IDirect3DRMViewport interface, 262
Render (IDirect3DRMViewport interface), 262-263
Reserve (IDirect3DMaterial interface), 353
ReserveSpace (IDirect3DRMMeshBuilder interface), 220
Save (IDirect3DRMMeshBuilder interface), 221
Scale
  IDirect3DRMMesh interface, 198
  IDirect3DRMMeshBuilder interface, 221
SetAppData (IDirect3DRMObject interface), 235-236
SetBack (IDirect3DRMViewport interface), 263
SetBackground (IDirect3DViewport interface), 367
SetBackgroundDepth (IDirect3DViewport interface), 367-368
SetBufferCount (IDirect3DRMDevice interface), 117
SetCamera (IDirect3DRMViewport interface), 263
SetColor
  IDirect3DRMFace interface, 130
  IDirect3DRMFrame interface, 161
  IDirect3DRMLight interface, 180
  IDirect3DRMMeshBuilder interface, 222
SetColorRGB
  IDirect3DRMFace interface, 131
  IDirect3DRMFrame interface, 161-162
  IDirect3DRMLight interface, 180-181
  IDirect3DRMMeshBuilder interface, 222-223
SetColors (IDirect3DRMTexture interface), 246

SetColorSource (IDirect3DRMMeshBuilder interface), 223
SetConstantAttenuation (IDirect3DRMLight interface), 181
SetDecalOrigin (IDirect3DRMTexture interface), 247
SetDecalScale (IDirect3DRMTexture interface), 247
SetDecalSize (IDirect3DRMTexture interface), 248
SetDecalTransparency (IDirect3DRMTexture interface), 248
SetDecalTransparentColor (IDirect3DRMTexture interface), 249
SetDefaultTextureColors (IDirect3DRM interface), 91
SetDefaultTextureShades (IDirect3DRM interface), 92
SetDither (IDirect3DRMDevice interface), 117
SetEmissive (IDirect3DRMMaterial interface), 188
SetEnableFrame (IDirect3DRMLight interface), 182
SetExecuteData (IDirect3DExecuteBuffer interface), 346-347
SetField (IDirect3DRMViewport interface), 264
SetFrame (IDirect3DRMAnimation interface), 99-100
SetFront (IDirect3DRMViewport interface), 264-265
SetGroupColor (IDirect3DRMMesh interface), 198-199
SetGroupColorRGB (IDirect3DRMMesh interface), 199
SetGroupMapping (IDirect3DRMMesh interface), 199-200

SetGroupMaterial (IDirect3DRMMesh interface), 200-201
SetGroupQuality (IDirect3DRMMesh interface), 201
SetGroupTexture (IDirect3DRMMesh interface), 201-202
SetLight (IDirect3DLight interface), 350-351
SetLinearAttenuation (IDirect3DRMLight interface), 182-183
SetMaterial
 IDirect3DMaterial interface, 354
 IDirect3DRMFace interface, 131
 IDirect3DRMMeshBuilder interface, 224
SetMaterialMode (IDirect3DRMFrame interface), 162-163
SetMatrix (IDirect3DDevice interface), 341-342
SetName (IDirect3DRMObject interface), 236-237
SetNormal (IDirect3DRMMeshBuilder interface), 224
SetOptions (IDirect3DRMAnimation interface), 100-101
SetOrientation (IDirect3DRMFrame interface), 163
SetPenumbra (IDirect3DRMLight interface), 183
SetPerspective (IDirect3DRMMeshBuilder interface), 225
SetPlane (IDirect3DRMViewport interface), 265
SetPosition (IDirect3DRMFrame interface), 164
SetPower (IDirect3DRMMaterial interface), 189
SetProjection (IDirect3DRMViewport interface), 266

SetQuadraticAttenuation (IDirect3DRMLight interface), 183-184
SetQuality (IDirect3DRMMeshBuilder interface), 225-226
SetRange (IDirect3DRMLight interface), 184
SetRotation (IDirect3DRMFrame interface), 164-165
SetSceneBackground (IDirect3DRMFrame interface), 165
SetSceneBackgroundDepth (IDirect3DRMFrame interface), 165-166
SetSceneBackgroundImage (IDirect3DRMFrame interface), 166-167
SetSceneBackgroundRGB (IDirect3DRMFrame interface), 167
SetSceneFogColor (IDirect3DRMFrame interface), 168
SetSceneFogEnable (IDirect3DRMFrame interface), 168
SetSceneFogMode (IDirect3DRMFrame interface), 169
SetSceneFogParams (IDirect3DRMFrame interface), 169-170
SetSearchPath (IDirect3DRM interface), 93
SetShades
  IDirect3DRMDevice interface, 119
  IDirect3DRMTexture interface, 249-250
SetSortMode (IDirect3DRMFrame interface), 170
SetSpecular (IDirect3DRMMaterial interface), 189-190
SetTexture
  IDirect3DRMFace interface, 132
  IDirect3DRMFrame interface, 170-171
  IDirect3DRMMeshBuilder interface, 226
SetTextureCoordinates
  IDirect3DRMFace interface, 132-133
  IDirect3DRMMeshBuilder interface, 227
SetTextureQuality (IDirect3DRMDevice interface), 119-120
SetTextureTopology
  IDirect3DRMFace interface, 133
  IDirect3DRMFrame interface, 171
  IDirect3DRMMeshBuilder interface, 227-228
SetTime
  IDirect3DRMAnimation interface, 101-102
  IDirect3DRMAnimationSet interface, 105-106
SetUmbra (IDirect3DRMLight interface), 185-186
SetUniformScaling (IDirect3DRMViewport interface), 266-267
SetVelocity (IDirect3DRMFrame interface), 172
SetVertex (IDirect3DRMMeshBuilder interface), 228
SetVertexColor (IDirect3DRMMeshBuilder interface), 229
SetVertexColorRGB (IDirect3DRMMeshBuilder interface), 229-230
SetVertices (IDirect3DRMMesh interface), 202
SetViewport (IDirect3DViewport interface), 368-369
SetZbufferMode (IDirect3DRMFrame interface), 172-173
SwapTextureHandles (IDirect3DDevice interface), 342-343
Tick (IDirect3DRM interface), 93-102
Transform
  IDirect3DRMFrame interface, 173-174
  IDirect3DRMViewport interface, 267-269

TransformVertices (IDirect3DViewport interface), 369-370
Translate
   IDirect3DRMMesh interface, 203-204
   IDirect3DRMMeshBuilder interface, 230-231
Unload (IDirect3DTexture interface), 358-359
Unlock
   (IDirect3DExecuteBuffer interface), 347-348
Unreserve (IDirect3DMaterial interface), 354-355
Update (IDirect3DRMDevice interface), 120-122
Validate (IDirect3DExecuteBuffer interface), 348-349

mipmapping, 13
Move method (IDirect3DRMFrame interface), 160-161
multi-dimensional arrays, 459
multiplying quaternions, 47

N

NextLight method (IDirect3DViewport interface), 366-367
NextViewport method (IDirect3DDevice interface), 339-340
normal vectors (normals), 8
normalizing vectors, 51

O

objects
   Animation
      adding to animation sets, 102
      deleting keys with specified time value, 98-99
      Frame object, setting, 99-100
      options, returning, 99
      position keys, 95-96, 98
      removing from animation set, 103
      rotation keys, 97
      scale keys, 97-98
      time, setting, 101-102
   array
      elements, retrieving, 64-65
      pick records, retrieving, 65-67
   collision computations, 52-53
   COM, 24-25
      accessing with C, 25
      creating instances, 39-40
      increasing reference counts, 37-38
      pointers, 38
   device, initializing, 116-117
   face, returning number of vertices, 128
   frame, combining transforms, 283-284
   IDirect3DRMAnimation, 68-69
   IDirect3DRMAnimationSet, 69
   IDirect3DRMDevice, 70-74
   IDirect3DRMDeviceArray, 85-86
   IDirect3DRMFace, 74
      colors, setting, 130-131
      material, setting, 131
      normal, adding, 123-124
      texture, setting, 132-133
      texture topology, retrieving, 127
      vectors, retrieving, 129-130
      vertex, adding, 123-124
   IDirect3DRMFrame, 75
   IDirect3DRMLight, 75-77
   IDirect3DRMMaterial, 77
      defined, 190-204
      retrieving, 124-125
   IDirect3DRMMesh, 78
   IDirect3DRMMeshBuilder, 78
   IDirect3DRMObject
      finding by name, 86
      loading, 87-89
   IDirect3DRMTexture, 81
      retrieving, 125

IDirect3DRMUserVisual, 82-83
IDirect3DRMViewport, 83
IDirect3DRMWrap, 84-85
loading, 297-299
material information, retrieving, 288
mesh, rendering quality, 290
mesh builder
    color sources, 283
    rendering quality, specifying, 290
reference counts, decreasing, 38-39
removing update callback functions, 107-108
Retained-Mode, 44
    enumerating, 85
Retained-Mode Device, 115-116
uninitialized objects, creating, 79
viewport, projection types, 289

objects (3D)
geometry, 5-9
    faces (polygons), 7
    lines, 7
    meshes, 9
    normal vectors (normals), 8
    vectors, 8
    vertices, 6
visual characteristics, 10-13
    lights, 10-12
    materials, 10
    textures, 12-14

opcodes
defining, 434-436
execute buffers, 32

open templates, 460
Optimize method (IDirect3DExecuteBuffer interfaces), 346
origins (coordinate systems), 6
orthographic (parallel) projection, 15
OSF's DCE standard, 485

P

painter's algorithm, 19
PaletteChanged method (IDirect3DTexture interface), 357-358
parallel (orthographic) projection, 15
parallel point lights, 11-12
perspective projection, 15
Phong shading, 18
Pick method
    IDirect3DDevice interface, 340-341
    IDirect3DRMViewport interface, 262
pick records, retrieving from picked objects, 65-67
point lights, 11
polygonal modeling, 5-6
polygons, 7
projection transform, defining values, 446-448

Q

Quaternion template reference guide, 465
quaternions
    computing from rotations, 46-47
    multiplying, 47
    rotation matrices, calculating, 46
    spherical linear interpolation, 48
QueryInterface method (IUnknown interface), 38

R

range (lights), 12
rasterization (rendering methods), 17-19
    backface culling, 19
    flat shading, 18
    Gouraud shading, 18
    painter's algorithm, 19
    Phong shading, 18

wireframe rendering, 17
z-buffering, 19
Rasterization Module (rendering engine), 32
record-bearing tokens, 483
    TOKEN_GUID, 485
    TOKEN_INTEGER, 485
    TOKEN_INTEGER_LIST, 486
    TOKEN_NAME, 484
    TOKEN_REALNUM_LIST, 486
    TOKEN_STRING, 484-485
Release method (IUnknown interface), 38-39
Render method (IDirect3DRMViewport interface), 262-263
render module states, defining values, 436-442
rendering engine, 30-32
    DirectDraw, 32
    execute buffers, 32
    Lighting Module, 31-32
    Rasterization Module, 32
    Transformation Module, 31
rendering methods, 17-19
    backface culling, 19
    flat shading, 18
    Gouraud shading, 18
    painter's algorithm, 19
    Phong shading, 18
    wireframe rendering, 17
    z-buffering, 19
Reserve method (IDirect3DMaterial interface), 353
reserved words (DirectX file format), 456
ReserveSpace method (IDirect3DRMMeshBuilder interface), 220
restricted templates, 460
restriction types (templates), 459-460
    closed, 460
    restricted, 460

Retained-Mode
  API, 29-32
  Array interfaces, 63-67
    GetElement method, 64-65
    GetPick method, 65-67
    GetSize method, 64
  callback functions, 56
    D3DRMDEVICEPALETTECALLBACK, 56-57
    D3DRMFRAMEMOVECALLBACK, 57
    D3DRMLOADCALLBACK, 58
    D3DRMLOADTEXTURECALLBACK, 58-59
    D3DRMOBJECTCALLBACK, 59-60
    D3DRMUPDATECALLBACK, 60
    D3DRMUSERVISUALCALLBACK, 61-62
    D3DRMWRAPCALLBACK, 62-63
  data types, return values, 303
  enumerated types
    D3DRCOLORSOURCE, 283
    D3DRMCOMBINETYPE, 283-284
    D3DRMFILLMODE, 284-285
    D3DRMFOGMODE, 285-286
    D3DRMFRAMECONTSRAINT, 286
    D3DRMLIGHTMODE, 287
    D3DRMLIGHTTYPE, 287-288
    D3DRMMATERIALMODE, 288
    D3DRMPALETTEFLAGS, 289
    D3DRMPROJECTIONTYPE, 289
    D3DRMRENDERQUALITY, 290
    D3DRMSHADEMODE, 291
    D3DRMSORTMODE, 292
    D3DRMTEXTUREQUALITY, 292-293
    D3DRMUSERVISUALREASON, 293-294
    D3DRMWRAPTYPE, 294
    D3DRMXOFFORMAT, 294-295
    D3DRMZBUFFERMODE, 295-296

functions, 43
- *D3DRMColorGetAlpha, 44-45*
- *D3DRMColorGetBlue, 44-45*
- *D3DRMColorGetGreen, 44-45*
- *D3DRMColorGetRed, 44-45*
- *D3DRMCreateColorRGB, 45*
- *D3DRMCreateColorRGBA, 45*
- *D3DRMMatrixFromQuaternion, 46*
- *D3DRMQuaternionFromRotation, 46-47*
- *D3DRMQuaternionMultiply, 47*
- *D3DRMQuaternionSlerp, 48*
- *D3DRMVectorAdd, 49*
- *D3DRMVectorCrossProduct, 49-50*
- *D3DRMVectorDotProduct, 50*
- *D3DRMVectorModulus, 51*
- *D3DRMVectorNormalize, 51*
- *D3DRMVectorRandom, 52*
- *D3DRMVectorReflect, 52-53*
- *D3DRMVectorRotate, 53*
- *D3DRMVectorScale, 54*
- *D3DRMVectorSubtract, 55-56*
- *Direct3DRMCreate, 44*

IDirect3DRM interface, 67-95
- *AddSearchPath method, 68*
- *CreateAnimation method, 68-69*
- *CreateAnimationSet method, 69*
- *CreateDevice method, 69*
- *CreateDeviceFromClipper method, 70-71*
- *CreateDeviceFromD3D method, 71-72*
- *CreateDeviceFromSurface method, 73-74*
- *CreateFace method, 74*
- *CreateFrame method, 75*
- *CreateLight method, 75-76*
- *CreateLightRGB method, 76-77*
- *CreateMaterial method, 77*
- *CreateMesh method, 78*
- *CreateMeshBuilder method, 78*
- *CreateObject method, 79*
- *CreateShadow method, 80-81*
- *CreateTexture method, 81*
- *CreateUserVisual method, 82-83*
- *CreateViewport method, 83*
- *CreateWrap method, 84-85*
- *EnumerateObjects method, 85*
- *GetDevices method, 85-86*
- *GetNamedObject method, 86*
- *GetSearchPath method, 86-87*
- *Load method, 87-89*
- *LoadTexture method, 90*
- *LoadTextureFromResource method, 90-91*
- *SetDefaultTextureColors method, 91*
- *SetDefaultTextureShades method, 92*
- *SetSearchPath method, 93*
- *Tick method, 93-95*

IDirect3DRMAnimation interface, 95-102
- *AddPositionKey method, 95-96, 98*
- *AddRotateKey method, 97*
- *AddScaleKey method, 97-98*
- *DeleteKey method, 98-99*
- *GetOptions method, 99*
- *SetFrame method, 99-100*
- *SetOptions method, 100-101*
- *SetTime method, 101-102*

IDirect3DRMAnimationSet interface, 102
- *AddAnimation method, 102*
- *DeleteAnimation method, 103*
- *Load method, 103-105*
- *SetTime method, 105-106*

IDirect3DRMDevice interface, 106
- *AddUpdateCallback method, 107*
- *DeleteUpdateCallback method, 107-108*
- *GetBufferCount method, 108*
- *GetColorModel method, 108-109*
- *GetDirect3DDevice method, 109*

GetDither method, 110
GetHeight method, 110
GetQuality method, 111-112
GetShades method, 112
GetTextureQuality method, 112-113
GetTrianglesDrawn method, 110-111
GetViewports method, 113-114
GetWidth method, 114
GetWireframeOptions method, 114-115
Init method, 115
InitFromClipper method, 115-116
InitFromD3D method, 116-117
SetBufferCount method, 117
SetDither method, 117
SetShades method, 119
SetTextureQuality method, 119-120
Update method, 120-122
IDirect3DRMFace interface, 122-123
  AddVertex method, 123
  AddVertexAndNormalIndexed method, 123-124
  GetColor method, 124
  GetMaterial method, 124-125
  GetNormal method, 125
  GetTexture method, 125
  GetTextureCoordinateIndex method, 126
  GetTextureCoordinates method, 126-127
  GetTextureTopology method, 127
  GetVertex method, 127-128
  GetVertexCount method, 128
  GetVertexIndex method, 128-129
  GetVertices method, 129-130
  SetColor method, 130
  SetColorRGB method, 131
  SetMaterial method, 131
  SetTexture method, 132
  SetTextureCoordinates method, 132-133
  SetTextureTopology method, 133

IDirect3DRMFrame interface, 135-136
  AddChild method, 136-137
  AddLight method, 137
  AddMoveCallback method, 137-138
  AddRotation method, 138-139
  AddScale method, 139-140
  AddTransform method, 140
  AddTranslation method, 140-141
  AddVisual method, 141-142
  DeleteChild method, 142
  DeleteLight method, 142-143
  DeleteMoveCallback method, 143
  DeleteVisual method, 143-144
  GetChildren method, 144
  GetColor method, 145
  GetLights method, 145
  GetMaterialMode method, 146
  GetOrientation method, 146-147
  GetParent method, 147
  GetPosition method, 148
  GetRotation method, 148-149
  GetScene method, 149
  GetSceneBackground method, 149-150
  GetSceneBackgroundDepth method, 150
  GetSceneFogColor method, 150-151
  GetSceneFogEnable method, 151
  GetSceneFogMode method, 151-152
  GetSceneFogParams method, 152
  GetSortMode method, 153
  GetTexture method, 153-154
  GetTextureTopology method, 154
  GetTransform method, 155
  GetVelocity method, 155-156
  GetVisuals method, 156
  GetZbufferMode method, 156-157
  InverseTransform method, 157
  Load method, 158-159
  LookAt method, 159-160

Move method, 160-161
SetColor method, 161
SetColorRGB method, 161-162
SetMaterialMode method, 162-163
SetOrientation method, 163
SetPosition method, 164
SetRotation method, 164-165
SetSceneBackground method, 165
SetSceneBackgroundDepth method, 165-166
SetSceneBackgroundImage method, 166-167
SetSceneBackgroundRGB method, 167
SetSceneFogColor method, 168
SetSceneFogEnable method, 168
SetSceneFogMode method, 169
SetSceneFogParams method, 169-170
SetSortMode method, 170
SetTexture method, 170-171
SetTextureTopology method, 171
SetVelocity method, 172
SetZbufferMode method, 172-173
Transform method, 173-174
IDirect3DRMLight interface, 174
  GetColor method, 174-175
  GetConstantAttenuation method, 175
  GetEnableFrame method, 176
  GetLinearAttenuation method, 176-177
  GetPenumbra method, 177
  GetQuadraticAttenuation method, 177-178
  GetRange method, 178
  GetType method, 179
  GetUmbra method, 179-180
  SetColor method, 180
  SetColorRGB method, 180-181
  SetConstantAttenuation method, 181
  SetEnableFrame method, 182
  SetLinearAttenuation method, 182-183
  SetPenumbra method, 183
  SetQuadraticAttenuation method, 183-184
  SetRange method, 184
  SetUmbra method, 185-186
IDirect3DRMMaterial interface, 186
  GetEmissive method, 186-187
  GetPower method, 187
  GetSpecular method, 187-188
  SetEmissive method, 188
  SetPower method, 189
  SetSpecular method, 189-190
IDirect3DRMMesh interface, 190
  AddGroup method, 191
  GetBox method, 192
  GetGroup method, 192-193
  GetGroupColor method, 193
  GetGroupCount method, 194
  GetGroupMapping method, 194-195
  GetGroupMaterial method, 195
  GetGroupQuality method, 196
  GetGroupTexture method, 196
  GetVertices method, 197
  Scale method, 198
  SetGroupColor method, 198-199
  SetGroupColorRGB method, 199
  SetGroupMapping method, 199-200
  SetGroupMaterial method, 200-201
  SetGroupQuality method, 201
  SetGroupTexture method, 201-202
  SetVertices method, 202
  Translate method, 203-204
IDirect3DRMMeshBuilder interface, 204-205
  AddFace method, 205
  AddFaces method, 205-207
  AddFrame method, 207
  AddMesh method, 207-208
  AddMeshBuilder method, 208

AddNormal method, 208-209
AddVertex method, 209
CreateFace method, 210
CreateMesh method, 210-211
GenerateNormals method, 211
GetBox method, 211-212
GetColorSource method, 212
GetFaceCount method, 212-213
GetFaces method, 213
GetPerspective method, 214
GetQuality method, 214-215
GetTextureCoordinates method, 215-216
GetVertexColor method, 216
GetVertexCount method, 216-217
GetVertices method, 217-218
Load method, 218-220
ReserveSpace method, 220
Save method, 221
Scale method, 221
SetColor method, 222
SetColorRGB method, 222-223
SetColorSource method, 223
SetMaterial method, 224
SetNormal method, 224
SetPerspective method, 225
SetQuality method, 225-226
SetTexture method, 226
SetTextureCoordinates method, 227
SetTextureTopology method, 227-228
SetVertex method, 228
SetVertexColor method, 229
SetVertexColorRGB method, 229-230
Translate method, 230-231
IDirect3DRMObject interface, 231
   AddDestroyCallback method, 231-232
   Clone method, 232-233
   DeleteDestroyCallback method, 233
   GetAppData method, 233-234
   GetClassName method, 234
   GetName method, 235
   SetAppData method, 235-236
   SetName method, 236-237
IDirect3DRMShadow interface, 237
   Init method, 237-239
IDirect3DRMTexture interface, 239
   Changed method, 239-240
   GetColors method, 240
   GetDecalOrigin method, 241
   GetDecalScale method, 241
   GetDecalSize method, 242
   GetDecalTransparency method, 242
   GetDecalTransparentColor method, 243
   GetImage method, 243
   GetShades method, 244
   InitFromFile method, 244-245
   InitFromResource method, 245
   InitFromSurface method, 245-246
   SetColors method, 246
   SetDecalOrigin method, 247
   SetDecalScale method, 247
   SetDecalSize method, 248
   SetDecalTransparency method, 248
   SetDecalTransparentColor method, 249
   SetShades method, 249-250
IDirect3DRMUserVisual interface, 250
   Init method, 250-251
IDirect3DRMViewport interface, 251
   Clear method, 252
   Configure method, 252
   ForceUpdate method, 253
   GetBack method, 253-254
   GetCamera method, 254
   GetDevice method, 254-255
   GetDirect3DViewport method, 255
   GetField method, 255-256
   GetFront method, 256
   GetHeight method, 256-257
   GetPlane method, 257

Index—Retained-Mode

GetProjection method, 258
GetUniformScaling method, 258-259
GetWidth method, 259
GetX method, 259-260
GetY method, 260
Init method, 260-261
InverseTransform method, 261
Pick method, 262
Render method, 262-263
SetBack method, 263
SetCamera method, 263
SetField method, 264
SetFront method, 264-265
SetPlane method, 265
SetProjection method, 266
SetUniformScaling method, 266-267
Transform method, 267-269
IDirect3DRMwinDevice interface, 269
   HandleActivate method, 269
   HandlePaint method, 270-271
IDirect3DRMWrap interface, 271
   Apply method, 271
   ApplyRelative method, 272
   Init method, 272-273
IUnknown interface
   AddRef method, 37-38
   CoCreateInstance method, 39-40
   CoInitialize method, 40-41
   CoUninitialize method, 41-42
   QueryInterface method, 38
   Release method, 38-39
structures
   D3DRMBOX, 275
   D3DRMIMAGE, 275-276
   D3DRMLOADMEMORY, 277
   D3DRMLOADRESOURCE, 277-278
   D3DRMPALETTEENTRY, 278-279
   D3DRMPICKDESC, 279-280
   D3DRMQUATERNION, 280
   D3DRMVECTOR4D, 280-281
   D3DRMVERTEX, 281
type definitions
   D3DRMANIMATIONOPTIONS, 296
   D3DRMCOLORMODEL, 297
   D3DRMLOADOPTIONS, 297-299
   D3DRMMAPPING, 299-300
   D3DRMMATRIX4D, 300
return values
   Immediate-Mode data type, 449-451
   Retained-Mode data type, 303
RGB colors
   creating from supplied color components, 45
   returning components, 44-45
RGB_GETBLUE macro (Immediate-Mode), 312
RGB_GETGREEN macro (Immediate-Mode), 312
RGB_GETRED macro (Immediate-Mode), 313
RGB_MAKE macro (Immediate-Mode), 313-314
RGB_TORGBA macro (Immediate-Mode), 314
RGBA_GETALPHA macro (Immediate-Mode), 315
RGBA_GETBLUE macro (Immediate-Mode), 315
RGBA_GETGREEN macro (Immediate-Mode), 316
RGBA_GETRED macro (Immediate-Mode), 316
RGBA_MAKE macro (Immediate-Mode), 317
RGBA_SETALPHA macro (Immediate-Mode), 317-318
RGBA_TORGB macro (Immediate-Mode), 318-319

right-handed coordinate systems, 4
rotating vectors, 53
rotation (geometric transformations), 15
rotation matrices, calculating for unit quaternions, 46

S

Save method (IDirect3DRMMeshBuilder interface), 221
scale (geometric transformations), 15
Scale method
   IDirect3DRMMesh interface, 198
   IDirect3DRMMeshBuilder interface, 221
scene hierarchy, 14
scenes (3D), 14-17
   converting to 2D representations, 16-17
   frames of reference, 14
   geometric transformations, 14-15
   rasterization, 17-19
      rendering methods, 17-19
   viewing volume, 15
search paths
   directories, adding, 68
   Retained-Mode, setting, 93
SetAppData method (IDirect3DRMObject interface), 235-236
SetBack method (IDirect3DRMViewport interface), 263
SetBackground method (IDirect3DViewport interface), 367
SetBackgroundDepth method (IDirect3DViewport interface), 367-368
SetBufferCount method (IDirect3DRMDevice interface), 117
SetCamera method (IDirect3DRMViewport interface), 263
SetColor method
   IDirect3DRMFace interface, 130
   IDirect3DRMFrame interface, 161
   IDirect3DRMLight interface, 180
   IDirect3DRMMeshBuilder interface, 222
SetColorRGB method
   IDirect3DRMFace interface, 131
   IDirect3DRMFrame interface, 161-162
   IDirect3DRMLight interface, 180-181
   IDirect3DRMMeshBuilder interface, 222-223
SetColors method (IDirect3DRMTexture interface), 246
SetColorSource method (IDirect3DRMMeshBuilder interface), 223
SetConstantAttenuation method (IDirect3DRMLight interface), 181
SetDecalOrigin method (IDirect3DRMTexture interface), 247
SetDecalScale method (IDirect3DRMTexture interface), 247
SetDecalSize method (IDirect3DRMTexture interface), 248
SetDecalTransparency method (IDirect3DRMTexture interface), 248
SetDecalTransparentColor method (IDirect3DRMTexture interface), 249
SetDefaultTextureColors method (IDirect3DRM interface), 91
SetDefaultTextureShades method (IDirect3DRM interface), 92
SetDither method (IDirect3DRMDevice interface), 117
SetEmissive method (IDirect3DRMMaterial interface), 188
SetEnableFrame method (IDirect3DRMLight interface), 182
SetExecuteData method (IDirect3DExecuteBuffer interface), 346-347
SetField method (IDirect3DRMViewport interface), 264

SetFrame method (IDirect3DRMAnimation interface), 99-100
SetFront method (IDirect3DRMViewport interface), 264-265
SetGroupColor method (IDirect3DRMMesh interface), 198-199
SetGroupColorRGB method (IDirect3DRMMesh interface), 199
SetGroupMapping method (IDirect3DRMMesh interface), 199-200
SetGroupMaterial method (IDirect3DRMMesh interface), 200-201
SetGroupQuality method (IDirect3DRMMesh interface), 201
SetGroupTexture method (IDirect3DRMMesh interface), 201-202
SetLight method (IDirect3DLight interface), 350-351
SetLinearAttenuation method (IDirect3DRMLight interface), 182-183
SetMaterial method
    IDirect3DMaterial interface, 354
    IDirect3DRMFace interface, 131
    IDirect3DRMMeshBuilder interface, 224
SetMaterialMode method (IDirect3DRMFrame interface), 162-163
SetMatrix method (IDirect3DDevice interface), 341-342
SetName method (IDirect3DRMObject interface), 236-237
SetNormal method (IDirect3DRMMeshBuilder interface), 224
SetOptions method (IDirect3DRMAnimation interface), 100-101
SetOrientation method (IDirect3DRMFrame interface), 163
SetPenumbra method (IDirect3DRMLight interface), 183

SetPerspective method (IDirect3DRMMeshBuilder interface), 225
SetPlane method (IDirect3DRMViewport interface), 265
SetPosition method (IDirect3DRMFrame interface), 164
SetPower method (IDirect3DRMMaterial interface), 189
SetProjection method (IDirect3DRMViewport interface), 266
SetQuadraticAttenuation method (IDirect3DRMLight interface), 183-184
SetQuality method (IDirect3DRMMeshBuilder interface), 225-226
SetRange method (IDirect3DRMLight interface), 184
SetRotation method (IDirect3DRMFrame interface), 164-165
SetSceneBackground method (IDirect3DRMFrame interface), 165
SetSceneBackgroundDepth method (IDirect3DRMFrame interface), 165-166
SetSceneBackgroundImage method (IDirect3DRMFrame interface), 166-167
SetSceneBackgroundRGB method (IDirect3DRMFrame interface), 167
SetSceneFogColor method (IDirect3DRMFrame interface), 168
SetSceneFogEnable method (IDirect3DRMFrame interface), 168
SetSceneFogMode method (IDirect3DRMFrame interface), 169
SetSceneFogParams method (IDirect3DRMFrame interface), 169-170
SetSearchPath method (IDirect3DRM interface), 93
SetShades method

IDirect3DRMDevice interface, 119
IDirect3DRMTexture interface, 249-250
SetSortMode method (IDirect3DRMFrame interface), 170
SetSpecular method (IDirect3DRMMaterial interface), 189-190
SetTexture method
IDirect3DRMFace interface, 132
IDirect3DRMFrame interface, 170-171
IDirect3DRMMeshBuilder interface, 226
SetTextureCoordinates method
IDirect3DRMFace interface, 132-133
IDirect3DRMMeshBuilder interface, 227
SetTextureQuality method (IDirect3DRMDevice interface), 119-120
SetTextureTopology method
IDirect3DRMFace interface, 133
IDirect3DRMFrame interface, 171
IDirect3DRMMeshBuilder interface, 227-228
SetTime method
IDirect3DRMAnimation interface, 101-102
IDirect3DRMAnimationSet interface, 105-106
SetUmbra method (IDirect3DRMLight interface), 185-186
SetUniformScaling method (IDirect3DRMViewport interface), 266-267
SetVelocity method (IDirect3DRMFrame interface), 172
SetVertex method (IDirect3DRMMeshBuilder interface), 228
SetVertexColor method (IDirect3DRMMeshBuilder interface), 229
SetVertexColorRGB method (IDirect3DRMMeshBuilder interface), 229-230

SetVertices method (IDirect3DRMMesh interface), 202
SetViewport method (IDirect3DViewport interface), 368-369
SetZbufferMode method (IDirect3DRMFrame interface), 172-173
shade modes, defining values, 442-443
shades (textures), setting usable shades, 92
shadows, creating, 80-81
sorting child frames, 292
specular color, 10
specular exponent, 10
spherical linear interpolation (quaternions), 48
spherical wrap (texture mapping), 13
spline-based modeling, 6
spot lights, 12
stand-alone tokens, 483-484
STRING data type, 458
strings, current search path, 86-87
structures
Immediate-Mode
D3DBRANCH, 371-372
D3DCOLORVALUE, 372-373
D3DDEVICEDESC, 373-375
D3DEXECUTEBUFFERDESC, 376-377
D3DEXECUTEDATA, 377-378
D3DFINDDEVICERESULT, 378
D3DFINDDEVICESEARCH, 379-382
D3DHVERTEX, 382-383
D3DINSTRUCTION, 383
D3DLIGHT, 384-385
D3DLIGHTDATA, 385-386
D3DLIGHTINGCAPS, 386-387
D3DLIGHTINGELEMENT, 387-388
D3DLINE, 388
D3DLINEPATTERN, 388-389
D3DLVERTEX, 389-390

D3DMATERIAL, 390-392
D3DMATRIX, 392
D3DMATRIXLOAD, 392-393
D3DMATRIXMULTIPLY, 393
D3DPICKRECORD, 394
D3DPOINT, 394-395
D3DPRIMCAPS, 395-403
D3DPROCESSVERTICES, 404-405
D3DRECT, 405-406
D3DSPAN, 406
D3DSTATE, 406-407
D3DSTATS, 407-408
D3DSTATUS, 408-411
D3DTEXTURELOAD, 411
D3DTLVERTEX, 412-413
D3DTRANSFORMCAPS, 413
D3DTRANSFORMDATA, 414-416
D3DTRIANGLE, 416-419, 421-422
D3DVECTOR, 420
D3DVERTEX, 420-422
D3DVIEWPORT, 422-423
Retained-Mode
D3DRMBOX, 275
D3DRMIMAGE, 275-276
D3DRMLOADMEMORY, 277
D3DRMLOADRESOURCE, 277-278
D3DRMPALETTEENTRY, 278-279
D3DRMPICKDESC, 279-280
D3DRMQUATERNION, 280
D3DRMVECTOR4D, 280-281
D3DRMVERTEX, 281
SwapTextureHandles method (IDirect3DDevice, 342-343)

T

templates
DirectX file format, 458-461
Animation, 479
AnimationKey, 478
AnimationOptions, 478-479
AnimationSet, 480
arrays, 459-461
binary format, 481-482
Boolean, 468
Boolean2d, 468-469
ColorRGB templates, 467
ColorRGBA templates, 466-467
Coords2d templates, 464-465
data types, 458-459
FloatKeys, 476-477
Frame, 476
FrameTransformMatrix, 475-476
Header templates, 461, 463-464
IndexedColor templates, 467-468
instances, 461-463
Material, 469-470
Matrix4x4 templates, 466
Mesh, 474-475
MeshFace, 470-471
MeshFaceWraps, 471
MeshMaterialList, 473-474
MeshNormals, 472-473
MeshTextureCoords, 472
MeshVertexColors, 473
Quaternion templates, 465
restriction types, 459-460
TextureFilename, 470
TimedFloatKeys, 477
Vector templates, 464

texture address modes, defining values, 443-444
texture filter modes, defining values, 445-446
texture-blending modes, defining values, 444-445
TextureFilename template reference guide, 470
textures, 12-14
   colors, setting, 91
   loading, 90
      from resources, 90-91
   mapping, mesh groups, 299-300
   mipmapping, 13
   shades, setting, 92
   texture coordinates, 13
   texture mapping, 13
three-dimensional objects
   coordinate systems, 4
      origin, 6
   geometry, 5-9
      lines, 7
      meshes, 9
      normal vectors (normals), 8
      vectors, 8
      vertices, 6
   visual characteristics, 10-13
      lights, 10-12
      materials, 10
      textures, 12-14
three-dimensional scenes, 14-17
   converting to 2D representations, 16-17
   frames of reference, 14
   geometric transformations, 14-15
   rasterization, 17-19
      rendering methods, 17-19
   viewing volume, 15

Tick method (IDirect3DRM interface), 93-102
TimedFloatKeys template reference guide, 477
TOKEN_GUID, 485
TOKEN_INTEGER, 485
TOKEN_INTEGER_LIST, 486
TOKEN_NAME, 484
TOKEN_REALNUM_LIST, 486
TOKEN_STRING, 484-485
tokens
   record-bearing, 483
      TOKEN_GUID, 485
      TOKEN_INTEGER, 485
      TOKEN_INTEGER_LIST, 486
      TOKEN_NAME, 484
      TOKEN_REALNUM_LIST, 486
      TOKEN_STRING, 484-485
   stand-alone, 483-484
Transform method
   IDirect3DRMFrame interface, 173-174
   IDirect3DRMViewport interface, 267-269
Transformation Module (rendering engine), 31
transforms, defining values, 446-448
TransformVertices method (IDirect3DViewport interface), 369-370
Translate method
   IDirect3DRMMesh interface, 203-204
   IDirect3DRMMeshBuilder interface, 230-231
translation (geometric transformations), 15
type definitions (Retained-Mode)
   D3DRMANIMATIONOPTIONS, 296
   D3DRMCOLORMODEL, 297
   D3DRMLOADOPTIONS, 297-299
   D3DRMMAPPING, 299-300
   D3DRMMATRIX4D, 300

U

UCHAR data type, 458
UNICODE data type, 459
uninitialized objects, creating, 79
unit quaternions
    computing from rotations, 46-47
    rotation matrices, calculating, 46
unit vectors, 8
Unload method (IDirect3DTexture interface), 358-359
Unlock method (IDirect3DExecuteBuffer interface), 347-348
Unreserve method (IDirect3DMaterial interface), 354-355
Update method (IDirect3DRMDevice interface), 120-122

V

Validate method (IDirect3DExecuteBuffer interface), 348-349
Vector template reference guide, 464
vectors, 8
    adding, 49
    components, multiplying by a scalar value, 54
    cross products, computing, 49-50
    dot products, computing, 50
    length, calculating, 51
    normalizing, 51
    random, 52
    reflections, calculating, 52-53
    rotating around an axis, 53
    subtracting, 55-56

Version Number-Major Number field (header elements), 457
Version Number-Minor Number field (header elements), 457
vertex normals, 8
vertices, 6
view transform, defining values, 446-448
viewing volume (frustum), 15
viewpoint (viewing volume), 15

W-Z

wireframe rendering, 17
WORD data type, 458
world transform, defining values, 446-448
wrapping (textures), 13

z-buffer algorithms, 427-428
z-buffering, 19
    frames, 295-296

 Support:

If you need assistance with the information in this book, please access the Knowledge Base on our Web site at **http://www.superlibrary.com/general/support**. Our most Frequently Asked Questions are answered there. If you do not find the answer to your questions on our Web site, you may contact Macmillan Technical Support **(317) 581-3833** or e-mail us at **support@mcp.com**.